Probabilistic Systems and Random Signals

Probabilistic Systems and Random Signals

Abraham H. Haddad

Henry and Isabelle Dever Professor and
Director, Master of Information Technology Program
Electrical and Computer Engineering Department
Robert R. McCormick School of Engineering and Applied Science
Northwestern University, Evanston, IL

Upper Saddle River, NJ 07458

Library of Congress Cataloging-in-Publication Data on file.

Vice President and Editorial Director, ECS: *Marcia Horton*
Associate Editor: *Alice Dworkin*
Executive Managing Editor: *Vince O'Brien*
Managing Editor: *David A. George*
Production Editor: *James Buckley*
Director of Creative Services: *Paul Belfanti*
Creative Director: *Jayne Conte*
Cover Designer: *Bruce Kenselaar*
Art Editor: *Greg Dulles*
Manufacturing Manager: *Alexis Heydt-Long*
Manufacturing Buyer: *Lisa McDowell*
Senior Marketing Manager: *Holly Stark*

© 2006 Pearson Education, Inc.
Pearson Education, Inc.
Upper Saddle River, New Jersey 07458

Pearson Prentice Hall™ is a trademark of Pearson Education, Inc.

Printed in the United States of America

10 9 8 7 6 5 4 3 2 1

ISBN 0-13-009455-2

Pearson Education Ltd., *London*
Pearson Education Australia Pty. Ltd., *Sydney*
Pearson Education Singapore, Pte. Ltd.
Pearson Education North Asia Ltd., *Hong Kong*
Pearson Education Canada Inc., *Toronto*
Pearson Educación de Mexico, S.A. de C.V.
Pearson Education—Japan, *Tokyo*
Pearson Education Malaysia, Pte. Ltd.
Pearson Education, Inc., *Upper Saddle River, New Jersey*

To
Carolyn

Contents

Preface

The purpose of this textbook on probability and random processes for electrical and computer engineering (ECE) undergraduates is to provide a text that addresses these important concepts at the junior (or even sophomore) level and to include applications as early as possible, rather than waiting for a course on random signals to discuss ECE applications. In addition to the applications to reliability, errors in communication systems, load distributions, among others, the text presents a short introduction to statistics, since many ECE students do not usually take a course in statistics. Furthermore, because statistics is considered a basic engineering subject, the inclusion of a brief introduction to statistics satisfies the basic engineering requirement. Since juniors who take the course may not have had a course in Fourier transform, the concepts involving frequency domain approaches and characteristic functions (requiring Fourier transforms) are isolated so as to allow the coverage of most concepts without the need for the Fourier transform. Actually, only Chapter 7, Chapter 14, and parts of Chapter 8 require such background. The subjects of linear systems and impulse functions also need not be taken by students before taking this course. Therefore, continuous time linear systems are covered only in the second half of Chapter 13 and the use of impulse functions is limited, with a short introduction in the Appendix to allow the possibility of using the impulse function in discrete densities. In order to make the subject more attractive to students, MATLAB examples and problems are included as part of the text to get students to observe the various distributions and to relate to the mathematical concepts. In the same vein the textbook does not rely a great deal on complex mathematical proofs. These are included in such a way that they can be skipped if desired, and in some cases references to detailed proofs are provided. My experience with undergraduate students is that they forget much of the math we teach them less than a semester after they take the appropriate course. Stressing proofs that they are soon going to forget is not an objective of this course. The objective is to get the students to understand the concepts and some key applications of such concepts in ECE. Most textbooks aimed at ECE students tend to rush through the probability and random variables parts of the instruction and quickly reach the random signal and noise applications. It is very difficult to reach the material on power spectra and even shallow coverage of random processes in one semester at the undergraduate level. That is the reason for trying to make the early concepts relevant, with examples in ECE, rather than wait until the random signals subjects. While these subjects are included in this text, they are aimed at those who plan to take a second course in random signals. In turn, this first introductory text would provide them with the link to the more advanced topics. If a two-semester sequence is offered on this subject, then the latter chapters may be used for such a purpose. An attempt is made here to reach undergraduate students and not to present the material to serve the intermediate levels for either graduate and undergraduate students.

There are several ways to use this text for a course at the level indicated for a one-semester course. If random processes are not covered, then the plan would be to cover in one semester Chapters 1 through 6 and parts of Chapters 8, 9, 10, and 11. If random signals are to be covered in the same semester, then we drop the subject on hypothesis testing in Chapter 10, restrict the coverage in Chapter 8, and cover instead Chapters 12 and parts of 13. For students with a background in linear systems and Fourier transforms, an alternative approach would be to cover Chapters 1 through 6, parts of Chapter 8, and then Chapter 12, with selections from Chapters 13 and 14.

I would like to acknowledge the many suggestions made by the reviewers: Philipos Loizou, Junshan Zhang, David L. Clark, Mikhail Matioutov, and Mahmood R. Azimi-Sadjadi. Their comments and suggestions added a great deal to the final version of this textbook. I also wish to thank Professor Martin Plonus for many helpful suggestions. He also provided the example that is used to illustrate the relation between Bernoulli trials and the number of trials until the first success (the apple example). Thanks are also due to Dr. Peter Alexic for many corrections and for the Matlab solutions. Finally, many thanks to students over the past five years for suggestions and corrections.

ABRAHAM H. HADDAD
Northwestern University

Probabilistic Systems and Random Signals

1

Introduction

1.1 WHY PROBABILISTIC METHODS IN ENGINEERING?

Probability and statistics are encountered in many engineering problems. They represent two aspects of the way we treat uncertainties in the analysis, design, operation, and production of many engineering systems. Statistics addresses the problem of how to derive useful information from data obtained in many situations. Data collected in economics and populations may be analyzed using statistics alone, as in many cases a model to assist in the interpretation of the data may not exist. However, in many man-made systems we can usually provide a probabilistic model that helps in analyzing the data and derive useful information despite the presence of uncertainties. We start by looking at various problems in which uncertainties occur. The obvious problem in which uncertainty plays a major role is in gambling, which is clearly not an engineering problem. Examples may include the case of how to play a hand of poker or black jack or the likelihood of winning the lottery or a roulette game. We shall see that the uncertainties encountered in engineering (especially in electrical, computer, or industrial engineering) are more complex, but also more interesting. The purpose of this section is to introduce various such problems and to show how they require probabilistic models for their solution.

1.1.1 Binary Communications and Signal Detection

We are all familiar with using the telephone, fax, the Internet, and other key telecom-munications media. The common element in all of these system is that voice, pictures, and other information are transmitted as "zeros" and "ones" over usually noisy chan-nels. Since the transmission is made via some form of electrical signal in a channel (copper wire, optical fiber, coaxial cable, or wireless), such channels usually contain disturbances in the form of signals from other users sharing the channel and the ther-mal (or optical) noise that exists in every electrical conductor, due to the random mo-tion of the free electrons, which carry the current in a non-regimented fashion. The problem is how to decide whether a "one" or a "zero" was sent when the receiver ob-serves a waveform such as the one shown in Figure 1.1. In this example the signal is shown by the smooth curve, while the jagged curve represents the signal plus noise. It is assumed for this illustration that a "one" is represented by half a sine wave, while a "zero" is represented by either a negative half sine wave or just by a signal with zero amplitude.

   Clearly, in this case, we can observe from the general shape of the signal that a "one" was transmitted. However, if the noise during a particular time frame is too large, the system may not be able to tell if the transmitted shape represents "one" or "zero." The questions that need to be answered is how to find the error rate if we know some information about the noise (also, what kind of information about the noise can be obtained) and if such an error rate is not acceptable, how to design the system so as to achieve an acceptable error rate. Similar and even more critical problems occur in radar receivers that are attempting to detect whether a signal re-ceived contains a reflection from a target or just plain noise. An incorrect decision in

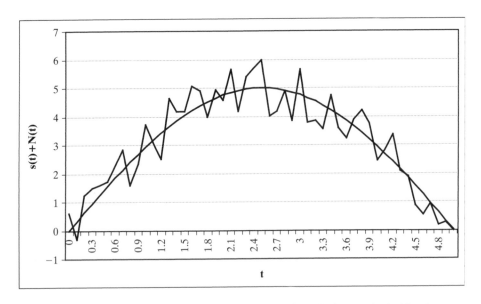

Figure 1.1   An example of a signal representing a transmitted "one" when received with noise

such a case may mean either a false alarm (saying a target is present when only noise is received) or a miss. Both kinds of errors in many civilian applications (detection of malignant tumors, for example) and military applications (radar detection of enemy aircraft, for example) can have serious implications.

1.1.2 System Reliability

All man-made systems or components are subject to failures. We can define such reliability by looking at the fraction of systems that fail in a given time period, and we may denote, for the present, the failure rate as the fraction of systems that fail per unit time. (A more precise definition of reliability will be provided in Chapter 11.) The question is how to design a system composed of many components so that its failure rate is acceptable. Also, assuming that we know the failure rates of its components, how can we compute the failure rate of the system as a whole without testing it after it is built? Usually a system can be considered as composed of parallel connections and series connections of several components, as well as more complex connections, as shown in Figure 1.2.

Let us suppose that these examples represent communication channels between two cities or locations. Then a parallel connection means that there are multiple ways of sending information between the cities or locations; a series connection means that we can reach a given location only through intermediate locations; the complex connection means that there are various possible ways to connect the two locations. Intuitively, we realize that a parallel connection is more reliable than a

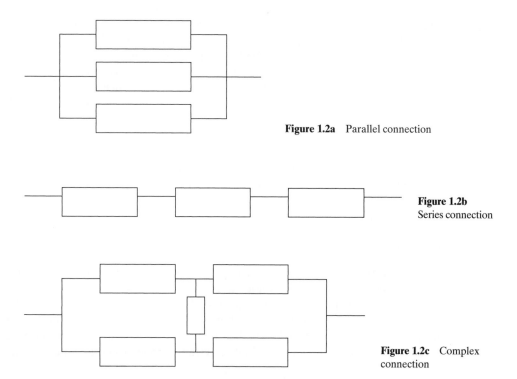

Figure 1.2a   Parallel connection

Figure 1.2b
Series connection

Figure 1.2c   Complex connection

series connection, for if one branch fails, then the system can still function via the other branches. The question is how to quantify the reliability (or failure rate) in this case or in the more complex cases.

1.1.3 Noise Models

As mentioned in Section 1.1.1, the free electrons in an electric conductor that conduct the electric current do not move in a regimented fashion. Even when there is no voltage applied to the terminals of conductors, the free electrons are always in random motion due to the fact that the temperature of the conductor is not absolute zero Kelvin. Such random motion causes the current, when a voltage is applied to the terminal of the conductor, to fluctuate about the value we expect. We call these fluctuations thermal noise. The question is how to model this noise and how to characterize it in a way that helps us extract useful information from the current signal despite the fluctuations. Similar noise models need to be considered for the random signals received by the antenna of a wireless telephone or the antenna of radar, TV, or radio receivers. The reason the problem is important in these cases is that the useful signal is usually weak, and hence, even though the noise may also be small, it can have an undesirable effect on the information we wish to receive.

1.1.4 Service Models

Suppose that a company has 1000 employees with each one having a phone on his or her desk. Suppose also that some "average" information about telephone usage for outside communications is available. The question is how many outside lines the company needs to acquire to satisfy the telephone usage. Obviously, it is too expensive to have 1000 lines (one for each phone). However, if the number of lines is less than 1000, the employees will experience busy tones occasionally when dialing for an outside line. Based on some measure of "quality of service," the company may decide that getting a busy tone 1% of the time is acceptable. How can such a measure be translated into the number of lines required? Probabilistic models can answer such questions. Similar problems exist when dealing with the number of servers required by a customer service desk at a store or a company. If we know the information about the average number of customers arriving per hour and the average number it takes to serve one customer, then in many cases, we can answer the question of how many servers are needed using probabilistic models. Obviously, such an answer depends on what we consider acceptable "quality of service" to the customers in terms of how long they have to wait to be served.

1.1.5 System Tolerances

Every man-made system is composed of components that are not as precisely manufactured as we wish. For example, in electrical circuits, the values of resistors or other components may have a tolerance of 1%, 5%, or 10%. This means that, when we pick a 5% quality resistor of 100 ohms, its value can be anywhere in the range of 95 ohms to 105 ohms. If we wish smaller tolerances, we have to pay a higher price. The question of interest is how we can build a system with an acceptable performance by using parts that have a range of values. Here again, probabilistic approaches come to the rescue. Similarly, if we wish to fit a peg with a given tolerance of production dimensions through a hole with a similar tolerance, how can we determine the success rate of doing so with acceptable result? We shall see, for example, that if we connect two resistors of tolerance 10% in series, then under some assumptions, 75% of the resulting resistors will have a tolerance of 5%.

1.1.6 Product Defects

In any manufacturing system, products usually have defects or do not conform to desired requirements. For example, if we make sheet metal, then we may characterize the quality by the number of defects per linear meter of the product. Similar characterization may apply to different products. Important questions in such cases are (a) How many samples of the product do we need to measure in order to get a good idea whether the product is acceptable? (b) How can we determine that the manufacturing process has changed significantly, so as to require adjustments? (c) How can we obtain a desired length of material without any defects? A similar problem involves the occurrence (arrival) of failures in a system in operation. If we characterize failure rate as the number of failures per hour, can we determine the length of time with no failures? We shall see that such problems may be handled by a well-known probabilistic model that helps answer some of the questions we raised.

1.1.7 Measurement Errors

When we measure a quantity, we usually can obtain a value with a certain accuracy, since no measurement device is perfectly accurate. If we repeat the measurement, we usually obtain a different answer. What we customarily do in such cases is add the measurements and divide by the number of measurements taken to provide our answer. The question is why this is an acceptable method. Also, how many measurements do we take to reduce the error to an acceptable level? Again, we shall answer these questions in later chapters using probabilistic methods.

1.2 DATA ANALYSIS

If we collect data without assuming any underlying model, we just obtain a sequence of numbers. For example, consider the temperature taken at various times of day or various days of the month. As another example, consider the number of failures during every month of a given system (such as a cable service provider or an Internet service provider). Finally, consider the measurement of a voltage produced by a voltage source or the measurements of resistance of a bunch of identically labeled resistors. What can we do with such data (other than just listing it or throwing it away)? We can plot it to see how many data values fall within certain intervals. We call such a plot a histogram. For example, the set of values shown in Table 1.1 may be viewed as the measurement of 20 different resistors whose nominal value is

TABLE 1.1   Values of 20 Resistors

i	x_i
1	109.29
2	107.22
3	97.12
4	104.1
5	95.96
6	106.26
7	91.45
8	103.4
9	102.62
10	91.57
11	106.87
12	107.66
13	107.09
14	92.2
15	91.95
16	109.93
17	102.84
18	96.24
19	104.11
20	106.14

$100 \pm 10\%$, where the measuring instrument is assumed to have an accuracy of two significant decimal digits.

Let us now divide the range of values (90, 110) into five ranges: (90, 94), (94, 98), (98, 102), (102, 106), (106, 110). If we plot a bar graph showing the number of measurements that fall in each range, we obtain a ***histogram*** as shown in Figure 1.3. In creating a histogram, the ranges that we use are also called bins. Note that instead of plotting the number of times each range occurs, we can plot the fraction of such numbers relative to the total number of measurements (20 in this case). In this case the Y-axis of the graph of Figure 1.3 will range from 0 to 0.40. Also note that even though the nominal value is 100, we had no values in the range 98 to 102 in this particular example.

If we do not need so much detail, we can try to summarize the results by a few representative numbers. Two such useful numbers are what we call the ***sample mean*** and ***sample standard deviation***. The sample mean is defined as the sum of all the

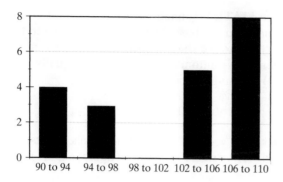

Figure 1.3 Histogram of the values of the resistors in Table 1.1

values divided by the number of data points. If we have n values $\{x_i\}$ for $i = 1, 2, \ldots, n$ (which in our case is $n = 20$), we denote the sample mean by $\bar{x}$ and define it by the following expression:

$$\text{Sample mean of } X = \bar{x} = \frac{1}{n}\sum_{i=1}^{n} x_i \tag{1.1}$$

In the preceding example, the sample mean is equal to 101.7, which is not equal to the nominal value of 100. The sample mean provides us with an indication of a central value of the data we measured. Another important attribute of the data is how it is dispersed around the sample mean. The *sample standard deviation*, which is denoted by s_x, is a parameter that provides a measure of such a spread and is defined by the following expression:

$$\text{Standard deviation of } X = s_x = \sqrt{\sum_{i=1}^{n} (x_i - \bar{x})^2 \Big/ (n - 1)} \tag{1.2}$$

The question is why do we divide by $(n - 1)$ instead of n to derive the standard deviation. We shall address this in more detail in Chapter 9, but we mention a simple explanation here. Since we used all the data points to obtain the sample mean, the n deviations from the sample mean are linearly related (the sum of the deviations is equal to zero!). We say, in this case, that the data after we computed the sample mean have only $(n - 1)$ degrees of freedom. That is the reason we do not divide by n, but by $(n - 1)$, since only $(n - 1)$ of the deviations provide "new" information about the spread. Intuitively, we know that if we have only one data point, we cannot obtain a valid standard deviation, since we cannot estimate two parameters from one point of data.

For our example, the standard deviation is found to be equal to 6.2. We cannot do much more with such data unless we are willing to assume some probabilistic models that would allow us to deal with such problems in a more systematic way.

1.2.1 Data Analysis Using MATLAB

How do we use MATLAB to generate information such as that presented in the preceding example? MATLAB provides a powerful tool for data analysis and simulation.

In the sequel, as we introduce MATLAB functions, we have to differentiate between functions that are available in the basic MATLAB program and those that are available in the statistics toolbox. We shall identify the toolbox functions with the superscript (§). We can generate random numbers that are equally likely to be anywhere in the interval $(0, 1)$ by using the command

$$X = \text{rand}(1, n) \tag{1.3}$$

The preceding command generates a vector X of dimension n; each of its entries is a random number between 0 and 1. If we wish to generate a number in the range (a, b), then we can use the command

$$X = a + (b - a) * \text{rand}(1, n) \tag{1.4}$$

If we wish to generate random integers in the range $[k, m]$, then we have to use the fix function as follows:

$$X = \text{rand}(1, n) \tag{1.5a}$$

$$Y = \text{fix}(k + (m - k + 1) * X) \tag{1.5b}$$

The vector Y will contain n random integers between k and m (inclusive).

Once we obtain the random numbers we can generate the appropriate histogram using the command

$$\text{hist}(X, m) \tag{1.6}$$

In the histogram command, m is equal to the number of bins into which we wish to subdivide the range of the values of X. We may wish to specify the bin size and the range for the histogram. In that case, we first specify the range and bin size by the variable y and then use the histogram command

$$y = \text{min:bin:max} \tag{1.7a}$$

$$\text{hist}(X, y) \tag{1.7b}$$

Here, y specifies the minimum value, the bin size, and the maximum value that are to be used in constructing the histogram.

Finally, we can derive the sample mean and the sample standard deviation by using the following two commands:

$$\text{Sample Mean} = \text{mean}(X) \tag{1.8a}$$

$$\text{Sample Standard Deviation} = \text{std}(X) \tag{1.8b}$$

We are now ready to start discussing the subject of probability models, which allows us to systematically handle problems of data and system analysis. We shall address the topic of data analysis in more depth in Chapter 9, where we consider an introduction to statistics.

1.3 WHAT IS PROBABILITY?

In the examples discussed in Sections 1.1 and 1.2, we have experiments whose outcome is not known in advance. Each time we measure a variable, receive a signal, or observe a system, we obtain an answer (or a value) that may be different. We call such an observation or measurement a ***random experiment***, since the outcome is not known in advance and can be one of several possibilities. Probability, which measures the likelihood that an outcome or collection of outcomes will occur, is represented by a number between zero (unlikely) and one (most likely) assigned to such an outcome or collection of outcomes. Such a number is supposed to express to us how likely such an outcome or collection of outcomes of the experiment are to occur. For example, when we toss a coin, we can say that heads or tails are equally likely to occur. On the other hand, when we roll a die, the outcome of even face values is three times more likely to occur than the outcome of face value equal to 1. How do we assign probabilities in a systematic way in general? There are three approaches to assigning probabilities to the outcome of random experiments:

a. Subjective: We assign probability based on our subjective feelings or belief. Such an approach is not pursued further here, but is very commonly practiced by gamblers or lottery players.

b. Empirical: We perform the experiment a number of times (as we have shown in the resistance case in Section 1.2) and try to infer some probabilistic model from the data. We assign a probability based on the relative frequency of the occurrence of the outcome. For example, if we toss a coin 100 times and we obtain 48 heads, we assign probability of 0.48 to the outcome heads.

c. Axiomatic: We study probability models in a more mathematical framework that provides all the rules that such models have to obey. This is the approach that is used in this text and in most engineering problems. The reason is that the approach provides a general framework for the subject and removes any inconsistent assumptions or rules. In general, the actual assignment of probabilistic values is based on some key assumptions. For examples, the assumption that certain outcomes are equally likely to occur. Again let us look at the example of the coin tossing. Since there are two outcomes and there is no reason to favor one over the other, we assign probability of 0.5 to the outcome heads.

However, in more complex problems, we usually combine the axiomatic and the empirical approaches. First, based on analytical assumptions, probability models and rules are established. Then, when we need to apply such rules to a given engineering problem, we do have to resort to empirical experiments to validate the applicability of the model and to infer some of the values, we assign to the various variables involved in the model. This means that once we have a model by using the axiomatic approach, we validate its parameters using the empirical approach. We call this ***inferential statistics***.

We are now ready to study the basic definition of probability and its properties.

1.4 PROBLEMS

1. Generate n random numbers that take values in the range $(0, 10)$, for $n = 100$ and $n = 1000$. Plot the histograms by using 10 equally spaced bins and compute the sample average and sample standard deviation. What can you say about the shape of the histogram as n becomes larger?

2. Repeat Problem 1 by generating integers between 1 and 10 (inclusive).

3. Repeat Problem 1 for the range $(100, 120)$.

4. Repeat Problem 2 for integers in the range from 20 to 40 (inclusive). Use 21 bins.

2

Basic Probability

2.1 INTRODUCTION

Probability is a number assigned to outcomes or collections of outcomes of random experiments to indicate how likely or unlikely these outcomes are to occur. Since we wish to assign probability to outcomes as well as to collections of outcomes, we need to study the way outcomes of random experiments are manipulated in order to define how probability is to be assigned. Here are some examples of random experiments and their outcomes.

Example 2.1

Toss a coin twice and list all possible outcomes as shown in the following illustration:

	First Toss	Second Toss
Outcome 1	*H*	*H*
Outcome 2	*H*	*T*
Outcome 3	*T*	*H*
Outcome 4	*T*	*T*

In addition to the basic four outcomes, we can define collections of outcomes that are combinations of those just shown, such as

{at least one Head}, {two tosses are equal}, {at least one Tail}, {two or more Tails}, {two or more Heads}

11

Example 2.2

Send a known block of bits (binary digits) from a server to a digital terminal. Observe the received block of bits as it arrives at the terminal. Since we know the transmitted block, for each bit we can define two outcomes: {the bit is received correctly} or {the bit is received in error}. Suppose that the block contains 1024 bits, for example. We can now define other collections, such as {at most three errors were received in the block}, {exactly two bits were received in error}, {all 1024 bits were received correctly}, and {more than 4 bits were received in error}.

Example 2.3

In the example of measuring the resistance whose value falls between the values of 90 and 110 (such as the small sample shown in Table 1.1), we may assume (before doing any measurements) that the value of the resistance can take any real number between 90 and 110. In such a case, we can define collections such as {resistance is between 95 and 105}, {resistance is greater than 100}, {resistance is less than 98}, and many others. The number of possibilities is very large if we do not confine ourselves to just a small sample of resistors, but consider all possible values we may encounter if we were to pick a resistor at random and measure its resistance.

In order to be able to manipulate such collections of outcomes, we need to discuss the basic elements of set theory. Sets in general are collections of elements. However, here they denote collections of outcomes of a random experiment and are also called *events*.

2.2 SET THEORY AND EVENTS

2.2.1 Set (Event) Definitions

We define the collection of all possible outcomes of a random experiment as the *sample space* and we denote it by S. An individual outcome maybe denoted by a letter, ζ, and we use subscripts to indicate a particular outcome. We show the sample space S as a rectangle whose points represent the outcomes we are dealing with. Collections of outcomes are called sets in general, but in our case we call them *events* and they are denoted by capital letters such as A, B, C. We call the figures showing the outcomes and collections of outcomes *Venn diagrams*. Figure 2.1(a) shows the sample space S, which contains all outcomes, and is therefore called the *certain* event, since one of its outcomes must occur. We define an event either by listing all the outcomes it contains or by providing a rule describing what outcomes it contains, as we have seen in the preceding examples.

Example 2.4

We refer to Example 2.3, but here we assume that we are not dealing with just a given sample of resistors. Instead we are picking a resistor that has a nominal value of 100 and has a tolerance of 10%. We know that its value could be any real number between

90 and 110. In this case we have for the certain event $S = \{\zeta|90 < \zeta < 110\}$. We may define events A, B, C, D, and E as follows:

$A = \{\zeta|\zeta < 98\}$, which means all values less than 98
$B = \{\zeta|\zeta \geq 98\}$, which means all values greater than or equal to 98
$C = \{\zeta|\zeta < 95\}$, which means all values less than 95
$D = \{\zeta|95 < \zeta < 100\}$, which means all values between 95 and 100
$E = \{\zeta|\zeta = 95\}$, which means the value is exactly equal to 95

We indicate that an outcome belongs to an event by using the "belongs" symbol, $\in$. Similarly, we use the symbol $\notin$ to denote "does **not** belong." Hence, in the preceding example, we say that the outcome $\zeta_1 = 97$ satisfies $\zeta_1 \in A$ while the outcome $\zeta_2 = 104$ satisfies $\zeta_2 \notin A$.

In particular, just as we defined the event S that contains **all** outcomes, we can define an event ϕ that contains **no** outcome, as the empty set or the **null** event. We may also call it the **impossible** event. Events are shown pictorially as enclosed areas of the rectangular sample space.

2.2.2 Events Algebra

Events may have relationships as they may or may not contain outcomes in common. The symbol $\subseteq$ is used to denote that an event is contained in another event. For example, in the preceding resistance case we have $C \subseteq A$. In set theory we say that C is a **subset** of A. In general all events are contained in S: $A \subseteq S, B \subseteq S, C \subseteq S$. If a set A is contained in another set B and B has at least one element that is not in A, we say that A is a proper subset of B and denote it as $A \subset B$. Two sets or events are equal if they contain the same elements or outcomes; thus we say $A = B$ if $A \subseteq B$ and $B \subseteq A$. The operation of contained in or contains is shown in Figure 2.1 (b). In the rest of this text we shall use the symbol $\subset$ instead of $\subseteq$ to denote the same meaning.

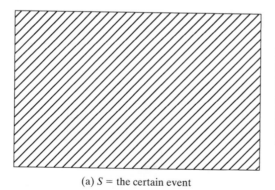

(a) S = the certain event

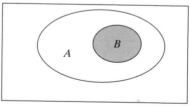

(b) Subset: B is contained in $A = B \subset A$

Figure 2.1   Event Relationships and Algebra

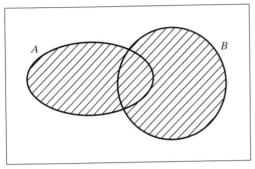

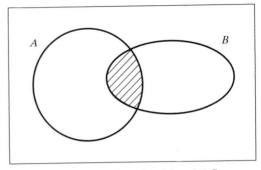

(c) Union: A or B (or both) = $A \cup B$

(d) Intersection: A and $B = A \cap B$

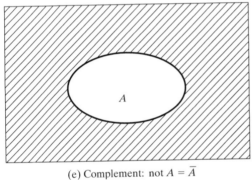

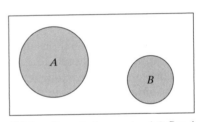

(f) Mutually exclusive events: $A \cap B = \phi$

(e) Complement: not $A = \bar{A}$

Distributive Rules

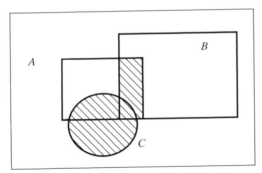

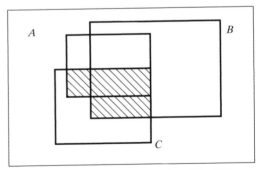

(g) C or (A and B) = (C or A) and (C or B)
$C \cup (A \cap B) = (C \cup A) \cap (C \cup B)$

(h) C and (A or B) = (C and A) or (C and B)
$C \cap (A \cup B) = (C \cap A) \cup (C \cap B)$

Figure 2.1   (Continued)

DeMorgan's Law

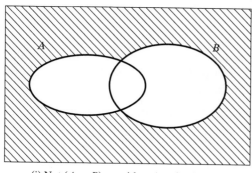

(i) Not $(A$ or $B) = $ neither A and neither B
$$(\overline{A \cup B}) = \overline{A} \cap \overline{B}$$

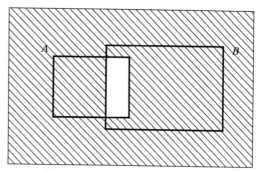

(j) Not $(A$ and $B) = $ not A or not B
$$(\overline{A \cap B}) = \overline{A} \cup \overline{B}$$

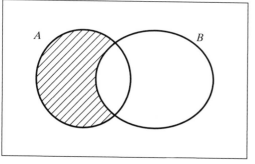

(k) A but not $B = A \cap \overline{B}$

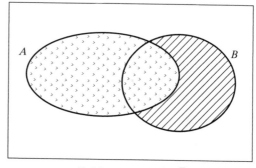

(l) B but not $A = B \cap \overline{A}$

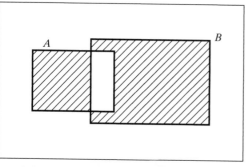

(m) A or B but not both: $(A \cap \overline{B}) \cup (B \cap \overline{A})$

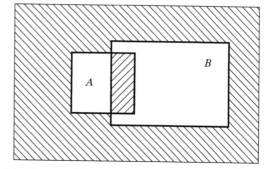

(n) Either A and B together or neither: $(A \cap B) \cup (\overline{A} \cap \overline{B})$

Figure 2.1 (Continued)

We are now ready to define the algebra of events to help us manipulate events and assign probabilities to such events.

Union

Given two events A and B, we define C as the union of A and B. C is the event that contains all the outcomes that are in either A or B or both. Another expression for the union is inclusive **or** and is denoted by the symbol, $\cup$:

$$C = A \cup B = (A \text{ or } B) = \{\text{outcomes that are in either } A, \text{ or } B, \text{ or both}\}$$

The union operation is illustrated in Figure 2.1(c).

Intersection

Given two events A and B, we define D as the intersection of A and B. D is the event that contains all the outcomes that are in both A and B. Another expression for the intersection is **and**, which is denoted by the symbol, $\cap$:

$$D = A \cap B = (A \text{ and } B) = \{\text{outcomes that are in both } A \text{ and } B\}$$

The intersection operation is illustrated in Figure 2.1(d).

Complement

Given an event A, we define its complement as the event containing all the outcomes that are not in A. The complement is denoted by $\overline{A}$. Another expression for the complement of A is **not** A:

$$\overline{A} = \{\zeta | \zeta \notin A\} = (\text{not } A) = \{\text{outcomes that are not in } A\}$$

The complement of an event is shown in Figure 2.1(e).

Mutually Exclusive Events

Events with no elements in common are called **mutually exclusive** or **disjoint**. For such events we have the expression

$$A \cap B = \phi$$

Mutually exclusive events are illustrated in Figure 2.1(f). It can be seen from Figure 2.1(e) that since A and its complement have no element in common, but together they contain all outcomes, we have

$$A \cap \overline{A} = \phi \quad \text{and} \quad A \cup \overline{A} = S \tag{2.1}$$

Example 2.5

We use the events defined in Example 2.4 to illustrate the preceding operations:

$$B = \overline{A}, B \cap A = \phi, B \cup A = S$$

Define $F = \{\zeta | \zeta < 100\}$ and $G = \{\zeta | 95 < \zeta < 98\}$, then we can see that

$$C \subset A, F = A \cup D, G = A \cap D$$

Properties

The intersection and union operations satisfy the following key properties:

Commutative property: The operations of union and intersection commute:

$$A \cup B = B \cup A \tag{2.2}$$

$$A \cap B = B \cap A \tag{2.3}$$

Associative property: The order of the operations is not important; hence we do not bother to use a bracket in operations involving more than two events:

$$(A \cup B) \cup C = A \cup (B \cup C) = A \cup B \cup C \tag{2.4}$$

$$(A \cap B) \cap C = A \cap (B \cap C) = A \cap B \cap C \tag{2.5}$$

When we have unions and intersections of a number of events, $A_1, A_2, \ldots A_n$, we use the following notation shown (since the order of the operation is not important):

$$B = A_1 \cup A_2 \cup A_3 \cup \ldots \cup A_n = \bigcup_{i=1}^{n} A_i \tag{2.6}$$

and

$$C = A_1 \cap A_2 \cap A_3 \cap \ldots \cap A_n = \bigcap_{i=1}^{n} A_i \tag{2.7}$$

Distributive rule: We can open the bracket when we perform unions of intersecting events or when we perform intersections involving a union of events:

$$A \cup (B \cap C) = (A \cup B) \cap (A \cup C) \tag{2.8}$$

$$A \cap (B \cup C) = (A \cap B) \cup (A \cap C) \tag{2.9}$$

The proofs of these properties can best be done by using the Venn diagram. Equation (2.8) is illustrated in Figure 2.1(g) and equation (2.9) is illustrated in Figure 2.1(h). The distributive property deserves the following comment (we are familiar with the distributive property of multiplications in regular algebra):

$$a \times (b + c) = a \times b + a \times c$$

However, unlike regular algebra, the distributive property holds also for unions, which is similar to addition, which does not hold for regular algebra:

$$a + (b \times c) \neq (a + b) \times (a + c)$$

Finally, we list additional properties of the two basic events: the certain event S and the null event ϕ. We have, in this case the following identities:

$$A \cap \phi = \phi \text{ and } A \cup \phi = A \qquad (2.10)$$

$$A \cap S = A \text{ and } A \cup S = S \qquad (2.11)$$

De Morgan's Law

De Morgan's law is a rule governing the complement of a union or an intersection. In this, case we can use Venn Diagrams to show that the following rules hold for every set or event:

$$\overline{(A \cup B)} = \overline{A} \cap \overline{B} \qquad (2.12)$$

$$\overline{(A \cap B)} = \overline{A} \cup \overline{B} \qquad (2.13)$$

The rule is illustrated in Figure 2.1(i) for equation (2.12) and in Figure 2.1(j) for equation (2.13).

Next we illustrate an additional relation or operation involving events, which in some textbooks is listed as "difference" between two events, but we shall not use this terminology here. This operation is

$$A \text{ and } (\textbf{not } B) = \{\text{All outcomes that are in } A \text{ but not in } B\} = A \cap \overline{B}$$

This operation and its symmetric operation involving $\{B \text{ and } (\text{not } A)\}$ are shown in Figures 2.1(k) and 2.1(l), respectively.

Finally, Figure 2.1(m) illustrates the operation "exclusive or" (i.e., the outcomes that are either in A or in B but not in both), and Figure 2.1(n) illustrates the operation of "either both A and B or neither one":

"Exclusive or" = $\{$outcomes in A or B, but not in both$\}$ = $(A \cap \overline{B}) \cup (B \cap \overline{A})$

$\{$Outcomes in $(A \text{ and } B)$ or (neither A and neither B)$\}$ = $(A \cap B) \cup (\overline{A} \cap \overline{B})$

Example 2.6

Consider the example of tossing two coins described in Example 2.1. Let A denote the event that coin #1 is Heads and let B denote the event that coin #2 is Heads. Then equation (2.12) implies that the event that complements the event $\{$either one coin or both coins are Heads$\}$, is the event $\{$neither coin is Heads$\}$. Similarly, equation (2.13) implies that the event that $\{\textbf{not} \text{ (both are Heads)}\}$ is really the event that $\{$either one or both are Tails$\}$.

Event Class

We are now ready to assign probabilities to events of a random experiment. It is important to note that there are some cases in which we cannot assign probabilities to every collection of outcomes. For example, if the number of outcomes is infinite and uncountable, there are many possibilities of defining collections that may cause mathematical difficulties. We therefore restrict ourselves to assigning probabilities to events that form a collection that is closed under union and intersection operations and contains the certain event S as well. What do we mean by the expression "closed under union and intersection"? We mean that when we specify the collection it must satisfy the following properties: (a) if an event belongs to the collection, then its complement also belongs to the collection; (b) if two events are in the collection, then their union and their intersection are also in the collection; and (c) the certain event S also belongs to the collection. At the level of coverage in this text, this should not be a problem and will not be discussed much further, other than to formally define an event class. The problems occur when we have to assign probabilities to cases in which the sample space contains an uncountable number of outcomes (e.g., Example 2.4). We therefore will assign probability to events that belong to an event class (collection of events), $\mathcal{F}$, defined as follows:

$$S \in \mathcal{F}$$

If $A \in \mathcal{F}$ and $B \in \mathcal{F}$, then $\overline{A} \in \mathcal{F}, \overline{B} \in \mathcal{F}, A \cap B \in \mathcal{F}$, and $A \cup B \in \mathcal{F}$

The formal definition of probability is carried out in the next section. We shall not return to the event class in subsequent chapters, but we note here that probability is defined only for events belonging implicitly to an event class. The key concept here is that the event class is a collection of events that is exhaustive; that is, it contains all outcomes. When dealing with an uncountable number of outcomes, as in Example 2.4, the event class may be defined as containing all possible intervals, namely $\{\zeta | a < \zeta \leq b\}$ with $a \geq 90$ and $b < 110$.

As a simple illustration of what we mean by an event class, consider the case of rolling a die once. We can assign probabilities to an event class containing the following four events:

$$\{S, \phi, \{\text{outcome is even}\}, \{\text{outcome is odd}\}\}$$

This is a valid event class. However, for such a case we cannot assign probability to the event that the outcome is less than 3. Our choice was to restrict ourselves to the four events just described, but we could have defined a different event class and assigned probability to its events. This is an artificially defined event class to illustrate the concept. We shall not address the problem further in this text.

2.3 AXIOMS OF PROBABILITY

We are now ready to define probability for the events resulting from a random experiment. As mentioned in Chapter 1, there are various ways of assigning probabilities to events. However, these assignments must obey certain rules, which are called the axioms of probability, since they cannot be proved right or wrong, as they are just a convention that is consistent with our intuitive understanding of what a probability measure is.

2.3.1 Probability Definition

Given a sample space S and given an event class that contains subsets of the sample space, then for any event A in the event class, we define the probability of A by $P(A)$ as a real number assigned to the event A and satisfying the following axioms:

$$\text{Axiom I: } P(A) \geq 0 \tag{2.14}$$

$$\text{Axiom II: } P(S) = 1 \tag{2.15}$$

Axiom III: If two events A and B are mutually exclusive ($A \cap B = \phi$), then

$$P(A \cup B) = P(A) + P(B) \tag{2.16}$$

Let us discuss these axioms. Axiom I just restricts the probabilities to be nonnegative, while Axiom II implies that the certain event has probability of 1. This is just as we expect in dealing with the way we express measures of likely or unlikely occurrences. Axiom III is also intuitively clear, since the probability of either of two events occuring is the sum of their probabilities, if these events cannot occur together. For example, if we assume that the probability of picking a card of a certain suit from a deck of cards is 0.25, then the probability of picking a red card is $P(\text{Red}) = P(\text{Heart}) + P(\text{Diamond}) = 0.25 + 0.25 = 0.5$, as we would expect.

2.3.2 Properties

These axioms help us derive more properties of probability, by using the rules of events algebra.

Property 1: $P(\overline{A}) = 1 - P(A)$ \hfill (2.17)

To prove this property, we use the fact that since $\overline{A}$ and A are mutually exclusive and their union is equal to S, then by Axiom II and III we have

$$1 = P(S) = P(A \cup \overline{A}) = P(A) + P(\overline{A})$$

which yields equation (2.17).

Property 2: $P(A) \leq 1$ \hfill (2.18)

This property follows directly from equation (2.17) and the fact that $P(A)$ is nonnegative, as stipulated by Axiom I.

Property 3: If $B \subset A$, then $P(B) \leq P(A)$ \hfill (2.19)

This property follows from Figure 2.1c, since A is the union of B and $(A \cap \overline{B})$ and these are mutually exclusive events. Hence, since $P(A \cap \overline{B}) \geq 0$, we have

$$P(A) = P(B) + P(A \cap \overline{B}) \geq P(B)$$

Property 4: $P(\phi) = 0$ $\hspace{3cm}$ (2.20)

This property follows from the fact that the null event is a complement of S, and we thus use equation (2.17) and Axiom II to obtain equation (2.20). It should be noted that while the impossible event has probability zero, not every event with probability zero is impossible. For example, if we consider Example 2.4 and assume that the probability of the events involving values taken by the resistance is proportional to the interval in question, then clearly the event $E = \{\zeta | \zeta = 95\}$ will have probability zero, as it involves an interval of length zero. However, the event can happen, since it is not impossible.

Property 5: $P(A \cup B) = P(A) + P(B) - P(A \cap B)$ $\hspace{1.5cm}$ (2.21)

This property follows from Figure 2.2, which illustrates the relation

$$A \cup B = A \cup (B \cap \overline{A})$$ $\hspace{3cm}$ (2.22)

where A and $(B \cap \overline{A})$ are mutually exclusive events. By using Axiom III we obtain the expression

$$P(A \cup B) = P(A) + P(B \cap \overline{A})$$ $\hspace{2cm}$ (2.23)

However, for B we also have the relationship

$$B = (B \cap A) \cup (B \cap \overline{A})$$ $\hspace{2.5cm}$ (2.24)

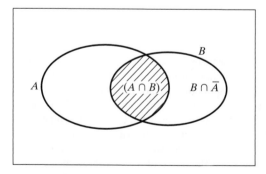

Figure 2.2   A graphical proof of property 5. The right ellipse is event B and A is the left ellipse. $(A \cap B)$ is the shaded area.

where the two events on the right side of equation (2.24) are also mutually exclusive. Again Axiom III yields

$$P(B) = P(B \cap A) + P(B \cap \overline{A}) \tag{2.25}$$

resulting in the expression

$$P(B \cap \overline{A}) = P(B) - P(B \cap A) \tag{2.26}$$

Now equations (2.26) and (2.23) yield the result shown in equation (2.21). Note that when the two events A and B are mutually exclusive, the probability of the intersection is zero and we obtain Axiom III again. We may look at this property in an intuitive fashion, in that when we add $P(A)$ and $P(B)$, we are adding the probability of the intersection twice, and hence to obtain the probability of the union, we need to subtract the probability of the intersection.

Now that we know the axioms of probability, how do we assign probability to a specific example? First we have to define the sample space and the possible events of interest. If we can divide the sample space into a number of mutually exclusive events that together form the entire sample space, then all we have to do is assign a value to the probability of each event such that the total is 1. Such an assignment satisfies the Axioms, and hence it is valid mathematically. However, whether such an assignment has any utility depends on how we pick these values. One way of picking these values is empirically, by performing the experiment a number of times and assigning probabilities to events based on the relative frequency of the occurrence of such events. Another way is geometric in nature, in that if we can subdivide the sample space into N events that would logically seem equally likely to occur, then we can assign probability of $1/N$ to each such event. What happens when the number of outcomes is uncountable such as in the measurements of voltages, currents, or resistance that take values in an interval? In such a case we may select the probability to be in some way related to the length of each subinterval of values.

We now illustrate some of these assignments, and their properties with some examples.

Example 2.7

We refer again to Example 2.1, in which we toss a coin twice and assign probabilities to the resulting outcomes. In this example, we have four individual outcomes, HH, HT, TH, TT, where the first letter shows the outcome of the first toss and the second letter shows the outcome of the second toss (consistent with Example 2.1). Clearly, there is no reason to favor one of these four outcomes if the coin is fair. Hence each of these events (events that contain a single outcome each) will have probability 0.25, so that the total indeed adds up to 1. We can then answer questions such as the probability of at least one Heads, and the answer is the union of the first three such events in the list and has probability 0.75. Similarly, the probability of exactly one Heads is the union of the middle two events in the list, and the answer is 0.5.

Example 2.8

Suppose we observe two components in a fixed length of time and see if they fail or do not fail during that time. The sample space also contains four mutually exclusive outcomes. Let F_1 denote the event that component #1 fails, and F_2 denote the event that component #2 fails. The four mutually exclusive outcomes that subdivide S for this case are

$$F_1 \cap F_2 = \{\text{both components fail}\}$$
$$F_1 \cap \overline{F_2} = \{\text{component #1 fails, but #2 does not fail}\}$$
$$\overline{F_1} \cap F_2 = \{\text{component #1 does not fail, but #2 fails}\}$$
$$\overline{F_1} \cap \overline{F_2} = \{\text{neither component fails}\}$$

How to assign probabilities to each of these events may depend on empirical tests. An example of a valid probability assignment to the four events may be as follows: 0.02, 0.20, 0.20, and 0.58. Let us call this ***Case 1***. Another assignment (which has different properties to be discussed later) is 0.02, 0.18, 0.08, and 0.72. Let us call this ***Case 2***. Using these assignments we can obtain probabilities such as shown in the following table:

	Case 1	*Case 2*
$P(F_1) = P(F_1 \cap F_2) + P(F_1 \cap \overline{F_2}) =$	0.22	0.20
$P(F_2) = P(F_1 \cap F_2) + P(\overline{F_1} \cap F_2) =$	0.22	0.10
$P(\text{exactly one component fails}) =$		
$P(F_1 \cap \overline{F_2}) + P(\overline{F_1} \cap F_2) =$	0.40	0.26

Example 2.9

If we roll a pair of dice, we can divide the sample space into 36 equally likely events, combining every face-up value of die #1 with every face-up value of die #2. If we define A_i for $i = 1, 2, \ldots, 6$, as the event that die #1 has face value of i, and similarly we define B_j for $j = 1, 2, \ldots, 6$, to denote the event that die #2 has face value j, then if we assume that each of the resulting 36 events is equally likely, we have a probability assignment of 1/36 for any one of these 36 individual events:

$$P(A_i \cap B_j) = 1/36, \text{ for } i, j = 1, 2, \ldots, 6 \tag{2.27}$$

Now let us try to find the probability that the face value of one of the dice is equal to 2. Clearly, such an event is equal to the union of A_2 and B_2 and is given by equation (2.21) as

$$P(A_2 \cup B_2) = P(A_2) + P(B_2) - P(A_2 \cap B_2) = 1/6 + 1/6 - 1/36 = 11/36 \tag{2.28}$$

We cannot use Axiom III directly here, since the two events are not mutually exclusive. If we just add the two probabilities we will be double counting the event that both dice roll a 2 together! This clearly explains why Property 5 is indeed based on the double counting of the events occurring together.

Example 2.10

Consider the case of measuring two resistors from a batch of 100-ohm resistors with tolerance of $\pm 10\%$. The sample space contains all possible pairs of values in the range (90, 110), thus forming a square. If we assume that there is no reason to favor any one pair of values over any other pair, then we may assume that the probability of any pair of values falling in any region in the square is proportional to the area of the region.

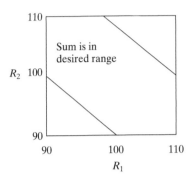

Figure 2.3   The values of two resistors and their sum

Since the probability of falling inside the square is equal to 1, the probability of a pair of values falling in a region is equal to the area of the region divided by the area of the square. The sample space is shown in Figure 2.3. If we now combine the two resistors in series and ask for the probability that the total is in the range $200 \pm 5\%$ (i.e., between 190 and 210), we can find the desired probability by drawing the region of interest (shown in the figure between the two diagonal lines) and dividing the area of the region by the area of the square.

The result is easily computed to be 0.75 (area of the square less areas of the two triangles divided by the area of the square):

$$P\{\text{sum is in range } (190, 210)\} = \frac{20 \times 20 - 2(10 \times 10)/2}{20 \times 20} = \frac{400 - 100}{400} = 0.75$$

2.4 CONDITIONAL PROBABILITY AND INDEPENDENCE

2.4.1 Conditional Probability

If we have two events A and B, we sometimes wish to know the probability of A if we already know that B has occurred. For example, if we roll two dice and we know that their sum is 5, we can ask about the probability that one of them rolled a 2. In an engineering setting, in a system composed of several components, we may compute the probability of failure of the system if we know the failure probabilities of each component. If the system fails and we are trying to perform diagnostics, we may wish to find the probability of failure of some critical component after the fact that the system has failed! We define such probabilities as *conditional probability*. Here is a formal definition:

Definition: Given two events A, B, in a sample space S with probability assignment P, such that $P(B) > 0$, we define the conditional probability of A given B by the following expression:

$$P(A|B) = \frac{P(A \cap B)}{P(B)} \qquad (2.29)$$

When we consider conditional probability, we are restricting ourselves to the case that B has occurred. The definition means that we are looking only at the outcomes

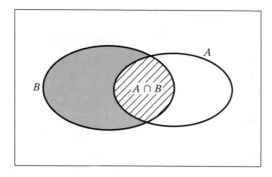

Figure 2.4 Description of Conditional Probability: ratio of dashed area to area of B (left ellipse)

in B in deriving the probability of the other event (in this case A) being conditioned on B. We can see that pictorially in Figure 2.4.

In the figure, if the probabilities are represented by the areas of the events, then in computing the conditional probability of A given B, we are restricting ourselves only to the shaded area that is in B. Hence, we take the common area of A and B and divide it by the area of B.

Several cases are of interest in this situation:

a. If A and B are mutually exclusive, then $P(A|B) = P(\phi)/P(B) = 0$. It is obvious that when both events cannot occur together, A cannot occur if B has occurred!

b. If $B \subset A$ (A contains all the outcomes of B), then $(A \cap B) = B$, which means that if B occurred, then A also must occur. In this case the conditional probability of A given B is $P(A|B) = 1$.

c. If $A \subset B$ (A is a subset of B) and $P(B) < 1$, then $(A \cap B) = A$, which means that $P(A|B) = P(A)/P(B) > P(A)$, since $P(B) < 1$. This case implies that the probability that A will occur is higher if we know that B has occurred.

In general, the conditional probability of A given B could be larger or smaller than or the same as the unconditional probability of A.

Example 2.11

Consider the preceding problem involving rolling two dice and we know that the sum of the roll values is 5 (we denote that as the event B). What is the probability that one of them rolled a 2, which we denote as event A? In this case we can show that the event B contains the following outcomes adding up to 5:

$$B = \{1 \text{ and } 4, 2 \text{ and } 3, 3 \text{ and } 2, 4 \text{ and } 1\}$$

This yields

$$P(B) = 4/36 = 1/9$$

The intersection of the event $A = \{\text{one or both the rolls is a 2}\}$ with B contains just the two outcomes

$$(A \cap B) = \{3 \text{ and } 2, 2 \text{ and } 3\}, \text{ with } P(A \cap B) = 2/36 = 1/18$$

Hence the resulting conditional probability of A given B results in

$$P(A|B) = P(A \cap B)/P(B) = (1/18)/(1/9) = 0.5$$

Note that we obtained the unconditional probability $P(A)$ earlier as 11/36, which is less than 0.5. Hence, knowledge that the sum is equal to 5, increased the probability of A. On the other hand, if we wished to find the conditional probability that one of the rolls is a 5 (we shall denote this event by C), we would obtain zero as $P(C|B)$, since the event of a roll of 5 is mutually exclusive with the event of the sum equal to 5.

Equation (2.29) that defines conditional probability is in many cases useful in deriving the joint probability of A and B. In such a case, if we know the conditional probability $P(A|B)$ (which may be obtained empirically, for example) and we know the probability of B, we can find the probability of their intersection:

$$P(A \cap B) = P(A|B)P(B) \tag{2.30a}$$

It should be noted that the preceding equation can also be written in terms of the conditional probability of B given A:

$$P(A \cap B) = P(B|A)P(A) \tag{2.30b}$$

The two equations may also be combined to yield

$$P(A|B)P(B) = P(B|A)P(A) \tag{2.30c}$$

An important note to remember is that all probability definitions are in some sense conditional probabilities. In most cases, the condition is left out, as it is implicitly assumed. For example, when we say that the probability of Heads is 0.5, we are assuming that the coin is fair. Hence, in cases in which we may be dealing with fair and unfair coins, we do then state the probability as a conditional probability, otherwise we do not write it as a conditional probability.

We have seen that sometimes the conditional probability of A given B results in a smaller probability (even zero) and sometimes results in a larger probability. In both cases, the knowledge of the fact that B has occurred improves or reduces the likelihood that A would have occurred. Obviously, the case in which there is no change in the probability of A merits consideration, as it implies that the occurrence of B has no influence (in the statistical sense) on the occurrence of A. We say in such a case that A and B are *independent*.

2.4.2 Independence

We state that two events A and B are independent if

$$P(A \cap B) = P(A)P(B) \tag{2.31}$$

If two events are independent, then we have

$$P(A|B) = P(A) \text{ and } P(B|A) = P(B)$$

The occurrence of one event does not influence the occurrence of the other statistically.

Many students confuse the properties of mutually exclusive events with independence. Since mutually exclusive events cannot occur together, then the occurrence of one implies that the other has zero probability of happening. Hence, mutually exclusive events are very much dependent.

Example 2.11 (continued):

In the example we denoted by B the event that the sum of the rolls of two dice is equal to 5 and by C the event that one of the rolls is 5. We know that B and C are mutually exclusive, as they cannot occur together, and hence

$$P(B \cap C) = 0 \neq P(B)P(C) = (1/9)(11/36)$$

It clearly means that the events B and C are dependent, since if we know that B occurred, then we know that C could not have occurred.

Example 2.9 (continued):

Consider, for, example, the rolling of two dice, with A_i ($i = 1, 2, 3, 4, 5, 6$) and B_j ($j = 1, 2, 3, 4, 5, 6$) as the events representing the rolls of the first and the second die, respectively. We may assume that the rolls are independent, which means that A_i and B_j are independent of each other, so that the probability that both rolls are equal to 3, for example, is the probability of $A_3 \cap B_3$ and is equal to 1/6 times 1/6. The same argument applies for any A_i with any B_j. However, A_3 and A_5, for example, are mutually exclusive, so that the probability of their intersection is zero.

The definition of independence can be used in two ways:

(A) The first is to help in assigning probabilities in complex situations by assuming that some events are independent (e.g., the toss of two coins, the roll of two dice, the failure of different components, the arrival of different packets at a router, the errors in consecutive binary digits in a channel, etc ...). In such cases we assume independence so that after assigning probabilities to A and B, we can easily assign a probability to their intersection.

(B) The second is to test if two events are independent. We first derive the probabilities, either through some geometric or physical argument or through experimental data, and then we test to see if equation (2.31) is satisfied. An example of the latter case is the finding that smoking and the occurrence of lung cancer are dependent events through experimental means.

Example 2.12

In tossing two coins, let us define the event

$A = \{\text{exactly one Head}\}$ and the event $B = \{\text{First toss is Heads}\}$

Are these events independent? It is easy to see that $P(A) = 0.5$ and $P(B) = 0.5$. The intersection of the two events is equal to the event HT, which has probability of 0.25. Hence we have

$$P(A \cap B) = P(\text{HT}) = 0.25 = P(A)P(B)$$

which proves that the two events are independent.

Example 2.8 (continued):

We can verify that the failures of the components in *Case 1* are dependent events, since

$$P(F_1 \cap F_2) = 0.02 \neq 0.0484 = (0.22)(0.22) = P(F_1)P(F_2)$$

On the other hand in *Case 2* these failures are independent, since we have

$$P(F_1 \cap F_2) = 0.02 = (0.2)(0.1) = P(F_1)P(F_2)$$

If we have two independent events A and B, we can show that their complements are also independent:

$$P(\overline{A} \cap \overline{B}) = P(\overline{A \cup B}) = 1 - P(A \cup B) = 1 - P(A) - P(B) + P(A \cap B)$$

$$= P(\overline{A}) - P(B) + P(A)P(B) = P(\overline{A}) - P(B)[1 - P(A)] = P(\overline{A})[1 - P(B)]$$

$$= P(\overline{A})P(\overline{B})$$

The first equality in this derivation is obtained by the use of De Morgan's Law (2.12), followed by the probability of a union of events, equation (2.21).

Independence of n *Events*

The property of independence can be extended to more than two events. If we have n events $\{A_i, i = 1, 2, \ldots, n\}$, we say that they are independent if the probability of the intersection of any k events is equal to the product of the probabilities of the k events for all $k = 2, 3, \ldots, n$.

We now illustrate the use of the concept of independence to compute the failure probability of simple systems composed of several components.

Parallel Connection of Systems

Consider the case in which a system is composed of n components connected in parallel. Let us denote by F_i (for $i = 1, 2, \ldots, n$) the event that component #i fails, and let us assume that the components fail independently of each other. If we denote the event that the system fails by F, then, since the system fails only if all components fail, we have

$$F = \{\text{all components fail}\} = \bigcap_{i=1}^{n} F_i \tag{2.32}$$

Since we assumed independence we obtain the failure probability as

$$P(F) = P(F_1)P(F_2)\ldots P(F_n) = \prod_{i=1}^{n} P(F_i) \tag{2.33}$$

For example, suppose that $n = 3$ and that $P(F_i) = 0.1$ for $i = 1, 2, 3$, then the failure probability of the system is 0.001. This means that a parallel connection improves the reliability of the system.

Series Connection of Systems

Consider the case in which a system is composed of n components connected in series. Let us denote by F_i (for $i = 1, 2, \ldots, n$) the event that component #i fails, and let us assume that the components fail independently of each other. If we denote the event that the system fails by F, then, since the system fails if any one (or more) of its components fail, we have

$$F = \{\text{either #1, or #2, or #3,} \ldots, \text{or #}n \text{ fails}\} = \bigcup_{i=1}^{n} F_i \qquad (2.34)$$

However, computing $P(F)$ is complicated, since we cannot just add the probabilities (here the events are independent and **not** mutually exclusive). In order to simplify our job, let us consider the probability of the event that the system does not fail, namely,

$$\overline{F} = \overline{\bigcup_{i=1}^{n} F_i} = \bigcap_{i=1}^{n} \overline{F_i} \qquad (2.35)$$

In order to obtain equation (2.35), we used De Morgan's laws. Equation (2.35) tells us that for the system not to fail, **all** components must not fail. We therefore can find the probability of failure more easily by using the independence of the component failures (which also implies independence of nonfailures). The result is seen to be

$$P(F) = 1 - P(\overline{F}) = 1 - P\left(\bigcap_{i=1}^{n} \overline{F_i}\right) = 1 - \prod_{i=1}^{n} P(\overline{F_i}) = 1 - \prod_{i=1}^{n} [1 - P(F_i)]$$

$$(2.36)$$

For the special case of $n = 3$ and $P(F_i) = 0.1$ for $i = 1, 2, 3$, then the failure probability of the system is given by

$$P(F) = 1 - (1 - 0.1)(1 - 0.1)(1 - 0.1) = 1 - 0.9 \times 0.9 \times 0.9 = 0.271$$

We see that the failure probability is almost three times the failure probability of one component, which means that the reliability gets much worse if the components are connected in series.

The derivation of failure probability of more complex systems is done in similar ways if we can reduce it to combinations of series and parallel connections. In cases for which this cannot be done, we have to resort to actual enumeration of the elements contained in the event that the system fails in terms of failure or nonfailure of each component.

2.5 TOTAL PROBABILITY AND BAYES' RULE

We shall consider the problem shown in Figure 2.5 in which the event A is divided into two mutually exclusive parts, based on its intersection with B or with the

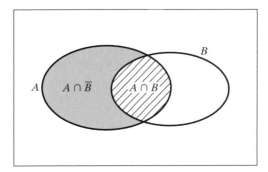

Figure 2.5   The event A (filled) is divided into two mutually exclusive events

complement of B. A situation like this occurs when we wish to obtain (or derive) information about A and we do that in two steps. In the first step we explore the case in which B would have occurred, and next we explore the case in which B would not have occurred, and in each case we find the conditional probability of the occurrence of A.

The two events whose union forms the event A are $(A \cap B)$ and $(A \cap \overline{B})$, and their probabilities add up to the probability of A (since they are mutually exclusive), and may be found using the conditional probability rule as expressed in equation (2.30):

$$P(A) = P(A \cap B) + P(A \cap \overline{B}) = P(A|B)P(B) + P(A|\overline{B})P(\overline{B}) \quad (2.37)$$

We call this the rule of **total probability**, as it allows us to find the "total" probability of A when we know its conditional probabilities given B and given the complement of B. This rule may be generalized to n mutually exclusive events B_i for $i = 1, 2, \ldots, n$, that together form the sample space S. We have in this case

$$B_i \cap B_j = \phi \text{ for } i \neq j; \quad \text{and} \quad S = \bigcup_{i=1}^{n} B_i \quad (2.38)$$

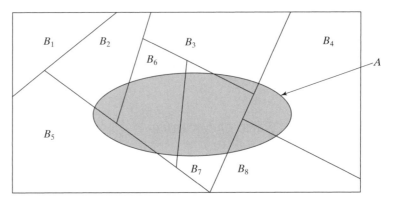

Figure 2.6   The event A (the oval) and the events B_i for $n = 8$

We therefore can express A as the union of mutually exclusive events obtained from the intersection of A with B_i as shown in Figure 2.6, and the result is

$$A = \bigcup_{i=1}^{n}(A \cap B_i) \tag{2.39}$$

The rule of total probability (for A) will therefore be derived the same way it was derived for $n = 2$, by using the fact that the union in equation (2.39) is of mutually exclusive events, and the probability of each such event may be obtained from the definition of the conditional probability as given by equation (2.30) to result in the rule of **total probability**:

$$P(A) = P\left\{\bigcup_{i=1}^{n}(A \cap B_i)\right\} = \sum_{i=1}^{n}P(A \cap B_i) = \sum_{i=1}^{n}P(A|B_i)P(B_i) \tag{2.40}$$

Example 2.13

Suppose that in a dial-up connection you may be connected through one of three types of channels with varying quality of transmission. In Type I the channel has an error probability of 0.01, in Type II the channel has an error probability of 0.005, and in Type III the channel has an error probability of 0.001. Suppose we assume (or we know) that for the service provider used, 20% of the channels are of Type I, 30% are of Type II, and 50% are of Type III. What is the probability of error for an arbitrary connection? Note that, when we specify an error probability, we mean that a transmitted bit or a transmitted block of data is received in error.

We define the events

$$A = \{\text{a bit is received in error}\}$$
$$B_i = \{\text{connection is made via channel of Type } i\}, i = 1, 2, 3.$$

We have, based on the definition of the problem, the following probabilities:

$$P(B_1) = 0.2, \quad P(A|B_1) = 0.01$$
$$P(B_2) = 0.3, \quad P(A|B_2) = 0.005$$
$$P(B_3) = 0.5, \quad P(A|B_3) = 0.001$$

We now can apply equation (2.40) to derive the error probability as a total probability:

$$P(A) = 0.01 \times 0.2 + 0.005 \times 0.3 + 0.001 \times 0.5 = 0.004$$

We should obtain the same type of problem if we wish to evaluate a number of different coins in terms of their fairness, and we pick a coin at random from a collection, and ask about the resulting probability of Heads.

Bayes' Rule

Let us discuss the problem in Figure 2.5 again. Now that we have found the probability of the event A, suppose that the event A did indeed occur. We may wish to know whether B or its complement has in fact occurred. In other words, we wish to find the probability of B given A, and the probability of $\overline{B}$ given A. In this case we just revert to the definition of the conditional probability to obtain

$$P(B|A) = \frac{P(A \cap B)}{P(A)} = \frac{P(A|B)P(B)}{P(A)} \tag{2.41}$$

Here we just used equation (2.30c) to express $P(B|A)$ in terms of $P(A|B)$. The probability of A in the denominator is obtained from equation (2.37):

$$P(A) = P(A|B)P(B) + P(A|\overline{B})P(\overline{B}) \tag{2.42}$$

Equations (2.41) and (2.42) together are called **Bayes' Rule**. In most texts these are written as a single equation. However, it is better not to combine the two equations, as most students tend to try to remember it as one large formula, with the result of using the wrong probabilities in the terms of the resulting equation. It should always be derived as two separate equations and then combined.

We can repeat the process for the general case when S is subdivided into n mutually exclusive events B_i and we may ask for the probability of any of the events B_j given that A has occurred. By the same argument used earlier, we obtain the general form of **Bayes' Rule**, as in the following expressions:

$$P(B_j|A) = \frac{P(A \cap B_j)}{P(A)} = \frac{P(A|B_j)P(B_j)}{P(A)} \tag{2.43a}$$

$$P(A) = \sum_{i=1}^{n} P(A|B_i)P(B_i) \tag{2.43b}$$

Here again we write the rule as a set of two equations so as not to be too confusing.

Example 2.13 (continued):

As an example, consider the channel problem just discussed. Suppose we observed an error. What is the probability that we were connected via a channel of Type I? Type II? Type III?

$$P(B_1|A) = P(A|B_1)P(B_1)/P(A) = 0.01 \times 0.2/0.004 = 0.50$$

$$P(B_2|A) = P(A|B_2)P(B_2)/P(A) = 0.005 \times 0.3/0.004 = 0.375$$

$$P(B_3|A) = P(A|B_3)P(B_3)/P(A) = 0.001 \times 0.5/0.004 = 0.125$$

Again, if we apply this rule to the coin-tossing problem, then based on whether the outcome was Heads or Tails, we can obtain the conditional probability that the coin we picked was fair or unfair.

Consider the failure probability of the system shown in Figure 2.7, which has five components. These components are assumed to fail independently of each other.

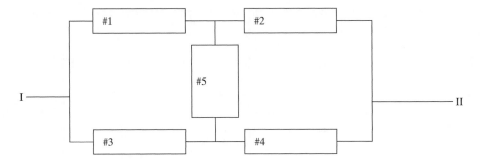

Figure 2.7   A system with complex connections

Let us define for $i = 1, 2, 3, 4, 5$

$P(F_i) = P\{\text{component } \#i \text{ fails}\} = p_i,$

$P(\overline{F_i}) = P\{\text{Component } \#i \text{ does not fail}\} = 1 - p_i = q_i,$

$P(F) = P\{\text{The system fails}\} = P\{\text{No connection between the end points I and II}\}.$

One way to find the probability of failure of the system is to enumerate all 32 possible events that are involved in the failure or nonfailure of the five components. However, there is an easier way by using Bayes' Rule.

   We see that component #5 causes us a problem, in that it causes the system to not be composed of just series and parallel connections that we studied earlier. However, if we can somehow get rid of #5, we revert back to series and parallel connections. Therefore we can find the conditional probability of failure under two mutually exclusive conditions, which also form the entire space S, namely, F_5 and $\overline{F_5}$. These two conditions are shown in Figures 2.8a and 2.8b, respectively.

   In this case, if #5 failed, we have from Figure 2.8a that components #1 and #2 are in series; also components #3 and #4 are in series, and the two branches are in parallel. The result is the conditional probability that the system fails given that #5 failed:

$$P(F|F_5) = P\{(F_1 \cup F_2) \cap (F_3 \cup F_4)\} = (1 - q_1 q_2)(1 - q_3 q_4)$$

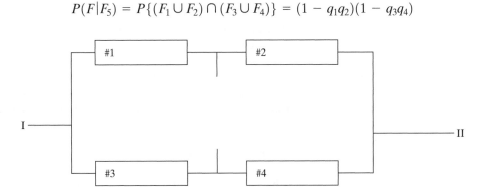

Figure 2.8a   The condition that component #5 failed (F_5)

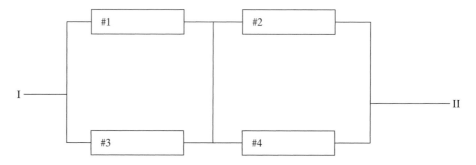

Figure 2.8b   The condition that component #5 did not fail ($\overline{F_5}$)

Similarly, if #5 did not fail, we have from Figure 2.8b that components #1 and #3 are in parallel, and components #2 and #4 are also in parallel, and the two branches are in series. The result is the conditional probability that the system fails given that #5 did not fail:

$$P(F|\overline{F_5}) = P\{(F_1 \cap F_3) \cup (F_2 \cap F_4)\} = 1 - (1 - p_1 p_3)(1 - p_2 p_4)$$

Finally, when we combine both using the total probability rule, we obtain

$$P(F) = P(F|F_5)P(F_5) + P(F|\overline{F_5})P(\overline{F_5})$$
$$= (1 - q_1 q_2)(1 - q_3 q_4)p_5 + [1 - (1 - p_1 p_3)(1 - p_2 p_4)]q_5$$

If we were to observe that the system failed, then we may ask about the probability that #5 has failed

$$P(F_5|F) = P(F|F_5)P(F_5)/P(F),$$

where all the quantities have already been derived.

Binary Communications Channel

As an important illustration of Bayes' rule, we consider a binary communications channel on which we transmit binary digits as "zeros" or "ones". However, we assume that there are transmission errors, so that a bit that was sent as "one" may be received as "zero" and a bit that was sent as "zero" maybe received as "one". We assume that through testing or analysis we can find the conditional probability of such errors. Let the event that a transmitted bit is zero be denoted by T_0 and let the event that the transmitted bit is a "one" be denoted by T_1. Similarly, we denote the events of a received bit being "zero" or "one" by R_0 or R_1, respectively. The conditional error probabilities are therefore given by

$$p_{10} = P\{R_1|T_0\} = \text{Probability that a transmitted "zero" is received as "one"}$$
$$p_{01} = P\{R_0|T_1\} = \text{Probability that a transmitted "one" is received as "zero"}$$

Since the sum of probabilities must add up to unity, we have, for the probabilities of correct reception for both cases, the following:

$$p_{00} = 1 - p_{10} = P\{R_0|T_0\} = \text{Probability that a transmitted "zero"}$$
$$\text{is received as "zero"}$$

$$p_{11} = 1 - p_{01} = P\{R_1|T_1\} = \text{Probability that a transmitted "one"}$$
$$\text{is received as "one"}$$

These events are illustrated in Figure 2.9.

Suppose we know the probability of a transmitted bit being a "zero" or a "one" (this maybe obtained from the ratios of "zeros" or "ones" to the total number of transmitted bits) as $p_0 = P\{T_0\}$ and $p_1 = P\{T_1\} = 1 - p_0$. The question is, What are the probabilities of a received bit being a "zero" or a "one"?

The rule of total probabilities will yield the answer:

$$P\{R_0\} = P\{R_0|T_0\}P\{T_0\} + P\{R_0|T_1\}P\{T_1\} = p_{00}p_0 + p_{01}p_1$$
$$= (1 - p_{10})p_0 + p_{01}(1 - p_0)$$

$$P\{R_1\} = P\{R_1|T_0\}P\{T_0\} + P\{R_1|T_1\}P\{T_1\} = p_{10}p_0 + p_{11}p_1$$
$$= p_{10}p_0 + (1 - p_{01})(1 - p_0) = 1 - P(R_0)$$

We now can ask the question that can be answered using Bayes' rule: Suppose we received a "zero." What is the probability that the transmitted bit was actually a "zero"? The answer is obtained by using Bayes' rule:

$$P\{T_0|R_0\} = P\{R_0|T_0\}P\{T_0\}/P\{R_0\} = (1 - p_{10})p_0/[(1 - p_{10})p_0 + p_{01}(1 - p_0)]$$

Using simple algebra we can verify that the probability of the transmitted bit was a "one" given that we received a "zero" is equal to

$$P\{T_1|R_0\} = P\{R_0|T_1\}P\{T_1\}/P\{R_0\} = 1 - P\{T_0|R_0\}$$

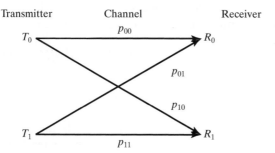

Transmitter   Channel   Receiver

Figure 2.9 An illustration of the binary channel

The same process can be repeated to obtain the conditional probability of the transmitted bit given that the received bit is a "one":

$$P\{T_0|R_1\} = P\{R_1|T_0\}P\{T_0\}/P\{R_1\} = p_{10}p_0/[p_{10}p_0 + (1 - p_{01})(1 - p_0)]$$
$$P\{T_1|R_1\} = P\{R_1|T_1\}P\{T_1\}/P\{R_1\} = 1 - P\{T_0|R_1\}$$

An especially interesting case is the binary symmetric channel, for which the two conditional error probabilities are equal: $p_{01} = p_{10} = p$. In this case we have

$$P\{R_0\} = (1 - p)p_0 + p(1 - p_0)$$
$$P\{R_1\} = pp_0 + (1 - p)(1 - p_0) = 1 - P(R_0)$$

Similarly, we get for the a posteriori probabilities

$$P\{T_0|R_0\} = (1 - p)p_0/[(1 - p)p_0 + p(1 - p_0)]$$
$$P\{T_1|R_1\} = (1 - p)(1 - p_0)/[pp_0 + (1 - p)(1 - p_0)]$$

If the probabilities of transmitting a "one" or a "zero" are equal ($p_0 = 0.5$), then we have

$$P\{R_0\} = (1 - p)0.5 + p(1 - 0.5) = 0.5 = P\{R_1\}$$

Similarly, we get for the a posteriori probabilities

$$P\{T_0|R_0\} = (1 - p)0.5/0.5 = (1 - p) = P\{T_1|R_1\}$$

2.6 INDEPENDENCE AND CONDITIONAL INDEPENDENCE

We defined the independence of two events on the basis that their joint probability is equal to the product of their individual probabilities. To understand what is meant by *conditional independence*, consider the following two cases, where we have two coins, one fair with $P(H) = 0.5$ and one unfair with $P(H) = 0.8$:

Case a. We pick one of the coins at random, toss it once, put it back, and repeat the experiment again. In this case both tosses are independent, since in each toss we are repeating the entire experiment. In each toss we may end up with the fair coin or with the unfair coin. In each toss we have

$$P(H) = P(H|\text{Fair})P(\text{Fair}) + P(H|\text{Unfair})P(\text{Unfair})$$
$$= 0.5 \times 0.5 + 0.8 \times 0.5 = 0.65$$
$$P(\text{both tosses are Heads}) = 0.65 \times 0.65 = 0.4225$$

Case b. We pick a coin at random and toss it twice. In this case, once we pick a coin, we are stuck with that same coin for both tosses. Clearly, if we picked the unfair coin we may have a higher probability of Heads in both tosses, while if we picked the fair coin the probability of Heads is not higher than that of Tails in both tosses. Hence, the two tosses are called **conditionally independent**. It means that under the condition that we picked the fair coin, the tosses are independent with probability of Heads of 0.5, and under the condition that we picked the unfair coin, the tosses are independent with probability of Heads of 0.8. In this case we have

$P(\text{both tosses are Heads}|\text{Fair}) = 0.5 \times 0.5 = 0.25$

$P(\text{both tosses are Heads}|\text{Unfair}) = 0.8 \times 0.8 = 0.64$

$P(\text{both tosses are Heads}) = P(\text{both are Heads}|\text{Fair})P(\text{Fair}) +$
$\quad P(\text{both are Heads}|\text{Unfair})P(\text{Unfair}) = 0.25 \times 0.5 + 0.64 \times 0.5 = 0.445$

For example, in the first case we cannot question which coin was used if both tosses are Heads, since we may not have used the same coin in both tosses. In the second case we can question which coin was likely to have been picked given that both tosses are Heads. Using Bayes' Rule, we obtain

$$P(\text{Fair}|\text{both tosses are Heads}) = \frac{P\,(\text{both are Heads}|\text{Fair})\text{P(Fair)}}{P(\text{both are Heads})}$$

$$= 0.25 \times 0.5/0.445 = 0.281$$

Similarly, for the unfair coin we have

$P(\text{Unfair}|\text{both tosses are Heads}) = 0.64 \times 0.5/0.445 = 0.719$

$$= 1 - P(\text{Fair}|\text{both are Heads})$$

We can discuss several more examples based on these principles in communication channels with errors, in component failures under different ambient conditions, and many others. The case in Example 2.13 is exactly one of conditional independence, since once we are connected, we are subject to the same channel throughout the session. In the next two examples we see the difference between independence and conditional independence.

Example 2.14

Suppose we send three packets of data through a switch with two packet-switched channels. Each packet is routed to one of the channels via a random assignment. Let the event that the packet is routed via Channel I be A and the event that it is routed via Channel II be $\overline{A}$. Define the event that a packet is lost by L. It is assumed that the channels have different probabilities of losing a packet, which may be due to different congestion conditions.

Suppose we know that 30% of the packets are routed via Channel I. Then we have

$$P(A) = 0.3, P(\overline{A}) = 0.7$$

Suppose that we also know that the loss probabilities in each channel are given by

$$P(L|A) = 0.01, P(L|\overline{A}) = 0.005$$

(A) If one packet is sent, what is the probability of its being lost?

$$P(L) = P(L|A)P(A) + P(L|\overline{A})P(\overline{A}) = 0.01 \times 0.3 + 0.005 \times 0.7$$
$$= 0.0065$$

(B) If a packet is lost, what is the probability that it was routed via Channel I? Here we apply Bayes' rule to obtain

$$P(A|L) = P(L|A)P(A)/P(L) = 0.01 \times 0.3/0.0065 = 0.46$$

(C) If three packets are sent, what is the probability of all three being lost?

Here, we are not obliged to route all packets through the same channel. Since each individual packet may be routed via either channel, we have independence. In this case we may define by L_i the event that packet #i is lost, for $i = 1, 2, 3$. Then we have

$$P(\text{all three of the packets are lost}) = P(L_1 \cap L_2 \cap L_3) = P(L_1)P(L_2)P(L_3)$$
$$= 0.0065 \times 0.0065 \times 0.0065 = 2.7 \times 10^{-7}$$

Example 2.15

Suppose we have a similar communications problem, except that we are connecting via modem, and we have a chance to connect via a high-quality line or via one of lower quality. Once we are connected, we stay with that same line throughout the session. This type of channel is also called a circuit-switched channel, since the entire session uses the same channel. Suppose we are sending three blocks of data using some protocol. We assume that a block has a different probability of being received in error in the two types of lines. We define the following events:

$A = \{$a single block sent is received in error$\}$

$B = \{$connected via a high quality line$\}$, $\overline{B} = \{$connected via a lower quality line$\}$

Suppose that 60% of the service provider's lines are of high quality. We also assume that blocks are received in error independently of each other, but since the blocks are sent via the same channel, this is a conditional independence case (i.e., it is conditional on the type of line that resulted from the connection). In this case suppose that we have the following probabilities, conditional on the line type:

$$P(A|B) = 0.01, P(A|\overline{B}) = 0.02$$

We also have, from the types of lines available, $P(B) = 0.6$ and $P(\overline{B}) = 0.4$.

(A) What is the probability of receiving a single block in error (when one block is sent)?

$$P(A) = P(A|B)P(B) + P(A|\overline{B})P(\overline{B}) = 0.01 \times 0.6 + 0.02 \times 0.4 = 0.014$$

This question is the same as the corresponding question in Example 2.14, since we are considering only a single block.

(B) If three blocks are sent, what is the probability that all three are received in error?

Here the errors in the blocks are conditionally independent, since they either all go through the good line or they all go through the bad line. Hence, if we denote by A_i the event that block #i is received in error, for $i = 1, 2, 3$, we have

$$P(A_1 \cap A_2 \cap A_3|B) = P(A_1|B)P(A_2|B)P(A_3|B)$$
$$= 0.01 \times 0.01 \times 0.01 = 10^{-6}$$
$$P(A_1 \cap A_2 \cap A_3|\overline{B}) = P(A_1|\overline{B})P(A_2|\overline{B})P(A_3|\overline{B})$$
$$= 0.02 \times 0.02 \times 0.02 = 8 \times 10^{-6}$$
$$P(A_1 \cap A_2 \cap A_3) = P(A_1 \cap A_2 \cap A_3|B)P(B)$$
$$+ P(A_1 \cap A_2 \cap A_3|\overline{B})P(\overline{B})$$
$$= 10^{-6} \times 0.6 + 8 \times 10^{-6} \times 0.4 = 3.8 \times 10^{-6}$$

(C) If we received all three blocks in error, what is the probability that we were connected via the lower quality line? (Note that it would have been meaningless to ask this question in the previous example, since each packet may have been sent via a different channel.)

$$P(\overline{B}|A_1 \cap A_2 \cap A_3) = P(A_1 \cap A_2 \cap A_3|\overline{B})P(\overline{B})/P(A_1 \cap A_2 \cap A_3)$$
$$= 3.2/3.8 = 0.84$$

Similarly, we find the conditional probability that the good line was used if all three blocks are received in error:

$$P(B|A_1 \cap A_2 \cap A_3) = P(A_1 \cap A_2 \cap A_3|B)P(B)/P(A_1 \cap A_2 \cap A_3)$$
$$= 8/38 = 0.16$$
$$= 1 - P(\overline{B}|A_1 \cap A_2 \cap A_3).$$

2.7 INDEPENDENT TRIALS (BERNOULLI TRIALS)

So far we have discussed the outcomes of a single experiment. In some cases we had more than one, such as the tossing of several coins or the rolling of two dice, but in those cases we solved the problem directly. Similarly, for a system with several components, the failure or normal operation of each component can be considered an experiment, so that the failure or normal operation of more than one component may be considered as a repetition of the experiment with a single component a number of times. If the experiments are repeated, they have to be repeated independently for us to be able to obtain a general solution for the probability of the intersection of events among the various experiments. Furthermore, the outcomes and the corresponding probabilities of a success or failure in each experiment have to be identical in all experiments if we wish to analyze such a case mathematically, without exhaustive enumeration of all possible outcomes. This process of repeated independent trials is also called *Bernoulli trials*.

The problem we consider is the following:

A random experiment has two possible outcomes, **success** and **failure**. The experiment is repeated *n* times under the following conditions:

a. The experiments are repeated **independently** of each other.

b. The probability of **success** in each experiment is *p* and is the same for all experiments.

For brevity, we denote the probability of **failure** by $q = 1 - p$.

We are interested in finding the probability of the event that exactly *k* successes occurs in the *n* trials.

Before we solve the problem, let us consider, for example, the case of $n = 4$. Clearly, there are 16 possible individual events (each containing a single outcome), as shown in Table 2.1, which provides a systematic way of enumerating all such individual

TABLE 2.1   All possible individual outcomes in the repeated trials experiment with **n = 4**

No. of successes	Experiment 1	Experiment 2	Experiment 3	Experiment 4	Probability
0	failure	failure	failure	failure	$qqqq$
1	success	failure	failure	failure	$pqqq$
1	failure	success	failure	failure	$qpqq$
1	failure	failure	success	failure	$qqpq$
1	failure	failure	failure	success	$qqqp$
2	success	success	failure	failure	$ppqq$
2	success	failure	success	failure	$pqpq$
2	success	failure	failure	success	$pqqp$
2	failure	success	success	failure	$qppq$
2	failure	success	failure	success	$qpqp$
2	failure	failure	success	success	$qqpp$
3	success	success	success	failure	$pppq$
3	success	success	failure	success	$ppqp$
3	success	failure	success	success	$pqpp$
3	failure	success	success	success	$qppp$
4	success	success	success	success	$pppp$

outcomes in the four experiments. In the column at the right in the table we also include the probability of each such event.

Now we are ready to find the probability that there are k successes in the four trials. The probability for zero successes, namely, $k = 0$, involves just the probability of a single event, shown in first row of the table:

$$P(0 \text{ successes}) = q^4 = (1 - p)^4$$

For $k = 1$ we see that there are four mutually exclusive individual events, shown in rows 2 to 5. The probability of each of these events is the same, so that in order to find the probability that either will occur, we just add the four probabilities. This means that we have to multiply by 4 the probability of a single event or outcome:

$$P(1 \text{ success}) = 4P(\text{a specific event with 3 failures and 1 success})$$
$$= 4pq^3 = 4p(1 - p)^3$$

We proceed in this fashion to the case of $k = 2$ (2 successes), and here we see six events contributing to $k = 2$, each having the same probability, so that we have

$$P(2 \text{ successes}) = 6P(\text{a specific event with 2 failures and 2 successes})$$
$$= 6p^2q^2 = 6p^2(1 - p)^2$$

We continue with $k = 3$, and here we also have four such possible mutually exclusive events, with all four having the same probability, leading to the result

$$P(3 \text{ successes}) = 4P(\text{a specific event with 1 failure and 3 successes})$$
$$= 4p^3q = 4p^3(1 - p)$$

Finally, the event of $k = 4$ (exactly 4 successes) includes only a single event, and the resulting probability is

$$P(4 \text{ successes}) = p^4$$

If we add all the probabilities, we obtain unity if we use the binomial expansion of $(p + q)^4 = 1$, which is exactly the sum of the five probabilities we obtained.

How do we extend this case to an arbitrary value of n?

In order to handle this, we first should note that a specific individual event containing k successes and $n - k$ failures has a probability (because of independence) of

$$P(\text{a single event with a specific occurrence of } k \text{ successes and } n - k \text{ failures})$$
$$= p^k q^{n-k} = p^k(1 - p)^{n-k}$$

We now have to count how many such individual events exist, as we enumerated in the table for $n = 4$. We refer here to the way we do counting of **permutations** and **combinations**.

Permutations: Suppose we have n distinct elements and we wish to form sets by selecting k of these elements without replacement (meaning no element is selected twice in the same set), and where we care about the order of the elements in the sets. We call the number of all such possible sets the number of **permutations** of size k from a population of size n, and we denote it by P_k^n.

As an example of permutations, we have 26 letters of the alphabet, and we want to form five-letter words where no letter is selected twice in the same word. The number of possible words that can be selected this way is equal to the number of permutations of size 5 out of 26 elements and is equal to P_5^{26}.

It is not too difficult to evaluate the expression for P_k^n:

> We have n choices of the first item in the set.
>
> Next, we have $n - 1$ choices for the second item in the set.
>
> Next, we have $n - 2$ choices for the third item in the set.
>
> We proceed in this manner, and we see that we have $(n - k + 1)$ choices for the kth element (last element) in the set.

The number of permutations we are seeking is just the product of all these possible choices:

$$P_k^n = n(n - 1)(n - 2)\ldots(n - k + 1) = n!/(n - k)! \qquad (2.44)$$

Here we simplified the formula in equation (2.44) by multiplying the numerator and denominator by $(n - k)(n - k - 1)\ldots(2)(1) = (n - k)!$ so that the numerator becomes $n!$ as shown. A special case of $k = n$ provides us with the number of different ways of just ordering a set of n elements, since all the sets will contain all n elements. In this case we have $P_n^n = n!$

Consider the example of the number of different words with five letters that do not contain the same letter twice:

$$P_5^{26} = 26 \times 25 \times 24 \times 23 \times 22 = 7,893,600$$

Note that the first expression in equation (2.44) is the one to be used for computation. The more compact second expression is easier to write but not very efficient for computation.

Listing of permutations in MATLAB: We can obtain a listing of all the permutations of n elements in MATLAB by using the function *perms(x)*, where x is a row vector of size n, and the result is a matrix having $n!$ rows, and each row contains one of the permutations of the elements of x.

Combinations: If we were to select sets of k elements out of n distinct elements, where the order of the elements in the resulting sets is unimportant, we define the number of all possible selections as the number of **combinations** of k elements out of n and we denote it by C_k^n or $\binom{n}{k}$ (both notations are used in many texts). Occasionally, this is also called **n choose k**.

As an example of combinations, consider the five-letter words that we previously considered. If we wanted only to distinguish the words by the letters they contain rather than by the order of the letters in the words, we would obtain combinations rather than permutations. In this case we do not have words, but we have sets of five letters that do not contain the same letter twice, and two sets are different only if they do not contain the same five letters.

In order to find C_k^n, let us suppose that we know what it is equal to. Suppose also that we obtained all the combinations of size k out of the n elements. Now, if we want to obtain all permutations of size k, all we have to do is to reorder the elements in each selected combination of size k. The reordering of the k elements in each such combination implies that each unordered combination can yield $k!$ such differently ordered sets (which is the number of permutations of k elements out of k). This means that if we multiply C_k^n by $k!$, we should obtain the number of permutations of k elements out of n:

$$P_k^n = C_k^n k! \tag{2.45}$$

We now solve for C_k^n to obtain

$$\binom{n}{k} = C_k^n = P_k^n/k! = n!/[k!(n-k)!] = \frac{n(n-1)(n-2)\ldots(n-k+1)}{k!} \tag{2.46}$$

We call the result the binomial coefficient because it appears in the binomial expansion

$$(a+b)^n = \sum_{k=0}^{n} C_k^n a^k b^{n-k} \tag{2.47}$$

Properties of the binomial coefficients are

$$C_0^n = 1, C_1^n = n, \quad C_k^n = C_{n-k}^n \tag{2.48}$$

Again we consider the five-letter sets we discussed previously. The number of different sets of five letters (not different words) taken out of the 26 letters of the alphabet is equal to

$$C_5^{26} = (26 \times 25 \times 24 \times 23 \times 22)/(5!) = 7{,}893{,}600/120 = 6580$$

This explains the approach we used to find the number of combinations in general. In the letters case there are 6580 different sets of letters of size five. Since, if we order each such set differently, there are $5! = 120$ different words for each set. Hence the product of (5!) by the number of different sets will yield the number of different words that was obtained earlier.

Computationally, it is not efficient to use the compact form of C_k^n as shown in the middle of equation (2.46). It is more efficient to compute C_k^n by using the expression at the right side of equation (2.46) for $k \leq n/2$. Then, for $k > n/2$, we use the symmetry property in equation (2.48).

How does this help solve the number of different ways of obtaining k success-es in n trials? It will be shown that the number of different ways of selecting the experiments in which the k successes occur is exactly $\binom{n}{k}$ or C_k^n.

We shall illustrate this in Figure 2.10 for the case $n = 5$ and $k = 2$. The fig-ure shows the number of trials, and marks with an S the location of the two suc-cesses. At the right, we indicate the two numbers identifying the location of the two successes.

It should be noted that when we identify the location of successes, we do not need to distinguish between $(1, 2)$ and $(2, 1)$, as they mean the same thing: Successes occurred at the first and second trial. Hence, in the preceding exam-ple, the number of different possible individual events containing two successes in five trials is equal to the number of combinations of size two out of five ele-ments and is equal to 10.

In the general case we have n distinct elements numbered from 1 to n (the number of experiments). We are looking to pick k of these elements to be the ones in which the k successes occur. Since having successes at j and m is the same as hav-ing successes at m and j, we have here a problem of selecting k combinations out of n elements.

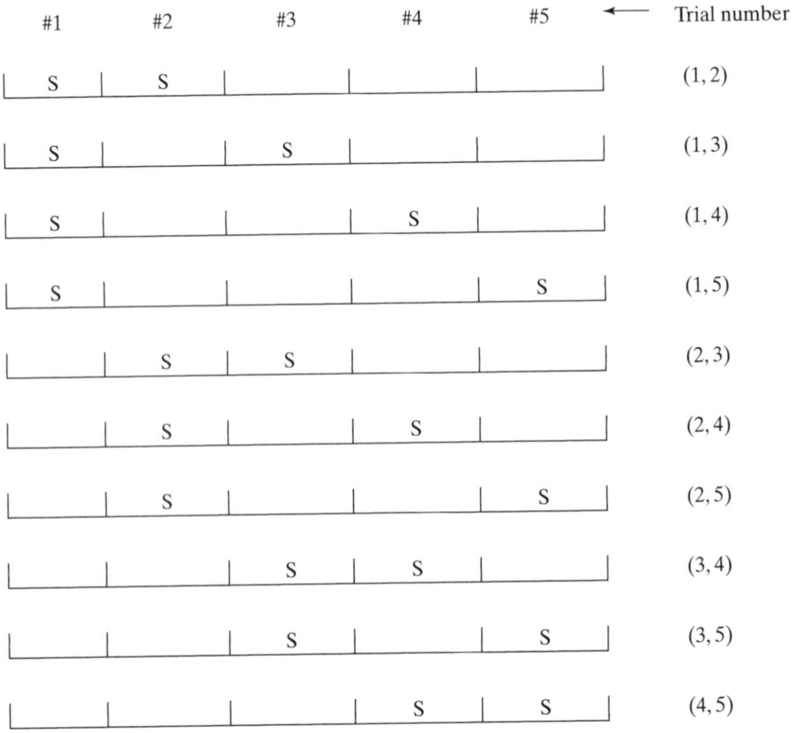

Figure 2.10   Listing of all possible ways to have two successes in five trials

Since we already know the probability of each specific way of having k successes and $n - k$ failures, all we have to do to obtain the final answer is to multiply the individual probability by C_k^n. The result is expressed as follows:

$$P(\text{Exactly } k \text{ successes in } n \text{ trials}) = C_k^n p^k (1 - p)^{n-k} \tag{2.49}$$

You may check this for the case of $n = 4$ we discussed previously.

Listing of combinations in MATLAB: We can obtain a listing of all combinations of size k out of n elements in MATLAB by using the function $nchoosek(x,k)$, where x is a vector of size n, and k is the number of elements in each combination. The result is a matrix having C_k^n rows, with each row containing one of the distinct combinations.

For example, in Table 2.1, we may obtain a listing of the six rows corresponding to two successes and two failures, by using the following MATLAB commands:

$$x = [1\ 2\ 3\ 4]$$

Here x provides the number assigned to each trial. We now use the command

$$nchoosek(x, 2)$$

to obtain the location of the possible two successes, corresponding to rows 6 through 11 in Table 2.1:

1	2
1	3
1	4
2	3
2	4
3	4

We also may obtain the number of combinations of size k out of n elements, C_k^n, by using the same command, where x is replaced by n:

$$nchoosek(n, k)$$

In the preceding example, if we use the command $nchoosek(4,2)$, we obtain the number 6.

Example 2.16

Suppose we have a system with five identical components, which are assumed to fail independently of each other. The system fails to operate only if three or more of the components fail. Let the probability of failure of each component be 0.1. Then the probability of failure of the system is obtained from independent trials with $n = 5$ and $p = 0.1$:

$$P(\text{Failure}) = P(3 \text{ or more components fail}) = \sum_{k=3}^{5} C_k^5 p^k (1 - p)^{5-k}$$
$$= 10(0.1)^3(1 - 0.1)^2 + 5(0.1)^4(1 - 0.1)^1 + (0.1)^5 = 0.00856$$

Example 2.17

We wish to reduce the error probability in a noisy binary channel. In order to achieve our objective, we repeat each bit three times, so that at the receiver we decide that a bit is a "one" if 2 or 3 "ones" are received, and we decide it is a "zero" if 2 or 3 "zeros" are received. Assume that each bit transmitted via the channel has an error probability of $p = 0.05$ and that the errors are independent. We therefore have a case of independent trials with $n = 3$ and $p = 0.05$. We obtain an error in the received bit if 2 or 3 of the three repeated bits are erroneous. Hence we have

$$P(\text{error}) = P(2 \text{ or } 3 \text{ bits received in error out of } 3) = 3p^2(1 - p) + p^3 = 0.00725$$

We see here that we improved the error probability of the channel at the cost of tripling the transmission rate. This is not the most efficient way of adding parity bits to improve the error rate in binary channels, but is used to illustrate the principle of coding.

So far we fixed the number of trials and have wanted to find the probability of a fixed number of successes. We next consider the case in which we wish to repeat the experiment until we obtain a success.

Number of Trials to First Success

We now consider the case in which we keep repeating the experiment until we achieve a success. What is the probability that we achieve the first success on the first trial? It is obvious from the definition of p that

$$P(\text{first success at the first trial}) = p$$

We achieve the first success at the kth trial, for $k > 1$, if we had failures at the first $k - 1$ trials and a success at the kth trial:

$$P(\text{first success at the } k\text{th trial}) = p(1 - p)^{k-1}$$

Since the preceding forms what is known as a "geometric series," it is sometimes called the geometric case, and will be discussed further in Chapter 3.

Example 2.18

If in an accelerator a particle has probability 0.01 of hitting a target material, what is the probability that the first particle to hit the target is the 100th?

$$P(\text{first to hit is the 100th}) = 0.01(1 - 0.01)^{99} = 0.00407$$

What is the probability that the target will be hit first by any of the first 100 particles?

$$P(\text{target is hit first by any of the first 100}) = \sum_{k=1}^{100} 0.01(1 - 0.01)^{k-1} = 0.6321$$

Example 2.19

Here we shall look at a simple example to illustrate the general approach previously discussed and also to relate it to the case of a fixed number of trials.

Suppose that there is an apple on a tree and you jump to try to get it. Suppose that the probability of success in each jump is $p = 0.6$. We shall denote a success in trial #i by S_i, and we assume that S_1 and S_2 are independent and have probability $p = 0.6$ each. We shall denote the complement of the events S_i by F_i.

What is the probability of getting the apple in the first trial?
Let us denote this event by A_1. Clearly the answer to this question is 0.6, since we have

$$P\{A_1\} = P\{S_1\} = 0.6.$$

What is the probability of getting the apple in the second trial?
Let us denote this event by A_2. Obviously you do not try again unless the first trial is unsuccessful, which means that the event A_2 can be written as the intersection of a failure during the first trial and a success during the second:

$$A_2 = F_1 \cap S_2$$

Since the events are independent, we obtain the probability

$$P\{A_2\} = P\{F_1 \cap S_2\} = P\{F_1\}P\{S_2\} = (0.4)(0.6) = 0.24$$

We now may ask about the probability that you get the apple in at most two trials, which we shall denote by B. This event is the union of A_1 and A_2 and therefore its probability is the sum of their probabilities, resulting in

$$P\{B\} = P\{A_1 \cup A_2\} = P\{A_1\} + P\{A_2\} = 0.6 + 0.24 = 0.84$$

We can also obtain this probability as the complement of the events of failure during the first two trials:

$$B = (\overline{F_1 \cap F_2})$$

We therefore have

$$P(B) = 1 - P(F_1 \cap F_2) = 1 - P\{F_1\}P\{F_2\} = 1 - (0.4)(0.4) = 0.84$$

The sample space for this problem is shown in Figure 2.11.
    The relation to independent trials with $n = 2$:
    We now relate it to the repeated trials case with $n = 2$. It is seen from the expression for B that it is the complement of the event of zero successes in two trials. Hence the complement B is the event that there are one or two successes in two trials for $n = 2$:

$$P(B) = P(1 \text{ or } 2 \text{ successes in } 2 \text{ trials}) = 2(0.6)(0.4) + (0.6)(0.6) = 0.84$$

Since we claimed that there was only one apple, how do we justify the statement that B means 1 or 2 apples in two jumps? The answer to the question is provided by the sample

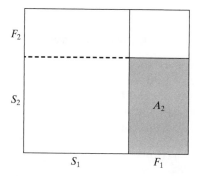

Figure 2.11   Successes and
Failures in Trials 1 and 2

space in Figure 2.11. If the first trial was a success, then it does not matter what happens at a second trial, if indeed there is one (that is why the outcomes of the second trials are shown via a dashed line in the figure). The large square on the left means that we would get two apples if there were two, and the smaller rectangle on the left (above the dashed line) means that we do not get a second apple. However, both of these events are included in the event of the first success S_1. We see therefore that the outcomes of the second trial if the first trial was a success are not relevant to the result, as both are included in the event S_1.

We can further illustrate this by the tree diagram (no pun intended) in Figure 2.12.

In the figure, successes are shown by a thicker arrow and failures by thinner arrows. Note that the second jump results (which need not occur, as the jump will not be taken) are shown via dashed lines. We may compute these probabilities and add them, but they will contribute only the value of 0.6 for the first success:

$$0.6(0.4 + 0.6) = 0.6$$

As we see, we need only add 0.6 to the probability of the top branch, and not worry about adding the probability of each branch of the dashed event:

$$(0.6)(0.6) + (0.6)(0.4) = 0.6$$

We would obtain the same answer if we were to use the repeated trials with $n = 2$, since then we will be adding the dashed lines individually, which, as seen from the figure, yields the same answer.

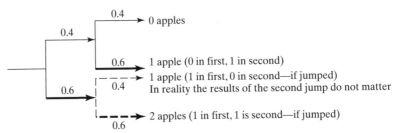

Figure 2.12   Tree diagram illustrating the two jumps

MATLAB commands to generate independent trials data

If we wish to generate two outcomes, success and failure, which we shall represent by "0" and "1," respectively, we can do so by generating a random number whose value is equally likely to be between 0 and 1, and then selecting the outcome as "1" if the number is between $1 - p$ and 1, and selecting "0" otherwise. Alternatively, we may use the *fix* command to achieve the same result:

$$x = fix(p + rand(1, n))$$

In this case, "1," which represents success, occurs with probability p, and the vector x will have n entries representing the success or failure at each trial. Consider, for example, the generation of $n = 20$ data values that represent the outcomes of n independent trials, where the probability of success is $p = 0.4$. The following commands provide the result:

$$x = fix(0.4 + rand(1, 20))$$

The results we obtained in one sample are

0 0 1 0 0 0 0 1 0 0 0 1 0 1 0 0 1 0 0 1

If we now wish to count the number of successes, we simply use the *sum* command:

$$y = sum(x)$$

In this example we obtain the outcome $y = 6$.

If now we wish to repeat our experiment 10 times, we can use an array of 10 by 20 random numbers, and when we sum over the outcomes of each set of 20 trials, we obtain 10 outcomes of the count of the number of successes in the 20 trials.

In this case we can use the following commands:

$$x = fix(0.4 + rand(20, 10));$$
$$y = sum(x)$$

In one case the results were as follows:

10   4   8   11   8   11   9   7   9   4

We see that even though all values from 0 to 20 are possible as outcomes of the 20 trials, we obtained only values between 4 and 11 successes when we used $p = 0.4$ and $n = 20$ and repeated the 20 trials 10 times.

2.8 SUMMARY

Events and their operations:

An event is a collection of outcomes of a random experiment.

$S = \{$a collection of all outcomes of the experiment$\}$ = **certain event**

$A \cup B = A$ **or** $B = \{$all outcomes that are in A or B or both$\}$

$A \cap B = A$ **and** $B = \{$all outcomes that are in both A and $B\}$

$\overline{A} = $ **not** $A = \{$all outcomes that are not in $A\}$

$\phi = \{$contains no outcomes$\}$ = **impossible event**

$A \cap B = \phi$: Mutually exclusive events; they have no outcome in common.

$A \subset B$: A is contained in B; B contains A; the outcomes of A are also outcomes in B.

Distributive rules: $A \cup (B \cap C) = (A \cup B) \cap (A \cup C)$ and
$A \cap (B \cup C) = (A \cap B) \cup (A \cap C)$

DeMorgan's Laws: $\overline{(A \cup B)} = \overline{A} \cap \overline{B}$ and $\overline{(A \cap B)} = \overline{A} \cup \overline{B}$

Probability—axioms and properties:

Axiom I: $P(A) \geq 0$, probability cannot be negative.

Axiom II: $P(S) = 1$, the certain event has probability 1.

Axiom III: If $A \cap B = \phi$ then $P(A \cup B) = P(A) + P(B)$

$P(\overline{A}) = 1 - P(A)$

$P(\phi) = 0$, the impossible event has probability zero.

$P(A) \leq 1$, probability cannot be larger than 1.

$P(A \cup B) = P(A) + P(B) - P(A \cap B)$

If $A \subset B$, then $P(A) \leq P(B)$

Conditional probability and independence:

$P(A|B) = P(A \cap B)/P(B) = $ conditional probability of A given that B has occurred.

$P(A \cap B) = P(A|B)P(B) = P(B|A)P(A)$

If $P(A \cap B) = P(A)P(B)$, then A and B are independent events.

In that case $P(A|B) = P(A)$ and $P(B|A) = P(B)$.

Conditional independence:

A and B are conditionally independent given event C if
$P(A \cap B|C) = P(A|C)P(B|C)$

Total probability and Bayes' rule:

Total probability:

If $B_i \cap B_j = \phi$ and $B_1 \cup B_2 \cup \ldots \cup B_{n-1} \cup B_n = S$ then: $P(A) = \sum_{i=1}^{n} P(A|B_i)P(B_i)$

Bayes' rule:

$P(B_k|A) = P(A|B_k)P(B_k)/\text{P}(A)$, where $P(A)$ is obtained from total probability rule.

Independent trials:

Random experiment is repeated n times with the following assumptions:

Each experiment has two outcomes: **success** and **failure.**

Probability of success is p and is the same in all trials, and probability of failure $q = 1 - p$.

The repeated experiments are independent of each other.

$$P(k \text{ successes in } n \text{ trials}) = C_k^n p^k (1 - p)^{n-k}.$$

Here $C_k^n = \binom{n}{k} = \dfrac{n!}{k!(n-k)!}$ (also called the binomial coefficient) is equal to the number of different combinations of choosing k elements out of n without regard to order. In this case, we are looking at the number of different ways we can select the k successes to occur among the n trials.

2.9 PROBLEMS

MATLAB Problems

1. a. Use MATLAB to generate 10 outcomes that reflect the results of tossing a coin 10 times, where the probability of heads in one toss is $p = 0.5$. Count the number of Heads you generated this way, which will be a number between 0 and 10.

   b. Repeat 200 times so that you will get 200 numbers (between 0 and 10) showing the number of Heads in 10 trials for each of the repeated experiment. Draw a histogram of the 200 outcomes you obtained. Compare the results to the mathematical expression for the probability of k Heads in 10 tosses. Find the sample average of the number of Heads in 10 trials and compare to $10p$.

2. Repeat Problem 1(a) for the case of simulating the failure of one of 25 components, where the failures are independent and the probability of failure is $p = 0.2$. Repeat problem 1(b) for this case with the number of repetitions equal to 500.

3. Use MATLAB to list all possible ways that if we send a block of 8 bits (1 byte) through a channel with errors, 2 errors can occur in the byte. Use MATLAB to list all possible ways that exactly 6 errors can occur in the byte, and then show that you get the same number of possible choices.

4. Simulate the errors in the 8 transmitted bits of Problem 3, by assuming a probability of error of $p = 0.1$. Generate 1000 samples of the 8 bits so that an error is described as 1 and no error is described by 0. Count the number of errors in the eight bits and draw a histogram of the relative frequency of errors in the 1000 samples. Compare with equation (2.49).

Regular Problems (advanced problems are marked with *)

5. A system with three components is shown in the diagram.

   Each component may fail or not fail in a given interval of time. Define the events

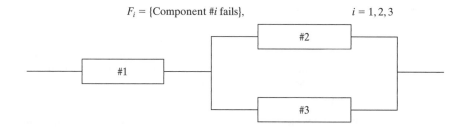

$$F_i = \{\text{Component \#}i \text{ fails}\}, \qquad\qquad i = 1, 2, 3$$

   a. List all eight individual and mutually exclusive events that make up the sample space involving the failures of the three components.

   b. Which events among those listed in (a) cause system failure (no connection between its terminals)?

6.   Repeat Problem 5 for the following system:

7.   Two resistors with resistance $10 \pm 10\%$ are picked at random. Their possible values R_1 and R_2 can be equally likely in the square $9 < R_1 < 11$ and $9 < R_2 < 11$ as shown in the following figure:

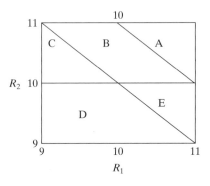

(a) Express the events A, B, C, D, E in terms of the values of the two resistors.
(b) Express the events $(C \cup D)$ and $(B \cup E)$ in terms of the values of the two resistors.
(c) Find the probabilities of the two events A, and $(C \cup D)$ if each area of the same size in the square is equally likely.
(d) Express the events $\{R_1 + R_2 < 21\}$ and $\{(R_1 + R_2 < 21) \cap (R_2 > 10)\}$ in terms of the events A, B, C, D, E.

8.   Given the sample space S containing all real numbers in the interval $[0, 20]$, the following events are defined: $A = \{0 \le \zeta \le 10\}$, $B = \{8 \le \zeta \le 19\}$, $C = \{19 < \zeta \le 20\}$, $D = \{8 \le \zeta \le 16\}$. Describe the following events (you may wish to use the Venn diagram) and then find their probabilities if we assume that the probability of an outcome in an interval is proportional to the length of the interval: a. $A \cup B$; b. $A \cup B \cup C$; c. $A \cap B$; d. $(A \cup B) \cap D$; e. $A \cap D$; f. $(A \cup B) \cap (D \cup C)$; g. $(A \cap B) \cup C$; h. $\bar{A}$; i. $\overline{(A \cup B)}$; j. $\overline{(A \cap B)}$

9.   A circuit contains electrical components resistors, capacitors, and inductors. Each component is one of two types: low tolerance and high tolerance. The number of each component and type in the circuit is shown in the table:

	Resistors	Capacitors	Inductors
High tolerance	120	75	15
Low tolerance	80	25	10

We pick a component in the circuit, and we define the following events:

A = {component is a resistor}, B = {component is a capacitor}, C = {component is an inductor} D = {component is of high tolerance}, E = {component is of low tolerance}

Find the probabilities of the following events: A, B, C, D, E, $A \cap D$, $A \cap E$, $B \cap D$, $B \cap E$, $C \cap D$, $C \cap E$, $A \cup B$, $(A \cup B) \cap D$. Explain what the events mean.

10. Assume that in Problem 5 we have the following probabilities: $P\{(F_2 \cap F_3) \cap F_1\}$ = 0.002, $P\{(F_2 \cap F_3) \cap \overline{F_1}\}$ = 0.018, and $P\{(\overline{F_2} \cup \overline{F_3}) \cap F_1\}$ = 0.008. Find $P\{F_2 \cap F_3\}$ and $P\{F_1\}$. Can you also find $P\{F_2\}$ or $P\{F_3\}$? Explain why or why not.

11. Two communication systems (shown in the two associated figures) are composed from several links, where, for proper operation, a connection must be available between the two end points of each system. For a link to work properly, it must provide a connection across its end points. The links are assumed to fail **independently** of each other. Each link is numbered with #i, and we assume that the probability that link #i fails is equal to p_i. Find the probability of failure of each system. Compute for the case

$$p_1 = 0.1,\ p_2 = p_3 = 0.05,\ p_4 = p_5 = 0.15,\ p_6 = p_7 = 0.2$$

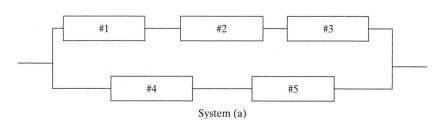

System (a)

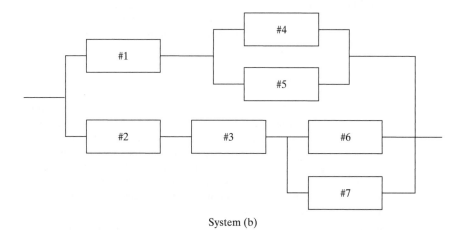

System (b)

12. A circuit contains components that come from one of three manufacturers: I, II, and III. When components are ordered, 50% are ordered from manufacturer I, 40% are from manufacturer II, and 10% are from manufacturer III. If a component is from manufacturer I, it has 0.001 probability of being defective. If it is from manufacturer II, it has 0.005 probability of being defective. If it is from manufacturer III, it has 0.01 probability of being defective.

   (a) We pick a circuit and check a component. What is the probability that it is defective?
   (b) If we found such a component defective, what is the probability that it came from manufacturer I? Manufacturer II? Manufacturer III?

13. Suppose that in Problem 12 each circuit contains two such components. What is the probability that both components are defective? Consider two cases:

   (a) The ordered parts from the three manufacturers are mixed before using the components in the circuit.
   (b) The parts from the three manufacturers are kept separately during the production, so that each circuit contains components from the same manufacturer.

14. In a binary communication channel the receiver sends "zero" or "one," but at the receiver there are three possibilities: a "zero" is received, a "one" is received, and an "undecided bit" is received (which means that the receiver will ask the transmitter to repeat the bit). Define the event $T_1 = \{1 \text{ is sent}\}$ and $T_0 = \{0 \text{ is sent}\}$ and assume that they are equally probable. At the receiver we have three events:

   $R_1 = \{1 \text{ is received}\}$, $R_0 = \{0 \text{ is received}\}$, $R_u = \{\text{cannot decide the bit}\}$. We assume that we have the following conditional probabilities:

   $$P\{R_0|T_0\} = P\{R_1|T_1\} = 0.9, P\{R_u|T_0\} = P\{R_u|T_1\} = 0.09$$

   (a) Find the probability that a transmitted bit is received as "undecided."
   (b) Find the probability that a bit is received in error.
   (c) Given that we received a "zero," what is the conditional probability that a "zero" was sent? What is the conditional probability that a "one" was sent?
   (d) Repeat (a), (b), and (c) if $P\{T_0\} = 0.6$.

15. An example of how we may obtain three possibilities at the receiver of a binary channel of Problem 14, consider the case in which we send each bit twice to improve the error performance. At the receiver, we decide that the bit is a "zero" if the two bits representing each transmitted bit are both "zero." We decide that the bit is a "one" if the two bits representing the transmitted bit are both "one." Consequently, when the two bits contain a "one" and a "zero," we declare the received bit as undecided and request retransmission. Suppose the probability of error in the channel in each bit is $p = 0.1$ (it does not matter whether it is a "one' received as a "zero" or a "zero" received as a "one"). Assume also that the number of transmitted "ones" and "zeros" is the same. Also assume that the errors are independent.

   (a) Find the probability that a transmitted bit is received in error.
   (b) Find the probability that a transmitted bit is received as undecided.
   (c) Find the probability that a transmitted bit is received correctly.

16. An air-to-surface missile can hit the target with probability 0.6. In a test, five missiles are fired at the target. What is the probability that at least one hits the target? The test is considered a failure if one or no missiles hit the target. What is the probability of failure of the test?

17. In order to detect errors over a noisy binary channel, to each 8 bits a parity bit is added so that the number of "ones" in the resulting 9-bit word is even (we call this even parity). At the receiver, if the received 9 bits contain odd number of "ones," we assume the word is in error and we request retransmission. The probability of an error in one bit transmitted over the channel is 0.02 and the errors in the bits are independent. Find and compare the probability that a transmitted 8-bit word is received in error for two cases: with the use of the even parity bit and without the use of the even parity bit.

18. For the following communication system with seven components that may fail independently of each other and where the definition of p_i is as in Problem 11,

   (a) Determine the probability of failure of the system by using conditional probability rules dependent on the failure or nonfailure of links #5 and #6.
   (b) Compute for $p_1 = p_2 = 0.1$, $p_3 = p_4 = 0.5$, $p_7 = 0.25$, and $p_5 = p_6 = 0.3$.
   (c) Given that the system failed, find the conditional probability that both links #5 and #6 failed
   (d) Given that the system failed, find the conditional probability that both links #5 and #6 did not fail.

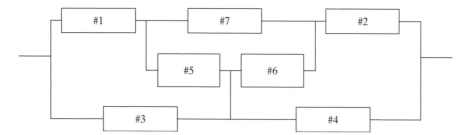

19. A round peg whose diameter of 5 cm has a dimensional tolerance of 2% (meaning that its value is equally likely to be between 4.9 and 5.1) is being matched with a round hole whose diameter of 5.1 cm has a similar tolerance, so that its value is equally likely to be between 5.0 and 5.2. The possible values of the two elements are shown in the following sample space, where the probability of being in an area is proportional to the area.

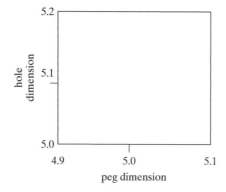

If an arbitrary peg and hole are picked at random, find the probability that the peg will not fit in the whole. Using MATLAB, generate 1000 pairs of random values, one in the range of $(4.9, 5.1)$ and the other in the range of $(5.0, 5.2)$, and find the fraction of pairs that do not fit (meaning that the diameter of the hole is smaller than that of the peg). Compare with the previous answer.

20.* An AND gate has two inputs and one output. The two inputs are pulses of widths 1.5 ms and random arrival times that vary between 0 ms and 2 ms that are independent of each other. The output is "one" only if both input pulses are present at the same time.

   (a) Draw a square sample space showing the arrival times of the two pulses, and assume that the probability of arrival times in an area is proportional to the area.
   (b) Draw the region in the arrival time sample space that will result in an output of "one."
   (c) Find the probability that the output is "zero."

21.* An exclusive OR gate has two inputs and one output. The two inputs are pulses of widths 0.5 ms and random arrival times that vary between 0 ms and 2 ms that are independent of each other. The output is "one" if either one (but NOT both) input pulse is present.

   (a) Draw a square sample space showing the arrival times of the two pulses, and assume that the probability of arrival times in an area is proportional to the area.
   (b) Draw the region in the arrival time sample space that will result in an output of "one."
   (c) Find the probability that the output is "one."

22. A fuse (or circuit breaker) can trip under normal current conditions with probability 0.01. It trips under overload conditions with probability 0.9999. If we assume that the current is normal 98% of the time, what is the probability that the fuse will trip? If the fuse has tripped find the conditional probability that the current was normal.

23.* A switch that is activated by a relay fails to function in some random fashion. When the power to the relay is ON it may fail to close, and similarly, when the power to the relay is OFF it may fail to open. Assume that the relay is ON 60% of the time. Let A be the event that the switch activated by the relay is closed. Then we have

$$P(A|ON) = 0.9 \text{ and } P(A|OFF) = 0.05$$

   (a) Find the probability that the switch is closed.
   (b) If the switch is closed, what is the conditional probability that the relay is ON?
   (c) Find the probability that the switch is open.
   (d) If the switch is open, what is the conditional probability that the relay is OFF?

24.* Suppose that we have two switches of the same properties as those in Problem 23 and they are controlled from the same relay coil (note that this implies conditional independence). Consider the following two connections of the switches in a circuit, and for each of the two cases, answer the following:

   (a) Find the probability that the circuit is "connected."
   (b) If the circuit is connected, find the conditional probability that the relay is ON.
   (c) Find the probability that the circuit is not connected.

Parallel Case   Series Case

(d) If the circuit is **not** connected, find the conditional probability that the relay is OFF.

25.* Solve Problem 24(a) and 24(c) if we know that the switches are controlled by two independent relay coils. Also assume that the ON probabilities of both relays are the same. Can you explain why we could not provide meaningful answers to questions 24(b) and 24(d) for this case?

26.* In trying to distinguish between two circuit-switched channels, one with probability of error of 0.01 (we shall denote this channel as channel I) and one with probability of error of 0.02 (we shall denote this channel as channel II), a test sample of 1000 bits is transmitted and we obtain k errors in the test sample. We know that when we make a connection, it is equally likely to be via either channel. Let A_k denote the event that exactly k errors will be received. Let B denote the event that the channel is channel I.

(a) Find the conditional probability of B given that k errors are received.
(b) Find the conditional probability of $\overline{B}$ given that k errors are received.
(c) What can you conclude for the following values of k: (i) $k = 20$, (ii) $k = 18$, (iii) $k = 15$, (iv) $k = 12$, and (v) $k = 10$?
(d) Use MATLAB to generate 1000 bits that can be "zero" with probability 0.99 and 1000 bits that can be "zero" with probability 0.98. How many "ones" did you obtain in the two cases?

3

A Single Random Variable

3.1 DEFINITION OF A RANDOM VARIABLE

So far we have dealt with random experiments, whose outcomes were defined in terms of the occurrence of some events, the appearance of Heads or Tails in coin tossing, the failure of a component or a link, an error in a transmitted bit, the loss of a packet, a warning light turning ON or OFF, etc. When we dealt with events and their probabilities, we dealt primarily with items that can be described in terms of set theory or with words. However, many problems involving random experiments lead to numerical answers. For example, in gambling an amount of money is won or lost as a result of the occurrence of an event. In engineering problems, for example, an error in a channel maybe translated into a change in the amplitude of the received digital signal. Such an error in the reception of a bit, may be translated into the reception of a wrong value if the value is being transmitted digitally. Similarly, a failure of one of the branches of a telecommunications network may result in reduced capacity of the channel, even though the network is not down. In all these problems, we are converting the events that may be described by words or sets into numerical values of interest to the user or the engineer. In order to achieve such a transformation, we need to define random variables.

Before we formally define what a random variable is, let us consider the very simple case of tossing two coins. There are four outcomes in the sample space: HH, HT, TH, and TT. We can define a random variable X that assigns a numerical value to each outcome, for example, we assign 0 to the outcome TT, we assign 1 to the outcome HT, and also 1 to the outcome TH, and finally we assign 2 to the outcome HH. We arrive at a random variable, which we shall call X, and which we can also describe in words as "the number of Heads in the two tosses." Thus instead of dealing with word-type of events, we deal with the numerical values that result from the occurrence of these events. If we take any of the systems composed of several links that we considered in Chapter 2, we can assign a capacity to each link in the system (messages or calls that each link can carry). Then we can define a variable that describes the capacity of the system, and it will be random as some of the branches may fail, in which case the capacity of the system changes. We shall discuss such an example in detail later on in this chapter.

Based on the preceding discussion, it appears that a random variable assigns numeric values to outcomes of a random experiment. Formally, we define a random variable as follows:

Definition: Given a sample space S with events and a probability assignment P on these events, a **random variable** $X(\zeta)$ is defined as a function that assigns a real number to every outcome ζ of S, such that the set

$$\{\zeta | X(\zeta) \le a\} \tag{3.1}$$

is an event for any real number a.

What the definition states is that a random variable is a function! It is a function of the outcomes of the sample space. We usually denote random variables by upper case letters such as $X(\zeta)$, $Y(\zeta)$, and $Z(\zeta)$. Since we understand that these are functions of the sample space, we do not always show the explicit dependence on the points ζ of S. Therefore, in most cases we just denote the random variables as X, Y, and Z. Figure 3.1 shows an abstract illustration of what a random variable is. S is shown in the rectangle at the top of the figure, and the points on the real line are shown at the bottom. The arrows show how each point (only a few are illustrated) in the sample space is assigned a real number by the random variable $X(\zeta)$.

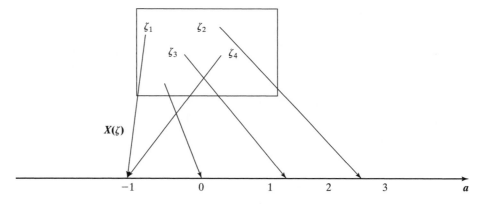

Figure 3.1   An abstract illustration of a random variable

Example 3.1

Consider the communications network shown in Figure 3.2. The network is composed of five links, connected as shown. In the figure each link is noted with the capacity of the link in packets per unit time. Our sample space consists of the 32 outcomes that result from the failure of one or more of the links. Let us define X as the capacity of the network between its two end points. Clearly, we can describe X as a mapping from one of the 32 outcomes, which shows the value it assigns to that outcome, as illustrated in Table 3.1. The table indicates each of the 32 outcomes, and the value assigned by X is displayed in the next to last column of the table.

Table 3.1 provides a list of the events resulting from to the possibility that each link may fail or not fail. In the table the failed links are identified by the letter F in the corresponding cells, while the working links are identified by blank cells. Let us assume that channels #1, #2, and #3 fail with probability 0.2, while channels #4 and #5 fail with probability of 0.1. We shall also assume that the links fail independently of each other, so that we can find the probability (labeled as P) of each of the 32 events, which is also listed in Table 3.1. Since the table provides the values taken by X as a function of the underlying events, we can find the probability of each value taken by X. Previously, we were concerned only with probability of failure of the network. Here we see that a failure of one link may not cause a failure of the network, but may result in lower capacity. The events leading to complete failure are identified by the events leading to a value of $X = 0$. We see that the random variable X takes the five values: 0, 4, 6, 8, and 12.

We can easily find the probability taken by each value of X by simply adding the probabilities of the disjoint events that lead to the corresponding value taken by X. We shall leave the actual evaluation of the probabilities to the next section, as this example was simply intended to illustrate how a random variable is defined.

In this example the random variable takes discrete values (in this case only five distinct values). In many cases, the random variable represents the measurement of a quantity that takes a range of continuous values. An example of a continuous random variable may be obtained if we define X as the value of the resistor picked from a bunch of resistors with nominal value of $100 \pm 10\%$. In such a case the random variable may take any real value in the range of 90 to 110.

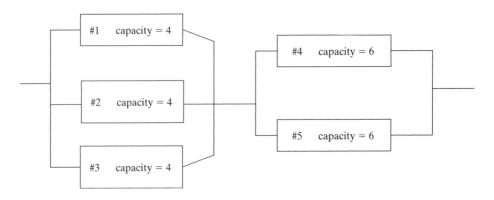

Figure 3.2   A network system with five links

TABLE 3.1 Definition of the random variable X of Example 3.1

Outcome #	Branch 1	Branch 2	Branch 3	Branch 4	Branch 5	X	P
1						12	$(0.8)^3(0.9)^2$
2	F					8	$0.2(0.8)^2(0.9)^2$
3		F				8	$0.2(0.8)^2(0.9)^2$
4			F			8	$0.2(0.8)^2(0.9)^2$
5				F		6	$0.1(0.8)^3(0.9)$
6					F	6	$0.1(0.8)^3(0.9)$
7	F	F				4	$(0.2)^20.8(0.9)^2$
8	F		F			4	$(0.2)^20.8(0.9)^2$
9	F			F		6	$0.1(0.2)(0.8)^20.9$
10	F				F	6	$0.1(0.2)(0.8)^20.9$
11		F	F			4	$(0.2)^20.8(0.9)^2$
12		F		F		6	$0.1(0.2)(0.8)^20.9$
13		F			F	6	$0.1(0.2)(0.8)^20.9$
14			F	F		6	$0.1(0.2)(0.8)^20.9$
15			F		F	6	$0.1(0.2)(0.8)^20.9$
16				F	F	0	$(0.1)^2(0.8)^3$
17	F	F	F			0	$(0.2)^3(0.9)^2$
18	F	F		F		4	$(0.1)(0.2)^2(0.8)0.9$
19	F	F			F	4	$(0.1)(0.2)^2(0.8)0.9$
20	F		F	F		4	$(0.1)(0.2)^2(0.8)0.9$
21	F		F		F	4	$(0.1)(0.2)^2(0.8)0.9$
22	F			F	F	0	$(0.1)^2(0.2)(0.8)^2$
23		F	F	F		4	$(0.1)(0.2)^2(0.8)0.9$
24		F	F		F	4	$(0.1)(0.2)^2(0.8)0.9$
25		F		F	F	0	$(0.1)^2(0.2)(0.8)^2$
26			F	F	F	0	$(0.1)^2(0.2)(0.8)^2$
27	F	F	F	F		0	$(0.1)(0.2)^3(0.9)$

TABLE 3.1 (Continued)

28	*F*	*F*	*F*		*F*	0	$(0.1)(0.2)^3(0.9)$
29	*F*	*F*		*F*	*F*	0	$(0.1)^2(0.2)^2(0.8)$
30	*F*		*F*	*F*	*F*	0	$(0.1)^2(0.2)^2(0.8)$
31		*F*	*F*	*F*	*F*	0	$(0.1)^2(0.2)^2(0.8)$
32	*F*	*F*	*F*	*F*	*F*	0	$(0.1)^2(0.2)^3$

3.2 DISTRIBUTIONS AND DENSITY FUNCTIONS

On the basis of the definition of a random variable, we can obtain probabilities of the form $P\{\zeta|X(\zeta) \le a\}$, for any real value of a that we may select. In shorthand notation, we may write this just as $P\{X(\zeta) \le a\}$ or just $P\{X \le a\}$, where we keep the dependence on the sample space outcomes implicit. We understand that the meaning of such an expression is the probability of the event defined in equation (3.1). We shall see that we do not need to return to the sample space to find probabilities of the random variable taking values in various ranges, once we find the probability of the event defined in equation (3.1) for all values of a. We call the function we obtain in this manner the probability distribution function, or *cumulative distribution function* (CDF), of the random variable X. Here is a formal definition of this function:

Definition: Given a sample space S and a random variable $X(\zeta)$, we define $F_X(a)$, for any real value a as the **cumulative distribution function** (CDF) of the random variable X by the following expression:

$$F_X(a) = P\{\zeta|X(\zeta) \le a\} = P\{X(\zeta) \le a\} = P\{X \le a\} \tag{3.2}$$

Note that the three expressions in equation (3.2) are just different shorthand ways of denoting the same thing. Also, it is customary to write the distribution function of the random variable X as $F_X(x)$, where x is any real number. The reason this text prefers not to do so is that it causes the students sometimes to confuse the X in the subscript (which is the name of the random variable) and the dummy variable x as the argument of the function, which is just any real number.

Example 3.2

We toss a fair coin twice and we define the random variable X as the number of Heads in two tosses.

Here the sample space contains just four outcomes: HH, HT, TH, and TT. The random variable X, as a function of the outcomes, takes the following values:

$$X(\text{TT}) = 0$$
$$X(\text{TH}) = X(\text{HT}) = 1$$
$$X(\text{HH}) = 2$$

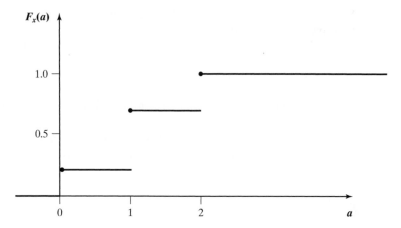

Figure 3.3 The distribution function, $F_X(a)$, of the random variable X = number of Heads in two tosses

We now try to find the distribution function $F_X(a)$ for any value of a.
For $a < 0$ we have no outcomes that yield values of X that are negative. Hence,

$$F_X(a) = 0, \text{ for } a < 0$$

For $0 \le a < 1$ the random variable takes values less than 1 but greater than or equal to zero, only for the event TT, which means that

$$F_X(a) = P\{TT\} = 0.25, \text{ for } 0 \le a < 1$$

For $1 \le a < 2$ the random variable takes values less than 2 but greater than or equal to 1, if either TT, or TH, or HT occurs. Hence the distribution function becomes

$$F_X(a) = P\{TT\} + P\{TH\} + P\{HT\} = 0.75, \text{ for } 1 \le a < 2$$

Finally, for $2 \le a$, the random variable takes all its values in the range that includes the values 0, 1, and 2. Hence for the preceding range of values of a, the distribution function is equal to 1:

$$F_X(a) = P\{TT\} + P\{TH\} + P\{HT\} + P\{HH\} = 1, \text{ for } 2 \le a$$

We plot the resulting distribution function in Figure 3.3.

Example 3.3

We consider here the distribution function of the random variable, which was defined in Example 3.1. It is easier to find the probability of each value taken by the random variable, and then we can construct the distribution function. The probabilities are found from Table 3.1 by computing the probabilities of each outcome included in each case. Let $p_i = P\{\text{link } \#i \text{ fails}\}$ and let $q_i = (1 - p_i) = P\{\text{link } \#i \text{ does not fail}\}$. We have, from the assumptions in the example, that $p_i = 0.2$ for $i = 1, 2, 3$ and $p_i = 0.1$ for $i = 4, 5$. We can find the probability of each value of X by looking at the table. After checking all possible values taken by X, we obtain the following result (X takes the value 12 when outcome listed as #1 occurs):

$$P\{X = 12\} = q_1 \, q_2 \, q_3 \, q_4 \, q_5 = (0.8)^3 (0.9)^2 = 0.41472$$

We proceed in the same manner to find the probabilities of other values by adding the probabilities of the disjoint events that result in the desired value of X. For the value $\{X = 8\}$ there are exactly three events that contribute to this value:

$$P\{X = 8\} = (q_4\, q_5)(p_1\, q_2\, q_3 + q_1\, p_2\, q_3 + q_1\, q_2\, p_3) = 3(0.2)(0.8)^2(0.9)^2 = 0.31104$$

For $\{X = 6\}$ there are eight such events in Table 3.1 that contribute to this value:

$$P\{X = 6\} = (p_4\, q_5 + q_4\, p_5)(p_1\, q_2\, q_3 + q_1\, p_2\, q_3 + q_1\, q_2\, p_3 + q_1\, q_2\, q_3)$$
$$= 2(0.1)(0.9)[3(0.2)(0.8)^2 + (0.8)^3] = 0.16128$$

For $\{X = 4\}$ there are exactly nine such events in the table that contribute to the result:

$$P\{X = 4\} = (p_4\, q_5 + q_4\, p_5 + q_4\, q_5)(p_1\, p_2\, q_3 + q_1\, p_2\, p_3 + p_1\, q_2\, p_3)$$
$$= [2(0.1)(0.9) + (0.9)^2][3(0.8)(0.2)^2] = 0.09504$$

Finally, the value $\{X = 0\}$ is the result of 11 individual events in the table. It can also be derived directly as the probability that the network fails completely:

$$P\{X = 0\} = p_1\, p_2\, p_3 + p_4\, p_5 - p_1\, p_2\, p_3\, p_4\, p_5 = 0.008 + 0.01 - 0.00008 = 0.01792$$

It is easy to check that we did not make any errors along the way, since the total probability that is taken by all values adds up to unity, as expected. We now can derive the distribution function of the random variable X. It is derived from the values obtained previously by adding cumulatively the probabilities as we move along the real line axis:

$$F_X(a) = 0, \text{ for } a < 0$$
$$F_X(a) = P\{X = 0\} = 0.01792, \text{ for } 0 \leq a < 4$$
$$F_X(a) = P\{X = 0\} + P\{X = 4\} = 0.11296, \text{ for } 4 \leq a < 6$$
$$F_X(a) = P\{X = 0\} + P\{X = 4\} + P\{X = 6\} = 0.27424, \text{ for } 6 \leq a < 8$$
$$F_X(a) = P\{X = 0\} + P\{X = 4\} + P\{X = 6\} + P\{X = 8\}$$
$$= 0.58528, \text{ for } 8 \leq a < 12$$
$$F_X(a) = 1, \text{ for } 12 \leq a$$

This example was intended to illustrate the direct relationship between how a random variable is defined and the way its distribution function is derived. We could have simplified our derivation if we had exploited the symmetry in the way the network was constructed.

Now that we have defined distribution functions for random variables, we have to study their properties. In particular, we have to show that once we know the distribution function, we can find every probability we need about the random variable X, and in many cases we can forget about how it was defined as a function of the sample space.

Properties of the Cumulative Distribution Function (CDF)

Here we discuss the properties that a function must satisfy in order to serve as a valid cumulative distribution function for a random variable:

1. If $a < b$, then $F_X(a) \leq F_X(b)$ (3.3)

   This property states that a distribution function is nondecreasing. It follows from the fact that the event $\{\zeta | X(\zeta) \leq a\}$ is contained in the event $\{\zeta | X(\zeta) \leq b\}$, namely, $\{\zeta | X(\zeta) \leq a\} \subset \{\zeta | X(\zeta) \leq b\}$.

2. $F_X(-\infty) = 0$ and $F_X(\infty) = 1$ (3.4)

   The first follows from the fact that the event $\{\zeta | X(\zeta) \leq -\infty\}$ is null, since X must take a real value, and the second follows from the fact that $\{\zeta | X(\zeta) \leq \infty\}$ is the certain event, for the same reason.

3. $\lim_{\varepsilon \to 0} F_X(a + \varepsilon) = F_X(a)$, for $\varepsilon > 0$ (3.5)

   This property means that the distribution function is continuous from the right.

   The preceding three properties simply state that a distribution function is a monotonic non-decreasing function starting at 0 and ending with 1. It may have jumps, but at the jumps the value of the distribution is equal to the value at the top of the jump.
   How do we use distribution functions to find the probability that X takes values in some range? We are looking for the probability of the event $\{\zeta | a < X(\zeta) \leq b\}$. It can be seen that the event in question is related to the events $\{\zeta | X(\zeta) \leq b\}$ and $\{\zeta | X(\zeta) \leq a\}$ by the expression

$$\{\zeta | a < X(\zeta) \leq b\} \cup \{\zeta | X(\zeta) \leq a\} = \{\zeta | X(\zeta) \leq b\}   \tag{3.6}$$

Since the event on the right of equation (3.6) is the union of mutually exclusive events, we obtain

$$P\{\zeta | X(\zeta) \leq b\} = P\{\zeta | a < X(\zeta) \leq b\} + P\{\zeta | X(\zeta) \leq a\}   \tag{3.7}$$

This yields the result we are looking for:

$$P\{\zeta | a < X(\zeta) \leq b\} = P\{\zeta | X(\zeta) \leq b\} - P\{\zeta | X(\zeta) \leq a\} = F_X(b) - F_X(a) \tag{3.8}$$

What is the probability of the random variable taking a specific real value? If we apply the preceding rule, we obtain

$$P\{X = a\} = F_X(a) - \lim_{\varepsilon \to 0} F_X(a - \varepsilon) = F_X(a) - F_X(a-)   \tag{3.9}$$

Here we use the notation $F_X(a-)$ to indicate the limit of the value of the distribution function as we approach the point a from the left. If the function is continuous at that point, the probability $P\{X = a\}$ is zero. If, on the other hand, the distribution has a jump at that point, the probability $P\{X = a\}$ is equal to the value of the jump at the point a.

As a result, we can have three types of distributions:

a. Piecewise constant distribution functions, which are distributions of discrete random variables. An example was shown in Figure 3.3.

b. Continuous distribution functions, which are distributions of continuous random variables. An illustration is shown in Figure 3.4(a).

c. Mixed distribution functions, which contain both continuous curves and jumps, and serve as distributions of random variables that take values both in continuous ranges and at a discrete number of real values. An illustration is shown in Figure 3.4(b). In the figure we also illustrate the meaning of $F_X(a-)$ defined previously.

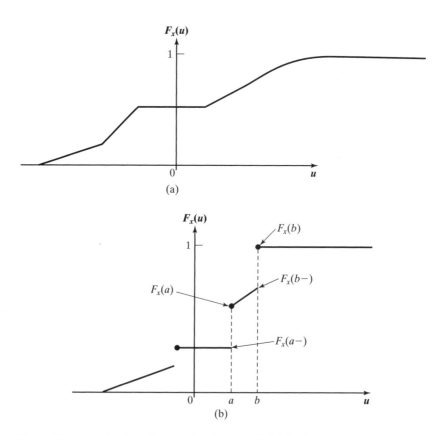

Figure 3.4 Examples of continuous (a) and mixed (b) distributions

We have seen in Figure 3.3 an example of a discrete distribution. Figure 3.4 shows examples of the other two types of distributions.

In Figures 3.3 and 3.4(b) the end of the jump is shown by a heavy bullet to indicate that, at the jump, the value of the distribution at that point is equal to the value at the top of the jump, to be consistent with the continuity from the right property. For example, in Figure 3.3 the value of $F_X(u)$ at $u = 1$ is 0.75, while its value before we reach $u = 1$ is 0.25:

$$F_X(1) = 0.75, \text{ and } F_X(1-) = 0.25.$$

The last expression really means that $F_X(0.99999\ldots9) = 0.25$, where the expression inside the brackets means a large but finite number of 9s after the decimal point.

Probability Mass Function

The cumulative distribution function provides all the information we need about the probabilities associated with the values taken by the random variables. In the discrete case, we have seen that we can simply provide the probabilities for each value taken by the random variables, as we observed from the several examples we considered. This affords us with an alternative way of providing the information contained in the distribution function. Instead of $F_X(\alpha)$, we can simply write the probabilities

$$p_X(\alpha_i) = P\{X = \alpha_i\}, \tag{3.10}$$

for all values $\{\alpha_i\}$ taken by the random variable X. We call the function defined in equation (3.10) the *probability mass function* (PMF) of the random variable. The rationale for the name PMF is that we may consider displaying the probabilities as point masses attached on a weightless wire at the points defined by the values taken by the random variable, as illustrated in Figure 3.5, where a random variable taking five values is shown. The size of the mass reflects the magnitude of the probability that the random variable takes that value. The only restriction is that the sum total of all the masses adds up to unity. It should be noted that if the random variable takes M values, the definition (3.10) implies

$$\sum_{i=1}^{M} p_X(\alpha_i) = 1 \tag{3.10a}$$

Figure 3.5   An illustration of a probability mass function

We can summarize the properties of the probability mass function of a discrete random variable as follows:

Properties of the Probability Mass Function (PMF)

1. $p_X(\alpha_i) > 0$. It must be a nonnegative function. $\hspace{2cm}$ (3.10b)

2. $\sum\limits_{i=1}^{M} p_X(\alpha_i) = 1$. It must add up to 1. $\hspace{2cm}$ (3.10c)

3. $F_X(\alpha) = \sum\limits_{\alpha_i \leq \alpha} p_X(\alpha_i)$. $\hspace{2cm}$ (3.10d)

4. $\mathrm{P}\{a < X \leq b\} = \sum\limits_{a < \alpha_i \leq b} p_X(\alpha_i)$. $\hspace{2cm}$ (3.10e)

The question is whether we can define something similar for a continuous random variable. Since a continuous random variable takes values in a range, we may use the wire analogy and assume that the wire is not weightless, but has a variable cross section, so that the total mass of the length of wire before reaching the point α, is equal to the mass of the wire until that point. Clearly, in such cases we can talk about the mass of the wire in terms of its mass density per unit length. Since the mass was just a representation of the probabilities involved, we can define a probability density function, which should have a role similar to that of the mass density in the wire case.

Probability Density Function

We define the *probability density function* (PDF) of a continuous random variable by

$$f_X(\alpha) = \frac{d}{d\alpha} F_X(\alpha) \hspace{2cm} (3.11)$$

On the basis of its definition, and the properties of the CDF, we can summarize its properties as follows:

Properties of the Probability Density Function (PDF)

1. $f_X(\alpha) \geq 0$. It must be a nonnegative function. $\hspace{2cm}$ (3.12)

2. $\int\limits_{-\infty}^{\infty} f_X(u)\, du = 1$. Its area must be equal to 1. $\hspace{2cm}$ (3.13)

3. $F_X(\alpha) = \int\limits_{-\infty}^{\alpha} f_X(u)\, du \hspace{2cm}$ (3.14)

4. $\mathrm{P}\{a < X \leq b\} = \int\limits_{a}^{b} f_X(u)\, du \hspace{2cm}$ (3.15)

Any nonnegative function whose area is equal to unity can serve as a probability density function of a random variable. In order to find the probability that the random variable takes values in an interval, all we have to do is find the area under the density function for that interval. A note on property 4 as given by equation (3.15) is in order. The property follows directly from the definition of the distribution function. However, if the distribution is continuous, the term on the left side of equation (3.15) is the same if we include the point $\{X = a\}$ or exclude it (as in equation (3.15)), or if we exclude the point $\{X = b\}$ or include it (as in equation (3.15)). The result is different only if the values $\{X = a\}$ or $\{X = b\}$ have nonzero probability (such as in mixed or discrete distributions). We can summarize this note by stating that, for continuous distributions, the following is true:

$$P\{a < X \le b\} = P\{a \le X \le b\} = P\{a < X < b\} = P\{a \le X < b\}.$$

What do we do in the mixed random variable case? If we are willing to be less rigorous with the mathematics, we can define a density function even in cases of discrete or mixed random variables. In such cases, we have to find a derivative of a jump at the jump point. Obviously, the derivative is infinite at that point. To that end we define an impulse function $\delta(x)$, which maybe drawn as an arrow whose magnitude is 1 occurring at $x = 0$. It is defined by its influence on other functions involving the following integral:

$$\int_{-\infty}^{\infty} g(x)\delta(x - a)\, dx = g(a) \tag{3.16}$$

Equation (3.16) is valid only if $g(x)$ is continuous at $x = a$. We can look at the impulse function as the derivative of a unit step function. Other properties are shown in Appendix D.

   If we are allowed the use of the impulse function, we can write the density function of a discrete random variable as

$$f_X(u) = \sum_{i=1}^{M} P\{X = \alpha_i\}\delta(u - \alpha_i) = \sum_{i=1}^{M} p_X(\alpha_i)\delta(u - \alpha_i) \tag{3.17}$$

The summation in equation (3.17) extends over all possible values taken by the random variable X, which are assumed to be M in this case.

   Now that we are done with the definitions of distribution and density functions, we can discuss key useful distributions and densities that are important in engineering problems.

3.3 EXAMPLES OF DISTRIBUTIONS

In this section we shall discuss various random variables and their distribution or density functions. When we just say *distribution* without specifying the word *function*, we mean the generic way a random variable is distributed. It may be described either by its probability density function (PDF) or its cumulative distribution function (CDF) or both.

3.3.1 Uniform Distribution

The continuous uniform distribution is the simplest continuous distribution. It is used when we have no information to go on other than the range of the random variable. Hence, if we know that the random variable takes values in the interval (a, b), we may assume for lack of any other knowledge that its density function is constant on the interval, which means that each value in the interval is equally likely.

Since the area under the density function must be unity, we have

$$f_X(u) = \frac{1}{(b - a)}, \qquad \text{for } a < u < b, \text{ and is zero elsewhere} \qquad (3.18)$$

The corresponding distribution function is easily found to be

$$F_x(u) = \begin{cases} 0, & \text{for } u < a \\ \dfrac{u - a}{b - a}, & \text{for } a \leq u < b \\ 1, & \text{for } b \leq u \end{cases} \qquad (3.19)$$

Figure 3.6 shows both the distribution function and its density function for the values $a = 5$ and $b = 7$. Example 2.10 that we considered in Chapter 2 about resistors with known tolerance assumed a uniform distribution for $a = 90$, and $b = 110$.

Another practical example of such a distribution is the one obtained when we quantize a continuous signal or variable (representing a continuous value by some

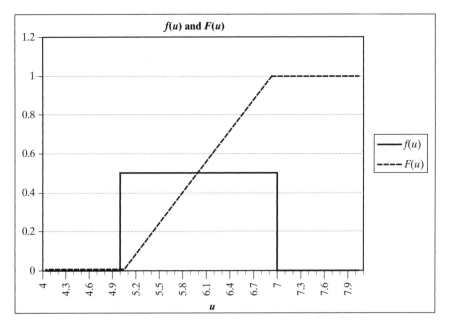

Figure 3.6   The uniform distribution: PDF (solid) and CDF (dashed)

binary code). In such a case, if the quantization is uniform with quantization level Δ, then we can assume that each digital representation can differ from the real value by at most $\pm\Delta$. Hence, in such a case we may assume that the quantization error is uniformly distributed in the interval $(-\Delta, +\Delta)$.

We can also consider discrete uniform distributions, in which the random variable X takes n discrete values with equal probability, so that in general they maybe described as

$$a + ib, \text{ for } i = 0, 1, 2, \ldots (n - 1).$$

Each value will have a probability of $1/n$, so that the probability mass function is given by

$$P\{X = a + ib\} = 1/n, \text{ for } i = 0, 1, 2, \ldots, n - 1.$$

The simplest case of such a random variable is when $a = b = 1$, so that X takes the values $1, 2, \ldots, n$. A practical example of such a random variable is the case in which a router can choose one of n possible channels for routing a packet. If the routes are not distinguishable, we may assume that the packet has equal probability of being routed via channel X, where X takes the values $1, 2, \ldots, n$.

3.3.2 Triangular Distribution

This is another continuous distribution. It can be derived from the uniform as we did in Chapter 2, Example 2.10, when we took two resistors at random and connected them in series. We assumed that each value of the two resistors falls equally likely in the square bounded by (a, b). In that example we found the probability that the sum falls inside the $\pm 5\%$ tolerance. Here we define the random variable X as the value of the sum of the values of the two resistors. We can look at the picture in Figure 3.7 in order to find the probability that X (which is the sum of the two resistances) takes values less than u_i for different ranges of the real variable u_i.

The figure shows the square $(a, b) \times (a, b)$ in which the values of the two resistors are distributed and also indicates by two lines when their sum is equal to a certain value (u_1 or u_2). Two values are shown: for the line labeled u_1 the sum falls between $2a$ and $(a + b)$, while for the line labeled u_2 the sum falls between $(a + b)$

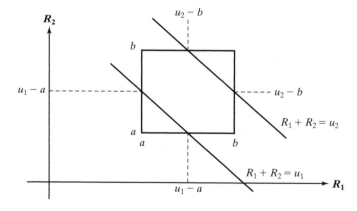

Figure 3.7 Illustrating the values of two resistors in the square and the value of the sum equal to a given number (u_1 or u_2)

and $2b$. On the basis of the illustration, we can derive the distribution functions $F_X(u)$ for several general key values of the variable u. Clearly, for values of $u < 2a$, the value of $F_X(u)$ is zero, since the sum can never be less than $2a$. Similarly, for values of $u > 2b$, the value of $F_X(u)$ is 1, since the sum is never larger than $2b$. It remains to find the value of $F_X(u)$ for the two regions shown in Figure 3.7. For the value of u between $2a$ and $(a + b)$ (as illustrated by u_1) the two values of the resistors must fall below the lower diagonal line marked by $u = u_1$. This implies that the probability that X is less than u, is equal to the area of the lower triangle divided by the area of the square. The triangle shown is bounded by the line $R_1 + R_2 = u_1 = u$ and is a right-angle triangle with two sides equal to $[(u - a) - a]$, as can be seen from the figure. The resulting value of the distribution is

$$F_X(u) = \frac{(u - 2a)^2}{2(b - a)^2}, \qquad \text{for } 2a < u < (a + b) \qquad (3.20)$$

Similarly, for the value of u between $(a + b)$ and $2b$, we take the area of the square bounded by the upper diagonal line marked by $u = u_2$ in the figure. This is the same as taking the area of the square and subtracting the upper triangle and then dividing by the area of the square. In other words, to find the probability that X (the sum) is less than u, we subtract from 1 the ratio of the areas of the upper triangle divided by the area of the square. The triangle shown is bounded by the line $R_1 + R_2 = u_2 = u$ and is also a right-angle triangle with two sides equal to $[b - (u - b)]$, as can be seen from the figure. The resulting value of the distribution function is as shown by

$$F_X(u) = 1 - \frac{(2b - u)^2}{2(b - a)^2}, \qquad \text{for } (a + b) < u < 2b \qquad (3.21)$$

We then can find the density function by taking the derivative of the distribution function to obtain

$$f_X(u) = \frac{u - 2a}{(b - a)^2}, \qquad \text{for } 2a < u < (a + b) \qquad (3.22)$$

$$f_X(u) = \frac{2b - u}{(b - a)^2}, \qquad \text{for } (a + b) < u < 2b \qquad (3.23)$$

Both the distribution function and the density function are shown in Figure 3.8 for $a = 2.5$, and $b = 3.5$.

3.3.3 Bernoulli Random Variable

The Bernoulli random variable is the simplest random variable, as it takes only two values, which for simplicity we assume are 0 and 1. Hence, we need only to provide the probability that $\{X = 1\}$ and the distribution will be completely defined. In this case we assume that

$$P\{X = 1\} = p$$

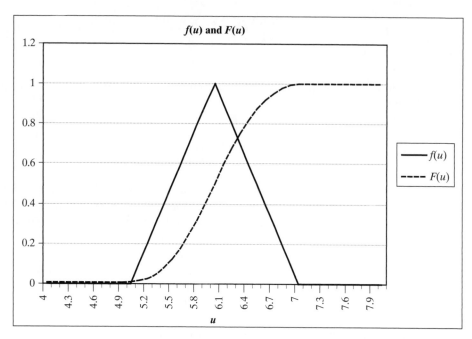

Figure 3.8   Illustrating the triangular distribution: CDF (dashed) and PDF (solid)

The probability that $\{X = 0\}$ will therefore be given by

$$P\{X = 0\} = q = (1 - p)$$

A practical example of this random variable may be obtained in the tossing of a single coin, and we define the value of X to be zero when the outcome is tails, and the value is one when the outcome is heads. A more practical example occurs in digital communications in the transmission of a single bit, since the value of the transmitted bit (1 or 0) can be used as the value taken by the random variable X. In another case of binary communications, the random variable X may represent the error in a transmitted bit, so that $X = 1$ when an error occurs and $X = 0$ when a bit is received correctly.

3.3.4 Binomial Distribution

We have discussed independent trials in Chapter 2. Suppose we perform n independent trials in which the probability of success in one experiment is p, and the probability of failure in one experiment is $q = 1 - p$. We define a random variable X as the number of successes in n trials. Clearly, X takes the $(n + 1)$ values $0, 1, 2, 3, \ldots, n$. We have already derived the probability of k successes in n trials in equation (2.49). Here such a probability is indeed equal to the probability mass function of the random variable X. We call the resulting distribution the binomial distribution, with probability mass function

$$p_X(k) = P\{X = k\} = \binom{n}{k} p^k q^{n-k} = \frac{n!}{k!(n-k)!} p^k q^{n-k}, \text{ for } k = 0, 1, 2, \ldots, n$$

$$(3.24)$$

The following notation is used for the binomial coefficient, C_k^n or $\binom{n}{k}$, discussed in Chapter 2:

$$C_k^n = \binom{n}{k} = \frac{n!}{k!(n-k)!} \qquad (3.24a)$$

There is no closed form expression for the cumulative distribution function. The value of the distribution function at a point u is equal to the sum of the probabilities in equation (3.24) over all integers k that are less than or equal to u. Since the probability mass function provides all the information we need, there is really no reason to actually evaluate the cumulative distribution function in general.

The binomial distribution is very important in telecommunications problems when the error in the transmission of one bit is known and we need to find the probability of errors when transmitting blocks of size n bits, assuming that the errors are independent. It should be noted that the Bernoulli random variable is a special case of the binomially distributed random variable for the case $n = 1$.

Example 3.4

Consider a binary communications channel with an error probability (probability of receiving a bit in error) of $p = 0.01$. We assume that, if we transmit n bits, the errors occur independently in each of the n bits. In order to reduce the error probability, consider using an error correcting code that adds 3 "parity" bits to every 4 data bits that are generated by the sender. Such a code (if properly designed) is capable of correcting one error in the 7 bits that are sent (4 data bits and 3 parity bits). What is the error probability in one 4-bit word without the error-correcting code and with the error-correcting code?

When we do not use error-correcting codes, we send only 4 bits when we want to send a 4-bit word. The word will be in error if one or more errors occur in the 4 bits:

$$P(\text{error in one word without coding}) = P(\text{one or more errors in four bits})$$

$$= \sum_{k=1}^{4} \binom{4}{k} (0.01)^k (0.99)^{4-k} = 1 - (0.99)^4 = 1 - 0.96056 = 0.039404$$

When we use the error-correcting code we add 3 bits to the 4-bit word, so we actually send 7 bits, which means we increase the load in the channel by 75%. Here, since the code can correct one error, the word is in error if 2 or more bits are in error in the 7 bits that are needed to send one word:

$$P(\text{error in one word with coding}) = P(\text{two or more errors in seven bits})$$

$$= \sum_{k=2}^{7} \binom{7}{k} (0.01)^k (0.99)^{7-k} = 1 - (0.99)^7 - 7(0.01)(0.99)^6 = 0.002031$$

Of course we achieved the lower error rate by decreasing the throughput in the channel.

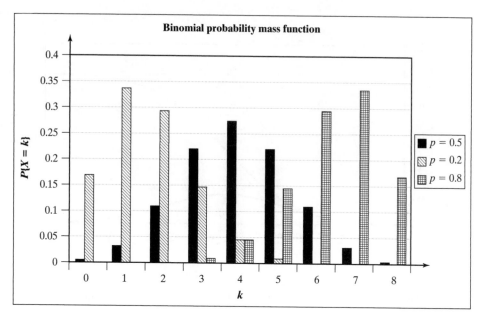

Figure 3.9   Examples of binomial probability mass functions for $n = 8$

An example of the binomial probability mass function is shown in Figure 3.9 for $n = 8$ and for three values of p: 0.5, 0.2, and 0.8. We see that when $p = 0.5$, the probability mass function is symmetric about $n/2 = 4$. However, when $p = 0.2$, it is skewed toward low values of k, while for $p = 0.8$, it is skewed to larger values of k.

Other examples of communications system problems involve the failures of links in channels with many parallel paths, the loss of packets that are sent via a packet-switched network, errors in blocks that are transmitted over a modem line, and many others.

3.3.5 Gaussian

The Gaussian distribution (also called "normal" in some textbooks) occurs in many practical problems, due to the central limit theorem, which we will study later, involving the sum of many random variables. A random variable is said to be Gaussian or to have a Gaussian distribution if its density function is given by the expression

$$f_X(u) = \frac{1}{\sqrt{2\pi}\sigma} e^{-\frac{(u-m)^2}{2\sigma^2}} \tag{3.25}$$

It is shown in Figure 3.10 for $m = 5$, and $\sigma = 2$ (Fig. 3.10a) and for $\sigma = 0.5$ (Fig. 3.10b). The parameter m represents the center of the bell-shaped curve of the Gaussian density, while the parameter σ represents how wide or narrow is the density.

In order to find the distribution function for Gaussian random variables, we have to use tables or computer programs. However, we do not need a table for every

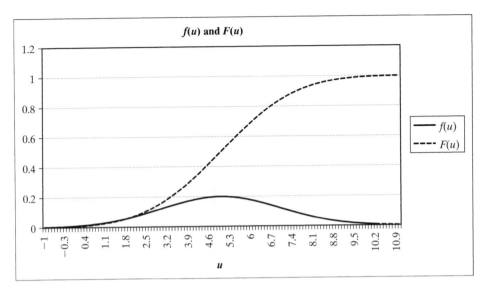

Figure 3.10a   The Gaussian distribution function and its density function for $\sigma = 2$

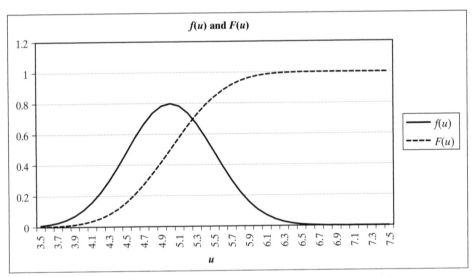

Figure 3.10b   The Gaussian distribution function and its density function for $\sigma = 0.5$

value of the parameters m and σ. It is sufficient to know the values of the distribution function for the parameters $m = 0$, and $\sigma = 1$. We call such a distribution the unit Gaussian distribution, or the normalized Gaussian distribution, or the unit normal distribution, or the standard Gaussian distribution. We denote the resulting distribution function by $\Phi(u)$, which is defined as

$$\Phi(u) = \frac{1}{\sqrt{2\pi}} \int_{-\infty}^{u} e^{-\frac{v^2}{2}} \, dv \qquad (3.26)$$

We can show that the value of the distribution function as u tends to infinity is indeed unity, as expected. The proof is mathematically tedious and is derived in Appendix A. If we wish to find the probability of a Gaussian random variable with parameters m and σ between a and b, we obtain it by changing the variable of integration to achieve the following result:

$$P\{a < X < b\} = \Phi\left(\frac{b-m}{\sigma}\right) - \Phi\left(\frac{a-m}{\sigma}\right) \tag{3.27}$$

It should be noted that important values of $\Phi(u)$ are the following:

$$\Phi(0) = 0.5, \ \Phi(-3) = 0.0013, \ \Phi(-2) = 0.02275, \ \Phi(-1) = 0.1587$$

Some tables tabulate only the values of $\Phi(u)$ for either positive or negative values of u, due to symmetry:

$$\Phi(+a) = 1 - \Phi(-a) \tag{3.28}$$

Table 3.2 shows the values of the standard normal distribution for the range 0 to 3.29.
The use of the symmetry and the values of Φ at -1, -2, and -3, can yield the following results:

$$P\{|X-m| < \sigma\} = \Phi(1) - \Phi(-1) = 0.6826$$
$$P\{|X-m| < 2\sigma\} = \Phi(2) - \Phi(-2) = 0.9545$$
$$P\{|X-m| < 3\sigma\} = \Phi(3) - \Phi(-3) = 0.9974$$

TABLE 3.2   The cumulative Gaussian distribution function for zero mean and unit variance

$$\Phi(x) = \int_{-\infty}^{x} \frac{\exp(-u^2/2)}{\sqrt{2\pi}} du$$

x	0.00	0.01	0.02	0.03	0.04	0.05	0.06	0.07	0.08	0.09
0.00	0.500000	0.503989	0.507978	0.511967	0.515953	0.519939	0.523922	0.527903	0.531881	0.535856
0.10	0.539828	0.543795	0.547758	0.551717	0.555670	0.559618	0.563559	0.567495	0.571424	0.575345
0.20	0.579260	0.583166	0.587064	0.590954	0.594835	0.596708	0.602568	0.606420	0.610261	0.614092
0.30	0.617911	0.621719	0.625516	0.629300	0.633072	0.636831	0.640576	0.644309	0.648027	0.651732
0.40	0.655422	0.659097	0.662757	0.666402	0.670031	0.673645	0.677242	0.680822	0.684386	0.687933
0.50	0.691462	0.694974	0.698468	0.701944	0.705402	0.708840	0.712260	0.715661	0.719043	0.722405
0.60	0.725747	0.729089	0.732371	0.735653	0.738914	0.742154	0.745373	0.748571	0.751748	0.754903
0.70	0.758036	0.761148	0.764238	0.767306	0.770350	0.773373	0.776373	0.779360	0.762305	0.785236
0.80	0.788145	0.791030	0.793892	0.796731	0.799546	0.802338	0.806108	0.807850	0.810570	0.813267
0.90	0.815940	0.818589	0.821214	0.823814	0.826391	0.828944	0.831472	0.833977	0.838457	0.838013
1.00	0.841345	0.843752	0.846136	0.848495	0.850830	0.853141	0.855428	0.657690	0.859929	0.862143

TABLE 3.2   (Continued)

x	0.00	0.01	0.02	0.03	0.04	0.05	0.06	0.07	0.08	0.09
1.10	0.864334	0.866500	0.868643	0.870762	0.872857	0.874928	0.876976	0.878999	0.881000	0.882977
1.20	0.884930	0.886860	0.888767	0.890651	0.892512	0.894350	0.896165	0.897958	0.899727	0.901475
1.30	0.903199	0.904902	0.906582	0.908241	0.909677	0.911492	0.913085	0.914856	0.916207	0.917736
1.40	0.919243	0.920730	0.922196	0.923641	0.925066	0.926471	0.927855	0.929219	0.930563	0.931888
1.50	0.933193	0.934478	0.935744	0.936992	0.938220	0.939429	0.940620	0.941792	0.942947	0.944083
1.60	0.945201	0.946301	0.947384	0.948449	0.949497	0.950529	0.951543	0.962540	0.953521	0.954486
1.70	0.955435	0.956367	0.957284	0.958185	0.959071	0.959941	0.960796	0.961836	0.962462	0.963273
1.80	0.964070	0.964852	0.965621	0.966375	0.967116	0.967843	0.968557	0.969258	0.969946	0.970621
1.90	0.971284	0.971933	0.972571	0.973197	0.973810	0.974412	0.975002	0.975581	0.976148	0.976705
2.00	0.977250	0.977784	0.978308	0.978822	0.979325	0.979618	0.980301	0.980774	0.961237	0.961691
2.10	0.982136	0.982571	0.982997	0.983414	0.963823	0.984222	0.984614	0.984997	0.985371	0.965738
2.20	0.986097	0.986447	0.986791	0.987126	0.987455	0.987776	0.988089	0.996396	0.968696	0.968989
2.30	0.989276	0.989556	0.989830	0.990097	0.990358	0.990613	0.990863	0.991106	0.991344	0.991576
2.40	0.991802	0.992024	0.992240	0.992451	0.992656	0.992857	0.993053	0.993244	0.993431	0.993613
2.50	0.993790	0.993963	0.994132	0.994297	0.994457	0.994614	0.994766	0.994915	0.995060	0.995201
2.60	0.995339	0.995473	0.995603	0.995731	0.995855	0.995975	0.996093	0.996207	0.996319	0.996427
2.70	0.996533	0.996636	0.996736	0.996833	0.996928	0.997020	0.997110	0.997197	0.997282	0.997365
2.80	0.997445	0.997523	0.997599	0.997673	0.997744	0.997814	0.997882	0.997948	0.998012	0.998074
2.90	0.996134	0.998193	0.996250	0.998305	0.998359	0.996411	0.998462	0.998511	0.996559	0.996605
3.00	0.998650	0.998694	0.998736	0.998777	0.998817	0.996856	0.998893	0.998930	0.998965	0.998999
3.10	0.999032	0.999064	0.999096	0.999126	0.999155	0.999184	0.999211	0.999238	0.999264	0.999289
3.20	0.999313	0.999336	0.999359	0.999381	0.999402	0.999423	0.999443	0.999482	0.999481	0.999499

The meaning of these numbers is that the random variable X takes values within 2σ of m with probability 95% and within 3σ of m with probability 99.7%. These are very important values, as they are used in defining our confidence in results based on measurements with random errors or other uncertainties.

Example 3.5

The amplitude of a noise signal is assumed to be Gaussian with $m = 0$ and $\sigma = 2$ volts. This noise is added to a constant voltage of magnitude 20 volts.

a. Find the probability that the total signal amplitude exceeds 25 volts.

Since we are adding the noise to the constant signal, the total amplitude will have a Gaussian distribution with $m = 20$ and $\sigma = 2$. Hence, we find

$$P(X > 25) = 1 - \Phi[(25 - 20)/2] = 1 - \Phi(2.5)$$
$$= 1 - 0.99379 = 0.00621$$

b. Find the probability that the total signal amplitude is less than 16 volts.

$$P(X < 16) = \Phi[(16 - 20)/2] = \Phi(-2) = 0.02275$$

c. Finally find the probability that the total signal amplitude is between 16 and 25 volts.

$$P(16 < X < 25) = \Phi(2.5) - \Phi(-2) = 0.97104$$

This example illustrates an important problem in communications. Suppose that we are trying to distinguish between a signal of magnitude 20 and one of magnitude 30. In such a case, suppose we decide that the signal is of magnitude 20 if the value of the received signal plus noise is less than 25 and we decide that it is 30 if the signal plus noise is larger than 25. In this case the result we obtained in part (a) is equal to the probability of making an error, when the true signal is 20 but we decide it is 30. For the values of the noise parameters we used here, this probability is equal to 0.00621. We shall address this type of problems in Chapter 10 in a more general framework.

MATLAB Evaluation of the Gaussian Density and Distribution Functions

The value of the density function is obtained by the following command, available in the statistics toolbox (note these commands are listed with the superscript § to so identify them):

$$Y = normpdf(X, m, sigma)^\S$$

Here, X and Y are vectors, such that $Y(i)$ = the value of the Gaussian density function with parameters m and σ evaluated at the point $X(i)$.

The value of the cumulative Gaussian distribution is obtained by the following command:

$$Y = normcdf(X, m, sigma)^\S$$

Here, $Y(i)$ = the value of the cumulative Gaussian distribution with parameters m and σ evaluated at the point $X(i)$.

In other words we have

$$\Phi(u) = normcdf(u, 0, 1)^\S$$

In the basic version of MATLAB, the function *normcdf* is not available. The function *erf* is used in that case. The function is called the error function and is defined as

$$\text{erf}(u) = \frac{2}{\sqrt{\pi}} \int_0^u e^{-v^2} \, dv$$

In this case we obtain the unit Gaussian CDF by the following MATLAB command (obtained by using change of variables in the integral):

$$\Phi(u) = 0.5*\left(1 + \text{erf}\left(u/\sqrt{2}\right)\right)$$

We sometimes are interested in the probability that a Gaussian random variable exceeds certain values. In this case, we are looking at the tails of the distribution. For such problems we define a new function $Q(u)$, which tabulates the values of

$$Q(u) = 1 - \Phi(u) = \frac{1}{\sqrt{2\pi}} \int_u^\infty e^{\frac{v^2}{2}} \, dv \tag{3.29}$$

Instead of $Q(u)$ in the basic version of MATLAB, a function erfc, which is called the complementary error function, is used. In this case we have

$$\text{erfc}(u) = 1 - \text{erf}(u) = \frac{2}{\sqrt{\pi}} \int_u^\infty e^{-v^2} \, dv$$

We therefore can evaluate the function $Q(u)$ using the following MATLAB command:

$$Q(u) = 0.5*\left(1 - \text{erf}\left(u/\sqrt{2}\right)\right) = 0.5 * \text{erfc}\left(u/\sqrt{2}\right)$$

We described in Chapter 1 how to generate uniformly distributed random numbers by using MATLAB. How do we generate random numbers having a Gaussian distribution? In this case we use the function randn. Specifically, we use the expression

$$X = \text{randn}(k,n)$$

Here X will be a matrix with $k \times n$ Gaussian random numbers. The matrix will have k rows and n columns. If we wish to generate just one set (i.e., one column) of numbers, we use $k = 1$. The random numbers so generated will have $m = 0$, and $\sigma = 1$. If we wish for a different m and σ, we multiply X by σ and add m to the result to obtain Y, with parameters m and σ:

$$Y = m + \sigma X$$

For example, the following command generates eight Gaussian random variables with $m = 2$ and $\sigma = 0.2$:

$$y = m + \sigma * \text{randn}(1,n) = 2 + 0.2 * \text{randn}(1,8)$$

The numbers generated in one example are

1.9135   1.6669   2.0251   2.0575   1.7707   2.2382   2.2378   1.9925

3.3.6 Cauchy Distribution

In order to illustrate the Cauchy distribution, consider the case of particles being emitted from a radioactive source equally likely in all directions in the half plane. To obtain a Cauchy distributed random variable, we place a sensitive screen at one side

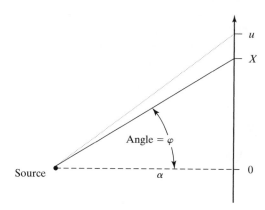

Figure 3.11   The definition of X as the vertical distance of impact from the origin 0

of the source at a distance α from the source and we define the distance of the impact on the screen from the center of the screen as the random variable X, as illustrated in Figure 3.11.

The figure shows one point of impact at a vertical distance X from the origin. The angle of emission for this example is shown as φ. Note that all angles between $-\pi/2$ and $+\pi/2$ are equally likely. We are now ready to derive the distribution of the random variable X. We use in the derivation the fact that the probability for the angle of the particle to fall in a certain range is equal to the angle divided by π. For the random variable X to fall below the value u, the angle, as seen in the figure, should be between $-\pi/2$ and $\tan^{-1}(u/\alpha)$:

$$F_X(u) = P\{X \le u\} = P\{-\pi/2 < \varphi \le \tan^{-1}(u/\alpha)\} = \frac{\tan^{-1}(u/\alpha) + \pi/2}{\pi}$$

(3.30)

The resulting density function is then obtained by taking the derivative

$$f_X(u) = \frac{1}{\alpha\pi[1 + (u/\alpha)^2]} = \frac{\alpha}{\pi(u^2 + \alpha^2)}$$

(3.31)

The distribution and its density is shown in Figure 3.12 for $\alpha = 0.4$.

The Cauchy density function has much larger tails than the Gaussian density function.

Example 3.6

Consider the particle emission problem and assume $\alpha = 0.5$. Find the probability that the vertical impact point is between -2 and $+2$.

$$P\{-2 < X < 2\} = [\tan^{-1}(2/0.5) - \tan^{-1}(-2/0.5)]/\pi = 0.8447$$

That is still not a very high probability, since we are four times away from the ± 0.5 points. We may note that the probability of hitting within -0.5 and $+0.5 = 0.5$
We shall not encounter this distribution in many applications, but it is important as it has a density function with very long tails, unlike the Gaussian density function.

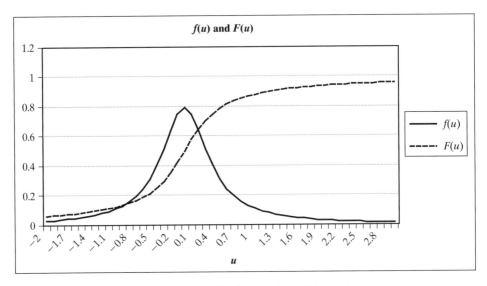

Figure 3.12   An example of the Cauchy distribution function and its density

3.3.7 Geometric Distribution

We considered the Binomial random variable in Section 3.3.4, which was defined as the number of successes in n independent trials. The geometric random variable is defined for the case in which we repeat the experiment until the first success occurs; hence the number of experiments is not fixed as in the Binomial case. Let X be defined as the experiment number at which the first success occurs. If we set the probability of a success in one experiment as p and of a failure as $q = 1 - p$, then the event $\{X = k\}$, for $k \geq 1$, will happen if there are exactly $(k - 1)$ failures during the previous $(k - 1)$ experiments, and a success occurs exactly at the kth experiment. We therefore have the following probability mass function for X:

$$p_X(k) = P\{X = k\} = p^1 q^{k-1} = p(1 - p)^{k-1}, \qquad k = 1, 2, 3, \dots. \qquad (3.32)$$

An example of such a random variable includes the case of a run of bits of size k without errors in a binary channel with an error probability of p.

Example 3.7

In an Ethernet network messages are divided into packets and transmitted through the network. If the Ethernet is congested, packets may be lost. Suppose that in a very congested network the probability that a packet is lost is $q = 0.8$. This means that the packet is not lost in a single transmission with probability $p = 0.2$. A packet is retransmitted repeatedly until it is received at its destination (the sender receives an acknowledgement signal from the destination).

a. Find the probability that a packet has to be sent at least three times until it is received.

In this case the number of transmissions is denoted by X and is geometrically distributed with parameter $p = 0.2$. We therefore have

$$P\{X \geq 3\} = 1 - P\{X < 3\} = 1 - P\{X = 1\} - P\{X = 2\}$$
$$= 1 - 0.2 - 0.2(0.8) = 0.64$$

b. Find the probability that a packet needs to be sent at most five times for successful reception:

$$P\{X \leq 5\} = \sum_{k=1}^{5} 0.2(0.8)^{k-1} = 0.2[1 + 0.8 + (.8)^2 + (0.8)^3 + (0.8)^4]$$
$$= 0.67232$$

We should note that we can find the probability that $X > n$ by using the expression

$$P\{X > n\} = \sum_{k=n+1}^{\infty} p(1-p)^{k-1} = (1-p)^n$$

We therefore obtain an expression for the distribution function for integer values, namely for $n \leq u < (n+1)$;

$$F_X(u) = P\{X \leq u\} = P\{X \leq n\} = 1 - P\{X > n\}$$
$$= 1 - (1-p)^n, \qquad \text{for } n = 0, 1, 2, \ldots \qquad (3.33a)$$

A typical example of the probability mass function of the geometric distribution is shown in Figure 3.13 for two values of the success probability p, one for $p = 0.2$ and one for $p = 0.4$. We see that for the case of the larger p, the probability mass function decays much faster than when p is smaller.

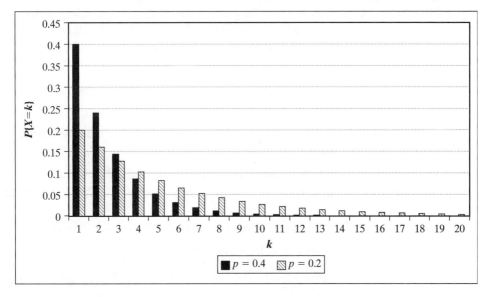

Figure 3.13 Examples of probability mass functions for geometric random variables for $p = 0.4$ (solid) and $p = 0.2$ (dashed)

The geometric distribution is important in many problems in communications when transmissions are repeated until a message is received correctly. This could be the transmission of packets as in the preceding example, the transmission of blocks via modems until they are received correctly, the retransmission of binary words when error-detecting codes are used, so that if a word is detected to have an error the receiver may request the retransmission of the word.

3.3.8 Poisson Distribution

The Poisson random variable is used to model many physical and practical phenomena. The Poisson model is useful whenever we have random occurrences of events of interest that satisfy certain assumptions, which we shall describe next. A few examples of applications of this random variable model are as follows:

a. The number of arrival of customers at a service desk or station
b. The number of arrivals of messages or calls to a switch or a router
c. The occurrence of failures in a product over a given time interval
d. The number of electrons or holes crossing a potential barrier (such as in a diode or a gate)
e. The number of defects in a roll of steel (or other material) of a given length
f. The number of accidents at an intersection in a given period of time

The Poisson random variable is a discrete random variable. However, since it involves the occurrence of events over an interval of time, we usually specify the time interval during which we are counting the number of such occurrences. Let us fix the length of the time interval under consideration as t. Then we define the random variable X as the number of occurrences (arrivals) during that interval. We define its probability mass function which provides the probability that exactly k arrive in the interval, which means that the probability (a function of k) also depends on the time interval in question as a parameter. We see therefore that the probability mass function depends on both k = number of arrivals, and t = length of interval in question:

$$P_k(t) = P\{X = k\} = P\{\text{exactly } k \text{ arrivals during an interval of length } t\}$$
(3.33)

We derive $P_k(t)$ under the following three assumptions that must be satisfied by the Poisson random variable:

Assumption I: Arrivals in nonoverlapping intervals are independent of each other.
Assumption II: $P\{\text{exactly one arrival in a small interval of length } \Delta t\} = \lambda(\Delta t) + o(\Delta t)$
Assumption III: $P\{\text{two or more arrivals in a small interval of length } \Delta t\} = o(\Delta t)$

From assumptions II and III we obtain

$$P\{\text{zero arrivals in a small interval of length } \Delta t\} = 1 - \lambda(\Delta t) + o(\Delta t)$$

In the preceding formula we use the notation $o(\Delta t)$ to indicate that the terms we are neglecting approach zero faster than Δt as Δt tends to zero.

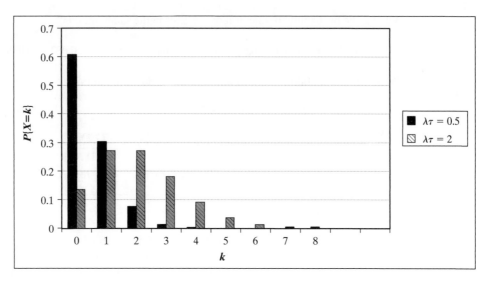

Figure 3.14   Examples of Poisson probability mass functions

Under these assumptions we can derive the Poisson distribution (as shown in Section 3.4 to avoid cluttering this section) to result in the expression for the probability mass function:

$$P_k(t) = \frac{(\lambda t)^k}{k!} e^{-\lambda t}, \qquad k = 0, 1, 2, 3, \ldots \tag{3.34}$$

It should be noted that λ represents an "average" arrival rate; hence it has dimensions of arrivals/time. The dimensions of the time t in equation (3.34) must be consistent with the dimension of λ. The distribution is therefore identified by a single parameter $\nu = (\lambda t)$, which represents the "average" number of arrivals during the interval of length t. We may therefore call λ the **arrival rate**.

An example of the probability mass function of the Poisson distribution is shown in Figure 3.14 for two values of the parameter λt, 0.5 and 2. We see that for the value of $\lambda t = 0.5$, the function is always decreasing and has its highest value at $k = 0$, while for $\lambda t = 2$, the function has its maximum at $k = 2$.

It can be shown that the maximum value of $P\{X = k\}$ indeed occurs at the value of k that is the closest integer to the value of λt. More precisely, the maximum value of $P\{X = k\}$ occurs at k_0 if the following is true:

$$(k_0 + 1) > \lambda t > k_0$$

That maximum is also achieved by the value at k_0 if $\lambda t = k_0 + 1$.

Example 3.8

If calls arrive at a switch at a rate of five per second, what is the probability that no call arrives in a half-second interval?

$$P\{0 \text{ in } t = 0.5\} = \frac{(5 \times 0.5)^0}{0!} e^{-5 \times 0.5} = e^{-2.5} = 0.082$$

What is the probability of one or more arrivals in the same interval?

$$P\{1 \text{ or more in } t = 0.5\} = 1 - P\{0 \text{ in } t = 0.5\} = 1 - 0.082 = 0.918$$

What is the probability of one or less arrivals in the same interval?

$$P\{1 \text{ or less in } t = 0.5\} = P\{0 \text{ in } t = 0.5\} + P\{1 \text{ in } t = 0.5\}$$

$$= \frac{(2.5)^0}{0!}e^{-2.5} + \frac{(2.5)^1}{1!}e^{-2.5}$$

$$= e^{-2.5}(1 + 2.5) = 0.2873$$

3.3.9 Exponential Distribution

The exponential random variable can be derived from the Poisson model in the same way as the derivation of the geometric from the binomial. Suppose that rather than asking for the number of arrivals in an interval of fixed length, we want to find the distribution of the time to the first arrival. We consider the Poisson model with parameter (arrival rate) λ and we define a random variable T as the time to the first arrival. In order to find the distribution function of the random variable T, we use the fact that T will be larger than a given time t, if there are zero arrivals during the time of length t, as seen in Figure 3.15. In the figure arrivals are marked with x's and T is shown as the time to the first arrival.

$$P\{T > t\} = P\{\text{zero arrivals in an interval of length } t\} = \frac{(\lambda t)^0}{0!}e^{-\lambda t} = e^{-\lambda t}$$

$$(3.35)$$

The distribution function of T will then be given by

$$F_T(t) = P\{T \le t\} = 1 - P\{T > t\} = 1 - e^{-\lambda t}, \qquad \text{for } 0 \le t \quad (3.36)$$

The corresponding density function is obtained by taking the derivative to obtain

$$f_T(t) = \lambda e^{-\lambda t}, \qquad \text{for } 0 \le t, \text{ and is zero for } t < 0 \qquad (3.37)$$

The exponential distribution is sometimes called a lifetime distribution. The reason for this is that if the arrivals are failures and a failure means the death of the system,

Figure 3.15   An illustration of the time to first arrival and its relation to the time t

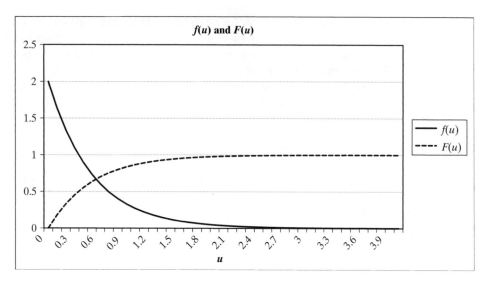

Figure 3.16   An example of the exponential distribution function $F(t)$ and its density function $f(t)$

then the time to the first failure is indeed the lifetime of the system or component. In communication systems or service system, the distribution is also called the inter-arrival time distribution. An example of an exponential distribution and density function is shown in Figure 3.16 for $\lambda = 2$.

Example 3.9

Consider the lifetime of a component, which is assumed to have an exponential density with failure arrival rate of $\lambda = 0.2$ per year.

a. What is the probability that the system lives five or more years?

$$P\{X > 5\} = 1 - [1 - \exp(-0.2 \times 5)] = \exp(-1) = 0.3679$$

b. What is the probability that the system fails between one and six years?

$$P\{1 < X < 6\} = [1 - \exp(-0.2 \times 6)] - [1 - \exp(-0.2 \times 1)]$$
$$= \exp(-0.2) - \exp(-1.2) = 0.5175$$

c. If we now have two identical systems that fail independently of each other, what is the probability that they both fail within five years?

First we find the probability that a single component fails within five years:

$$P(X < 5) = [1 - \exp(-0.2 \times 5)] = 0.6321$$

This failure probability is for each single component. If we assume that they fail independently of each other, then the probability that both fail before five years is

$$P\{\text{both fail before five years}\} = [P(X < 5)]^2 = (0.6321)^2 = 0.4$$

The exponential model is also a useful model for "departure" or "service times." In this case, if we have customers waiting in line to be served, we may consider the times between departures, which are the same as the service times, to be exponentially distributed. Let us denote the service times thus defined by the random variable X. If the service rate (which is the same as departure rate from the line) is assumed to be μ per unit time (we do not use λ, since in most such cases we have both arrivals and departures), then the probability density function of the service time is

$$f_X(t) = \mu \exp(-\mu t), \text{ for } t > 0, \text{ and is zero elsewhere} \tag{3.38}$$

If we are dealing with a communication system, then the same model maybe used for length of calls or length of messages, since the "service time" is proportional to message lengths.

3.4 DERIVATION OF THE POISSON DISTRIBUTION

In order to derive the Poisson distribution discussed in Section 3.3.8, based on Assumptions I, II, and III, we shall consider an interval of length $(t + \Delta t)$ where Δt is very small and approaches zero. Consider the probability that there are k arrivals in the interval of length $(t + \Delta t)$ for $k > 0$, and identify the two possible ways such an event can occur based on the assumptions as illustrated in Figure 3.17. Since the probability of more than one arrival in the small interval Δt is negligible (goes to zero fast as Δt approaches zero), then the event of k arrivals in $(t + \Delta t)$ is the union of two mutually exclusive events:

$\{k \text{ arrivals in } (t + \Delta t)\} =$
$\{k \text{ arrivals in } t \textbf{ and } \text{zero arrivals in } \Delta t\} \cup \{k - 1 \text{ arrivals in } t \textbf{ and } 1 \text{ arrival in } \Delta t\}$
$$\tag{3.39}$$

Now each of the events in equation (3.39) can be written as an intersection of independent events based on Assumption I:

$\{k \text{ arrivals in } t \textbf{ and } \text{zero arrivals in } \Delta t\} = \{k \text{ arrivals in } t\} \cap \{\text{zero arrivals in } \Delta t\}$
$\{k - 1 \text{ arrivals in } t \textbf{ and } 1 \text{ arrival in } \Delta t\} = \{k - 1 \text{ arrivals in } t\} \cap \{1 \text{ arrival in } \Delta t\}$
$$\tag{3.40}$$

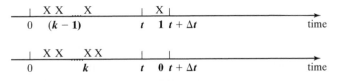

Figure 3.17   Two possible scenarios for k arrivals in an interval of length $(t + \Delta t)$. Number of arrivals in $(0, t)$ and in $(t, t + \Delta t)$ is shown in bold. Arrivals are marked by x's.

We now use the mutually exclusive and independent properties to arrive at the probability of $\{k$ arrivals in $(t + \Delta t)\}$:

$$P_k(t + \Delta t) = P\{k \text{ arrivals in } t\}P\{\text{zero arrivals in } \Delta t\}$$
$$+ P\{k - 1 \text{ arrivals in } t\}P\{1 \text{ arrival in } \Delta t\}$$
$$= P_k(t)P_0(\Delta t) + P_{k-1}(t)P_1(\Delta t) = P_k(t)[1 - \lambda\Delta t + o(\Delta t)]$$
$$+ P_{k-1}(t)[\lambda\Delta t + o(\Delta t)] \tag{3.41}$$

Here we have used Assumptions II and III as discussed in Section 3.3.8.

We now move $P_k(t)$ to the left side and divide both sides by Δt and let Δt approach zero to result in

$$[P_k(t + \Delta t) - P_k(t)]/\Delta t = -\lambda P_k(t) + \lambda P_{k-1}(t) + o(\Delta t)$$
$$\frac{dP_k(t)}{dt} = -\lambda P_k(t) + \lambda P_{k-1}(t), P_k(0) = 0, \qquad \text{for } k = 1, 2, 3, \ldots \tag{3.42}$$

It should be noted that for $k = 0$, the event as shown in Figure 3.17 can include only a single case, namely that there are zero arrivals at both intervals. We therefore obtain, using the same approach, the following equation for $k = 0$:

$$\frac{dP_0(t)}{dt} = -\lambda P_k(t), \qquad P_0(0) = 1 \tag{3.43}$$

The solution of the differential equation (3.43) with initial condition $P_0(0) = 1$, is obtained using standard solutions of linear differential equations:

$$P_0(t) = P_0(0)\exp(-\lambda t) = \exp(-\lambda t), \qquad \text{for } t \geq 0. \tag{3.44}$$

The solution of the differential equation (3.42) is similarly obtained and provides an expression for $P_k(t)$ in terms of $P_{k-1}(t)$. This means that we can solve for $k = 1$ using $P_0(t)$, and continue to solve for $P_2(t)$ in terms of $P_1(t)$, and so on. In general, the expression for $P_k(t)$ is obtained from equation (3.42) (using standard solution methods for first order linear differential equations) as

$$P_k(t) = \int_0^t \exp[-\lambda(t - \tau)]\lambda P_{k-1}(\tau)\, d\tau, \qquad \text{for } k = 1, 2, \ldots \tag{3.45}$$

We obtain for $k = 1$ the expression

$$P_1(t) = \int_0^t \exp[-\lambda(t - \tau)]\lambda\exp(-\lambda\tau)\, d\tau = (\lambda t)\exp(-\lambda t), \tag{3.46}$$

We can now use induction to show that the general expression for $P_k(t)$ given in equation (3.34) is indeed correct. We assume that the expression for $P_k(t)$, as given in equation (3.34), is correct for k, and use equation (3.45) to show that it will be also true for $(k + 1)$.

3.5 SUMMARY

Definition of random variables:

A random variable X is a real-valued function of the outcomes of a random experiment with a given probability assignment.

Distribution function of a random variable:

Definition:

$$F_X(u) = P\{X(\zeta) \le u\} = P\{X \le u\}$$

Properties:

$$F_X(-\infty) = 0, F_X(\infty) = 1$$

$$\lim_{\varepsilon \to 0} F_X(a + \varepsilon) = F_X(a), \qquad \text{where } \varepsilon > 0.$$

$$F_X(a) \le F_X(b), \text{ if } a < b. \text{ It is nondecreasing.}$$

$$P\{X = a\} = F_X(a) - F_X(a-)$$

where $F_X(a-)$ is the value of $F_X(u)$ just before reaching the point $u = a$.

$$P\{a < X \le b\} = F_X(b) - F_X(a)$$

$$P\{X > a\} = 1 - F_X(a)$$

Probability mass function:

If a random variables takes only discrete values $\{a_i\}$, for $i = 1, 2, 3, \ldots$, then its probability mass function is defined by the values

$$p_X(a_i) = P\{X = a_i\}$$

Probability density function:

If a random variable takes values only in a continuous range, then we may define (under some restrictions) a probability density function

$$f_X(u) = \frac{d}{du} F_X(u)$$

Properties of the density function:

$$f_X(u) \ge 0. \text{ It must be a nonnegative function.}$$

$$\int_{-\infty}^{\infty} f_X(u) \, du = 1. \text{ Its area must be equal to 1.}$$

$$F_X(\alpha) = \int_{-\infty}^{\alpha} f_X(u)\, du$$

$$P\{a < X \le b\} = \int_{a}^{b} f_X(u)\, du$$

Binomial distribution:

X = the number of successes in n trials:

$$P\{X = k\} = \binom{n}{k} p^k q^{n-k}, \qquad \text{for } k = 0, 1, 2, \ldots, n, \text{ where } \binom{n}{k} = \frac{n!}{k!(n-k)!}$$

Geometric distribution:

X = the number of trials until the first success:

$$P\{X = k\} = p(1 - p)^{k-1}, \qquad \text{for } k = 1, 2, 3, \ldots$$

Poisson distribution:

X = number of arrivals in a given time interval t when the arrival rate is λ:

$$P\{X = k\} = \frac{(\lambda t)^k}{k!} e^{-\lambda t}, \, k = 0, 1, 2, 3, \ldots$$

Uniform distribution:

X is equally likely to take any value in the interval $[a, b]$:

$$f_X(u) = \frac{1}{(b - a)}, \qquad \text{for } a < u < b, \text{ and is zero elsewhere}$$

$$F_X(u) = \begin{cases} 0, & \text{for } u < a \\ \dfrac{u - a}{b - a}, & \text{for } a < u < b \\ 1, & \text{for } b < u \end{cases}$$

Triangular distribution:

If we add two uniformly distributed random variables, we obtain a triangular density function, which takes value only in the interval $[2a, 2b]$:

$$f_X(\alpha) = \frac{\alpha - 2a}{(b - a)^2}, \qquad \text{for } 2a < \alpha < (a + b)$$

$$f_X(\alpha) = \frac{2b - \alpha}{(b - a)^2}, \qquad \text{for } (a + b) < \alpha < 2b$$

Gaussian or normal distribution:

The Gaussian density function with parameters m and σ is given by

$$f_X(u) = \frac{1}{\sqrt{2\pi}\sigma} e^{-\frac{(u-m)^2}{2\sigma^2}}$$

Unit Gaussian (or normal) density function:

$$f_X(u) = \frac{1}{\sqrt{2\pi}} e^{-\frac{u^2}{2}}$$

Cumulative unit Gaussian (or normal) distribution $\Phi(u)$, used to compute the following probability for any arbitrary Gaussian random variable:

$$P\{a < X < b\} = \Phi\left(\frac{b-m}{\sigma}\right) - \Phi\left(\frac{a-m}{\sigma}\right)$$

Exponential distribution:

X = time to first arrival or time to failure, where arrival rate is λ:

$$f_X(t) = \lambda e^{-\lambda t}, \text{ for } t > 0 \text{ and is zero elsewhere.}$$

$$F_X(t) = 1 - \exp(-\lambda t), \text{ for } t > 0 \text{ and is zero elsewhere.}$$

X = service time or departure time with departure rate μ, and will have the same density with parameter μ instead of λ.

3.6 PROBLEMS

MATLAB Problems:

1. Generate 1000 random numbers having a normal (Gaussian) distribution with parameters (mean) $m = 1$ and (standard deviation) $\sigma = 1$. Plot the histograms by using bins of size 0.1 and compare to the computed probability density function.

2. Repeat problem 1 by generating 5000 normal random numbers with $m = 2$, and $\sigma = 0.5$. The bin size you should use for this case is 0.05. In which case is the comparison to the computed density function better?

3. In Problem 2, find the fraction of the outcomes that are outside the range of $2(\sigma)$ from the mean and compare to the computed answer of 0.0454.

4. Generate one sample of a Poisson random variable with rate of $\lambda = 0.5$ and time interval $t = 10$, so that $\lambda t = 5$. This is how you generate the sample:

   Divide $t = 10$ into 1000 subintervals of length $\Delta t = 0.01$. In each subinterval generate a Bernoulli random variable that is equal to "one" with probability $\lambda \Delta t = 0.005$ and equal to zero with probability $(1 - \lambda \Delta t) = 0.995$. The locations of the "ones" are the time instants of the Poisson arrivals. If you place an "x" at these locations, you obtain a sample of the Poisson arrivals. Count the number of "ones" and that would be the number of arrivals for this sample.

Now generate 1000 such samples as you did for the first sample. Draw a histogram of the number of "ones" in each sample and compare it with the Poisson PMF.

5.   Generate 1000 samples of a geometric random variable with success probability of 0.2. Each sample will provide you with the number of trials until you obtained a success. Draw a histogram of the number of trials required to achieve the first success of the 1000 samples and compare it with the geometric PMF.

Regular Problems:

6.   Two communication systems with three links are shown in the diagrams:

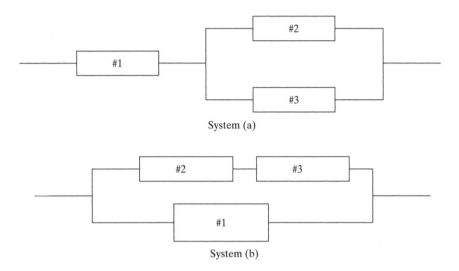

System (a)

System (b)

Each link may fail or not fail independently of the other links in a given interval of time. Define the events

$$F_i = \{\text{Component } \#i \text{ fails}\}, \qquad i = 1, 2, 3$$

Let M_i denote the capacity of link $\#i$ in megabits per second, and assume that $M_1 = 10$, $M_2 = 6$, and $M_3 = 4$. Also assume that $P\{F_i\} = p_i$ with $p_1 = 0.01$, $p_2 = 0.1$, $p_3 = 0.2$. For each system, let the capacity of the system be denoted by X, which in this case is a random variable due to the failures of the links.

a.   Define the values that X takes as a function of the sample space generated by the failures of the links.

b.   Derive the probability mass function and cumulative distribution function for this random variable.

7.   Four resistive loads are connected to a standard power outlet with voltage $V = 120$ volts as shown in the accompanying figure. Each resistive load has resistance of 24 Ω. The switches can be ON or OFF independently of each other, and the probability that a switch is ON is p = 0.4. The current through the power outlet is defined as a random variable X. Define the values that X takes as a function of the sample space, and derive the probability mass function and cumulative distribution function of X.

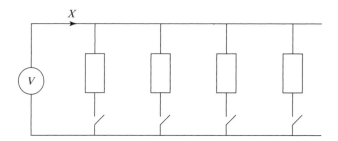

8. A resistor of nominal value $20 \pm 10\%$ Ω is selected at random and measured using a digital multimeter that displays only two digits after rounding off (for example instead of 18.56 or 19.43, it displays 19). Let the displayed value be denoted by X, which is a random variable, since we assume that the resistance is uniformly distributed in the range of $20 \pm 10\%$ Ω. Find the probability mass function of X and its cumulative distribution function.

9. Explain whether any of the four functions listed are valid cumulative distribution functions of a random variable. For those that are not valid, explain why. For those that are valid, find the following probabilities:

$$P\{0 < X < 1\}, \ P\{0 < X \le 1\}, \quad P\{1 < X < 2\}, \quad P\{1 \le X < 2\},$$
$$P\{1 \le X \le 2\}, P\{X = 2\}$$

a. $F_X(u) = \begin{cases} 0, & \text{for } u < -1 \\ 0.2(u + 1), & \text{for } -1 \le u < 1 \\ 0.5, & \text{for } 1 \le u < 2 \\ 0.2(u + 1), & \text{for } 2 \le u < 3 \\ 1, & \text{for } 3 \le u \end{cases}$

b. $F_X(u) = \begin{cases} 0, & \text{for } u \le -1 \\ 0.2(u + 1), & \text{for } -1 < u \le 1 \\ 0.5, & \text{for } 1 < u \le 2 \\ 0.2(u + 1), & \text{for } 2 < u \le 3 \\ 1, & \text{for } 3 < u \end{cases}$

c. $F_X(u) = \begin{cases} 0, & \text{for } u < 0 \\ 2[\sin(\pi u/4)]^2, & \text{for } 0 \le u < 3 \\ 1, & \text{for } 3 \le u \end{cases}$

d. $F_X(u) = \begin{cases} 0, & \text{for } u < 0 \\ [\sin(\pi u/4)]^2, & \text{for } 0 \le u < 2 \\ 1, & \text{for } 2 \le u \end{cases}$

10. Explain whether any of the four listed functions can be made into valid probability density functions of a random variable by a proper choice of C. For those that are not valid, explain why. For those that can be made valid, find the value of C and find the following probabilities:

$$P\{0 < X < 0.5\}, \qquad P\{0 < X \le 0.5\}, \qquad P\{X = 0.6\}$$

a. $f_X(u) = C \sin(\pi u)$, for $0 < u < 2$ and is zero elsewhere
b. $f_X(u) = C \sin(\pi u)$, for $0 < u < 1$ and is zero elsewhere
c. $f_X(u) = C \exp(-2u)$, for $0 < u < 1$ and is zero elsewhere
d. $f_X(u) = C(1 - u)$, for $-1 < u < 1$ and is zero elsewhere
e. $f_X(u) = C(1 - u)$, for $-1 < u < 2$ and is zero elsewhere

11. Let X be a random variable with a Gaussian distribution and with parameters $m = 2$ and $\sigma = 3$. Find the following probabilities:

$$P\{0 < X < 3\}, \qquad P\{-1 < X < 3\}, \quad P\{X < 5\}, \quad P\{-1 < X\}$$

12. Calls arrive at a switch at a rate of $\lambda = 2$ per second, and the arrivals obey the Poisson model.

a. What is the probability that there are no calls in a one-second interval?
b. What is the probability that there are more than five calls in a two-second interval?
c. What is the probability that there are exactly four calls in a two-second interval?
d. What is the probability that there are less than three calls in one second?
e. What is the length of the interval such that the probability of getting zero calls is exactly 0.9?

13. In a congested packet-switched network, a packet has a probability 0.6 of being dropped and having to be retransmitted. Packets are dropped at each transmission independently of each other.

a. What is the probability that a packet has to be retransmitted more than four times?
b. What is the probability that a packet has to be retransmitted exactly five times?
c. What is the probability that a packet has to be retransmitted less than six times?

14. The length of calls in a voice communications system is assumed to be exponentially distributed with departure rate $\mu = 0.5$ per minute.

a. Find the probability that a call lasts longer than two minutes.
b. Find the probability that a call will last less than one minute.
c. Find the probability that a call lasts between one and two minutes.

15.* Consider the two systems shown in Problem 6, and assume that each component fails independently of the other components with failure rate $\lambda = 0.5$ per year.

a. Consider any single component (all three components have the same failure rate) and find the probability that it fails during a two-year period.
b. Using the answer in (a), find the probability that the system fails during a two-year period.
c. Repeat (a) and (b) using a 1-year failure period.

16.* A unit in a factory has eight identical machines, which can be on or off independently of each other. A machine is on only 20% of the time on average. Each machine draws a current of 15 amps. The single power line feeding all the machines has a circuit breaker.

a. Suppose that the rating of the circuit breaker is 30 amps. Find the probability that it will trip.
b. What should be the rating of the circuit breaker so that it trips with probability of 0.01 or less?
c. Repeat (a) and (b) assuming that there are 16 machines but that each draws a current of 7.5 amps.

17.* Messages of the same length arrive at a switch to await transmission in a queue. Arrival rate is one message every two ms. Assume that the length of each message, in terms of time required for transmission, is 1.5 ms.

    a.   What is the probability that the queue length is larger than three messages?
    b.   What is the probability that exactly three messages wait in the queue?
    c.   What is the probability that there are zero messages in the queue?
    d.   What is the probability that the queue contains more than five messages?

18.* Two types of messages arrive at a switch: long and short. Each message can be long or short independently of the others, and 80% of the messages are short. The message arrival rate is equal to 10 per second. If we assume that the message arrival model satisfies the Poisson assumption, show that the model for the arrival of short messages is also Poisson with arrival rate of 8 messages per second. Generalize to the case of arbitrary arrival rate of λ and probability of a message being short is p.

19.* When we receive a signal, it is usually corrupted by noise, which we assume to be Gaussian with $m = 0$ and $\sigma = 0.1$. We are trying to distinguish between the case in which the signal is present at the receiver (in this case the signal amplitude is assumed to be Gaussian with $m = 0.5$ and the same $\sigma = 0.1$) and the case in which noise only is present. We do so by comparing the received signal to 0.25, and if the received signal is larger than 0.25, we claim that it is indeed present. Find the probability of the following two types of errors: (a) a miss, when we say the signal is absent but it is present; and (b) a false alarm, when we say that the signal is present but it is not.

4

Functions of a Random Variable and Expectations

4.1 FUNCTIONS OF A RANDOM VARIABLE

4.1.1 General Formulation

In many practical problems we do more with a random variable than compute its distribution or density functions. If the random variable is the amplitude of an electrical signal (voltage or current), we may wish to find the power dissipated when such a signal is applied to a circuit (even just a single resistance). If we pass such a signal through a rectifier or an amplifier with saturation, we may obtain as an output a signal with a different distribution function. Sometimes we receive sinusoidal signals whose phase is random (when the phase is unknown we usually assume it is random). The question is to find the way the random phase affects the signal amplitude and its distribution function. For the preceding examples, we need to address the question of how to derive the density or distribution function of a random variable if it is described as a function of another random variable.

Suppose X is a random variable with known distribution or density functions. A new random variable Y is defined as a function of the random variable X, namely $Y = g(X)$. We would like to find the distribution function of Y.

In order to do so, we use the definition of the distribution function of Y:

$$F_Y(v) = P\{Y \le v\} = P\{g(X) \le v\} \qquad (4.1)$$

Equation (4.1) implies that for every value of v, we have to find (1) the values of X that satisfy the relation $\{g(X) \le v\}$ and (2) the probability of the event so defined by using the distribution of X. Before providing a general expression for such a distribution, we shall consider two examples.

Example 4.1

Let the random variable X have a uniform distribution in the interval $(9, 11)$. We define the random variable $Y = 9/X$, and we wish to find the distribution of Y. The example is of a resistor of nominal value 10 Ω, with tolerance of $\pm 10\%$ (its value is represented by X) and Y is the current in the resistor when a 9-volt battery is applied at its terminals. It is easy to see that Y takes values only in the interval $(9/11, 9/9) = (0.8182, 1)$, as shown in Figure 4.1. Therefore the value of the distribution function of Y, $F_Y(v)$, is zero for $v < 0.8182$ and is 1 for $v > 1$. What happens between these two values can be inferred from the figure, where a line of a value of $v = 0.918$ is shown, so that we see that for Y to fall below this value, the value of X has to be higher than $9/v$, a point obtained by finding the inverse value of the function $9/X$. The resulting distribution function is obtained as follows:

$$F_Y(v) = P\left\{\frac{9}{X} \le v\right\} = P\left\{X \ge \frac{9}{v}\right\} = (11 - 9/v)/2 = 5.5 - 4.5/v,$$

$$\text{for } 0.8182 < v < 1$$

$$F_Y(v) = 0, \text{ for } v < 0.8182 \quad \text{and} \quad F_Y(v) = 1, \text{ for } v > 1 \qquad (4.2)$$

The density function of Y is obtained by taking the derivative of the distribution function; for the values in the range $(0.8182, 1)$ it has the expression

$$f_Y(v) = 4.5/v^2, \text{ for } 0.8182 < v < 1 \text{ and is zero elsewhere} \qquad (4.3)$$

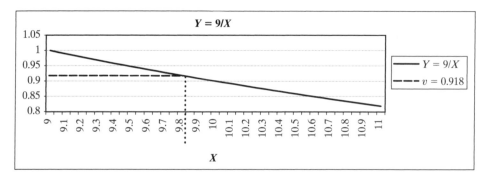

Figure 4.1 Y as a function of X, and a line showing one value of v

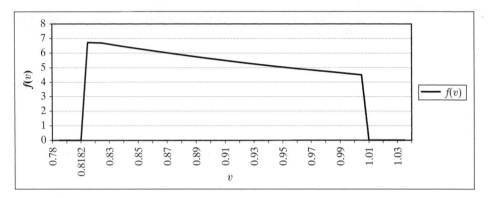

Figure 4.2(a) The probability density functions of Y

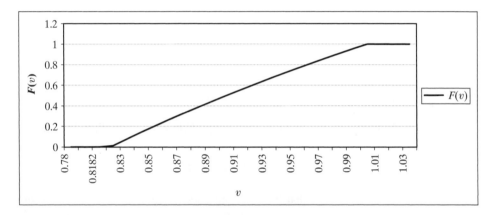

Figure 4.2(b) The cumulative distribution function of Y

The distribution and density functions are shown in Figure 4.2. It is interesting to note that even though X is uniformly distributed in the interval $(9, 11)$, the resulting current is not uniformly distributed (not that we expected it to be so).

Example 4.2

Here we consider the case of a saturation amplifier operating on a Gaussian random variable. This may represent the action of an amplifier–limiter on a noise whose amplitude is a random variable with a Gaussian distribution. In this case we assume that the input noise X has a Gaussian density function, with parameters $m = 0$, and $\sigma = 0.5$ (i.e., $f_X(u) = \{[2\exp(-2u^2)]/\sqrt{2\pi}\}$). The amplifier, whose output is assumed to be Y, is expressed by the following function:

$$Y = g(X) = \begin{cases} -a, & X < -1 \\ aX, & -1 < X < 1 \\ +a, & 1 < X \end{cases} \qquad (4.4)$$

It is relatively easy to see that when we use a value $v < -a$, we obtain no value of Y, since Y takes values only between $-a$ and $+a$, meaning that the probability

$$F_Y(v) = P\{Y \le v\} = 0, \quad \text{for } v < -a \tag{4.5}$$

Similarly, for $v \ge +a$, all values of Y will fall below the value of v, which means that the probability

$$F_Y(v) = P\{Y \le v\} = 1, \quad \text{for } +a \le v \tag{4.6}$$

Finally, for the values of v in the range $(-a, +a)$, we have the following relation for the probability:

$$F_Y(v) = P\{Y \le v\} = P\{aX \le v\} = P\{X \le v/a\} = F_X(v/a) \tag{4.7}$$

If we now differentiate the distribution function of Y, we obtain the value of the density function for the interval $(-a, +a)$:

$$f_Y(v) = f_X(v/a)/a = \frac{1}{a0.5\sqrt{2\pi}} \ exp\left\{-\frac{v^2}{2(a0.5)^2}\right\}, \text{for } -a < v < a \tag{4.8}$$

Note that the density expression in equation (4.8) is valid only for values of Y inside the interval $(-a, a)$. Also, since we have a jump in $F_Y(v)$ at $v = -a$ and $v = +a$, Y has a mixed distribution. The value of the jumps may be obtained from

$$P\{Y = -a\} = F_Y(-a) - F_Y(-a-) = F_X(-a/a) - 0 = F_X(-1) = \Phi(-2) = 0.0227$$

$$P\{Y = a\} = F_Y(a) - F_Y(a-) = 1 - F_X(a/a) = 1 - F_X(1)$$
$$= 1 - \Phi(2) = 1 - 0.9773 = 0.0227 \tag{4.9}$$

The result means that if we use impulses to represent the density function, then the density function will be given by equation (4.8) plus two impulses at $+a$ and $-a$ of magnitude 0.0227.

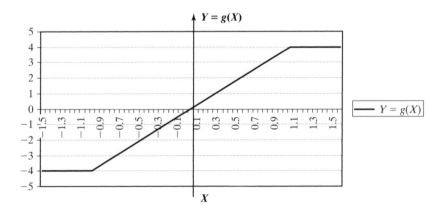

Figure 4.3(a)   The saturation amplifier function for $a = 4$

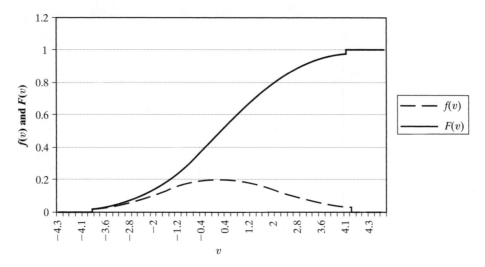

Figure 4.3(b)   The distribution $F(v)$ and density $f(v)$ functions for the example

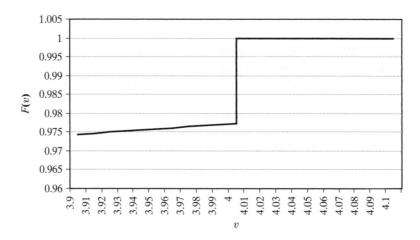

Figure 4.3(c)   A blow-up version of the distribution function near the value $v = 4$

The saturation function, the density function, and the distribution function are shown in Figure 4.3 for the value $a = 4$. The two impulses at $v = +a$ and $v = -4$ are not displayed in the figure for the density function.

The figures for the distribution function and the continuous part only of the density function are shown both for the entire interval and also in a blow-up version of the values near where a jump occurs, namely at $v = 4$ (for the distribution) and at $v = -4$ (for the density).

The preceding two examples illustrate how to obtain the distribution function and the density function (when it exists) when we transform a random variable through a nonlinear operation. The second example also shows how we may obtain

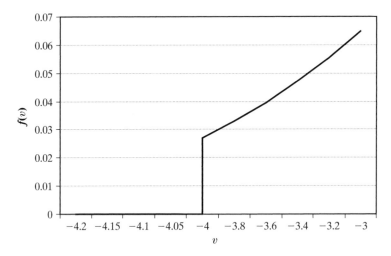

Figure 4.3(d)   A blow-up version of the density function near the value $v = -4$.

mixed random variables when we operate on continuous random variables by special operations such as saturation, or dead zone, among others.

   We next discuss a general approach to the derivation of the distribution and density functions when we operate on random variables by some nonlinear functions. The general approach can lead to difficulties, unless the function has special properties. In other cases we should revert to the special way we obtained the distribution in the foregoing examples.

4.1.2 Monotonically Increasing Function

We first consider the case in which the function $g(X)$ is monotonically increasing, as shown in Figure 4.4. The shaded parts in the figure are just our way of marking parts of the axes X and Y.

   In order to find the distribution function $F_Y(v)$, we use its definition as follows:

$$F_Y(v) = P\{Y \le v\} = P\{g(X) \le v\} = P\{X \le u = g^{-1}(v)\} = F_X[g^{-1}(v)] \tag{4.10}$$

The notation we use in equation (4.10) is that of the inverse function of $g(X)$, so that if $v = g(u)$, then we say that $u = g^{-1}(v)$. What we used to derive equation (4.10) is illustrated in Figure 4.4: The values that Y will take will be less than a variable v (the dashed part of the Y-axis) if the values of X fall below the value $u = g^{-1}(v)$ (the dashed part of the X-axis). We now can find the density function of X by differentiating equation (4.10). If we have $v = g(u)$ and $u = g^{-1}(v)$, then

$$\frac{du}{dv} = \frac{1}{g'[g^{-1}(v)]} \tag{4.11}$$

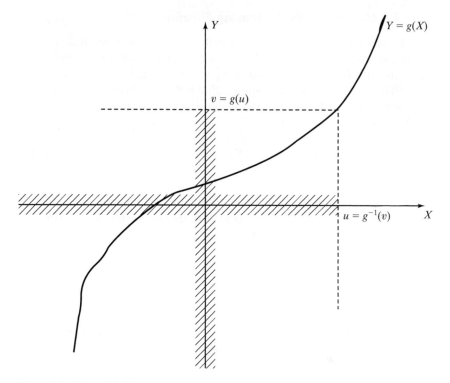

Figure 4.4 $Y = g(X)$, for a monotonically increasing g

We therefore obtain as the derivative of equation (4.10) with respect to v

$$f_Y(v) = \frac{d}{dv}F_X[g^{-1}(v)] = F'_X[g^{-1}(v)]\frac{d}{dv}\{[g^{-1}(v)]\} = f_X[g^{-1}(v)]/g'[g^{-1}(v)]$$

$$(4.12)$$

which can be written simply as

$$f_Y(v) = \left[\frac{f_X(u)}{g'(u)}\right]_{u=g^{-1}(v)}$$

$$(4.13)$$

Consider for example the case $Y = X^3$. Then the density function of Y can be expressed as

$$f_Y(v) = \left[\frac{f_X(u)}{3u^2}\right]_{u=\sqrt[3]{v}} = \frac{f_X(v^{1/3})}{3v^{2/3}}$$

$$(4.14)$$

4.1.3 Monotonically Decreasing Function

We next consider the case of a monotonically decreasing function $g(X)$. An example is illustrated in Figure 4.5. The figure also shows that if we want to find the values of Y that are less than some value v (shown by the dashed part of the Y-axis), then X will have to be higher than some value $u = g^{-1}(v)$ (shown by the dashed part of the X-axis). This fact leads us to the following expression for the distribution function of Y (based on its definition):

$$F_Y(v) = P\{Y \le v\} = P\{g(X) \le v\} = P\{X \ge u = g^{-1}(v)\} = 1 - F_X[g^{-1}(v)]$$
(4.15)

The derivation of the density function of Y is similarly obtained by differentiation. The derivation is exactly the same as in the increasing case, except for the negative sign appearing before the entire expression:

$$f_Y(v) = -\left[\frac{f_X(u)}{g'(u)}\right]_{u=g^{-1}(v)}$$
(4.16)

It should be noted that because $g(v)$ is monotonically decreasing, its derivative is negative! Therefore, instead of writing equation (4.16) with a negative sign, we use

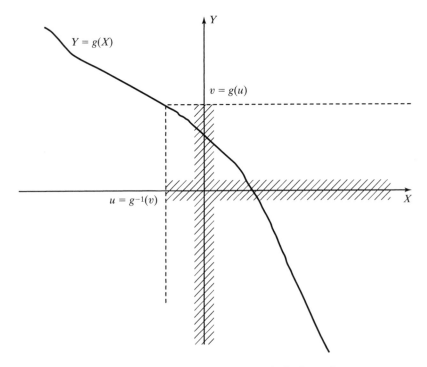

Figure 4.5   An illustration of $Y = g(X)$ that is monotonically decreasing

the absolute value of the derivative rather than its negative value, since they are the same:

$$-g'[u] = |g'[u]|$$

We therefore obtain

$$f_Y(v) = \left[\frac{f_X(u)}{|g'(u)|}\right]_{u=g^{-1}(v)} \tag{4.17}$$

In view of the fact that in the increasing case the derivative of $g(X)$ is positive, we can use equation (4.17) for both cases, as long as we are dealing with a monotonic function $g(X)$.

The earlier Example 4.1 demonstrates the case of a monotonically decreasing function and we could use the result to find the density function directly. In this case $g(u) = 9/u$, so that $g'(u) = -9/u^2$ and the inverse of $v = g(u)$ is $u = 9/v$. Hence the density of Y becomes

$$f_Y(v) = \left[\frac{f_X(u)}{|g'(u)|}\right]_{u=g^{-1}(v)} = \left.\frac{0.5}{\left[\dfrac{9}{u^2}\right]}\right|_{u=\frac{9}{v}} = 0.5/\{9/(9/v)^2\} = 0.5 \times 9/v^2 = 4.5/v^2$$

$$\text{for } 9/12 < v < 1.0$$

The result is exactly the same as the one derived directly.

An important special case of a monotonic function is the linear one:

$$Y = aX + b$$

In this case g is monotonically increasing if $a > 0$, and it is decreasing if $a < 0$, and we have $g'(v) = a$. The inverse function of $v = au + b$ is $u = (v - b)/a$. The resulting density function is obtained from equation (4.17) as

$$f_Y(v) = \frac{f_X[(v - b)/a]}{|a|}$$

4.1.4 Nonmonotonic Functions

Finally, we consider the case in which the function g has more than one inverse (an example is a quadratic function). An illustration of such a case is shown in Figure 4.6. It is possible to derive some general formulas for these cases. My preference is simply to show how it is done for this illustration and suggest that other cases of this kind in which the inverse of g is multiple-valued should be solved by using the definition of the distribution function directly. We shall consider two examples later in this section.

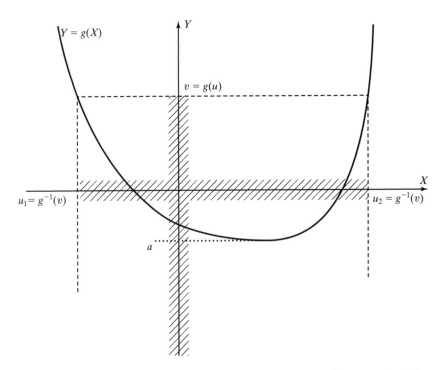

Figure 4.6   An illustration of $Y = g(X)$ whose inverse has two values for every value of Y

In this generic example of the multiple-valued inverse shown in Figure 4.6, we should mention one additional element besides the multiplicity. We see that, for values of u that are smaller than a (where the value a is the minimum point of the function), there are no values taken by the random variable Y. Hence we can state that

$$F_Y(v) = P\{Y \le v\} = P\{g(X) \le v\} = 0, \text{for } v < a \qquad (4.18)$$

We now consider the case in which $v \ge a$. In this region, for every value of $v = g(u)$, we have two values of u which are shown in the figure as u_1 and u_2. Hence, Y will take values less than the value of v (shown by the dashed part of the Y-axis) only when X takes values between u_1 and u_2 (shown by the dashed part of the X-axis). With the help of the figure, we can now find the distribution of Y:

$$F_Y(v) = P\{Y \le v\} = P\{g(X) \le v\} = P\{u_1 \le X \le u_2\} = F_X(u_2) - F_X(u_1) \qquad (4.19)$$

In equation (4.19) the values of u_1 and u_2 are the two solutions of $v = g(u)$, where $u_1 < u_2$. We can substitute the inverse function of g in equation (4.19) and take the derivative to obtain the density function of Y. If the student tries to use a general formula for such a case, he or she may make more mistakes than by simply solving each case directly and then taking the derivative.

Example 4.3

Let X be the amplitude of a random signal, which is assumed to be Gaussian, with parameters $m = 0$, and $\sigma = 2$. If we apply the signal to a 1-ohm resistor, we can define the dissipated power in the resistor as a random variable Y given by

$$Y = X^2$$

In this case we get a picture of $g(X)$ similar to the one shown in Figure 4.6, with $a = 0$ and with the two inverse values of $v = u^2$ equal to $u_1 = -\sqrt{v}$ and $u_2 = +\sqrt{v}$. For positive values of v the distribution function of Y is then obtained from the definition, with the help of Figure 4.6, to yield

$$
\begin{aligned}
F_Y(v) = P\{Y \le v\} = P\{X^2 \le v\} &= P\{-\sqrt{v} \le X \le +\sqrt{v}\} \\
&= F_X(+\sqrt{v}) - F_X(-\sqrt{v})
\end{aligned}
\tag{4.20}
$$

Now we can readily derive the density function of Y by taking the derivative and recognizing that the derivative of F_X is the density of X given by the Gaussian expression:

$$f_Y(v) = f_X(+\sqrt{v})/(2\sqrt{v}) - f_X(-\sqrt{v})/(-2\sqrt{v}) = \frac{f_X(\sqrt{v}) + f_X(-\sqrt{v})}{2\sqrt{v}} \tag{4.21}$$

Recall that the density of X is Gaussian with $m = 0$, $\sigma = 2$, so that when it is substituted in equation (4.21), we obtain

$$f_Y(v) = \frac{e^{-(v/8)}}{2\sqrt{2\pi v}}, \qquad 0 < v \tag{4.22}$$

The resulting density is called the chi-square density function with one degree of freedom and is shown in Figure 4.7. We see that it approaches infinity as v approaches zero.

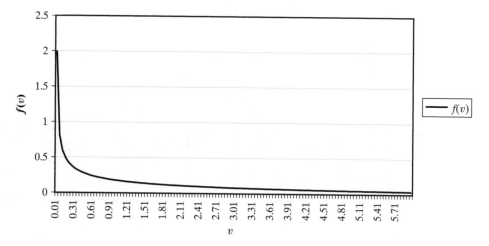

Figure 4.7   The chi-square density function $f(v)$ for $\sigma = 2$

Example 4.4

This example considers a sinusoidal signal with a random phase. We shall assume that the phase X is a random variable that is uniformly distributed in the interval $(-\pi, \pi)$, and let $Y = \cos(X)$. The signal is shown in Figure 4.8.

In order to find the distribution of Y, we see that here, as in Example 4.3, for every value of v there are two values of u solving the equation $v = \cos(u)$. Hence if we define the arccos function as the value that is between zero and π, the other solution is its negative value. Hence, the distribution function of Y can be derived as described next. Again, we select a value of v in the region of values that Y can take (in this case between -1 and $+1$) and find the probability that Y falls below that value of v. In this case it is easier to find the values of Y that are larger than the specified value of v, which is equal to $\{1 - F_Y(v)\}$. The random variable Y takes values larger than v shown in the figure if X takes values between the two inverses u_1 and u_2, where $u_2 = \arccos(v)$ and $u_1 = -u_2$. We obtain

$$1 - F_Y(v) = P\{Y \geq v\} = P\{\cos(X) \geq v\} = P\{u_1 \leq X \leq u_2\}$$
$$= P\{-\arccos(v) \leq X \leq \arccos(v)\} \tag{4.23}$$

Since the angle X is uniformly distributed between $(-\pi, \pi)$, the probability on the right side of equation (4.23) is just the length of the interval divided by 2π, so that the distribution becomes

$$F_Y(v) = 1 - P\{-\arccos(v) \leq X \leq \arccos(v)\} = 1 - 2\arccos(v)/(2\pi)$$
$$= 1 - \arcos(v)/\pi \tag{4.24}$$

The resulting distribution is called the arcsine distribution (for obvious reasons) and is shown in Figure 4.9. The density function is obtained by differentiating the distribution function to yield

$$f_Y(v) = \frac{1}{\pi\sqrt{(1 - v^2)}}, \qquad -1 < v < 1 \tag{4.25}$$

The density function is shown in Figure 4.10.

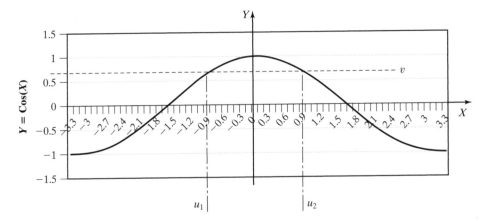

Figure 4.8   The sinusoidal function $Y = \cos(X)$

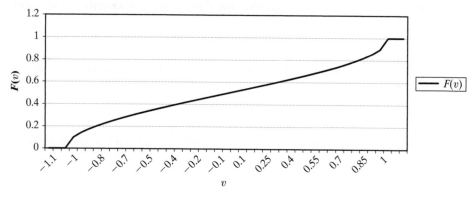

Figure 4.9   The arcsine distribution function

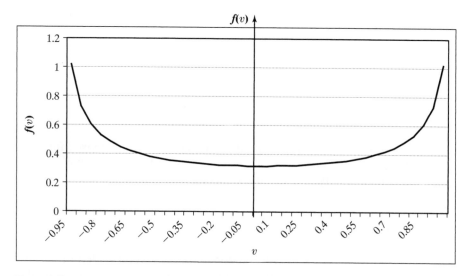

Figure 4.10   The density of the arcsine distribution function

Using the basic approach that utilizes the definition of the distribution function, we can derive in principle the distribution and density functions of any nonlinear operation that we care to define of a random variable of interest.

4.1.5 Computer Generation of Random Variables

If we wish to generate a sample of a random variable with a given distribution function, we can start with a uniformly distributed random variable X in the interval $(0, 1)$, and then use a transformation $Y = g(X)$, so that Y will have the desired distribution. Using the expression for monotonic functions, we can show (it is left as an exercise) that if we wish Y to have the distribution function $F_Y(v)$, then we should select $g(u)$ to have the form

$$g(u) = F_Y^{-1}(u)$$

As an example, suppose that we wish Y to have an exponential distribution

$$F_Y(v) = 1 - \exp(-\lambda v), \qquad v > 0$$

Then we can select g as the inverse function of the preceding equation:

$$v = g(u) = -\frac{\ln(1 - u)}{\lambda}, \text{ for } 0 < u < 1$$

Since this is a monotonic function, we can check the resulting density by using equation (4.17):
    We have $g'(u) = 1/[\lambda(1 - u)]$ and $g^{-1}(v) = F_Y(v) = 1 - \exp(-\lambda v)$, so the result is

$$f_Y(v) = \frac{1}{|g'[g^{-1}(v)]|} = \lambda[1 - g^{-1}(v)] = \lambda[1 - (1 - e^{-\lambda v})] = \lambda \exp(-\lambda v)$$

We can use MATLAB to generate samples of a uniformly distributed random variable $\{X_i\}$. Then we define

$$Y_i = -\frac{\ln(1 - X_i)}{2}$$

In this case the sample $\{Y_i\}$ will have the exponential density function $2 \exp(-2v)$. This approach can be used to generate samples of a random variable having any arbitrary density or distribution function.

4.2 EXPECTATIONS

So far, when we dealt with random variables, we provided the probability density and/or the cumulative distribution functions, which contained all the information that we can acquire about the random variables. In this manner we could find distributions of functions of such random variables, and the probability that the random variables take values in any range of interest. There are many cases in which we do not need that much information. Suppose we are trying to choose between two systems on the basis of downtime and the cost of parts for repairs. We try in such a case to convert the problem into one of costs: the costs of the downtime and the costs of repairs. Since there are probabilities associated with these events, we may be interested in finding some measure of the "average" cost to operate the system based on the preceding two factors. We can compare this problem to the problem of playing a game of chance, such that if we bet a certain amount, we can lose it with a given probability, and we can win a certain amount with a given probability. Obviously, in such a case we are also interested in our "average" gain (or loss). As an example, consider the case of a roulette wheel when one bets on red or black. The wheel has 18 red slots, 18 black slots, and 2 green slots (marked 0 and 00). If the bet is $1, then the probability of losing $1 is equal to 20/38 and the probability of winning $1 is

18/38. We can compute our average gain by multiplying each amount with the probability and adding

$$-1 \times 20/38 + 1 \times 18/38 = -0.0526$$

This means that for every \$1 we bet, we expect to lose on average about 5 cents.

We see here that we used the probabilities involved to compute just one value of interest, and in this case the value reflected our expected gain (or loss). This notion can be defined formally for any random variable so that we can provide information using just a few parameters or just a few values of interest about the random variable.

> **Definition:** Let X be a discrete random variables taking n values x_i with probabilities p_i for $i = 1, 2, \ldots, n$, and let $g(X)$ be a function of the random variable. We define the **expected value** (or the **expectation**) of $g(X)$ by the expression

$$E\{g(X)\} = \sum_{i=1}^{n} g(x_i) P\{X = x_i\} = \sum_{i=1}^{n} g(x_i) p_i \qquad (4.26)$$

If we wish to extend this definition to continuous random variables, we observe that the probability that $P\{X = x_i\}$ is zero for any particular value. Therefore we instead need to look at the probability that X falls within a small interval around the points $\{x_i\}$, which can be approximated by the value of the density function multiplied by the interval in question:

$$E\{g(X)\} = \sum_{i=1}^{n} g(x_i) P\{x_i \le X \le x_i + \Delta x\} = \sum_{i=1}^{n} g(x_i) f_X(x_i)\, \Delta x$$

$$= \sum_{i=1}^{n} g(x_i)[F_X(x_i + \Delta x) - F_X(x_i)]$$

It can be shown that as we make such intervals smaller and increase the value of n, the limiting behavior of the expectation becomes (assuming that the limit converges)

$$E\{g(X)\} = \int_{-\infty}^{\infty} g(u)\, dF_X(u) \qquad (4.27)$$

If the limit does not converge, then the expectation for that case does not exist. The existence and convergence of such integrals are quite mathematically complex and will not be addressed further in this text. The integral defined in equation (4.27) for the continuous random variable case (when the probability density function is assumed to exist) will have the form

$$E\{g(X)\} = \int_{-\infty}^{\infty} g(u) f_X(u)\, du \qquad (4.28)$$

In sum, an expectation is obtained by multiplying the values taken by the random variable with the probabilities of those values. In discrete cases we use equation (4.26) while in continuous cases we use equation (4.28). The mixed case is covered by the integral given in equation (4.27). However, in such a case we may use a combination of both equation (4.26) and equation (4.28), or we may use impulses in the expression for the density function and use equation (4.28) if we are careful.

Example 4.5

Consider the case in which a battery of 9 volts is applied to the terminals of a 10-ohm resistor, which was selected from a bunch of resistors with tolerance of $\pm 10\%$. We would like to find the expected value of the current in the resistor.

We let X be the value of the resistor, which is a random variable uniformly distributed between 9 and 11. The current, which we shall call Y, is given as

$$Y = 9/X$$

(In Section 4.1, we found its distribution and density functions. Here we wish only to find its expectation.) We now apply the definition for the expected value to obtain

$$E\{Y\} = E\{9/X\} =$$

$$\int_{-\infty}^{\infty} \frac{9}{u} f_X(u) \, du = \int_{9}^{11} \frac{9}{u} \frac{1}{2} du = 4.5[\ln(11) - \ln(9)] = 4.5 \ln(11/9) = 0.903 \qquad (4.29)$$

Note that in actually carrying out the integration, the limits on the integral are restricted to the region where the density function is not zero. It should be noted that if we try to find the expected value of the resistance X, we should obtain the value of 10. Hence, the expected value of the current is not equal to 9 volts divided by the average value of the resistance, which would have yielded an average of 0.9 instead of 0.903. In this case the difference is small, but it may not be that small in general.

Example 4.6

A system consists of three components, each having a probability $p = 0.1$ of failing. The cost of repairing a failed component is $100. The system is down if two or more components fail and the cost of down time during the repairs is $1000 in addition to the cost of repairing the failed components. Find the average (expected) value of the cost of failures. Here we use the definition of expectation for the discrete case. Let X denote the number of components failing, which means that it takes values 0, 1, 2, 3, and has a binomial distribution with $n = 3$ and $p = 0.1$. The cost of repairs, $g(X)$, can be expressed as

$$g(0) = 0, g(1) = 100, g(2) = 1200, g(3) = 1300.$$

The average cost becomes

$$E\{\text{cost}\} = E\{g(X)\} = 0 \times P\{X = 0\} + 100 \times P\{X = 1\}$$
$$+ 1200 \times P\{X = 2\} + 1300 \times P\{X = 3\} =$$
$$= 100 \times 3 \times 0.1 \times (0.9)^2 + 1200 \times 3 \times 0.01 \times 0.9 + 1300 \times 0.001 = \$58.00$$

Properties of Expectations

We see that the expectation is defined by either a sum or an integral involving the probabilities or distribution functions of the random variable. In many cases we can avoid performing messy operations if we utilize the properties of expectations that simplify many problems. The properties follow directly from the definition of the integral in equation (4.28) and the fact that the density function is always nonnegative.

Property 1: $E\{C\} = C$, where C is a constant.

Property 2: $E\{a\, g(X)\} = a\, E\{g(X)\}$, where a is a constant.

Property 3: $E\{g(X) + h(X)\} = E\{g(X)\} + E\{h(X)\}$

Properties 2 and 3 are also called the linearity property of the expectation.

Property 4: If $g(X) \geq 0$, then $E\{g(X)\} \geq 0$

From property 4 we can easily derive an additional property:

Property 5: If $g(X) \geq h(X)$, then $E\{g(X)\} \geq E\{h(X)\}$

We now consider special cases of the expectations, namely, the moments of a random variable or its distribution.

4.3 MOMENTS, MEAN, AND VARIANCE

Given a random variable X, we define its nth moment as the expected value of X^n:

$$m_n = E\{X^n\} \tag{4.30}$$

Note that in order to evaluate the moments, we need to use either equation (4.26) or equation (4.28) or both, depending on the type of the random variable. It should be noted that $m_0 = 1$, which follows from property 1.

Special cases of the moments are obtained for $n = 1$ and for $n = 2$. In the case of $n = 1$, we obtain the expected value of the random variable X itself and we denote it by m_X:

$$m_X = m_1 = E\{X\} = \int_{-\infty}^{\infty} u f_X(u)\, du \tag{4.31}$$

We call the expected value of X the **mean** of X or the mean of the distribution or density functions of X. It represents a kind of central value around which X takes its values (i.e., X takes values both larger and smaller than the mean). If the density function is symmetric, then the mean indeed falls in the center of the density function range. Another physical interpretation is that, if we make the density function of cardboard, then the mean is the center of gravity of the density function. The density function that is made of cardboard will balance if placed at a point equal to its mean value.

For $n = 2$, we obtain the second moment of X, which, when one is dealing with signal amplitudes (such as in volts), represents the average power of the signal, since the power is obtained by squaring the amplitude (assuming it is operating on a 1-ohm resistor).

Since the mean represents the center of the distribution or density functions, it is more interesting to show another average value that reflects the shape of the density. Note that the second moment by itself is not a good measure, since if we translate the mean of the same density, we get a different value of the second moment even though the shape of the density remains the same. We therefore define second central moments by finding the moments after we subtract the mean from the values taken by the random variable.

Hence, we define the nth central moment by the expression

$$\mu_n = E\{[X - m_X]^n\} \tag{4.32}$$

It is clear from the definition that $\mu_0 = 1$ and $\mu_1 = 0$. Of particular interest is the second central moment, μ_2, which we call the **variance** of the random variable X and denote by σ_X^2. The square root of the variance, σ_X, is called the **standard deviation** of the random variable X. It can be easily shown using the linearity property of expectations that we can obtain the variance either directly from the definition or via the second moment as follows:

$$\sigma_X^2 = E\{[X - m_X]^2\} = E\{X^2 - 2Xm_X + m_X^2\} = E\{X^2\} - m_X^2 \tag{4.33}$$

What Does the Variance Represent?

While the mean represents the center of gravity of the density function, the variance and the standard deviation reflect the spread of the density function around the mean. If it is narrowly distributed around the mean, it will have a smaller variance and vice versa. This property is best illustrated by finding the means and variances of the various random variables we derived earlier in Section 3.3.

Before we consider any examples, we shall derive two important properties of the mean and variance of random variables after a linear transformation. Let X denote a random variable with mean m_X and variance σ_X^2. Let $Y = aX + b$, where a and b are constants. We now use the linearity property of the expectation to show that

$$m_Y = E\{Y\} = E\{aX + b\} = am_X + b \tag{4.34}$$

Similarly, for the variance of Y we have

$$\sigma_Y^2 = E\{[Y - m_Y]^2\} = E\{[aX + b - (am_X + b)]^2\} = E\{a^2[X - m_X]^2\}$$
$$= a^2\sigma_X^2$$
$$\sigma_Y = |a|\sigma_X \tag{4.35}$$

A linear transformation of a random variable results in the same linear transformation of its mean. The standard deviations are related by the absolute value of the multiplicative part of the transformation. We now consider several examples of random variables and their means and variances.

4.3.1 Binomial Random Variable

If X has a binomial distribution with parameters p and n, its mean and variance are obtained as follows:[1]

$$m_X = \sum_{k=0}^{n} kP\{X = k\} = \sum_{k=0}^{n} k\binom{n}{k}p^k(1 - p)^{n-k} = np$$

$$\sigma_X^2 = E\{X^2\} - (m_X)^2 = \sum_{k=0}^{n} k^2P\{X = k\} - (np)^2$$

$$= \sum_{k=0}^{n} k^2\binom{n}{k}p^k(1 - p)^{n-k} - (np)^2 \tag{4.36}$$

$$= n(n - 1)p^2 + np - (np)^2 = np(1 - p) \tag{4.37}$$

For the Bernoulli random variable (i.e., when $n = 1$), we obtain a mean of p and variance of $p(1 - p)$.

For the general case, for example, if $p = 0.5$, then the mean is $0.5n$ and the variance is $0.25n$. We see that the mean of the random variable grows linearly with the number of trials, n, while the standard deviation grows as the square root of n. This has very strong implications about our confidence in performing trials as a way of estimating the value of p. Consider the next example as a demonstration.

Example 4.7

In order to find the probability of errors in transmitted blocks, we send n blocks and count how many were received in error, and we use the ratio as a measure of p. Let X denote the number of blocks in error among the n transmitted blocks. Define Y (to serve as an estimate of p) as the ratio of the number of blocks in error to the number of blocks transmitted: $Y = X/n$. We know that the mean of X is pn and its variance is $np(1 - p)$. We now use the linearity property of the mean and standard deviation to show that

$$m_Y = m_X/n = p \tag{4.38}$$
$$\sigma_Y^2 = \sigma_X^2/n^2 = p(1 - p)/n \tag{4.39}$$

[1]The summations in equations (4.36) and (4.37) may be derived by using the book by L.B.W. Jolley, "Summation of Series." These expressions are evaluated in Section 7.2 in this text as well.

We therefore have the following bound on the standard deviation of Y, where we use the fact that the function $p(1 - p)$ ranges between 0 and 0.25 and achieves its largest value when $p = 0.5$, so that $p(1 - p) = 0.25$ with a square root of 0.5:

$$\sigma_Y = \sqrt{\frac{p(1 - p)}{n}} \leq \frac{1}{2\sqrt{n}} \qquad (4.40)$$

Hence, we see that the mean of Y is indeed equal to the probability p we are trying to estimate, while its standard deviation becomes smaller and is inversely proportional to the square root of n. This means that for $n = 100$ the standard deviation of Y is less than 0.05, while for $n = 10,000$ the standard deviation is less than 0.005. Since the standard deviation serves as a measure of how wide or narrow the distribution is, we see that as we increase n, the density of Y gets narrower about the value of p we are trying to estimate.

4.3.2 Geometric Random Variable

Let X denote a random variable with geometric distribution. In this case it has the following probability mass function:

$$P\{X = k\} = p(1 - p)^{k-1}, \qquad \text{for } k = 1, 2, 3, \ldots \qquad (4.41)$$

The mean of the random variable is given by

$$m_X = \sum_{k=1}^{\infty} kP\{X = k\} = \sum_{k=1}^{\infty} kp(1 - p)^{k-1} = 1/p \qquad (4.42)$$

It is seen therefore that if $p = 0.2$, then the average number of trials until the first success is $1/p = 5$, which agrees with our intuitive expectation in this case. The variance in this case may be expressed as

$$\sigma_X^2 = \sum_{k=1}^{\infty} k^2 P\{X = k\} - m_X^2 = \sum_{k=1}^{\infty} k^2 p(1 - p)^{k-1} - 1/p^2 = \frac{1 - p}{p^2} \qquad (4.42a)$$

(See footnote 1 on page 115 for how to derive the summations in equations (4.42) and (4.42a) in this case). It is seen from equation (4.42a) that the variance increases as the value of p decreases. For example, for $p = 0.2$ we have a variance of 20, while for $p = 0.5$ we have a variance of 2.

Example 4.8

If we a send message over an Ethernet, the message has a certain probability of colliding with messages of other users. If the message collides, then we have to resend it. What is the average number of times we have to resend a message if we know the probability of collision? Usually the probability of collision can be inferred from the number of users on the Ethernet and the average volume of messages per user. Suppose that the probability of collision is 0.6 (60%). What is the average number of times that a message has to be retransmitted?

We use the result given in equation (4.42) to obtain the average number of trials until the first success, which we found to be given as $1/p$, where p is the probability of success. Here the probability of success is $p = 0.4$. Hence the average number of transmission until the first success is equal to $(1/0.4) = 2.5$. However, here we asked for the average number of retransmissions, so we have to subtract 1 for the first time we send the message. The answer is then 1.5. Suppose that it takes a message an amount of time equal to T for a successful transmission with no collisions. We learn about a collision only after $2T$ because it may take a full round trip around the network before we note the collision. What is the average time it takes a message for a successful transmission? Since we repeat the message an average of 1.5 times, and each such repetition takes $2T$, and the final successful transmission takes T, the average time for a successful transmission of a message is $T + 1.5 \times 2T = 4T$.

4.3.3 Poisson Random Variable

If we assume that X is a Poisson-distributed random variable with parameter $\alpha = \lambda t$, then its mean and variance are derived from the following expressions:

$$m_X = \sum_{k=0}^{\infty} k P\{X = k\} = \sum_{k=0}^{\infty} k \frac{\alpha^k}{k!} e^{-\alpha} = \alpha = \lambda t \qquad (4.43)$$

The variance is similarly derived:

$$\sigma_X^2 = E\{X^2\} - (m_X)^2 = \sum_{k=0}^{\infty} k^2 P\{X = k\} - \alpha^2 = \sum_{k=0}^{\infty} k^2 \frac{\alpha^k}{k!} e^{-\alpha} - \alpha^2 = \alpha = \lambda t \tag{4.44}$$

(See the footnote on page 115 about the summations in this case.) It is interesting that for the Poisson case the mean and the variance are identical. We shall discuss the implications of this property at a later stage when we discuss inference.

4.3.4 Gaussian Random Variable

Consider the Gaussian random variable X with density function

$$f_X(u) = \frac{1}{\sqrt{2\pi}\sigma} e^{\frac{(u-m)^2}{2\sigma^2}} \qquad (4.45)$$

The mean is obtained from

$$m_X = \int_{-\infty}^{\infty} u \frac{1}{\sqrt{2\pi}\sigma} e^{\frac{(u-m)^2}{2\sigma^2}} \, du = \int_{-\infty}^{\infty} (u - m) \frac{1}{\sqrt{2\pi}\sigma} e^{\frac{(u-m)^2}{2\sigma^2}} \, du$$

$$+ m \int_{-\infty}^{\infty} \frac{1}{\sqrt{2\pi}\sigma} e^{\frac{(u-m)^2}{2\sigma^2}} \, du$$

$$= 0 + m \times 1 = m \qquad (4.46)$$

We can also show that the variance is indeed equal to the parameter σ^2, which appears in the expression for the density function. We see that the Gaussian distribution is completely determined by its mean and standard deviation. We also know from the cumulative Gaussian distribution, that the probability of a Gaussian random variable taking values within $\pm 3\sigma$ of its mean is more than 99% (about 99.7%).

4.3.5 Uniform Random Variable

Let X be uniformly distributed in the interval (a, b). Then we have the following expression for its mean and variance:

$$m_X = \int_{-\infty}^{\infty} u f_X(u)\, du = \int_a^b u \frac{1}{b-a}\, du = \frac{a+b}{2} \tag{4.47}$$

$$\sigma_X^2 = E\{X^2\} - (m_X)^2 = \int_{-\infty}^{\infty} u^2 f_X(u)\, du - \left(\frac{a+b}{2}\right)^2$$

$$= \int_a^b u^2 \frac{1}{b-a}\, du - \left(\frac{a+b}{2}\right)^2 = \frac{(b-a)^2}{12} \tag{4.48}$$

Again, the mean is equal to the midpoint of the range of the random variable, while the standard deviation is proportional to the width of the range $(b-a)$.

4.3.6 Exponential Random Variable

Let X be a random variable with exponential distribution $f_X(t) = \lambda e^{-\lambda t}$. Then its mean can be found as follows:

$$m_X = \int_0^{\infty} u \lambda e^{-\lambda u}\, du = \frac{1}{\lambda} \tag{4.49}$$

This is expected, since λ represents the arrival rate. Therefore the average time to first arrival is the inverse of the arrival rate. Again, if the arrivals represent failures, then the average lifetime is inversely proportional to the failure rate. Similarly, we find the variance by finding the second moment:

$$E\{X^2\} = \int_0^{\infty} u^2\, \lambda e^{-\lambda u}\, du = \frac{2}{\lambda^2} \tag{4.50}$$

The variance is therefore equal to

$$\sigma_X^2 = E\{X^2\} - (m_X)^2 = \frac{2}{\lambda^2} - \frac{1}{\lambda^2} = \frac{1}{\lambda^2} \tag{4.51}$$

For this case the mean and the standard deviation are equal, while for the Poisson case the mean and variance are equal. These two related distribution cases should not be confused.

If we try to find the mean or variance of a Cauchy random variable, we find that the integrals involved do not converge since the density goes to zero very slowly as the values become very large. This is an example of a density that is easy to construct both mathematically and physically, yet its mean and variance do not exist.

4.3.7 Chebyshev's Inequality

We noted that for Gaussian random variables the variance (and the standard deviation) relate explicitly to the probability of being inside (or outside) a certain range of a number of standard deviations around the mean. For example, the probability of a Gaussian random variable taking values outside two standard deviations from the mean is less than 5%. While if we increase the interval to three standard deviations, the probability is less than 0.3%.

What can we say about other random variables whose distribution or density functions may not even be known but whose mean and variance are known?

An answer to this question is provided by Chebyshev's inequality, which can be stated as follows:

Given a random variable X with mean m_X and variance σ_X^2, then the following inequality holds:

$$P\{|X - m_X| > k\sigma_X\} < 1/k^2 \qquad (4.52)$$

Note that this bound is very pessimistic. For example, for Gaussian random variables we have exact values for the probability described in equation (4.52). For $k = 2$, the probability is less than 0.05, while the bound is equal to 0.25. Similarly, for $k = 3$, the exact value is less than 0.003 while the bound is equal to 0.111.

The inequality (4.52) can also be described in absolute terms, rather than relative to the standard deviation:

$$P\{|X - m_X| > b\} < (\sigma_X/b)^2 \qquad (4.53)$$

The Chebyshev inequality can be used to prove the behavior of certain random variables as some parameters are changed. For example, consider the previous example of estimating p by using n trials. We found that the variance of the estimate behaves as $1/(4n)$. Hence, the probability that Y is outside some interval, say 0.01, around the mean value is bounded by

$$P\{|Y - p| > 0.01\} < 10{,}000/(4n) = 2500/n$$

Hence, for $n = 10^6$, the probability that we make an error of 0.01 or larger in estimating p is less than 0.0025.

The proof of the inequality will now be derived. We wish to find a bound for the following probability, which is expressed in terms of a new random variable Y:

$$P\{|X - m_X| > k\sigma_X\} = P\{|X - m_X|/(k\sigma_X) > 1\} = P\{|Y| > 1\} \qquad (4.54)$$

Here we defined a new random variable $Y = (X - m_X)/(k\sigma_X)$. In order to simplify equation (4.54) we define a new function $g_1(Y)$ as follows:

$$g_1(Y) = \begin{cases} 1, & \text{for } |Y| > 1 \\ 0, & \text{for } |Y| \leq 1 \end{cases}$$

In this case we can write the expectation of this function as

$$E\{g_1(Y)\} = 1 \times P\{|Y| > 1\} + 0 \times P\{|Y| \leq 1\} = P\{|Y| > 1\} \quad (4.55)$$

The function $g_1(Y)$ is shown in Figure 4.11 together with the function Y^2, and it is easily verified that they satisfy the relation

$$g_1(Y) \leq Y^2 \tag{4.56}$$

Therefore, by Property 5 of the expectation and equations (4.55) and (4.56), we obtain

$$P\{|Y| > 1\} = E\{g_1(Y)\} \leq E\{Y^2\} = E\{[(X - m_X)/(k\sigma_X)]^2\}$$
$$= E\{(X - m_X)^2\}/(k\sigma_X)^2 = 1/k^2 \tag{4.57}$$

This proves the Chebyshev inequality.

As we see from the example, it is in our interest to obtain results based on experiments that have as small a variance as we could get. Obviously, we pay for

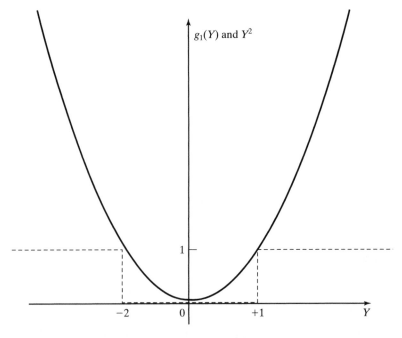

Figure 4.11   The relation between the function $g_1(Y)$ (dashed line) and Y^2 (solid line)

smaller variance (as illustrated in the example of estimating the value of p) by higher costs, in terms of repeating the experiment many times, where, presumably, each repetition has a cost.

4.4 SUMMARY

Functions of one random variable:

If $Y = g(X)$, where X is a random variable, then

$$F_Y(v) = P\{Y \le v\} = P\{g(X) \le v\}$$

If $g(u)$ is a monotonic function, then

$$f_Y(v) = \left[\frac{f_X(u)}{|g'(u)|} \right]_{u=g^{-1}(v)},$$

where $g'(u)$ is the first derivative of $g(u)$ and where $u = g^{-1}(v)$ means the inverse function of $v = g(u)$.

Expectations:

The expectation of a function of a random variable is given by

$$E\{g(X)\} = \int_{-\infty}^{\infty} g(u) f_X(u) \, du$$

The integral is replaced with the sum for discrete random variables, unless we use impulse functions.

Properties:

$$E\{C\} = C$$

$$E\{ag(X) + bh(X)\} = aE\{g(X)\} + bE\{h(X)\}$$

$$\text{If } g(X) \ge 0, \text{ then } E\{g(X)\} \ge 0$$

Mean and variance:

$$\text{Mean of } X = m_X = E\{X\} = \int_{-\infty}^{\infty} u f_X(u) \, du$$

$$\text{Variance of } X = \sigma_X^2 = E\{[X - m_X]^2\} = E\{X^2\} - m_X^2$$

Properties:

If $Y = aX + b$, then $m_Y = am_X + b$, $\sigma_Y^2 = a^2 \sigma_X^2$

Means and variances of special distributions:

Binomial with parameters n and p: $m_X = np$, $\text{Var}(X) = np(1 - p)$

Poisson with arrival rate λ and time t: $m_X = \text{Var}(X) = \lambda t$

Geometric with success probability p: $m_X = 1/p$, $\text{Var}(X) = (1 - p)/p^2$

Uniform in interval $[a, b]$: $m_X = (a + b)/2$, $\text{Var}(X) = (b - a)^2/12$

Exponential with parameter λ: $m_X = \sigma_X = 1/\lambda$

For a Gaussian, the parameters m and σ are the mean and standard deviation as well. The Cauchy distribution has no mean or variance.

4.5 PROBLEMS

MATLAB Problems:

1. Generate 2000 random numbers $\{X_i\}$ having a uniform distribution in the range $[0, 1]$. Then use the logarithmic function described in Section 4.1.5 to obtain 2000 random variables $\{Y_i\}$ having an exponential density function $2e^{-2u}$. Find the sample mean and sample standard deviation, and compare it with the mean and standard deviation of the preceding mathematical density function. Plot the histograms using bins of size 0.1, and compare them with the preceding exact probability density function.

2. Generate 2000 samples of a Cauchy-distributed random variable Y whose density is described in Section 3.3.5. First generate uniformly distributed random variables $\{X_i\}$ in the range $[-0.5\pi, +0.5\pi]$, and use $Y_i = 2\tan(X_i)$, where we are using equation (3.31) with $\alpha = 2$. Plot the histogram using bin sizes of 0.5 in the range from -10 to $+10$. What does the histogram tell you about the tails of the Cauchy density function? (You may confirm your conclusion by finding the sample standard deviation of Y). Also, plot the mathematical density function (equation (3.31) for $\alpha = 2$) and compare it with the histogram.

3. Use the same approach derived in Section 4.1.5 to generate a sample of size 2000 of a random variable that has the arcsine distribution function. (Use the function from Example 4.4 for this purpose.) Find the sample mean and sample standard deviation, and compare them with the theoretical value.

4. Generate 1000 samples of a Poisson random variable, as in Problem 3-4. Determine for each sample the time between the arrival times. Draw a histogram of the length of time between arrivals and compare it with the exponential density function.

5. Generate 1000 samples $\{X_i\}$ of a Gaussian random variable with mean zero and variance of 4. Now operate on the samples by a square-law device to generate samples $Y_i = X_i^2$. Draw a histogram of the sample Y_i and compare it with the chi-square density function.

Regular Problems:

6. In a congested packet-switched network, a packet has a probability of 0.8 of being in a collision and having to be retransmitted. Collisions at each transmission are independent events.

   a. Find the average number of **re**transmissions.
   b. Find the average number of total transmissions.

7. Calls arrive at a switch at an average rate of 2 per second, and the arrivals obey the Poisson model.

    a.   What is the mean and standard deviation of the number of calls in a 2-second interval? In a 1-minute interval? In a 10-minute interval? What can you conclude from the results?

    b.   Use Chebyshev's inequality to find a bound on the probability that the number of calls in a 10-minute interval is between 1100 and 1300.

8. A random signal whose amplitude is assumed to be a random variable X with density function $f_X(u) = \exp\{-2|u|\}$ is amplified by an amplifier with both dead zone and saturation so that the output is given by the expression $Y = g(X)$, where

$$g(X) = \begin{cases} -10, & \text{for } X < -2.1 \\ 5(X + 0.1), & \text{for } -2.1 < X < -0.1 \\ 0, & \text{for } -0.1 < X < +0.1 \\ 5(X - 0.1), & \text{for } 0.1 < X < 2.1 \\ 10, & \text{for } 2.1 < X \end{cases}$$

    a.   Find the distribution function of Y.

    b.   Find the mean and variance of Y.

    c.   Repeat part (a) if the random variable X is Gaussian with zero mean and standard deviation 1.5.

9. Suppose that in Problem 8 the signal is passed through a square-law detector, which means that the output Y is given as $Y = g(X)$, where $g(X) = 0.5X^2$.

    a.   Find the density function of Y.

    b.   Find the mean of Y.

10. An amplifier with a bias has an input signal whose amplitude is described as a random variable X with mean 0.5 and variance 9. The output Y is given by

$$Y = 5X - 1.5$$

    a.   Find the mean, variance, and standard deviation of Y.

    b.   If the random variable X is Gaussian, write the density function of Y.

11. A power supply is connected to six equal loads. Each load is ON 20% of the time and OFF 80% of the time, and draws a current of 5 amps. The loads are ON or OFF independently of each other. Let the current through the power supply be denoted by a random variable X, find the mean, variance, and standard deviation of X.

12. * Repeat Problem 11 assuming that we have 20 loads instead of 6, and compare the standard deviation of the current as a fraction of the average current for both cases. What can you conclude from this observation?

13. The time to failure, X, of a component is assumed to follow the exponential distribution, with failure rate $\lambda = 0.5$ per year. The cost Y of operating the component during the first year can be expressed as $2X$, while after one year, the cost becomes $4X + 2$.

a.   Find the average cost of operating the component.
b.   Find and sketch the density and distribution functions of Y.

14.* A signal whose amplitude X is a random variable having a Gauassian density with mean zero and standard deviation 3, is passed through a square-law detector with saturation, so that the output Y is given by

$$Y = \begin{cases} 0.25X^2, & \text{for } |X| < 6 \\ 9, & \text{for } |X| > 6 \end{cases}$$

a.   Find the distribution function of Y.
b.   Find the probability that $Y = 9$.
c.   Find and sketch the density of Y for the region $[0, 9)$.

15.* In the target model that resulted in the Cauchy density of equation (3.31) for the random variable X consider the case with $\alpha = 0.5$. The target has a fixed vertical dimension at 4, so that the impact distance is given by the function

$$Y = X, \text{for } |X| < 2 \text{ and } Y = 2\,\text{sgn}(X), \text{for } |X| > 2$$

a.   Find the mean and variance of Y.

b.   Find the distribution function of Y.

16.* Consider the packet-switched network of Problem 6. Assume that it is very congested, so that the probability of collisions is 0.8. If we assume that X is the number of retransmissions (taking values $0, 1, 2, 3, \ldots$), the delay involved in retransmission (due to the random time the network waits before retransmission) is equal to Y, which follows the following pattern:

$$Y = 0, \text{when } X = 0$$
$$Y = T\,2^{X-1}, \text{when } 1 \le X \le 10$$
$$Y = 512T, \text{when } 10 < X$$

Here T is the time it takes to transmit a single packet.

a.   Find the average delay involved in retransmission.
b.   Find the probability mass function of the delay Y.

17.* In an RLC circuit the natural frequency ω_0 is given by the expression

$$\omega_0 = \frac{1}{\sqrt{LC}}$$

Assume that the capacitance $C = 10\ \mu\text{F}$ but that the value of L is assumed to be a random variable uniformly distributed in the range $9 \pm 10\%$ mH.

a.   Find the probability density function of the natural frequency.
b.   Find the average frequency, and compare it with the nominal frequency (the frequency obtained with $L = 9$ mH).

18.[*] A signal whose amplitude is assumed to be a random variable X is quantized using a 3-bit quantizer. The output of the quantizer is denoted by Y, and we can write $Y = g(X)$, where g(u) is symmetric, and its values for a positive argument are given as follows:

$$g(u) = +q, \qquad 0 < u < 1$$
$$g(u) = +2q, \qquad 1 < u < 3$$
$$g(u) = +3q, \qquad 3 < u < 5$$
$$g(u) = +4q, \qquad 5 < u < \infty$$

For the two following cases, find the distribution function, probability mass function, mean and variance of the random variable Y:

a.   X is Gaussian with mean zero and variance 4.
b.   X has a probability density function $f_X(u) = 0.25 \exp\{-0.5|u|\}$

5

Two Random Variables

5.1 INTRODUCTION

So far we have learned how to handle one random variable when it is considered only by itself. We have discussed random variables that were defined in various ways such as the number of successes in n trials, the value of a resistor selected at random, the amplitude of a noise signal, the time to first arrival of random events, etc. However, in many cases more than a single random variable needs to be reckoned with. For example, whenever we receive a weak signal with unknown amplitude (and hence may be assumed to be random), the signal is usually corrupted by noise with some random amplitude as well. Whenever we receive a sinusoidal signal, we have to consider its amplitude and phase as two random variables if the signal is unknown in advance. When dealing with arrivals of events or failures, we may need to find the arrivals of subsequent events (times to first and second arrivals). When we roll two dice, we have the outcomes of both dice, so we naturally have two random variables. If we pick two resistors, we have two random values to contend with. We therefore need to study how to handle two random variables when considered together, since we already know how to treat them when we consider each one separately. To this purpose, we see that we need to define distributions and densities for more than one random variable, which we shall tackle next.

5.2 JOINT DISTRIBUTION FUNCTION

We first have to redefine what we mean by two random variables taken together. The definition of two random variables is exactly the same as the definition of a single random variable, except that we have two of them. We therefore need to consider values that are taken in a two-dimensional space (namely a plane) rather than on just the real line.

> **Definition:** Given a sample space S and a probability P defined on the events associated with the sample space, we define **two random variables** $X(\zeta)$ and $Y(\zeta)$ that assign two real numbers to every outcome ζ in the sample space such that the collection of outcomes
>
> $$\{\zeta|[X(\zeta) \le u] \cap [Y(\zeta) \le v]\}$$
>
> is an event.

In Figure 5.1, we show the region in the (X, Y) plane that is described in the definition. It is indicated by the shaded area defining the lower quadrant of the (X, Y) plane.

Example 5.1

As an example, consider the rolling of two dice with the 36 events described by the intersection of $(A_i \cap B_j)$ for $i, j = 1, 2, 3, 4, 5, 6$. Here we define the A_i as the outcome of the first die, and the B_j as the outcome of second die. We can define several random variables using this sample space. For example, we can define X as the sum of the face values of the two dice and Y as the absolute value of the difference of the rolls of the two dice. Clearly, we have the result given in Table 5.1, which shows the assignment that (X, Y) make to each of the 36 outcomes.

The table provides a better way of showing the assignment than drawing arrows from S to the two-dimensional real plane, as we did for the single random variable case.

We already know how to define the distribution function for a single random variable. Since two random variables take values in a plane, we define the **joint distribution function** in the same manner as for a single random variable by specifying the probability of each event that is mentioned in the definition of the two random variables, for every value of the real variables (u, v).

> **Definition:** The **joint cumulative distribution function**, $F_{XY}(u, v)$ of two random variables X and Y is defined as
>
> $$\begin{aligned} F_{XY}(u, v) &= P\{\zeta|[X(\zeta) \le u] \cap [Y(\zeta) \le v]\} \\ &= P\{[X(\zeta) \le u] \cap [Y(\zeta) \le v]\} = P\{X \le u, Y \le v\} \end{aligned} \quad (5.1)$$

The first line in equation (5.1) is the formal definition of the joint distribution function. The expressions in the second line of the equation represent shorthand notations that are usually used, rather than the cumbersome one used in the definition (the first line). As we have done in the case of one random variable, we usually omit the

TABLE 5.1   The definition of X and Y as functions of the outcome of the sample space

	A_1	A_2	A_3	A_4	A_5	A_6
B_1	$X = 2$	$X = 3$	$X = 4$	$X = 5$	$X = 6$	$X = 7$
	$Y = 0$	$Y = 1$	$Y = 2$	$Y = 3$	$Y = 4$	$Y = 5$
B_2	$X = 3$	$X = 4$	$X = 5$	$X = 6$	$X = 7$	$X = 8$
	$Y = 1$	$Y = 0$	$Y = 1$	$Y = 2$	$Y = 3$	$Y = 4$
B_3	$X = 4$	$X = 5$	$X = 6$	$X = 7$	$X = 8$	$X = 9$
	$Y = 2$	$Y = 1$	$Y = 0$	$Y = 1$	$Y = 2$	$Y = 3$
B_4	$X = 5$	$X = 6$	$X = 7$	$X = 8$	$X = 9$	$X = 10$
	$Y = 3$	$Y = 2$	$Y = 1$	$Y = 0$	$Y = 1$	$Y = 2$
B_5	$X = 6$	$X = 7$	$X = 8$	$X = 9$	$X = 10$	$X = 11$
	$Y = 4$	$Y = 3$	$Y = 2$	$Y = 1$	$Y = 0$	$Y = 1$
B_6	$X = 7$	$X = 8$	$X = 9$	$X = 10$	$X = 11$	$X = 12$
	$Y = 5$	$Y = 4$	$Y = 3$	$Y = 2$	$Y = 1$	$Y = 0$

outcome of the sample space that is describing the random variables. We just call them X and Y, and we use the comma to indicate that we mean by the expression $\{X \leq u, Y \leq v\}$ that X takes values less than or equal to the number u and Y takes values less than or equal to the number v, as shown in Figure 5.1.

We see from the definition of the distribution function that if we know the distribution function for all possible values of u and v, we should be able to find the probability that X and Y take values in any area of the two dimensional plane.

How do we obtain such a probability? In order to find the probability that X and Y take values in some area of the plane, we can always approximate such an area by rectangles, so that we can reduce the problem to that of finding the probability that X and Y take values in a rectangle as shown in Figure 5.2, where the rectangle is defined by $(a < X \leq b)$ and $(c < Y \leq d)$. Let us find this probability. We see that we can write such a probability as the difference between the probabilities of being in various areas of the plane. The figure illustrates these areas by different shadings to help explain the mathematical derivations. From the figure we see that the probability we need is given by

$$\begin{aligned}
P\{(a < X \leq b) \text{ and } (c < Y \leq d)\} &= P\{(X \leq b) \text{ and } (Y \leq d)\} \\
&\quad -P\{(X \leq a) \text{ and } (Y \leq d)\} - P\{(a < X \leq b) \text{ and } (Y \leq c)\} \\
&= F_{XY}(b, d) - F_{XY}(a, d) - P\{(a < X \leq b) \text{ and } (Y \leq c)\} \quad (5.2)
\end{aligned}$$

We now find the probability of the last term in equation (5.2) to be again the difference of probabilities of X and Y taking values in the quadrant $(X \leq b, Y \leq c)$, less

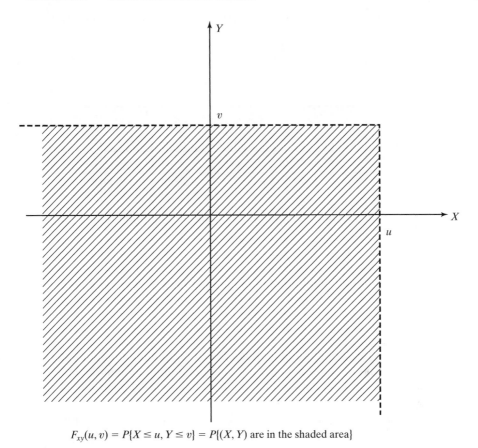

$$F_{xy}(u, v) = P\{X \le u, Y \le v\} = P\{(X, Y) \text{ are in the shaded area}\}$$

Figure 5.1   Definition of the distribution function

the probability that (X, Y) take values in the quadrant $(X \le a, Y \le c)$, as shown in Figure 5.2 in the areas bounded by $Y = c$:

$$P\{(a < X \le b) \text{ and } (Y \le c)\} = P\{(X \le b) \text{ and } (Y \le c)\}$$
$$-P\{(X \le a) \text{ and } (Y \le c)\}$$
$$= F_{XY}(b, c) - F_{XY}(a, c) \qquad (5.3)$$

If we now substitute equation (5.3) into equation (5.2), we obtain the answer we are after:

$$P\{(a < X \le b) \text{ and } (c < Y \le d)\} = F_{XY}(b, d) - F_{XY}(a, d)$$
$$- F_{XY}(b, c) + F_{XY}(a, c) \qquad (5.4)$$

Since the joint distribution function is a function of two variables, it is not easy to draw or visualize, unlike the single random variable case.

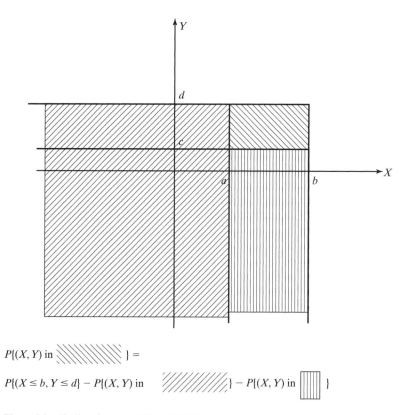

$P\{(X, Y) \text{ in } \diagdown \} =$

$P\{(X \le b, Y \le d\} - P\{(X, Y) \text{ in } \diagup \} - P\{(X, Y) \text{ in } |||| \}$

Figure 5.2   Finding the probability of X, Y in a rectangle

Example 5.2

As an example of a joint distribution function, consider the case of two resistor values, which we picked at random from a collection with values of 10 ohm and $\pm 10\%$ tolerance. If we define X and Y as the respective values of each resistor, then as we saw earlier, it is easy to assume that each value in the square bounded by $(9, 11)$ on the X axis, and by $(9, 11)$ on the Y axis is equally likely, so that the probability of being in any area of the square is equal to that area divided by the area of the square (which is equal to 4 in this case).

The way we find the distribution function is shown in Figure 5.3. We see that if we choose values of u or v that are less than 9, we get zero probability. Furthermore, if both values of u and v are larger than 11, we obtain 1 for the probability. We shall first find the value of the distribution function for both u and v between 9 and 11:

$$F_{XY}(u, v) = P\{(X \le u) \text{ and } (Y \le v)\} = (u - 9)(v - 9)/4,$$
$$\text{for } 9 < u < 11 \text{ and } 9 < v < 11$$

We now consider the case of u between 9 and 11 and v greater than 11:

$$F_{XY}(u, v) = P\{(X \le u) \text{ and } (Y \le v)\} = (u - 9)(11 - 9)/4$$
$$= (u - 9)/2, \quad \text{for } 9 < u < 11 \text{ and } 11 < v$$

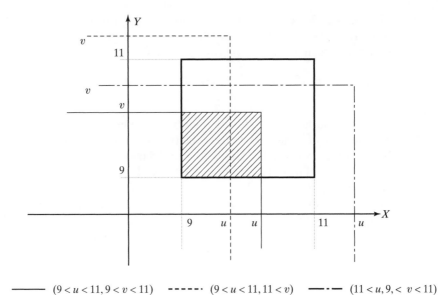

$$\text{———}\quad (9 < u < 11, 9 < v < 11)\qquad \text{- - - - -}\quad (9 < u < 11, 11 < v)\qquad \text{—·—}\quad (11 < u, 9, < v < 11)$$

Figure 5.3   Two random variables uniformly distributed in a square

Similarly, we obtain the distribution function for v between 9 and 11 and u greater than 11:

$$F_{XY}(u, v) = P\{(X \leq u) \text{ and } (Y \leq v)\} = (11 - 9)(v - 9)/4$$
$$= (v - 9)/2, \qquad \text{for } 11 < u \text{ and } 9 < v < 11$$

We thus have the complete picture of the joint distribution function for this simple case.

Properties of the Distribution Function

Just as we did for the one random variable case, we need to find out the properties of a function so that it can serve as a cumulative joint distribution function. Just as in the one-dimensional case, the distribution function must start at 0 and end at 1:

$$F_{XY}(-\infty, v) = 0, \; F_{XY}(u, -\infty) = 0$$
$$F_{XY}(\infty, \infty) = 1 \tag{5.5}$$

What happens if only one of the variables in the distribution function tends to infinity? Suppose that v tends to infinity. What $F_{XY}(u, v)$ then means is the probability that X is less than u and Y is anywhere. This is precisely the definition of the distribution of X alone. We can make a similar statement about the Y variable. Hence we have

$$F_{XY}(u, \infty) = F_X(u)$$
$$F_{XY}(\infty, v) = F_Y(v) \tag{5.6}$$

Finally, how do we describe the nondecreasing property of the distribution function? It is best described as in Figure 5.2, since stating the probability of X and Y taking values in any rectangle cannot be negative:

$$F_{XY}(b, d) - F_{XY}(a, d) - F_{XY}(b, c) + F_{XY}(a, c) \geq 0, \qquad \text{for } a < b \text{ and } c < d \tag{5.7}$$

Now that we have defined the distribution function and its properties, we really have to find an easier way to describe the probabilities associated with values taken by two random variables. Unlike the one dimensional case, where we had discrete, continuous and mixed distributions, here we have all these combinations and more, since one random variable can be discrete and the other continuous, while if two random variables are related through some equation, this relation will result in a jump in the distribution function along a line or a curve. We mention this in passing just to alert you to the many complex issues arising in describing joint distribution functions. In what follows we shall concentrate on reasonably well-behaved cases.

5.3 JOINT PROBABILITY MASS FUNCTION

If both random variables are discrete, which means that they take only distinct values and take no values in a continuous range (such as an interval), then we can describe the two random variables by their joint probability mass function. In this case, assume that X takes the values $\{a_i\}$ for $i = 1, 2, \ldots, n$, and Y takes the values $\{b_j\}$, for $j = 1, 2, \ldots, m$. Then all we need to do to define the probabilities of the values taken by X and Y is to use the probability mass function

$$P\{X = a_i, Y = b_j\} = p_{XY}(a_i, b_j), \qquad \text{for } i = 1, 2, \ldots, n \text{ and } j = 1, 2, \ldots, m \tag{5.8}$$

In this case, to find the probability that X and Y take values in a region, we simply add the probabilities for the values that fall within that region

Example 5.1 (continued):

A good example of such a case is the X and Y defined in Table 5.1 for the rolling of two dice. On the basis of the table, we can find the probability mass function and we can present it as a table involving the 11 values taken by X (from 2 to 12—in this case $n = 11$) and the 6 values taken by Y (from 0 to 5—in this case $m = 6$). The probability mass function in this case is shown in Table 5.2. It is obtained directly from the assignments in Table 5.1 with the knowledge that every event in the table has probability of 1/36.

How do we obtain the distribution function for such a case? The value of $F_{XY}(u, v)$ for given values of u and v is obtained by adding all the probabilities $P\{X = a_i, Y = b_j\}$ for all $a_i \leq u$ and $b_j \leq v$. For the case of Example 5.1 the function will be just a staircase type of function with steps at the points where X and Y take their discrete values. The distribution function in such a case contains no new information beyond the probability mass function, and it is more difficult to use. Hence we shall not even bother to derive it for the example, but will just display it in Figure 5.4(a). Since it takes the form of a staircase function, we show just the points in the plane with nonzero probability,

TABLE 5.2 Probability mass function for Example 5.1

X = Y =	2	3	4	5	6	7	8	9	10	11	12
0	1/36	0	1/36	0	1/36	0	1/36	0	1/36	0	1/36
1	0	2/36	0	2/36	0	2/36	0	2/36	0	2/36	0
2	0	0	2/36	0	2/36	0	2/36	0	2/36	0	0
3	0	0	0	2/36	0	2/36	0	2/36	0	0	0
4	0	0	0	0	2/36	0	2/36	0	0	0	0
5	0	0	0	0	0	2/36	0	0	0	0	0

and between them, we show the value of the distribution function. The heavy dots in Figure 5.4(a) represent the points at which the joint probability mass function is not zero. The staircase distribution function is also shown in Figure 5.4(b), where a three-dimensional figure is needed to fully describe the distribution function. The figure is shown only for the low values of u and v, as it becomes very complicated otherwise. It does not provide any additional information beyond that given by Figure 5.4(a).

We can obtain the one-dimensional probability mass function for the case of Example 5.1 by simply adding all the probabilities taken by Y for any of the values taken by X. Hence, if we add the values in Table 5.2 using the vertical columns, we obtain the probability mass function of the random variable X, while if we add the values using the horizontal rows, we obtain the probability mass function of Y. The result is shown in Table 5.3. We call these probability mass functions the marginal probability mass functions of X and Y. The corresponding distribution functions for each variable alone are called the marginal distribution functions.

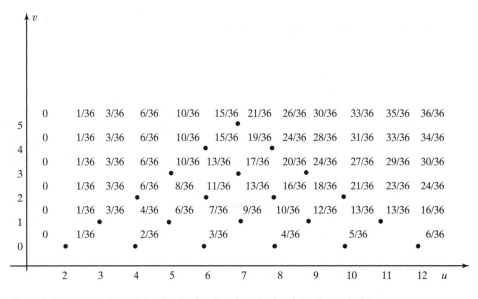

Figure 5.4(a)   The values of the distribution function $F_{XY}(u, v)$ for Example 5.1

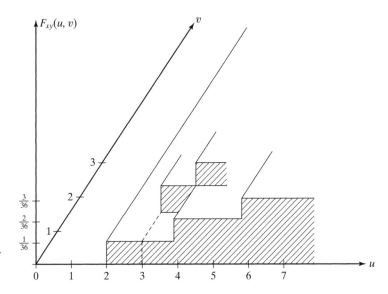

Figure 5.4(b)
$F_{XY}(u, v)$ for Example 5.1 for low values of u, v

TABLE 5.3   The probability mass functions for X and for Y for Example 5.1

a_i	2	3	4	5	6	7	8	9	10	11	12
$P\{X = a_i\}$	1/36	2/36	3/36	4/36	5/36	6/36	5/36	4/36	3/36	2/36	1/36

b_i	0	1	2	3	4	5
$P\{Y = b_i\}$	6/36	10/36	8/36	6/36	4/36	2/36

5.4 JOINT PROBABILITY DENSITY FUNCTION

We now consider two continuous random variables and we would like to describe their distribution in terms of a probability density function for two variables. We call such a density function the joint probability density function, and it is defined as the probability per unit area (just as the one-dimensional density function was a probability per unit length). One way of describing the density function is to find the probability that X and Y take values in a small rectangle of width Δu and Δv around the point (u,v), and then divide by the area of the rectangle and take the limit as Δu and Δv tend to zero.

Definition: The joint **probability density function** $f_{XY}(u, v)$ of two random variables X and Y is defined as the limit of the following expression as Δu and Δv tend to zero:

$$f_{XY}(u, v) = \lim_{\substack{\Delta u \to 0 \\ \Delta v \to 0}} \frac{P\{u < X \leq u + \Delta u, v < Y \leq v + \Delta v\}}{\Delta u \, \Delta v} \tag{5.9}$$

The numerator, before taking the limit of the expression (after the limit sign), is obtained from equation (5.4), and can be expressed as

$$[F_{XY}(u + \Delta u, v + \Delta v) - F_{XY}(u, v + \Delta v)] - [F_{XY}(u + \Delta u, v) - F_{XY}(u, v)] \tag{5.10}$$

When we divide equation (5.10) by $\Delta u \Delta v$ and take the limit, we obtain the second partial derivative of the distribution function with respect to its two variables:

$$f_{XY}(u, v) = \frac{\partial^2 F_{XY}(u, v)}{\partial u \, \partial v} \tag{5.11}$$

The density function can then be used to find the probability that X and Y take values in any region by integrating the density function over that region. We shall illustrate this relation only for a rectangular region in the following expression:

$$P\{(a < X \leq b) \text{ and } (c < Y \leq d)\} = \int_c^d \int_a^b f_{XY}(u, v) \, du \, dv \tag{5.12}$$

In particular, the distribution function can be similarly obtained from the density function by the expression

$$F_{XY}(u, v) = \int_{-\infty}^{v} \int_{-\infty}^{u} f_{XY}(\alpha, \beta) \, d\alpha \, d\beta \tag{5.13}$$

Properties of the density function

Just as in the one-dimensional case, the density function must be nonnegative and its integral must add up to 1. Any surface that is nonnegative and that encloses a volume equal to 1 could serve as a valid joint density function. We can summarize the properties directly from those of the distribution function in the following:

$$f_{XY}(u, v) \geq 0$$

$$\int_{-\infty}^{\infty} \int_{-\infty}^{\infty} f_{XY}(u, v) \, du \, dv = 1 \tag{5.14}$$

Since, if we integrate equation (5.13) over one of the variables from $-\infty$ to ∞ we obtain the marginal distribution function of the other variable, we can then obtain the marginal density function of the other random variable by taking the derivative. We derive the marginal CDF of X by integrating over the values taken by the Y variable:

$$F_X(u) = F_{XY}(u, \infty) = \int_{-\infty}^{\infty} \int_{-\infty}^{u} f_{XY}(\alpha, \beta) \, d\alpha \, d\beta \qquad (5.15)$$

Now by taking the derivative with respect to u, we obtain the marginal density of X:

$$f_X(u) = \int_{-\infty}^{\infty} f_{XY}(u, v) \, dv \qquad (5.16a)$$

We similarly have for the marginal density of Y:

$$f_Y(v) = \int_{-\infty}^{\infty} f_{XY}(u, v) \, du \qquad (5.16b)$$

Example 5.2 (continued):

Consider the two resistors of Example 5.2. In this case we can take the derivative of the distribution function derived in that example, and we find that the joint density function is zero everywhere outside the rectangle $9 < u < 11$ and $9 < v < 11$, where, after we take the derivative with respect to both u and v, we obtain

$f_{XY}(u, v) = 0.25,$ for $9 < u < 11$ and $9 < v < 11$, and is zero elsewhere.

We see that in this case the random variables are uniformly distributed in the square! We shall see in the next example that the region where the density function is not zero is quite important in how we carry out the analysis.

Example 5.3

Let X and Y be uniformly distributed in the triangle shown in Figure 5.5.

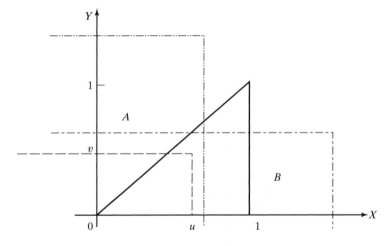

Figure 5.5   A uniform density function in a triangle

The figure also shows a point with coordinates (u, v) inside the triangle. Since the random variables are uniformly distributed in the triangle, the density function is constant in the triangle and zero outside of it.

The area of the triangle is equal to 0.5, so that the value of the density function must be 2 inside the triangle:

$$f_{XY}(u, v) = 2, \quad 0 < v < u < 1; \quad \text{and is zero elsewhere.}$$

We now can derive the distribution function for values of the point (u, v). If $u < 0$ or $v < 0$, the value of the distribution function is zero, since the values taken by X and Y are only in the positive region. For values of (u, v) with both $u > 1$ and $v > 1$, we have $F_{XY}(u, v) = 1$.

For the point (u, v) inside the triangle shown in the figure, using the rule of the area of a trapezoidal shape whose parallel sides have lengths u and $(u - v)$ and whose height has a value of v, we obtain

$$F_{XY}(u, v) = 2[(u - v) + u]v/2 = 2uv - v^2, \quad \text{for } 0 < v < u < 1$$

For $0 < v < 1$ and $u > 1$ (i.e., the point (u, v) is in region B in the figure and the area is bounded by the dashed and one-dotted lines), we have (since there are no additional values beyond $u = 1$)

$$F_{XY}(u, v) = 2[(1 - v) + 1]v/2 = 2v - v^2, \quad \text{for } 0 < v < 1 \text{ and } 1 < u$$

Finally, for $0 < u < 1$ and $v > u$ (i.e., the point (u, v) is in region A in the figure, and the area is bounded by the dashed and two-dotted lines), we have (since there are no additional values of the density beyond $v = u$)

$$F_{XY}(u, v) = 2[u^2/2] = u^2, \quad \text{for } u < v \text{ and } 0 < u < 1$$

These expressions also provide us with the marginal distributions of X and Y as we let u and v become large $(u > 1$ or $v > u)$ while the other variable stays within $(0, 1)$:

$$F_Y(v) = 2v - v^2, \quad \text{for } 0 < v < 1$$

$$F_X(u) = u^2, \quad \text{for } 0 < u < 1$$

The corresponding marginal density functions are obtained by taking the derivatives:

$$f_Y(v) = 2(1 - v), \quad \text{for } 0 < v < 1$$

$$f_X(u) = 2u, \quad \text{for } 0 < u < 1$$

We can also derive the marginal densities directly, rather than via the distribution function. For $0 < u < 1$, we have (since the density is nonzero only for $v < u$)

$$f_X(u) = \int_{-\infty}^{\infty} f_{XY}(u, v)\, dv = \int_0^u 2\, dv = 2u$$

Similarly, for $0 < v < 1$, we have (since the density is nonzero only for $u > v$)

$$f_Y(v) = \int_{-\infty}^{\infty} f_{XY}(u, v) \, du = \int_{v}^{1} 2 \, du = 2(1 - v)$$

It is interesting to note that even though (X, Y) are together uniformly distributed in the triangle, each one alone is not uniformly distributed in its interval $(0, 1)$. This is clear from the picture of the triangle, which shows that small values of Y are more probable than larger ones (at the bottom of the triangle), while larger values of X are more probable, as we see from the right boundary of the triangle.

5.5 INDEPENDENCE

We have already defined independence for events in a sample space. Two random variables are called independent if the value taken by one random variable is independent of the value taken by the other. In other words, two random variables are independent if, for all values of u and v, the two events $\{X \leq u\}$ and $\{Y \leq v\}$ are independent. Since the probability of the values taken by the random variables together is determined by the joint distribution function, the independence property means that the joint distribution function is given as a product.

Definition: Two random variables are **independent** if and only if their joint distribution function satisfies the following:

$$F_{XY}(u, v) = P\{[X \leq u] \cap [Y \leq v]\} = P\{X \leq u\}P\{Y \leq v\} = F_X(u)F_Y(v)$$
(5.17)

Since we deal most of the time with density functions, by taking the derivative of the distribution function, we obtain the joint density function. Hence, we can check for independence by using the densities. Two random variables are independent if and only if their joint density function satisfies the relationship

$$f_{XY}(u, v) = f_X(u)f_Y(v)$$
(5.18)

Let us check the two cases we observed in Examples 5.2 and 5.3. In Example 5.2 we have indeed two independent random variables, since the joint density is 0.25 in the square while the marginal densities are 0.5 each in the same region. In Example 5.3 we see that if we multiply the two marginal densities, we do not obtain the joint density. Hence, in the latter case the two random variables are dependent.

Example 5.4

Consider two components whose lifetimes are two random variables X and Y with the following joint density function:

$$f_{XY}(u, v) = 4e^{-2(u+v)}, \qquad 0 < u, 0 < v$$

Let us check to see whether they are independent. First we find the marginal densities, and we start with $f_X(u)$:

$$f_X(u) = \int_0^\infty 4e^{-2(u+v)}\, dv = 2e^{-2u}, 0 < u$$

Similarly, we find that the marginal density of Y is

$$f_Y(v) = 2e^{-2v}, \quad \text{for } 0 < v$$

Hence, the joint density is indeed the product of the two marginal densities. The random variables are therefore independent.

If we want to find the probability that both components fail within one year, all we have to do is integrate the joint density from 0 to 1:

$$P\{\text{both fail within one year}\} = P\{X < 1, Y < 1\} = \int_0^1 \int_0^1 4e^{-2(u+v)}\, du\, dv$$

$$= (1 - e^{-2})(1 - e^{-2}) = 0.7476$$

For the discrete random variables case, it can be shown that independence implies that the joint probability mass function of the two variables is represented by the product of the two probability mass function of each random variable:

$$P\{X = a_i, Y = b_j\} = P\{X = a_i\}P\{Y = b_j\}$$

It should be noted that for this case we do not need any tools other than those we used when we dealt with independence of events.

5.6 CONDITIONAL DENSITIES

When working with more than one random variable, we also wish to define the conditional densities associated with the random variables. In many applications, one of the random variables may represent observations or measurement values and the other may represent the signal we wish to estimate or recover from the observations. Hence, we define conditional distributions and conditional densities in the same manner in which conditional probability was defined. The conditional distribution of X given an event A is defined as

$$F_{X|A}(u|A) = P\{X \le u|A\} = P\{(X \le u) \cap A\}/P\{A\} \qquad (5.19)$$

If we now take the derivative of the conditional distribution function, we call the result the conditional density function of the random variable X given the event A.

Let us first consider conditional densities when the event conditioned upon, A, involves an interval of values taken either by X or by Y.

We have two general cases when the event A involves a random variable in an interval. The first case is when $A = \{a < X \leq b\}$, and the second case is when $A = \{a < Y \leq b\}$.

Case I: $A = \{a < X \leq b\}$:

$$F_{X|A}(u|A) = P\{X \leq u|A\}$$

$$= P\{(X \leq u) \cap (a < X \leq b)\}/P\{a < X \leq b\}$$

$$F_{X|A}(u|a < X \leq b) = \begin{cases} 0, & \text{for } u < a, \text{ since} \\ & (X \leq u) \cap (a<X \leq b) = \phi \\[2mm] \dfrac{\displaystyle\int_a^u f_X(x)\,dx}{\displaystyle\int_a^b f_X(x)\,dx}, & \text{for } a < u \leq b \\[2mm] & \text{for } b < u, \text{ since} \\ 1.0, & (X \leq u) \cap (a<X \leq b) = (a<X \leq b) \end{cases}$$

$$(5.19a)$$

The conditional density function will then be nonzero only in the interval $a < u \leq b$ and will be given by the derivative of equation (5.19a):

$$f_{X|A}(u|a < X \leq b) = \frac{f_X(u)}{\displaystyle\int_a^b f_X(x)\,dx}, \qquad a < u \leq b, \text{ and is zero elsewhere.}$$

$$(5.19b)$$

Example 5.5

Consider as an example the lifetime distribution function discussed in Section 3.3.9 and its density function as given by equation (3.37). We wish to show the memoryless property of the exponential distribution. Suppose we pick the event A for this case to be given by $A = \{T > t_0\}$. We wish to find the conditional density of T given A. This conditional density is the conditional density of the system's lifetime, given that the system lives longer than time t_0. In this case, if we use the result of equation (5.19b) together with equation (3.37), we obtain

$$f_{T|A}(u|t_0 < T) = \frac{f_T(u)}{\displaystyle\int_{t_0}^\infty f_T(u)\,du} = \frac{\lambda \exp(-\lambda u)}{\displaystyle\int_{t_0}^\infty \lambda \exp(-\lambda u)\,du} = \frac{\lambda \exp(-\lambda u)}{\exp(-\lambda t_0)}$$

$$= \lambda \exp[-\lambda(u - t_0)], \qquad \text{for } t_0 < u, \text{ and is zero elsewhere.}$$

We see that the density function for the time after t_0 is exactly the same as the original density function, except that it starts at t_0 instead of zero. We call this property the memoryless property of the exponential distribution, since the density is unchanged for the rest of the time, regardless of how long the system has lived already.

Case II: $A = \{a < Y \le b\}$:

$$F_{X|A}(u|a < Y \le b) = P\{X \le u|a < Y \le b\}$$
$$= P\{(X \le u) \cap (a < Y \le b)\}/P\{a < Y \le b\}$$

$$= \frac{\displaystyle\int_{-\infty}^{u} \int_{a}^{b} f_{XY}(\alpha, v)\, dv\, d\alpha}{\displaystyle\int_{a}^{b} f_Y(v)\, dv} \qquad (5.19c)$$

The conditional density is obtained by taking the derivative, yielding the expression

$$f_{X|A}(u|a < Y \le b) = \frac{\displaystyle\int_{a}^{b} f_{XY}(u, v)\, dv}{\displaystyle\int_{a}^{b} f_Y(v)\, dv} \qquad (5.19d)$$

We now define conditional densities involving one random variable, given a specific value taken by the other random variable. The event A then becomes

$$A = \{Y = v\}$$

Since, if Y is continuous, the probability of such an event is zero, we approximate it by the probability of the event A involving a small interval near the point $Y = v$ and then let the interval approach zero. In this case the event A becomes the limit of the following event:

$$A = \{v < Y \le v + \Delta v\}$$

The result is defined as the conditional density of X given Y and is derived as follows:

$$f_{X|Y}(u|v) = \frac{d}{du}\left\{\frac{P\{[X \le u] \cap [v \le Y \le v + \Delta v]\}}{P\{v \le Y \le v + \Delta v\}}\right\} \qquad (5.20)$$

Now we approximate the $P\{v \le Y \le v + \Delta v\}$ by taking the value of the density of Y and multiplying by the width of the interval, and if we approximate the numerator in the same manner, we obtain

$$f_{X|Y}(u|v) = \frac{d}{du} \left\{ \frac{\displaystyle\int_{v}^{v+\Delta v} \int_{-\infty}^{u} f_{XY}(\alpha, \beta)\, d\alpha\, d\beta}{\displaystyle\int_{v}^{v+\Delta v} f_Y(\beta)\, d\beta} \right\} = \frac{\displaystyle\int_{v}^{v+\Delta v} f_{XY}(u, \beta)\, d\beta}{\displaystyle\int_{v}^{v+\Delta v} f_Y(\beta)\, d\beta}$$

$$\cong \frac{f_{XY}(u, v)\Delta v}{f_Y(v)\Delta v} \tag{5.21}$$

The final result is as follows:

$$f_{X|Y}(u|v) = \frac{f_{XY}(u, v)}{f_Y(v)} \tag{5.22}$$

Similarly, we can define the conditional density of Y given the random variable X by

$$f_{Y|X}(v|u) = \frac{f_{XY}(u, v)}{f_X(u)} \tag{5.22a}$$

The preceding equations can be used in two ways: If we know the joint density function, we can find the conditional density function; if we know the conditional density, we can find the joint density function, as in the following expression:

$$f_{XY}(u, v) = f_{X|Y}(u|v)f_Y(v) = f_{Y|X}(v|u)f_X(u) \tag{5.23}$$

It should be noted that if one of the variables is discrete, then instead of a density function, we obtain a probability mass function. Otherwise, equations (5.22) and (5.23) can be applied to both cases if care is taken in the definition of the various variables.

If we do have the conditional density of Y given X and we wish to find the conditional density of X given Y, we get the continuous version of Bayes' rule. In this case, we use equation (5.23) to obtain the joint density, from which we can obtain the marginal density of the random variable Y and then apply the definition of the conditional density, equation (5.22), to conclude the solution of the problem. We first find the marginal density of Y, using equation (5.23):

$$f_Y(v) = \int_{-\infty}^{\infty} f_{XY}(u, v)\, du = \int_{-\infty}^{\infty} f_{Y|X}(v|u)f_X(u)\, du \tag{5.24}$$

From equation (5.22), the conditional density of X given Y then becomes

$$f_{X|Y}(u|v) = \frac{f_{XY}(u, v)}{f_Y(v)} = \frac{f_{Y|X}(v|u)f_X(u)}{f_Y(v)} \tag{5.25}$$

Equations (5.24) and (5.25) form Bayes' rule for the case of two random variables.

We now return to equation (5.19d), which provided us with an expression for the conditional density of X given Y in an interval. The equation can now be expressed in terms of the conditional densities involving X and Y. In this case we just utilize equation (5.23) for the joint density to obtain from two expressions from equation (5.19d), depending on which conditional density is provided:

$$f_{X|A}(u|a < Y \le b) = \frac{\displaystyle\int_a^b f_{X|Y}(u|v)f_Y(v)\,dv}{\displaystyle\int_a^b f_Y(v)\,dv} \tag{5.26a}$$

$$f_{X|A}(u|a < Y \le b) = \frac{\displaystyle\int_a^b f_{Y|X}(v|u)f_X(u)\,dv}{\displaystyle\int_a^b f_Y(v)\,dv} \tag{5.26b}$$

In the preceding expressions, the denominator involving $f_Y(v)$ can be obtained from the joint density function by integrating the X variable out:

$$f_Y(v) = \int_{-\infty}^{\infty} f_{XY}(u, v)\,du = \int_{-\infty}^{\infty} f_{Y|X}(v|u)f_X(u)\,du \tag{5.26c}$$

In particular, if $a = v$ and $b = v + \Delta v$, we obtain the usual expression for the conditional density of X given $Y = v$, that we derived earlier.

Example 5.6

For the two random variables in Example 5.3, we wish to find the conditional density of Y given X and of X given Y. We already know the joint density, which is equal to 2 inside the triangle. We also know that the marginal densities are

$$f_X(u) = 2u, \qquad \text{for } 0 < u < 1$$
$$f_Y(v) = 2(1 - v), \qquad \text{for } 0 < v < 1$$

The conditional densities will be defined by simply dividing the joint density by the marginal density while paying attention to the limits:

$$f_{Y|X}(v|u) = 2/(2u) = 1/u, \qquad \text{for } 0 < v < u < 1$$
$$f_{X|Y}(u|v) = 2/[2(1 - v)] = 1/(1 - v), \text{ for } 0 < v < u < 1$$

As we expect, the conditional densities are also uniformly distributed within the range in which they are nonzero, for any given value of the other variable. Since X is always larger than Y, we see that Y given $X = u$ is uniformly distributed in the interval $(0, u)$. Similarly, we see that X given $Y = v$ is uniformly distributed in the interval $(v, 1)$.

The expressions we defined for the conditional densities and its relations to the marginal densities work for the case in which one of the random variables is discrete. In such a case we replace densities for the discrete random variable with probabilities, and replace integrals with summations over all the values taken by the discrete random variable. Examples will be provided later in this chapter that illustrate the two cases.

5.7 GAUSSIAN RANDOM VARIABLES

A special joint density function arises for the case in which X and Y are jointly Gaussian random variables. In this case the joint density function is given by the expression

$$f_{XY}(u, v) = \frac{\exp\left\{-\dfrac{\left(\dfrac{u - m_x}{\sigma_X}\right)^2 - 2\rho\left(\dfrac{u - m_x}{\sigma_X}\right)\left(\dfrac{v - m_Y}{\sigma_Y}\right) + \left(\dfrac{v - m_Y}{\sigma_Y}\right)^2}{2(1 - \rho^2)}\right\}}{2\pi\sigma_X\sigma_Y\sqrt{1 - \rho^2}} \tag{5.27}$$

It can be shown that if we integrate the Y variable we obtain the marginal Gaussian density for X, and vice versa. If we now divide the joint density function to obtain the conditional density function, we can simplify the result to the following expression:

$$f_{X|Y}(u|v) = f_{XY}(u, v)/f_Y(v) = \frac{\exp\left\{-\dfrac{[u - m_X - \rho\dfrac{\sigma_X}{\sigma_Y}(v - m_Y)]^2}{2\sigma_X^2(1 - \rho^2)}\right\}}{\sigma_X\sqrt{2\pi(1 - \rho^2)}} \tag{5.28}$$

It is clear from the expression of the conditional density that it is also Gaussian with a mean that depends on the value of $Y = v$ and a variance that is constant. The mean of the conditional density is denoted by $E\{X|Y = v\}$ and is given by

$$E\{X|Y = v\} = m_X + \rho\frac{\sigma_X}{\sigma_Y}(v - m_Y) \tag{5.29}$$

It is also called the conditional mean of X given Y. The corresponding variance of the conditional density (which is also called the conditional variance) is given by

$$\text{Var}\{X|Y = v\} = \sigma_X^2(1 - \rho^2) \tag{5.30}$$

What can we say about the jointly Gaussian random variables? We see that they are related only through the parameter ρ, which, as we shall see in Chapter 6, is a very important parameter relating two random variables. In this case we see that when $\rho = 0$, the joint Gaussian density becomes the product of the two marginal densities, which means that they become independent. Also, it is clear from the square root expression that the parameter ρ cannot be larger than 1 nor smaller than -1. When ρ is equal to 1 or -1, the values of Y and X fall on a straight line, which relates the two random variables X and Y.

Figure 5.6 shows examples of how the joint density function looks like when $\rho = 0$ and when $\rho = \pm0.9$. We see from the figure that for a large value of ρ the function looks squished in one direction along a diagonal line. The density is shown for the case $m_X = m_Y = 0$ and $\sigma_X = \sigma_Y = 1$. We see that when $\rho = 0$, the density is a symmetric bell-shaped surface, whose cross sections are circles. The line along which the density takes its values has a positive slope when ρ is positive and has a negative slope when ρ is negative.

Another way of displaying the density function is to show contours of equal values of the density. For $\rho = 0$, these contours are circles, and are shown in Figure 5.7(a). For $\rho > 0$ and large, the contours become ellipses, which indicate the case in which X and Y take values in the same direction: When X is large, Y is large. When $\rho < 0$ and large, the ellipses indicate that as X grows, Y decreases, and vice versa. These contours are shown in Figures 5.7(b) through 5.7(e) for two positive values of ρ and two negative values of ρ. In the figures, the increasing value of the density is shown by inner circles or ellipses that are closer to the origin, and the values become smaller for the outer circles or ellipses.

5.8 EXAMPLES OF CONDITIONAL DENSITIES

We now consider several examples of how the conditional densities are used in obtaining information about one variable, when the value of the other variable is known (i.e., it is measured or observed).

Example 5.7

Consider the case in which we are observing the lifetime Y (time to failure) of a component whose average lifetime is unknown. Since the failure rate is unknown, let us assume that it is a random variable X, uniformly distributed in the interval $(0.1, 0.3)$. In this case, if we know the value of the failure rate $X = u$, then the conditional density of the random variable Y given X is exponentially distributed with parameter u:

$$f_{Y|X}(v|u) = ue^{-uv}, \qquad \text{for } 0 < v, \text{ and } 0.1 < u < 0.3$$

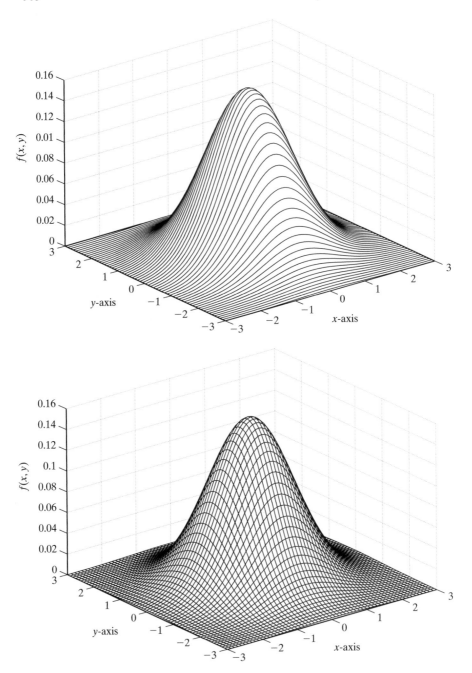

Figure 5.6(a)   Two renditions of the joint Gaussian density function for $\rho = 0$

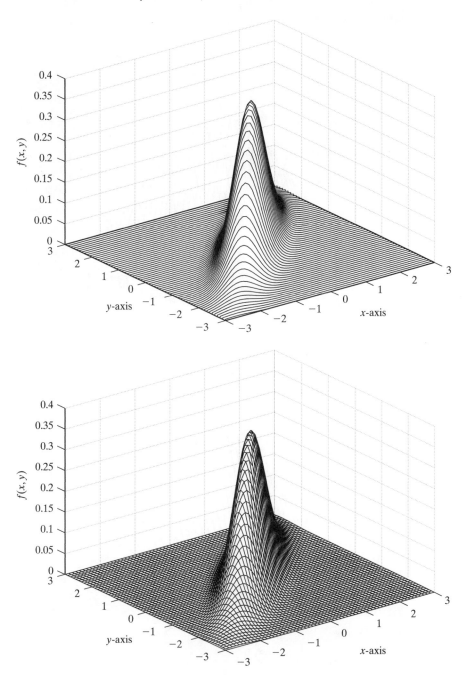

Figure 5.6(b)   Two renditions of the joint Gaussian density function when $\rho = 0.9$

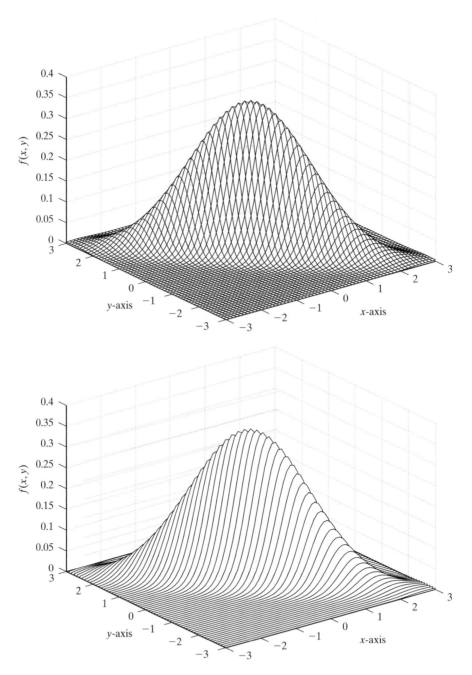

Figure 5.6(c)   Two renditions of the joint Gaussian density function when $\rho = -0.9$

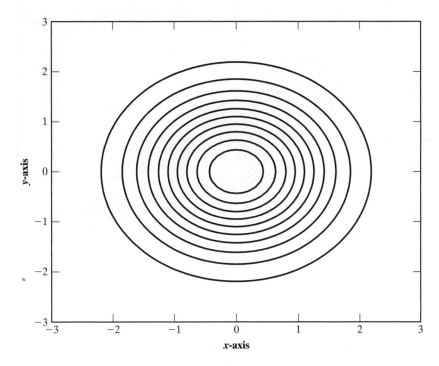

Figure 5.7(a) Equal-density contours of the joint Gaussian density function for $\rho = 0$

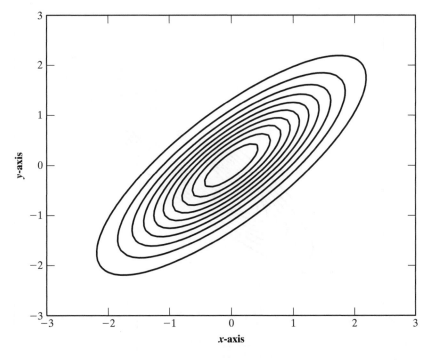

Figure 5.7(b) Equal-density contours of the joint Gaussian density function for $\rho = 0.8$

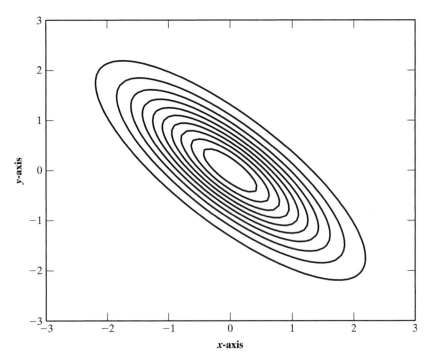

Figure 5.7(c)   Equal-density contours of the joint Gaussian density function for $\rho = -0.8$

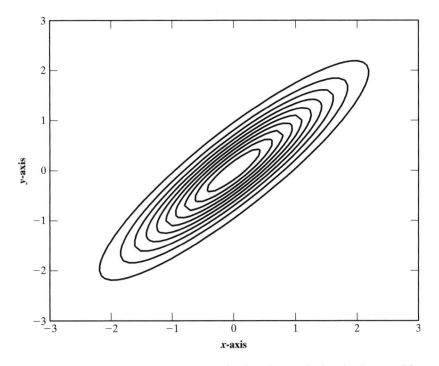

Figure 5.7(d)   Equal-density contours of the joint Gaussian density function for $\rho = 0.9$

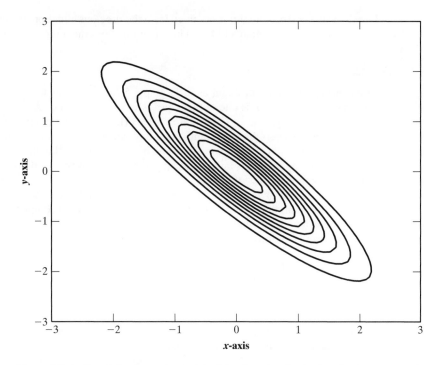

Figure 5.7(e)   Equal-density contours of the joint Gaussian density function for $\rho = -0.9$

Since we assumed that the density of X is uniform in the interval $(0.1, 0.3)$, the joint density of X and Y is given by

$$f_{XY}(u, v) = f_{Y|X}(v|u)f_X(u) = 5ue^{-uv}, \qquad \text{for } 0 < v, \text{ and } 0.1 < u < 0.3$$

If we observe Y (the time when the system actually fails), what is the conditional probability density of the failure rate X, given the value of $Y = v$?

Here we use the definition of the conditional density, after first integrating the joint density to obtain the density of Y, which we shall need for the denominator. The result is as follows:

$$f_Y(v) = \int_{0.1}^{0.3} f(u, v) \, du = \int_{0.1}^{0.3} 5ue^{-uv} \, du = \frac{5}{v^2}[e^{-0.1v}(1 + 0.1v) - e^{-0.3v}(1 + 0.3v)]$$

$$\text{for } 0 < v$$

Do not be concerned about the complicated expressions. After all, we assume that the value of Y is observed. Hence, in practice, we should know the value v that Y takes in any specific experiment. The conditional density of X given the value of $Y = v$ is therefore given as

$$f_{X|Y}(u|v) = \frac{5ue^{-uv}}{f_Y(v)}, \qquad \text{for } 0.1 < u < 0.3$$

Here the value of denominator is obtained from the previous equation. We may use the conditional density to obtain additional information about the unknown failure rate X.

Example 5.8

We reconsider the same problem as in Example 5.7, except that we assume that we know that our component is one of two types, where the first type has a failure rate of 0.1 and the second type has a failure rate of 0.3. (The rate may be per year or day or month, as long we keep the same units in all our calculations.) Suppose that we have two-thirds components of the second type and only one-third of the first type. If we observe that the component has failed at exactly $Y = v$, what is the conditional probability that the component was of type II?

Here again we have a conditional density of Y given the component type. If we define a discrete random variable X whose value is 0.1 when the component is of type I and whose values is 0.3 when the component is of type II, then we have the following probabilities and conditional densities:

$$P\{X = 0.1\} = 1/3 \quad \text{and } P\{X = 0.3\} = 2/3$$
$$f_{Y|X}(v|0.1) = 0.1e^{-0.1v}$$
$$f_{Y|X}(v|0.3) = 0.3e^{-0.3v}$$

Now we can obtain the unconditional density of Y by multiplying by the probabilities of values taken by X and adding to obtain

$$f_Y(v) = f_{Y|X}(v|0.1)P\{X = 0.1\} + f_{Y|X}(v|0.3)P\{X = 0.3\}$$
$$= 0.1e^{-0.1v}(1/3) + 0.3e^{-0.3v}(2/3)$$

Now if the component failed at time $Y = v$, we can find the conditional probability that it was of type II by the following expression:

$$P\{X = 0.3|Y = v\} = \frac{0.3e^{-0.3v}\,2/3}{f_Y(v)} = \frac{0.6}{0.1e^{0.2v} + 0.6}$$

Similarly, we can find the probability that the component was of type I (or we simply can subtract the results obtained for type II from 1):

$$P\{X = 0.1|Y = v\} = \frac{0.1}{0.1 + 0.6e^{-0.2v}}$$

We now consider the case in which a discrete random variable depends on the value of a continuous random variable. The basic process and the principles are the same, but the integrals are replaced by sums and the densities are replaced by probabilities. This is all that must remembered when dealing with both discrete and continuous random variables at the same time.

Example 5.9

Consider the case in which the probability of a message to be delivered intact is a function of the length of the message. Suppose the length of the message is defined as the random variable X and is assumed to have an exponential density function with parameter

μ, where $1/\mu$ is the average length of the message. Suppose that we define Y as a discrete random variable, which is equal to 0 if the message is delivered without a loss and is equal to 1 if one or more of its packets are lost. Suppose that the conditional probability of the loss given the length is given by the expression

$$P\{Y = 1|X = u\} = 0.2, \qquad \text{for } u > 5$$
$$P\{Y = 1|X = u\} = 0.1, \qquad \text{for } u < 5$$

We also assume that $\mu = 0.4$, so that the density function of X is given by

$$f_X(u) = 0.4e^{-0.4u}$$

We first find the probability that a message is lost:

$$P\{Y = 1\} = \int_0^\infty P\{Y = 1|X = u\}f_X(u)\, du$$

$$= \int_0^5 0.1 \times 0.4e^{-0.4u}\, du + \int_5^\infty 0.2 \times 0.4e^{-0.4u}\, du$$

$$= 0.1(1 - e^{-2}) + 0.2(e^{-2}) = 0.1(1 + e^{-2})$$

We now may ask the question that if a packet is lost what is the conditional probability density function of its length X?

$$f_{X|Y}(u|Y = 1) = \frac{P\{Y = 1|X = u\}f_X(u)}{P\{Y = 1\}} = \begin{cases} \dfrac{0.1 \times 0.4e^{-0.4u}}{0.1(1 + e^{-2})}, & \text{for } 0 < u < 5 \\[3ex] \dfrac{0.2 \times 0.4e^{-0.4u}}{0.1(1 + e^{-2})}, & \text{for } 5 < u \end{cases}$$

We can easily verify that the preceding is indeed a density function and that its integral is equal to 1. In a similar fashion, we can derive the probability that a message is received without loss, and then are can find the conditional density function of the message length given that there was no loss.

5.9 SUMMARY

Joint distribution function of two random variables X and Y:

$$F_{XY}(u, v) = P\{X \leq u, Y \leq v\}$$

Properties:

$$P\{(a < X \leq b) \text{ and } (c < Y \leq d)\} = F_{XY}(b, d) - F_{XY}(a, d)$$
$$- F_{XY}(b, c) + F_{XY}(a, c) \geq 0$$

$$F_{XY}(-\infty, v) = 0, F_{XY}(u, -\infty) = 0$$
$$F_{XY}(\infty, \infty) = 1$$

Marginal distributions:

$$F_{XY}(u, \infty) = F_X(u)$$
$$F_{XY}(\infty, v) = F_Y(v)$$

Joint probability mass function:

$p_{XY}(a_i, b_j) = P\{X = a_i, Y = b_j\}$, where X and Y take the values $\{a_i\}$ and $\{b_j\}$

Joint probability density function:

$$f_{XY}(u, v) = \frac{\partial^2 F_{XY}(u, v)}{\partial u\, \partial v}$$

Properties:

$$f_{XY}(u, v) \geq 0$$

$$\int_{-\infty}^{\infty} \int_{-\infty}^{\infty} f_{XY}(u, v)\, du\, dv = 1$$

$$P\{(a < X \leq b) \text{ and } (c < Y \leq d)\} = \int_{c}^{d} \int_{a}^{b} f_{XY}(u, v)\, du\, dv$$

$$F_{XY}(b, d) = \int_{-\infty}^{d} \int_{-\infty}^{b} f_{XY}(u, v)\, du\, dv$$

Marginal densities:

$$f_X(u) = \int_{-\infty}^{\infty} f_{XY}(u, v)\, dv \text{ and } f_Y(v) = \int_{-\infty}^{\infty} f_{XY}(u, v)\, du$$

Independent random variables:

$$f_{XY}(u, v) = f_X(u) f_Y(u)$$
$$F_{XY}(u, v) = F_X(u) F_Y(u)$$

Conditional densities:

$$f_{X|A}(u) = \frac{d}{du} P\{X \leq u | A\} = \frac{d}{du} P\{(X \leq u) \cap A\}/P\{A\}$$

Two cases:

a. $A = \{a < X \leq b\}$: $f_{X|A}(u|A) = f_X(u)/P\{A\}$, for $a < u \leq b$, and is zero elsewhere
b. $A = \{Y = v\}$: $f_{X|Y}(u|v) = f_{XY}(u, v)/f_Y(v)$

The second case can be expressed in two ways:

$$f_{XY}(u, v) = f_{X|Y}(u|v) f_Y(v) = f_{Y|X}(v|u) f_X(u)$$

Total probability and Bayes' rule for random variables:

$$f_X(u) = \int_{-\infty}^{\infty} f_{X|Y}(u|v) f_Y(v)\, dv$$

$$f_{Y|X}(v|u) = f_{X|Y}(u|v) f_Y(v)/f_X(v)$$

In the preceding expressions, if the values taken by one random variable are discrete, then the integrals are replaced by summation, and the densities are replaced by probabilities.

Jointly Gaussian random variables:

$$f_{XY}(u, v) = \frac{\exp\left\{-\dfrac{\left(\dfrac{u - m_X}{\sigma_X}\right)^2 - 2\rho\left(\dfrac{u - m_X}{\sigma_X}\right)\left(\dfrac{v - m_Y}{\sigma_Y}\right) + \left(\dfrac{v - m_Y}{\sigma_Y}\right)^2}{2(1 - \rho^2)}\right\}}{2\pi\sigma_X\sigma_Y\sqrt{1 - \rho^2}}$$

Conditional densities:

$$f_{X|Y}(u|v) = \frac{\exp\left\{-\dfrac{[u - m_X - \rho\dfrac{\sigma_X}{\sigma_Y}(v - m_Y)]^2}{2\sigma_X^2(1 - \rho^2)}\right\}}{\sigma_X\sqrt{2\pi(1 - \rho^2)}}$$

5.10 PROBLEMS

MATLAB Problems:

1. Generate 5000 random numbers $\{X_i\}$ with uniform distribution in the interval between 9 and 11. Generate another 5000 numbers $\{Y_i\}$ with the same distribution. Now add the two to form a third random variable: $\{Z_i = X_i + Y_i\}$. Draw a histogram of $\{Z\}$, and show that it is approximately triangular with mean 20 and range (18 to 22). Find the mean, the variance, and standard deviation for Z and compare to that of the triangular density with the same mean and range. Also, show that the mean of Z is equal to the sum of the means of X and Y and that the variance of Z is also equal to the variances of X and Y.

2. Use MATLAB to simulate the data in Example 5.9. Generate 50,000 random variables that have an exponential density function with $\lambda = 0.4$ and that represent the random variable X. For each value of X that is larger than 5, generate a binary random variable that takes the value of 1 with probability 0.2. For each value of X that is less than 5, generate a binary random variable that takes the value of 1 with probability 0.1. This will represent the values of the random variable Y. Find the relative frequency of the value 1 taken by the random variable Y you generated, and show that it is approximately equal to the value obtained in the example:

$$P\{Y = 1\} = 0.1(1 + e^{-2})$$

Plot two histograms for the values of X, one for all the values for which $Y = 1$ and one for all the values for which $Y = 0$, and compare with the conditional density functions obtained in the example.

3. Use MATLAB to simulate the rolling of two dice, and generate two random variables as in Example 5.1—one equal to the sum and the other equal to the difference. Generate 2000 samples, and compare the simulated relative frequency with the joint pmf as shown in Table 5.2.

4. Simulate the two random variables in Example 5.3 by generating two random variables uniformly distributed in a square $(0, 1) \times (0, 1)$, and eliminate all values in which Y is

larger than X. This means that if you start with 4000, you should end up with approximately 2000 samples as you remove the ones that do not qualify. Using the two random variables, plot the histogram representing the conditional density of X given Y and of Y given X, and compare with the mathematical results.

Regular Problems:

5. A DC power supply that can have three different input voltages is connected via a switch to one of four resistive loads as shown in the figure. The input voltage can take the values 6, 12, and 24 volts with probabilities 0.25, 0.50, and 0.25 respectively. The four loads are 3, 6, 12, and 24 ohms (as shown in the figure), with the switch closing on any load with equal probability. The switch closings are independent of the input voltage. Two random variables are defined: X is the current through the power supply, and Y is the input voltage.

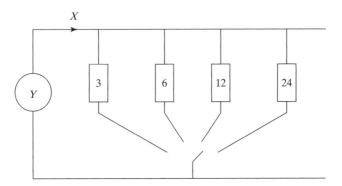

   a. Find the joint probability mass function and the marginal probability mass functions of X and Y.
   b. Find the joint distribution function of X and Y and the marginal distribution functions of X and Y.
   c. Find the following probabilities: $P\{X \le 1, Y \le 12\}; P\{0.5 < X \le 2, 10 < Y \le 12\}$.

6. The following density function (which is zero outside the rectangle defined) is a joint probability density function of the random variables X and Y:

$$f_{XY}(u, v) = C(2u + v), \qquad 0 < u < 1, 0 < v < 2$$

   a. Find the value of C that will make $f_{XY}(u, v)$ a valid density function.
   b. Find the marginal densities of X and Y.
   c. Find the joint distribution function of X and Y.
   d. Find the marginal distribution function of X and Y.
   e. Find the following probabilities: $P\{0.25 < X < 0.5, 1 < Y < 1.5\}$;

$$P\{0.5 < X < 1.2, 1 < Y < 1.5\}; P\{0.25 < X < 0.5, 1 < Y < 2.5\}.$$

7. The following function is a joint distribution function of X and Y, and it is shown only in the region where the density function is not zero:

$$F_{XY}(u, v) = u^2\{1 - \exp(-2v)\}, \qquad 0 < u < 1, \text{ and } 0 < v < \infty$$

  a. Show the values of the distribution function for the other regions of (u, v).
  b. Find the marginal distribution functions of X and Y.
  c. Find the joint density function of X and Y.
  d. Find the marginal density functions of X and Y.
  e. Find the following probabilities:

$$P\{0.5 < X < 0.8, 1 < Y < 2\}; P\{0.5 < X < 1.5, 1 < Y < 2\}.$$

8.* Two random variables (X, Y) are uniformly distributed inside a circle of radius 3.

  a. Find the marginal densities of X and Y.
  b. Find the distribution function of (X, Y).
  c. Find the conditional density of X given Y.

9.* Messages that arrive at a switch satisfy the Poisson model with an arrival rate of $\lambda = 5$ messages per second. Suppose that the switch combines every two messages to send together. We are, therefore, interested in the joint probability density function of the time to first arrival X, and the time to the second arrival Y. It can be shown that the joint density function has the following form:

$$f_{XY}(u, v) = 25 \exp(-5v), \text{ for } 0 < u < v < \infty, \text{ and is zero elsewhere.}$$

  a. Find the joint distribution function of X and Y.
  b. Find the marginal density functions of X and Y. Are they independent?
  c. Find the probability that the first message arrives within 0.4 sec and the second message arrives within 0.8 sec.
  d. Find the probability that the second message arrives within 0.8 sec.

10. Errors occur in a communication channel with probability that depends on the signal power in the channel. Suppose that the signal power is a random variable X assumed to be Gaussian with mean 10 and variance 4. (Usually, since X is power, then we know that $P\{X < 0\} = 0$, which is approximately true for this Gaussian model.) The errors are represented by the random variable Y that takes the value 1, if a bit is in error, and the value 0, if a bit is received correctly. Suppose we observe the following conditional probability of error (i.e, the probability of $Y = 1$ given that the value of X is equal to u):

$$P\{Y = 1 | X = u\} = 0.1 \exp\{-(u - 4)/4\}$$

  a. Find the total probability of error (namely, that $Y = 1$).
  b. What is the conditional density function of the power X given that we observed an error?
  c. If we observed an error, what is the probability that the power was larger than 10?

11.* Consider the figure of Problem 5, where the switch can be in any of four positions with equal probability. Define the following two random variables:

$$X = \text{The value of the resistive load connected to the power supply.}$$
$$Y = \text{The value of the current through the power supply.}$$

Let the voltage source be a Gaussian random variable with mean 12 and variance 9. Hence, if the switch connects the load of $X = 6$, then the current will be Gaussian with mean 12/6 and standard deviation of 3/6.

   a. Using the same arguments as for the case of $X = 6$, find the conditional density function of Y given the value of X.

   b. Find the unconditional density of Y.

   c. Find the conditional probabilities of the four values of X given that we observed a value of the current $Y = y$. Compute for $y = 1, 2, 3, 4$.

12.* Let X and Y have the following joint probability density function:

$$f_{XY}(u, v) = C \exp\{-2(u + v)\}, \text{ for } 0 < 0.5u < v < 2u < \infty$$

   a. Find the marginal density functions of X and Y.

   b. Find the distribution function of X and Y.

   c. Find the following probabilities: $P\{0 < X < 1 \text{ and } Y < 1\}$; $P\{0 < X < 1 \text{ and } Y < 3\}$; $P\{0 < X < 1 \text{ and } 2 < Y\}$; and $P\{0 < X < 1 \text{ and } 1 < Y\}$.

   d. Find the conditional density of Y given X.

13.* In a channel having five links, the probability that a link will be available is $p = 0.6$, and the links may or may not be available independently of each other. Let X denote the number of links that are available. The delay in sending a message is a random variable Y whose density depends on the number of available links, such that the conditional density of the delay given that $X = k$ is given by

$$f_{Y|X}(v|k) = 2k \exp(-2kv)$$

   a. Find the unconditional density of the delay Y.

   b. Find the condition probability that $X = k$ given that the delay value was $Y = v$. Compute for $v = 0.5$, $v = 1$, and $v = 0.25$.

   c. Find the conditional probability that $X = k$ given the event $\{Y > 1\}$.

   d. Find the conditional probability that $X = k$ given the event $\{Y < 1\}$.

14.* Messages waiting in a queue at a network node are a mix of voice and data messages. The length of the messages is a random variable with an exponential density function, but the average length of a message depends on whether it is a voice message or a data message. The average length of a voice message is 30 seconds, while the average length of a data message is 10 seconds. (Length is defined here in terms of transmission time.) Of the total number of messages, 70% are data messages and 30% are voice messages.

   a. Find the unconditional density of an arbitrary message in the queue.

   b. If we know that a message is 20 seconds long, what is the conditional probability that it is a data message? A voice message?

   c. If we know that a message is less than 15 seconds long, what is the probability that it is a data message?

   d. If we know that a message is longer than 25 second, what is the probability that it is a voice message?

15. Random variables X and Y take values on an ellipse as follows:

$$X^2/a^2 + Y^2/b^2 = 1$$

Find the conditional probability density function of Y given X.

16. The random variables X and Y are uniformly distributed inside a triangle, as shown in the figure.

$$(u + v) \leq a, \text{ with } u > 0 \text{ and } v > 0$$

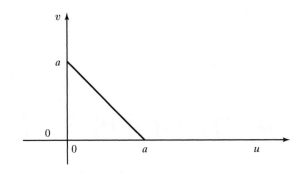

a. Find the joint distribution function of X and Y.
b. Find the marginal distributions and density functions of X and Y.
c. Find the conditional density function of X given Y and of Y given X.

6

Expectations
and Functions

6.1 EXPECTATIONS OF TWO RANDOM VARIABLES

Just as in the one random variable case, we may need to find the average of functions that depend on the values of two random variables. As an example, consider the case of connecting two resistors in series when each one is a random variable with known distribution. We may wish to find the resulting mean and variance if we know these parameters for each resistor. Expectations or statistical averages are defined in the same way as for the one random variable case. If the two random variables X and Y are discrete and we know the probabilities of the values they take, then the expectation of the function $g(X, Y)$ is defined as

$$E\{g(X, Y)\} = \sum_j \sum_i g(a_i, b_j) P\{X = a_i, Y = b_j)$$ (6.1)

The summation is over all values that X and Y take. For continuous random variables, the summation over all probabilities becomes an integral in the limit: We first divide the range of the values taken by X and Y into small rectangles of size $\Delta u \, \Delta v$ around every point (u, v) in the plane. Next, we approximate the expectation by multiplying the value of the function $g(u, v)$ by $f_{XY}(u, v) \, \Delta u \, \Delta v$, since the probability of being in this rectangle is approximately $f_{XY}(u, v) \, \Delta u \, \Delta v$. Finally, we take the limit to obtain the general expression for the expectation of $g(X, Y)$ if the resulting integral converges:

$$E\{g(X,Y)\} = \int_{-\infty}^{\infty} \int_{-\infty}^{\infty} g(u, v) f_{XY}(u, v) \, du \, dv \qquad (6.2)$$

Example 6.1

As an example, let us consider the average current in a resistor whose value is a random variable R with uniform density function in the interval $(9, 11)$, and V is the voltage signal applied to the resistor, which is also assumed to be random with Gaussian density having mean 9 and standard deviation 2. We also assume that the value of the resistor is independent of the value of the voltage signal. The current, is

$$I = g(R, V) = V/R$$

The average current then becomes

$$E\{I\} = E\{V/R\} = \int_{-\infty}^{\infty} \int_{9}^{11} \frac{v}{u} f_V(v) f_R(u) \, du \, dv$$

$$= \left[\int_{-\infty}^{\infty} v f_V(v) \, dv \right] \left[\int_{9}^{11} \frac{1}{2u} \, du \right]$$

The first term is just the expected value of V, so we do not even need to perform the integral, since we know the mean value of V, and we can write the answer for the first term as 9. The second term can be integrated to yield

$$E\{I\} = 9 \int_{9}^{11} \frac{1}{2u} \, du = 4.5 \ln(11/9) = 0.903$$

Example 6.1 illustrates two important properties of expectations, which we shall define shortly. We see that the independence assumption resulted in a product of two integrals, saving us a lot of work. The second thing we note is that in many cases we do not need to actually perform any integration if we can identify the expected value in question as one of the quantities we know already (in this case the mean of V). We are ready now to discuss properties of expectations. Some of these have already been considered in the one random variable case.

Property 1: $E\{C\} = C$. The expectation of a constant is still the same constant.

Property 2: $E\{ag(X,Y)\} = aE\{g(X,Y)\}$. A constant comes outside the expectation sign.

Property 3: $E\{g(X,Y) + h(X,Y)\} = E\{g(X,Y)\} + E\{h(X,Y)\}$. The expectation is linear.

Property 4: If $g(X,Y) \geq 0$, then $E\{g(X,Y)\} \geq 0$.

This property means that when averaging nonnegative quantities, the result is also non-negative.

Property 5: If X and Y are independent, then

$$E\{g(X)h(Y)\} = E\{g(X)\}E\{h(Y)\}$$

This property follows from the fact that the density in such a case is a product of the marginal densities, so the double integral becomes the product of two integrals.

We now consider special cases of expectations, as we have done in the case of one random variable.

6.1.1 Moments

Just as in the case of one random variable, we define moments as the expectations of the random variables raised to some power. Since we have two random variables here, we can define the $(m + n)$th moment as

$$M_{mn} = E\{X^m Y^n\} = \int_{-\infty}^{\infty} \int_{-\infty}^{\infty} u^m v^n f_{XY}(u, v) \, du \, dv \qquad (6.3)$$

Clearly the cases $m = 0$ or $n = 0$ reduce to the moments of Y and X, respectively. The first moment that involves both random variables is the case $m = n = 1$. We define the resulting moment as the ***correlation*** between X and Y:

$$R_{XY} = E\{XY\} \qquad (6.4)$$

Just as in the case of one random variable, it is more informative to consider the moments after we have shifted the values of X and Y by the means of X and Y, since the mean itself just defines the central values taken by the random variables rather than how widely they are distributed. The result is what we call the $(m + n)$th central moments of X and Y:

$$\mu_{mn} = E\{(X - m_X)^m (Y - m_Y)^n\} \qquad (6.5)$$

Again we see that for $m = 0$ or $n = 0$ we obtain the central moments of Y and X individually.

In this case we obtain the value zero for $m = 0$ and $n = 1$ or $m = 1$ and $n = 0$.

For $m = 0$ and $n = 2$ or $m = 2$ and $n = 0$, we obtain the variances of Y and X, respectively.

These are summarized as follows:

$$\mu_{01} = E\{(X - m_X)^0 (Y - m_Y)^1\} = 0 \qquad \mu_{10} = E\{(X - m_X)^1 (Y - m_Y)^0\} = 0 \qquad (6.6)$$

$$\sigma_X^2 = \mu_{20} = E\{[X - m_X]^2\}$$

$$\sigma_Y^2 = \mu_{02} = E\{[Y - m_Y]^2\} \qquad (6.7)$$

6.1.2 Covariance and Correlation Coefficient

The first central moment involving both variables is also a second-order moment with $m = n = 1$; it is defined as the **covariance** between X and Y and is denoted by

$$\text{Cov}(X, Y) = C_{XY} = E\{(X - m_X)(Y - m_Y)\} = R_{XY} - m_X m_Y \quad (6.8)$$

The last expression in equation (6.8) was obtained by using the linearity property of the expectation, as we expand the product inside the expectation.

What Does the Covariance Tell Us?

If we look at how it is defined, we can tell that when Y increases away from its mean, X also increases away from its mean, and vice versa, then the average of the product defining the covariance will be large. On the other hand, when Y increases, X can either increase or decrease, then we expect the covariance to be small. In this sense, the covariance tells us whether there is a linear relationship between X and Y (i.e., whether they grow together or not). We are speaking here about a statistical relation and not a causal relation. In order to further quantify the strength of such a relation, we need to normalize the covariance. We see that for the same problem, if, for example, we change dimensions from meters to centimeters (for either X or Y), the covariance will be 100 times larger since the units are smaller by a factor of 100. We therefore need a nondimensional number that expresses the strength of the correlation better. We call the resulting parameter the **correlation coefficient**, which is defined as

$$\rho_{XY} = \frac{\text{Cov}(X, Y)}{\sigma_X \sigma_Y} = \frac{E\{\{X - m_X)(Y - m_Y)\}}{\sigma_X \sigma_Y} = \frac{R_{XY} - m_X m_Y}{\sigma_X \sigma_Y} \quad (6.9)$$

It should be noted that the correlation coefficient is the same coefficient that related two jointly Gaussian random variables in equation (5.27). Before we consider the properties of the correlation coefficient, let us look at an example. We shall use the same example we considered in Example 6.1, with a resistor and a random voltage applied to it.

Example 6.2

Consider the problem posed in Example 6.1. We already know the average value of the voltage V (given as 9) and its variance (given as 4). We found the mean of the current I as well. We now would like to find the variance of the current I and its correlation with the voltage V. We have

$$E\{I^2\} = E\{V^2/R^2\} = E\{V^2\}E\{1/R^2\}$$

We used the fact that R and V are independent in order to factor the expectation into a product of two terms. Now we have to find each of the terms in the preceding expression:

$$E\{V^2\} = m_Y^2 + \sigma_Y^2 = 9^2 + 2^2 = 85$$

Here we used the relation between the second moment and the variance. Now we derive the second term directly:

$$E\left\{\frac{1}{R^2}\right\} = \int_9^{11} \frac{1}{u^2} 0.5\, du = -\frac{0.5}{11} + \frac{0.5}{9} = \frac{1}{99}$$

Hence we have the following value for the second moment of I:

$$E\{I^2\} = 85/99 = 0.858586$$

The variance of the current is therefore given by (where we use the mean derived in Example 6.1)

$$\sigma_I^2 = E\{I^2\} - m_I^2 = 0.858586 - (0.903)^2 = 0.043177$$

The standard deviation of the current is then equal to

$$\sigma_I = 0.208$$

In order to find the correlation coefficient, we need first to find the correlation or the covariance between V and I:

$$R_{VI} = E\{VI\} = E\{V^2/R\} = E\{V^2\}E\{1/R\}$$

Here we again used the fact that R and V are independent. Both terms in the preceding equation are already known from Example 6.1, so that we obtain

$$R_{VI} = 85[0.5\ln(11/9)] = 8.5285$$

The correlation coefficient can then be obtained from equation (6.9), to yield

$$\rho_{VI} = \frac{R_{VI} - m_V m_I}{\sigma_V \sigma_I} = \frac{8.5825 - 9 \times 0.903}{2 \times 0.208} = 0.965$$

We see that, as expected, there is a strong correlation between the voltage and the current.

In order to determine whether a correlation between two variables is strong or weak, we need to establish a key property of the correlation coefficient.

Properties of the Correlation Coefficient

The correlation coefficient takes values in the range $[-1, +1]$, namely,

$$|\rho_{XY}| \leq 1 \tag{6.10}$$

We can prove this bound by considering the following expectation:

$$E\left\{\left[\frac{X - m_X}{\sigma_X} \pm \frac{Y - m_Y}{\sigma_Y}\right]^2\right\} \geq 0 \tag{6.11}$$

If we now open the bracket on the left side and identify each term in the expectation, we obtain

$$E\left\{\left(\frac{X - m_X}{\sigma_X}\right)^2\right\} \pm 2E\left\{\left(\frac{X - m_X}{\sigma_X}\right)\left(\frac{Y - m_Y}{\sigma_Y}\right)\right\} + E\left\{\left(\frac{Y - m_Y}{\sigma_Y}\right)^2\right\} \geq 0$$

(6.12)

The preceding expression reduces to

$$1 \pm 2\rho_{XY} + 1 \geq 0 \tag{6.13}$$

When the $\pm$ sign is taken into account, the final inequality becomes

$$1 \geq \rho_{XY} \geq -1 \tag{6.14}$$

This is but another way of expressing equation (6.1), which proves the property.

If the correlation coefficient is close to ± 1, then we say that there is a strong correlation between X and Y. If it is close to zero, there is no or very weak correlation between the variables. If it is positive, then X and Y increase or decrease together (i.e., there is positive correlation between them). If it is negative, then when X increases, Y decreases, and vice versa. We say in such a case that X and Y are negatively correlated. Notice that when the correlation coefficient is zero, we say that X and Y are uncorrelated. If, in addition, one of them has zero mean, we say that X and Y are orthogonal and write

$$E\{XY\} = 0. \tag{6.15}$$

In general, for uncorrelated random variables, we have

$$E\{XY\} = E\{X\}E\{Y\} = m_X m_Y \tag{6.16}$$

which reduces to equation (6.15) if one or both means are zero.

What Does Weak or Strong Correlation Imply?

We shall see in Section 6.2 that correlation implies a linear relation between the two random variables. A strong correlation means that such a straight line fit between the two variables is a better fit or approximation than the case of a weak correlation. The stronger the correlation, the better fit the straight line becomes. We shall also quantify what is meant by a "strong" or "weak" correlation.

Example 6.3

Consider the following joint density function of two random variables X and Y:

$$f_{XY}(u, v) = \lambda^2 \exp(-\lambda v), \qquad 0 < u < v < \infty \text{ and is zero elsewhere.}$$

This density represents the joint density of the time to the first arrival (X) and the time to the second arrival (Y) of Poisson-distributed events.

Figure 6.1 illustrates the region in which the preceding joint density is nonzero. Since Y represents the time of the second arrival, it must therefore always be larger than the time of the first arrival X, so that the density is nonzero only for values of Y (represented by v) that are larger than values of X (represented by u).

We can find the marginal densities as follows, where we use the nonzero region in Figure 6.1 to determine the limits of the integrals:

$$f_X(u) = \int_u^\infty \lambda^2 \exp(-\lambda v)\, dv = \lambda \exp(-\lambda u), \qquad 0 < u < \infty \text{ and is zero elsewhere}$$

The limits of the preceding integral are obtained from the dashed vertical line in Figure 6.1. We then have

$$f_Y(v) = \int_0^v \lambda^2 \exp(-\lambda v)\, du = \lambda^2\, v \exp(-\lambda v), \quad 0 < v < \infty \text{ and is zero elsewhere}$$

The limits of the preceding integral are obtained from the dashed horizontal line in Figure 6.1.

The means and variances of X and Y can be obtained directly by integration to yield

$$m_X = E\{X\} = \int_0^\infty u\lambda \exp(-\lambda u)\, du = \frac{1}{\lambda}$$

$$m_Y = E\{Y\} = \int_0^\infty v\lambda^2 v \exp(-\lambda v)\, dv = \frac{2}{\lambda}$$

$$E\{X^2\} = \int_0^\infty u^2\lambda \exp(-\lambda u)\, du = \frac{2}{\lambda^2}, \qquad \sigma_X^2 = E\{X^2\} - m_X^2 = \frac{1}{\lambda^2}$$

$$E\{Y^2\} = \int_0^\infty v^2\lambda^2 v \exp(-\lambda v)\, dv = \frac{6}{\lambda^2}, \qquad \sigma_Y^2 = E\{Y^2\} - m_Y^2 = \frac{2}{\lambda^2}$$

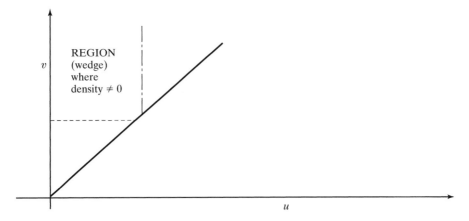

Figure 6.1   Region where the joint density of arrival times is not zero

Finally, we are ready to find the correlation between X and Y:

$$R_{XY} = E\{XY\} = \int_0^\infty \int_0^v uv\lambda^2 \exp(-\lambda v)\, du\, dv$$

$$= \int_0^\infty 0.5v^2 v\lambda^2 \exp(-\lambda v)\, dv = \frac{3}{\lambda^2}$$

The resulting covariance and correlation coefficient are obtained by using equations (6.8) and (6.9), and are expressed as

$$C_{XY} = R_{XY} - \frac{1}{\lambda} \times \frac{2}{\lambda} = \frac{1}{\lambda^2},$$

$$\rho_{XY} = \frac{C_{XY}}{\sigma_X \sigma_Y} = \frac{1/\lambda^2}{(1/\lambda)\left(\sqrt{2}/\lambda\right)} = \frac{1}{\sqrt{2}} = 0.707$$

We see that there is a reasonable correlation between the two variables, as expected, since if the first arrival time is large, we expect the time to the second arrival to be large as well, as it also includes the first arrival time.

The definition of the correlation and covariance between two random variables shows that if the two random variables are independent, then they are definitely uncorrelated, since the expected value of the product becomes a product of the expected values. However, uncorrelated random variables may still be dependent in general, but the dependence would be in some nonlinear form. This observation holds in general, except for some important cases we shall consider in Section 6.3. In the next example, we consider a case in which two random variables are very strongly dependent but are uncorrelated.

Example 6.4

Consider a Gaussian random variable X with mean zero and variance σ^2, and let Y be given by the relation

$$Y = X^2$$

We know by the definition of X that it has mean 0 and variance σ^2. By the definition of Y, we can easily find that its mean is

$$m_Y = E\{Y\} = E\{X^2\} = \sigma^2$$

Now we find the covariance between X and Y:

$$C_{XY} = E\{X(Y - m_Y)\} = E\{X^3\} - E\{X\}m_Y = 0$$

The reason the preceding expectations are both zero is the fact that the mean of X is zero as given and the expected value of X^3 is also zero, because the Gaussian density with zero mean is symmetric, so that all odd moments are zero. We see in this example that two strongly related random variables (after all $Y = X^2$) have zero covariance and hence are uncorrelated. We conclude that in general, when two random variables are uncorrelated, they may still be dependent. We shall see that the jointly Gaussian case is an exception to this general property.

6.1.3 Mean and Variance of a Sum of Two Random Variables

A very important result is involved with the effect of the correlation on the variance of a sum of two correlated random variables. Suppose that X and Y are random variables with known means, variances, and covariance. Let Z be defined as their sum:

$$Z = X + Y \tag{6.17}$$

We already know that the mean of Z is equal to the sum of the means of X and Y:

$$m_Z = E\{Z\} = E\{X + Y\} = m_X + m_Y \tag{6.18}$$

This expression always holds, regardless of the density or the dependence of the two random variables. It also holds for more than two random variables, as we shall observe later.

What about the variance of the sum, Z? Here we have

$$\sigma_Z^2 = E\{[Z - (m_X + m_Y)]^2\} = E\{[(X - m_X) + (Y - m_Y)]^2\}$$
$$= E\{[X - m_X]^2\} + E\{[Y - m_Y]^2\} + 2E\{(X - m_X)(Y - m_Y)\}$$
$$= \sigma_X^2 + \sigma_Y^2 + 2C_{XY} = \sigma_X^2 + \sigma_Y^2 + 2\rho_{XY}\sigma_X\sigma_Y \tag{6.19}$$

We see that the variance of a sum of two variables involves three terms, with the most interesting part being the term with the covariance or the correlation coefficient. It means that if the random variables are correlated, then the variance of their sum may be larger or smaller than the sum of their variances, depending on whether they are positively or negatively correlated.

On the other hand, we come to a very important result: If two random variables are uncorrelated, then the variance of their sum is equal to the sum of their variances, or

$$\text{Var}(X + Y) = \text{Var}(X) + \text{Var}(Y), \text{ if } X \text{ and } Y \text{ are uncolrerelated.} \tag{6.19a}$$

This result of the variance of a sum can be generalized to the n variable case. As we shall see later, even though we are considering n variables, if we are only concerned with the mean and variance of the sum, then we need only know their correlation, which means that we need only know how they behave two at a time.

We next address one of the key uses of correlation, namely that of estimating the value of one random variable if we know the value of another correlated random variable using straight line approximations.

6.2 LINEAR ESTIMATION

6.2.1 Linear Fit Between X and Y

We shall assume that we observe Y and would like to approximate the values of X by a straight line function of Y. We shall call the approximating line $\hat{X}$, and we assume that it is linear in the Y variable with coefficients yet to be determined. Our objective is to determine the coefficients of the linear approximation so as to minimize the error in our approximation in some sense. Our approximating line is assumed to have the general form

$$\hat{X} = aY + b \tag{6.20}$$

The coefficients a and b are to be determined to minimize the error in some sense.

The deviation from the straight line by the true values taken by X is $(\hat{X} - X)$, and we would like to minimize the expected value of the square of the error. We pick such a measure for convenience, and we need a measure that is nonnegative, since the error can be either positive or negative and we wish to minimize either deviation. In other words we wish to find the coefficients a and b such that the following mean-squared error (MSE) is minimized:

$$\text{MSE} = E\{(\hat{X} - X)^2\} = E\{[aY + b - X]^2\} \tag{6.21}$$

We now expand the terms inside the expectation and identify each term by using the means, variances, and the correlation coefficient to obtain

$$\text{MSE} = a^2E\{Y^2\} + b^2 + E\{X^2\} + 2abE\{Y\} - 2bE\{X\} - 2aE\{XY\}$$

Differentiation with respect to b to obtain the value of b that minimizes the expression yields

$$2b + 2aE\{Y\} - 2E\{X\} = 0$$

The preceding equation yields the value for $b = b_0$ that minimizes the error:

$$b_0 = E\{X\} - aE\{Y\} = m_X - am_Y \tag{6.22}$$

If we now substitute the value of b_0 from equation (6.22) into equation (6.21) and collect terms appropriately, we obtain

$$\text{MSE} = E\{[a(Y - m_Y) - (X - m_X)]^2\} = a^2\sigma_Y^2 - 2a\rho_{XY}\sigma_X\sigma_Y + \sigma_X^2 \tag{6.2.23}$$

Now we differentiate with respect to the slope of the linear approximation a, so that the MSE is minimized to obtain an equation for the optimal $a = a_0$:

$$2a_0\sigma_Y^2 - 2\rho_{XY}\sigma_X\sigma_Y = 0$$

The final result for the optimal slope is

$$a_0 = \rho_{XY}\frac{\sigma_X}{\sigma_Y} \tag{6.24}$$

We now use equations (6.22) and (6.24) in equation (6.20) to obtain the final expression for the "best" linear approximation of the values of X in terms of Y:

$$\hat{X} = m_X + \rho_{XY}\frac{\sigma_X}{\sigma_Y}(Y - m_Y) \tag{6.25}$$

It is easy to see that the mean of the approximation error is zero, so the MSE may also be interpreted as the variance of the error (obtained by substituting the optimal value of $a = a_0$ in equation (6.23)) and is given by

$$\text{MSE} = \text{Var}[\hat{X} - X] = \sigma_X^2(1 - \rho_{XY}^2) \tag{6.26}$$

Equation (6.26) shows that as the correlation coefficient approaches ± 1, the approximation gets better, as its error variance becomes closer to zero. As a matter of fact, the approximation MSE is zero when the correlation coefficient is ± 1, which means that almost all of the values of X and Y fall on a straight line. (Those which fall outside such a line contribute zero to the MSE.) We call X and Y in such a case perfectly correlated random variables.

Equation (6.26) provides us with a way of measuring strong or weak correlation. As a result of the straight line approximation, we were able to reduce the original variance of X by a factor of

$$\text{MSE}/\sigma_X^2 = (1 - \rho_{XY}^2)$$

For example, if the correlation coefficient is 0.9, then the variance of X as a result of the linear approximation is reduced to 19% of its original value. On the other hand, a correlation coefficient of 0.707, reduces the variance by only a factor of 50%. The strength or weakness of the correlation is a matter of practical definition of what percent reduction in the variance is considered good or bad. It becomes a subjective matter and depends on the utility of the estimated variable.

In statistics we call such a straight-line approximation of data involving two variables "regression." Some well-known regressions are the ones linking height and weight of people, and linking age and length in infants. Just to verify that what we are doing makes sense, let us consider Example 6.2 further.

Example 6.2 (continued)

In the example we derived the correlation between V and I. Here we wish to approximate the current I from the voltage V using linear estimation. In this case we have

$$I = 0.903 + 0.965\frac{0.208}{2}(V - 9) = 0.1003V$$

The answer is equal to the value of V multiplied by the average value of $1/R$, where R is the value of the resistance. This simple example illustrates that the correlation coefficient and its use in linear approximation leads to intuitively expected results.

6.2.2 Linear Estimation of Signal Amplitude

We can apply the result of best linear fit to estimate the amplitude of a signal, which we shall denote by X, when it is observed in additive noise errors, which we shall denote by N. The observation is denoted by the random variable Y. Hence we have

$$Y = X + N \tag{6.27}$$

We shall assume for simplicity that the signal and noise, X and N, are independent random variables with means m_X and $m_N = 0$, and variances σ_X^2 and σ_N^2, respectively. We now wish to estimate the value of X from the observations Y using linear approximation, such that the MSE is minimized. We know the answer to this problem from Section 6.2.1, so we only need to find the variances and the correlation coefficient involved.

We know the variance of X, so we need to find the variance of Y. Since Y is the sum of two independent random variables, its variance is equal to the sum of the variances of X and N:

$$\sigma_Y^2 = \sigma_X^2 + \sigma_N^2 \tag{6.28}$$

We also know that, due to the sum, the mean of Y is the sum of the means; hence mean of Y is equal to the mean of X (since the mean of N is zero). We now find the covariance between X and Y, which is equal to

$$
\begin{aligned}
C_{XY} &= E\{(X - m_X)(Y - m_Y)\} = E\{(X - m_X)[(X - m_X) + (N - m_N)]\} \\
&= E\{(X - m_X)^2\} + E\{(X - m_X)N\} \\
&= E\{(X - m_X)^2\} + E\{(X - m_X)\}E\{N\} = \sigma_X^2 + 0 = \sigma_X^2
\end{aligned}
\tag{6.29}
$$

The correlation coefficient is then obtained by normalizing with respect to the standard deviations of X and Y:

$$\rho_{XY} = \frac{C_{XY}}{\sigma_X \sigma_Y} = \frac{\sigma_X^2}{\sigma_X \sqrt{\sigma_X^2 + \sigma_N^2}} = \frac{\sigma_X}{\sqrt{\sigma_X^2 + \sigma_N^2}} \tag{6.30}$$

The estimation of X from the observations Y then can be derived as in Section 6.2.1 by using equation (6.25) and substituting the values of the correlation coefficient and the standard deviations:

$$\hat{X} = m_X + \frac{\sigma_X}{\sqrt{\sigma_X^2 + \sigma_N^2}} \frac{\sigma_X}{\sigma_Y}(Y - m_X) = m_X + \frac{\sigma_X^2}{\sigma_X^2 + \sigma_N^2}(Y - m_X) \tag{6.31}$$

The MSE of the approximation for this case can therefore be obtained from equation (6.26) and is expressed as

$$\text{MSE} = \sigma_X^2\left(1 - \frac{\sigma_X^2}{\sigma_X^2 + \sigma_N^2}\right) = \frac{\sigma_X^2 \sigma_N^2}{\sigma_X^2 + \sigma_N^2} = \sigma_X^2/(1 + \text{SNR}) \tag{6.32}$$

In this equation we defined the signal-to-noise ratio (SNR) by

$$\text{SNR} = (\sigma_X^2/\sigma_N^2)$$

It represents the average varying signal power (not including the constant mean) divided by the average measurement errors or noise power.

A more meaningful expression for the MSE is obtained when we normalize it by the variance of the signal to be estimated (to avoid the problem of the dimensions used). In this case, for the normalized MSE for this problem, we obtain

$$\text{MSE}/\sigma_X^2 = 1/(1 + \text{SNR})$$

We see that our approximation in terms of the resulting normalized MSE gets better as the SNR becomes larger. As the SNR tends to infinity, the MSE tends to zero as expected.

6.3 GAUSSIAN RANDOM VARIABLES

We studied the joint Gaussian density function in the Chapter 5, and it is represented by equation (5.27). What we notice when we take another look at it is that the parameter ρ in the joint density function is indeed the correlation coefficient between X and Y. It means that two jointly Gaussian random variables are completely specified (their joint density is known exactly) if we know their means, variances, and correlation coefficient. In this case we can state that Gaussian random variables are independent if they are uncorrelated, since if $\rho = 0$, then the density becomes a product of the two marginal densities. We also wrote the expressions for the conditional density of X given Y in equation (5.28). We found that it is also Gaussian, but its mean is a linear relation of Y, which is exactly the same relation we derived in equation (6.25) for the best linear fit. We also found that the variance of the conditional density of X given Y as given in equation (5.30) is identical to the expression for the variance of the error we obtained in equation (6.26). Finally, the variance of the conditional density as expressed in equation (5.30) tends to zero as the correlation coefficient approaches 1 or -1.

In general, uncorrelated random variables are not independent, since they may be related through some nonlinear relationship. Correlation measures only linear relations between the two variables. However, for Gaussian random variables, if they are uncorrelated, they are also independent.

In order to illustrate how correlated Gaussian random variables behave, we simulated the generation of 1000 sample values of two random variables X and Y. Both were selected to have zero mean, and X was selected to have variance equal to 1. Figures 6.2(a) through 6.2(d) show the scatter diagrams, where every pair of values of X and Y are shown as one point in the graph with X on the horizontal axis and Y on the vertical axis. The figures show different correlation coefficients and, in some cases, different variances for Y. We see in the scatter plots that as the correlation coefficient approaches 1, the graph concentrates more and more along some diagonal line in the first and third quadrants of the (X,Y) plane. As the coefficient gets

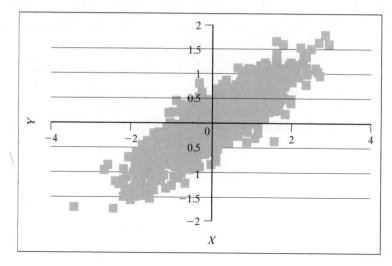

Figure 6.2(a) $\rho_{XY} = 0.86, \sigma_Y = 0.6$

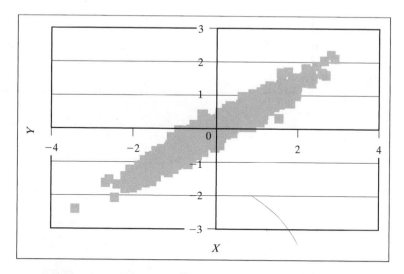

Figure 6.2(b) $\rho_{XY} = 0.96, \sigma_Y = 0.73$

close to zero, the scatter diagram looks just like a circle and appears almost symmetric about the X axis. We used here only positively correlated variables. If they were negatively correlated, the figures would be almost the same, except that they would be along a line with a negative slope. This means that most values will be in the second and fourth quadrant of the (X,Y) plane.

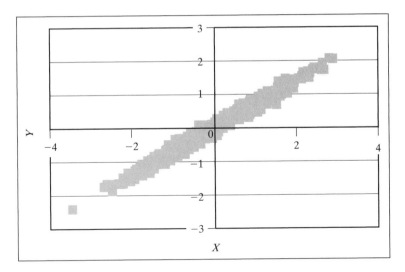

Figure 6.2(c) $\rho_{XY} = 0.99, \sigma_Y = 0.71$

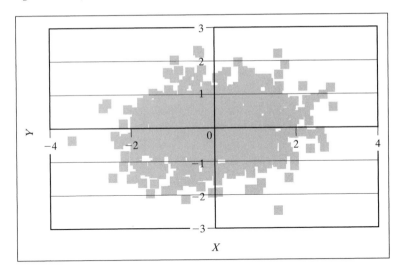

Figure 6.2(d) $\rho_{XY} = 0.14, \sigma_Y = 0.71$

Figure 6.2   Scatter diagrams of simulated Gaussian random variables

6.4 ONE FUNCTION OF TWO RANDOM VARIABLES

When dealing with functions of two or more random variables, the problems involving densities and distribution functions become very complicated and rather
unwieldy mathematically. Hence, in many of these cases we have to rely on expectations on the one hand, involving means, variances, and correlation. On the other
hand, we can do more if we assume that the random variables are independent. We
shall consider these two cases, then generalize them to the case of multiple random

variables, and finally consider two major applications in future chapters: applications to statistics and inference, and applications to reliability.

Since we are dealing with simplified cases, we shall concentrate on simple functions, such as the sum of random variables, and then address the case of other functions of interest. We also can distinguish between two major cases: whether we have one function of two random variables or two functions of two random variables.

6.4.1 Sums of Two Random Variables

Density of a Sum

When do we encounter sums involving several random variables? Such a case occurs whenever we wish to estimate some value and our measurements are noisy. What we do in such a case is add all the measurements and divide by the number of measurements. Why does such an approach work? If we need certain accuracy in the results, how many measurements should we take? Considering the properties of sums will help answer these questions.

Let us consider the case of two random variables. We have two independent random variables X and Y, and we wish to find the density function of their sum Z:

$$Z = X + Y \tag{6.33}$$

One way of finding the density of Z is to first find the conditional density of Z given X. If $X = u$ is known, then Z is simply a shifted version of the density of Y, since for known $X = u$, we have

$$Z = u + Y \tag{6.34}$$

This is just a linear transformation of the density of Y given X (as we assume that the value of X is known), and since Y is independent of X, the result for the conditional density of Z given X becomes

$$f_{Z|X}(w|X = u) = f_{Y|X}(w - u|X = u) = f_Y(w - u) \tag{6.35}$$

Therefore, the joint density function of X and Z is obtained by multiplying the conditional density of Z in equation (6.35) by the density of X to yield

$$f_{Z,X}(w, u) = f_Y(w - u)f_X(u) \tag{6.36}$$

If we now integrate over the values of X, we obtain the density of the sum Z:

$$f_Z(w) = \int_{-\infty}^{\infty} f_{Z,X}(w, u) \, du = \int_{-\infty}^{\infty} f_Y(w - u)f_X(u) \, du \tag{6.37}$$

As an example, consider the density of the time to the second arrival Z in a Poisson arrival problem. Define X as the time to first arrival, and let Y be the time between

Figure 6.3   Arrival times X, Y, and Z

the first and second arrivals. We know that both X and Y are independent random variables and that their density is exponential with arrival rate λ. Hence, the time to second arrival is exactly the sum of X and Y, as shown in Figure 6.3.

In this case we have

$$f_X(u) = \lambda \exp(-\lambda u), \qquad 0 < u$$
$$f_Y(v) = \lambda \exp(-\lambda v), \qquad 0 < v \tag{6.38}$$

Consequently, the expression for the density of Z is obtained from equation (6.37) as follows:

$$f_Z(w) = \int_0^w \lambda \exp[-\lambda(w - u)] \, \lambda \exp(-\lambda u) \, du = \lambda^2 w \exp(-\lambda w), 0 < w \tag{6.39}$$

The reason for the limits in equation (6.39) is the fact that the density of X is zero for negative values of u in the preceding expression, while the density of Y is zero for negative values of its argument $(w - u)$. Hence the upper limit on the value of u is w. We have seen this density before in Example 6.3 when we considered the joint density of Z and X. (At the time, we called the time to second arrival Y rather than Z.)

We can derive the density of a sum of random variables directly by using the definition of the distribution function. In this case we want to find the probability that

$$F_Z(w) = P\{Z \le w\} = P\{X + Y \le w\} \tag{6.40}$$

The probability defined in equation (6.40) is the volume under the joint density function of X and Y bounded by the area in the X, Y plane shown in Figure 6.4.

The area over which the density needs to be integrated is shaded in the figure (both vertical and horizontal shading). The probability is obtained as follows:

$$F_Z(w) = P\{X + Y \le w\} = \int_{-\infty}^{\infty} \int_{-\infty}^{w-u} f_Y(v) f_X(u) \, dv \, du \tag{6.41}$$

In order to find the density function, we have to take the derivative with respect to w, resulting in exactly the same expression as equation (6.37), since the argument of the density of Y inside the integral is to be replaced with $(w - u)$. It is left as an

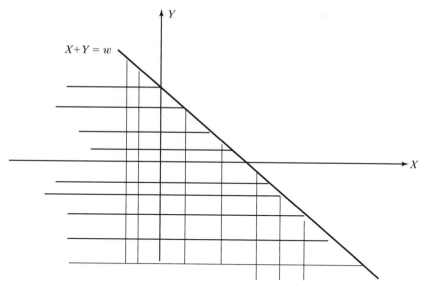

Figure 6.4   Area of $(X + Y) \le w$

exercise to derive the density of the sum of two resistors in series when each is uniformly distributed in the interval $(9, 11)$. We should obtain the same answer we derived in Section 3.3.2.

If we wish to find the density function of other functions of two random variables, we usually should rely on the definition of the distribution function and then take the derivative to obtain the density.

How do we handle sums of more than two random variables? If the random variables are independent, then we just have to evaluate the density two at a time. For example, if we wish to find the time to the third arrival in the Poisson problem, we first find the time to second arrival, then when we add an independent random variable reflecting the time between the second and third arrivals, we obtain the time to the third arrival. There is no conceptual difficulty here. The major difficulty in such problems is in evaluating the results using multiple integrations, which can be very tedious if the limits are finite, such as when we add a third resistor to the two resistors in series.

Due to the fact that such problems become tedious and may not provide any useful information beyond what we could obtain from the mean and variance, we tend to be satisfied in many cases with just the mean and variance of sums of random variables, as we discussed in Section 6.1.3.

The Gaussian Case

If the two random variables are jointly Gaussian, then we can show that if we use equation (6.37), we find that the density of the sum is also Gaussian. Therefore, all we need to do to find the density function of $Z = X + Y$, when X and Y are jointly Gaussian is to find the mean and variance of Z using equations (6.18) and (6.19), and we then can write the density of Z as a Gaussian density with mean m_Z and variance σ_Z^2. The result for jointly Gaussian random variables is proved in Chapter 7.

6.4.2 Other Functions

Another important function in communication systems is the envelope of a narrow band signal. In its simplest form, it considers a sinusoidal signal with a known frequency but whose amplitude is random, which may be described as

$$S(t) = X \cos(\omega t) + Y \sin(\omega t) = Z \cos(\omega t + \varphi) \qquad (6.42)$$

Here the amplitude Z is given by the expression

$$Z = \sqrt{X^2 + Y^2} \qquad (6.43)$$

If we are interested only in the amplitude (or as it is sometimes called the envelope) of the signal and not in its precise phase, then instead of the original amplitudes X and Y of the two components of the signal, we consider the amplitude Z. Suppose that X and Y are Gaussian, uncorrelated with zero means and identical variances of σ^2. Then the distribution of Z is obtained as the probability of the event $\{Z \le w\}$, which is the same as the probability of (X, Y) falling in a circle of radius w, as shown in Figure 6.5.

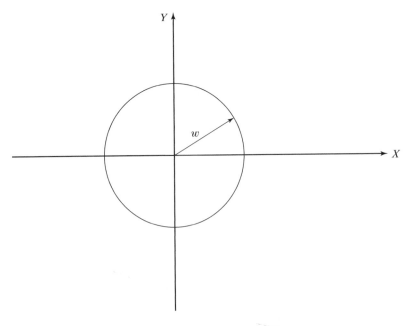

Figure 6.5   The region where $Z = \sqrt{X^2 + Y^2} \le w$

We therefore have the following expression for the distribution function:

$$F_Z(w) = P\{Z \le w\} = P\{\sqrt{X^2 + Y^2} \le w\} = \iint\limits_{\sqrt{u^2+v^2} \le w} f_{XY}(u, v)\, du\, dv \quad (6.44)$$

Due to the Gaussian assumption and the independence of X and Y we have

$$f_{XY}(u, v) = \frac{\exp\left\{-\dfrac{u^2 + v^2}{2\sigma^2}\right\}}{2\pi\sigma^2} \quad (6.45)$$

Since we are integrating inside a circle, it is easier to use polar coordinates such that

$$u = r\cos(\varphi),\ v = r\sin(\varphi),\ dudv = r\, dr\, d\varphi \quad (6.46)$$

Hence the integral in equation (6.44) becomes

$$F_Z(w) = \int_0^w \int_0^{2\pi} \frac{\exp\left(-\dfrac{r^2}{2\sigma^2}\right)}{2\pi\sigma^2} r\, d\varphi\, dr = \int_0^w \frac{\exp\left(-\dfrac{r^2}{2\sigma^2}\right)}{\sigma^2} r\, dr$$

$$= 1 - \exp\left(-\frac{w^2}{2\sigma^2}\right), \text{ for } w \ge 0 \quad (6.47)$$

This is what is called the Rayleigh distribution. The corresponding density is obtained by differentiating the distribution function, resulting in

$$f_Z(w) = \frac{w}{\sigma^2}\exp\left(-\frac{w^2}{2\sigma^2}\right), \text{ for } w \ge 0 \quad (6.48)$$

The density and its distribution are shown in Figure 6.6 for $\sigma = 2$.

If we are interested only in the density of the power of the signal, namely, Z^2, we can find the density of the power using a nonlinear (in this case quadratic) function of Z. Let the power be denoted by $V = Z^2$. Then we can find the distribution of V as follows:

$$F_V(v) = P\{V \le v\} = P\{Z^2 \le v\} = P\{Z \le \sqrt{v}\} = F_Z(\sqrt{v})$$

$$= 1 - \exp\left(-\frac{\sqrt{v}^2}{2\sigma^2}\right)$$

$$= 1 - \exp[-v/(2\sigma^2)], \text{ for } v \ge 0 \quad (6.49)$$

We see that the distribution of the power of the signal in this case is an exponential distribution, which we considered earlier in connection with arrival times and lifetime.

It should be noted that the Rayleigh density also occurs in target practice and missile accuracy problems. If an error in hitting a target has two components—horizontal

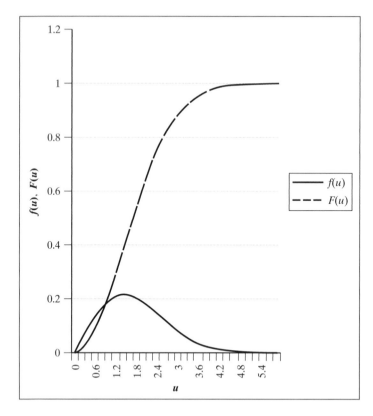

Figure 6.6 The Rayleigh density and its distribution function

(X) and vertical (Y) (or latitude and longitude)—and both of these errors are assumed to be Gaussian with zero mean and variance σ^2, then the miss distance from the target is the same random variable Z defined above. In such cases we find that the term **circular error probability** (CEP) distance is used to denote the distance within which the target is hit with 50% probability. This distance is then obtained from the Rayleigh distribution:

$$1 - \exp\left(-\frac{w^2}{2\sigma^2}\right) = 0.5, \qquad w = 1.1774\sigma$$

This is the way (using the basic definition of the distribution) we should handle any other function of two random variables. We have simply to use the definition of the distribution; therefore we can obtain the distribution function first and then derive the density function.

6.5 TWO FUNCTIONS OF TWO RANDOM VARIABLES

So far we have considered a single function of two random variables. The approach we used was of course to rely on the definition of the distribution function. When we have two functions that transform two random variables to other two random variables, we can still use the definition of the joint distribution function. However, the result is rather complex mathematically, unless the transformation is unique and has a unique inverse. We shall address this problem only in this important special case. If the uniqueness property is not satisfied, then each set of functions needs to be handled as a special case and will not be considered further in this text.

Consider the two random variables X and Y, which are transformed into the random variables U and V by the following functions:

$$U = g(X, Y)$$
$$V = h(X, Y) \qquad (6.50)$$

Since we assume that the functions are unique and have a unique inverse, let us define the inverse functions as

$$X = g_1(U, V)$$
$$Y = h_1(U, V) \qquad (6.51)$$

We can now try to find the distribution function of U and V if we know the joint density function $f_{XY}(\alpha, \beta)$ of X and Y. In this case, if we use the definition of the distribution function of U and V, we obtain

$$F_{UV}(u, v) = P\{U \le u, V \le v) = P\{g(X, Y) \le u, h(X, Y) \le v\}$$
$$= \iint\limits_{\substack{g(\alpha, \beta) \le u \\ h(\alpha, \beta) \le v}} f_{XY}(\alpha, \beta) d\alpha \, d\beta \qquad (6.52)$$

We now change the variables of integration by using the functions g and h as follows:

$$\eta = g(\alpha, \beta), \qquad \zeta = h(\alpha, \beta)$$
$$\alpha = g_1(\eta, \zeta), \qquad \beta = h_1(\eta, \zeta) \qquad (6.53)$$

Then we also have to change the differential $d\alpha \, d\beta$ by using the following expression that is valid for double integrals:

$d\alpha \, d\beta = |J(\eta, \zeta)| \, d\eta \, d\zeta$, where $|J|$ is given by

$$|J(\eta, \zeta)| = \det \begin{bmatrix} \dfrac{\partial g_1(\eta, \zeta)}{\partial \eta} & \dfrac{\partial g_1(\eta, \zeta)}{\partial \zeta} \\ \dfrac{\partial h_1(\eta, \zeta)}{\partial \eta} & \dfrac{\partial h_1(\eta, \zeta)}{\partial \zeta} \end{bmatrix} \qquad (6.54)$$

The integral in equation (6.52) then becomes

$$F_{UV}(u, v) = \int_{-\infty}^{v} \int_{-\infty}^{u} f_{XY}[g_1(\eta, \zeta), h_1(\eta, \zeta)] |J(\eta, \zeta)| \, d\eta \, d\zeta \qquad (6.55)$$

If we now take the derivative of the joint distribution function, we obtain the expression for the joint density function of U and V:

$$f_{UV}(u, v) = f_{XY}[g_1(u, v), h_1(u, v)]|J(u, v)| \tag{6.56}$$

An important note of caution in using this general expression is that it is useful only when the functions and their inverses are unique. Let us consider an example to illustrate this approach.

Example 6.5

Here we use the same example that resulted in the Rayleigh distribution (Section 6.4.2); however, we wish to look not just at the amplitude but also at the phase angle of the signal in question. Consider the sinusoidal signal given in equation (6.42), where the amplitudes X and Y of the sine and cosine components are assumed to be Gaussian with zero mean and equal variances. In equation (6.42) we defined only the overall amplitude of the resulting sinusoidal signal. Here we wish to consider the phase angle as well. We can rewrite equation (6.42) in terms of two new random variables Z and Θ as shown in the following expression:

$$S(t) = X \sin(\omega t) + Y \cos(\omega t) = Z \sin(\omega t + \Theta) \tag{6.57}$$

Here the expressions for the envelope Z and phase Θ are easily shown to be

$$Z = \sqrt{X^2 + Y^2}, \qquad \Theta = \arctan(Y/X) \tag{6.58}$$

The inverse transformations that provide us with the values of X and Y as a function of the new variables Z and Θ are obtained directly:

$$X = Z \cos(\Theta), \qquad Y = Z \sin(\Theta) \tag{6.59}$$

In order to find the joint density function $f_{Z\Theta}(w, \varphi)$ of Z and Θ, we use equation (6.56) with the inverse functions used as in equation (6.59):

$$|J(w, \varphi)| = \det\begin{bmatrix} \dfrac{\partial[w \cos \varphi]}{\partial w} & \dfrac{\partial[w \cos \varphi]}{\partial \varphi} \\ \dfrac{\partial[w \sin \varphi]}{\partial w} & \dfrac{\partial[w \sin \varphi]}{\partial \varphi} \end{bmatrix} = \det\begin{bmatrix} \cos \varphi & -w \sin \varphi \\ \sin \varphi & w \cos \varphi \end{bmatrix} = w \tag{6.60}$$

We now substitute the expressions for the functions in equation (6.59) together with equation (6.60) into equation (6.56) for the joint density, where we use the fact that the joint density of X and Y is Gaussian with means zero and variances σ^2:

$$f_{Z\Theta}(w, \varphi) = \frac{\exp\left\{ -\dfrac{(w \cos \varphi)^2 + (w \sin \varphi)^2}{2\sigma^2} \right\}}{2\pi\sigma^2} |J(w, \varphi)|$$

$$= \frac{w}{2\pi\sigma^2} \exp\left(-\frac{w^2}{2\sigma^2} \right), \quad \text{for } 0 < w \text{ and } 0 < \varphi < 2\pi \tag{6.61}$$

We can obtain the marginal densities of Z and Θ by integrating one of the variables out, and we find that the envelope Z will have the Rayleigh density and the phase angle will be uniformly distributed in $(0, 2\pi)$. We can easily verify then that the two variables are independent.

6.5.1 Linear Function of Two Variables

The special case in which the transformation is linear (i.e., it can be represented as a 2×2 matrix A multiplying the vector composed of the two variables) is given by

$$\begin{bmatrix} U \\ V \end{bmatrix} = A \begin{bmatrix} X \\ Y \end{bmatrix} \tag{6.62}$$

In this case it is easy to obtain the inverse function, as it is simply the inverse of the matrix A, where it is assumed that the inverse exists:

$$\begin{bmatrix} X \\ Y \end{bmatrix} = A^{-1} \begin{bmatrix} U \\ V \end{bmatrix} = \begin{bmatrix} a_1 & a_2 \\ a_3 & a_4 \end{bmatrix} \begin{bmatrix} U \\ V \end{bmatrix} \tag{6.63}$$

In this case the expression for $|J|$ is simply the inverse of the absolute value of the determinant of A, so that from equation (6.56), the expression for the density of U and V becomes

$$f_{UV}(u, v) = f_{XY}[a_1u + a_2v, a_3u + a_4v)]|[\det(A)]|^{-1} \tag{6.64}$$

An important special case is the one in which X and Y have a joint Gaussian density. The resulting density function of U and V is also Gaussian, and we can derive it directly by finding the means, variances, and covariance of U and V rather than using equation (6.64). We shall illustrate this property with an example. We also shall use this approach for the generation of correlated Gaussian random variables for simulation purposes.

Example 6.6

Let X and Y be Gaussian random variables with means zero and variances 4 and 9, respectively, and correlation coefficient 0.25. We now define two new variables U and V as follows:

$$U = X + Y, \quad V = Y - X$$

We can find the inverse transformation easily as

$$X = 0.5U - 0.5V, \quad Y = 0.5U + 0.5V$$

We know that the density of X and Y is given as

$$f_{XY}(x, y) = \frac{\exp\left\{ -\dfrac{\left(\dfrac{x}{2}\right)^2 - 2 \times 0.25\left(\dfrac{x}{2}\right)\left(\dfrac{y}{3}\right) + \left(\dfrac{y}{3}\right)^2}{2(1 - 0.0625)} \right\}}{2\pi \times 2 \times 3\sqrt{1 - 0.0625}}$$

We can use this result together with equation (6.64) to obtain the density of U and V, also using the fact that the determinant of the transformation matrix is equal to 2:

$$f_{UV}(u, v)$$

$$= \frac{\exp\left\{-\dfrac{\left(\dfrac{0.5u - 0.5v}{2}\right)^2 - 2 \times 0.25\left(\dfrac{0.5u - 0.5v}{2}\right)\left(\dfrac{0.5u + 0.5v}{3}\right) + \left(\dfrac{0.5u + 0.5v}{3}\right)^2}{2(1 - 0.0625)}\right\}}{2\pi \times 2 \times 3\sqrt{1 - 0.0625}} \cdot \frac{1}{2}$$

We can show after tedious algebra that the density may be obtained directly by first finding the means and variances of U and V and their correlation coefficient, and then substituting into the general form of the joint Gaussian density. In this case we have zero means for both U and V, and their variances are given by:

$$\text{Var}(U) = E\{[X + Y]^2\} = 4 + 9 + 2 \times 2 \times 3 \times 0.25 = 16$$

$$\text{Var}(V) = E\{[Y - X]^2\} = 9 + 4 - 2 \times 2 \times 3 \times 0.25 = 10$$

$$\rho = \frac{E\{(X + Y)(Y - X)\}}{\sqrt{\text{Var}(U)\text{Var}(V)}} = \frac{9 - 4}{4\sqrt{10}} = \frac{\sqrt{10}}{8}$$

The density of U and V obtained directly is given as

$$f_{UV}(u, v) = \frac{\exp\left\{-\dfrac{\left(\dfrac{u}{4}\right)^2 - 2 \times \dfrac{\sqrt{10}}{8}\left(\dfrac{u}{4}\right)\left(\dfrac{v}{\sqrt{10}}\right) + \left(\dfrac{v}{\sqrt{10}}\right)^2}{2\left(1 - \dfrac{10}{64}\right)}\right\}}{2\pi \times 4\sqrt{10}\sqrt{1 - \dfrac{10}{64}}}$$

Both expressions can be shown to be identical. However, it is much easier to derive the density by using the means, variances, and correlation coefficients of U and V.

6.5.2 Generation of Correlated Gaussian Random Variables

The linear transformation can be useful in generating Gaussian random variables that are correlated. We first invoke the **randn** command in MATLAB twice to generate two vectors $X(i)$ and $Y(i)$, each having zero mean and unit variance and having dimension n. We thus obtain two sets of n Gaussian random numbers, which are uncorrelated. We now can convert these uncorrelated random numbers into correlated random numbers with means m_U and m_V, variances σ_U^2 and σ_V^2, and correlation coefficient ρ by the following linear transformation of the X and Y variables:

$$U(i) = m_U + \sigma_U X(i)$$

$$V(i) = m_V + \sigma_V\left[\rho X(i) + \sqrt{1 - \rho^2}Y(i)\right]$$

It is left as an exercise to check that the two variables U and V indeed have the appropriate means, variances, and correlation coefficient. It should be noted that such a transformation is not unique, and we may find others that yield the same parameters.

6.6 INTRODUCTION TO ESTIMATION

In Section 6.2, we discussed linear minimum mean-squared error (MMSE) estimation, when we wished to estimate the value of a variable from observed data. At that time we discussed only the use of linear estimates (i.e., the variable is estimated using a linear transformation of the observed data). We considered as an example the estimation of a signal amplitude from measurements that were corrupted by additive noise. In Section 5.6 we discussed conditional densities, which provide us with all the information we need about one variable if we know the value of another variable. The question is whether we can utilize such conditional densities to derive an estimate of one variable given that we observed the value of the other variable. The purpose of this section is first to describe the use of conditional densities for estimation in a more general framework and then to relate the results to the linear MMSE estimate we considered in Section 6.2. We shall end by applying the results to the case of estimating a signal amplitude when the measurements are corrupted by additive Gaussian noise.

6.6.1 Estimation Using the Conditional Density

Suppose we have two random variables, X and Y, and we wish to obtain information about X after we have observed the value of Y. Clearly, the conditional density of X given Y (obtained in equation (5.25) as in Bayes' rule for conditional probabilities) provides the most detailed information on X when we know the value of Y. It provides us with a density function of X for each value of Y that we observe. Suppose we start by knowing how Y depends on X (i.e., we assume that we know the conditional density of Y given X, $f_{Y|X}(v|u)$). Such a density may be obtained by calibrating our measurement device or instrument. We also know that the density of X is $f_X(u)$ when we do not have any observations. Let us elaborate on how we may come to know the conditional density of Y given X. Suppose X is a signal we are transmitting via a noisy environment. Before using the system, we start by sending signals that we know and observe the values received for Y. After performing many such experiments, we may obtain empirically the conditional density function of Y given X. If X is a voltage we are measuring with a voltmeter, and assuming that the voltmeter just adds measurement errors, we start by calibrating the voltmeter to obtain the density function of its measurement errors, and then, as we shall see later, we can derive the conditional density of Y given X. The next question one may ask is how to obtain the unconditional density function of X. We also call this density the *a-priori* density of X. In this case, we assume that we know how our signal is generated, and we can derive its density on the basis of either empirical experiments or by theoretical means. Now we can use the information so obtained to find information about the value of X when we use the system to estimate X after Y is observed. Once we know the conditional density of Y given X and the a-priori density function of X, we then use Bayes' rule for the continuous case to obtain the conditional density of X given Y as in equation (5.25):

$$f_{X|Y}(u|v) = \frac{f_{XY}(u, v)}{f_Y(v)} = \frac{f_{Y|X}(v|u)f_X(u)}{f_Y(v)} \tag{6.65a}$$

The denominator in equation (6.65a) is obtained by integrating the numerator over all values that X takes, namely,

$$f_Y(v) = \int_{-\infty}^{\infty} f_{XY}(u, v)\, du = \int_{-\infty}^{\infty} f_{Y|X}(v|u)f_X(u)\, du \tag{6.65b}$$

It should be noted that the two parts of equation (6.65) together form Bayes' rule for the continuous random variables case. Now that we have the conditional density function of X given the value of Y (it is also called the *a-posteriori* density of X), we can use it in several ways to obtain an estimate of the value of X, depending on the cost of making a wrong estimate. We shall discuss just two such cases.

Maximum A-Posteriori Probability (MAP) Estimate

Since the conditional density of X given Y provides us with information on what values of X are more probable or less probable for the particular value of Y, one way of estimating the value of X is to use the value that makes the conditional density the largest, meaning, the value of X that is most probable given a particular value of Y. In Figure 6.7, we illustrate the conditional density for a hypothetical case, plotting several densities for various values of Y. In each case we indicate the value of X that maximizes the value of the conditional density, and hence may be used as an estimate of X.

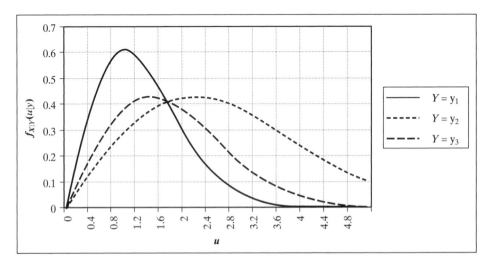

Figure 6.7   Conditional density of X given Y for three values of Y

We can see from the figure that for $Y = y_1$, the value of X that maximizes the conditional density is approximately 1.1. This means that our estimate of X (the most likely value of X) when $Y = y_1$ is $\hat{X} = 1.1$. Similarly, we can observe that the most probable value of X, for $Y = y_2$, is $\hat{X} = 2.1$, and for $Y = y_3$, is $\hat{X} = 1.4$. Of course, in a more general problem we would like to obtain some formula that relates our estimate to the observed value of Y.

It should be noted that the maximization of the conditional density with respect to the value of X is the same as the maximization of the numerator in equation (6.65a), since the denominator does not depend on the value of X. This obviously simplifies our problem, as we need not perform the integration in equation (6.65) to find the density of Y in order to substitute in the denominator. Since the conditional density of X given Y in such a case is called the ***a-posteriori*** probability density function of X, the resulting estimate is called the maximum a-posteriori probability (MAP) estimate.

MMSE Estimate

Another alternative to obtaining an estimate of X is to use the mean obtained from the conditional density. We know from the definition of the mean and variance that the mean obtained from a density function is the value that minimizes the spread (as defined by the variance or standard deviation of the random variable) of the density function. Since here we are dealing with a conditional density, we call such a mean a ***conditional mean*** and the resulting variance a ***conditional variance***. Also, the resulting mean minimizes the mean-squared error, since the variance of the estimate is indeed equal to the mean-squared error of the estimate. If we consider the densities given in Figure 6.7, in such a case we should compute the mean for each of the three densities to obtain the estimate of X. If these curves had the same shape and had a single maximum, but were also symmetric, then we know that the mean and the maximum value would have been identical. In the preceding illustration this is not the case, as is seen from the shape of the curves. In general we obtain the conditional mean by using the following expression:

$$\hat{X} = E\{X|Y = v\} = \int_{-\infty}^{\infty} u f_{X|Y}(u|v)\, du = \frac{\int_{-\infty}^{\infty} u f_{Y|X}(v|u) f_X(u)\, du}{f_Y(v)} \tag{6.66}$$

Here, we used equation (6.65) and we should use equation (6.65b) to substitute for the density of Y in the denominator of equation (6.66). The conditional variance, which provides a measure of the width of the spread of the resulting estimate, is obtained in the same manner as the variance of the conditional density:

$$\text{Var}\{X|Y = v\} = \int_{-\infty}^{\infty} (u - \hat{X})^2 f_{X|Y}(u|v)\, du = \int_{-\infty}^{\infty} u^2 f_{X|Y}(u|v)\, du - (\hat{X})^2 \tag{6.67}$$

We shall illustrate two examples using both approaches before relating the results to the linear MMSE estimates discussed in Section 6.2. It should be noted that the resulting estimates we have just discussed are in general nonlinear functions of the observations.

Example 6.7

Consider the case in which X and Y are jointly Gaussian, as given in equation (5.26). We need to find an estimate of X using the conditional mean approach and then compare it with the estimate obtained from the maximum of the conditional density (the MAP approach).

In this case we found the conditional density in equation (5.28), which has a conditional mean of

$$\hat{X} = E\{X|Y = v\} = m_X + \rho \frac{\sigma_X}{\sigma_Y}(v - m_Y) \tag{6.68}$$

This was derived in equation (5.29) with conditional variance as given in equation (5.30). If we try to find the maximum of the expression of the conditional density shown in equation (5.28), we obtain exactly the same result, since the Gaussian density has its maximum at the mean and is symmetric about the mean. In general, the position of the maximum of a density function and the position of the mean for that density are different. It is fortuitous that these positions are identical for the jointly Gaussian case. However, this is not the case in general.

Example 6.8

Consider the case in which the conditional density of X given Y has the following expression:

$$f_{X|Y}(u|Y = v) = \frac{u}{v^2} e^{-\frac{u^2}{2v^2}} \tag{6.69}$$

In this case, if we take the derivative of the conditional density and set it equal to zero to find the maximum, we obtain

$$0 = e^{-\frac{u^2}{2v^2}}\left(\frac{1}{Y^2} - \frac{u^2}{Y^4}\right)\Bigg|_{u=\hat{X}} \tag{6.70}$$

In equation (6.70), we substituted the random variable Y for the value it takes v, to emphasize the dependence of the estimate on the observed random variable Y. The maximum occurs at

$$\hat{X} = Y \tag{6.71}$$

If we now try to find the conditional mean of the density, we obtain as an estimate

$$\hat{X} = E\{X|Y\} = \int_0^\infty u \frac{u}{Y^2} e^{-\frac{u^2}{2Y^2}}\, du = \sqrt{\frac{\pi}{2}}Y = 1.25Y \tag{6.72}$$

We see that in this case the estimates are different.

We now compare what we obtained to the linear MMSE before we consider again our signal and additive noise example.

6.6.2 Estimation Using Linear MMSE

We discussed the linear MMSE in Section 6.2, where we wished to estimate the value of X from observation Y, but we wanted to use a linear estimate and we wished the expected value of the squared error to be the smallest. The estimator form was restricted to a straight line as given by equation (6.20), and we wished to minimize the MSE as given in equation (6.21). The resulting estimate becomes as it was in equation (6.25), which is shown again here:

$$\hat{X} = m_X + \rho_{XY}\frac{\sigma_X}{\sigma_Y}(Y - m_Y) \tag{6.73}$$

The resulting minimum value of the MSE was also obtained in equation (6.26) as shown here:

$$\text{MSE} = E\{[\hat{X} - X]^2\} = \text{Var}[\hat{X} - X] = \sigma_X^2(1 - \rho_{XY}^2) \tag{6.74}$$

It should be noted that for the linear MMSE estimator, we need only the information about the means, the variances, and the correlation coefficient between the variable we wish to estimate X and the observed variable Y. On the other hand, when we wish to use the conditional density (whether we use the conditional mean or the MAP estimate), we need to know the joint density of the two variables X and Y. In many cases, the information about the joint density may not be known or may be difficult to derive.

In general there is no direct relation between the two approaches to the estimation of X. However, when both X and Y are jointly Gaussian, as we saw in Example 6.7, the most probable estimate of X and the conditional mean estimate of X (which are equal) are given by equation (6.68). When we compare these estimates with the linear MMSE estimate of X, as was given in equation (6.73), we observe that the estimates are identical. We conclude that the two approaches yield identical results for the jointly Gaussian case. We therefore prefer to use the linear MMSE to derive the estimate in such a case, as it is simpler and does not require us to use the densities (joint or conditional). However, in the general case the two approaches yield different results.

6.6.3 Estimation of Signal from Additive Noise

We now reconsider the case we used in Section 6.2.2 of estimating the magnitude of a signal from additive noise, as shown in equation (6.27):

$$Y = X + N \tag{6.75}$$

At the time, we used only linear MMSE, and the resulting estimate was given by equation (6.31), and its MSE was given by equation (6.32).

Before comparing the result with the approaches described in this section, let us study this estimate briefly. We see that when the SNR is large (approaching infinity), we simply use the value of Y as the estimate:

$$\hat{X} = Y$$

The MSE in this case is also zero, as there is practically no noise. On the other hand, when the SNR is very small (approaching zero), the estimate is just the value of the mean of X, and the observation is ignored:

$$\hat{X} = m_X$$

In this case the MSE is equal to the variance of X, since we simply ignore the observations.

We now compare this result with the case in which we know the density functions of the signal and noise and we wish to use the conditional density for the estimation. If both the signal X and the noise N are Gaussian, we expect to obtain the same result as in equation (6.30). We shall assume that the noise is always Gaussian, with zero mean and variance σ_N^2, but we shall consider two cases for the signal density: the Gaussian case and a non-Gaussian case.

In this case the conditional density of Y given X is obtained by assuming that the value of X is known and obtaining the density of Y as a linear transformation of N:

$$f_{Y|X}(v|u) = f_N(v - u) = \frac{e^{\frac{(v-u)^2}{2\sigma_N^2}}}{\sigma_N \sqrt{2\pi}} \tag{6.76}$$

We now can find the conditional density of X given the observation Y by using equation (6.64) to obtain

$$f_{X|Y}(u|v) = \frac{f_{Y|X}(v|u)f_X(u)}{f_Y(v)} = \frac{f_X(u)e^{\frac{(v-u)^2}{2\sigma_N^2}}}{f_Y(v)\sigma_N \sqrt{2\pi}} \tag{6.77}$$

In order to obtain the estimate of X as the value that maximizes the conditional density of X, all we have to do is maximize the numerator of equation (6.77), since the denominator does not depend on the value taken by X. It is easier to maximize the logarithm of the numerator (so we do not have to deal with exponents all the time), since the logarithm is a monotonic function. Hence, the estimate $\hat{X}$ of X is obtained as the value of u that maximizes the expression

$$\max_u \left\{ \ln[f_X(u)] - \frac{(Y - u)^2}{2\sigma_N^2} \right\} \tag{6.78}$$

In the preceding expression, we substituted Y for the value it takes v, to make it clear that the estimate is indeed is a function of the observed value of Y.

Let us first consider the Gaussian case, in which X is Gaussian with mean m_X and variance σ_X^2. In this case the expression (6.78) becomes

$$\max_u \left\{ -\frac{(u - m_X)^2}{2\sigma_X^2} - \frac{(Y - u)^2}{2\sigma_N^2} \right\} \tag{6.79}$$

In the preceding expression, we ignored the constant that is part of the denominator of the Gaussian density of X, since it does not affect the maximization. If we now differentiate the expression (6.79) and equate to zero, we obtain

$$0 = -\frac{(u - m_X)}{\sigma_X^2} + \frac{(Y - u)}{\sigma_N^2} \bigg|_{u = \hat{X}} \tag{6.80}$$

It is left as an exercise to verify that the solution of equation (6.80) is exactly given by equation (6.30), as expected. This shows us again that for the jointly Gaussian case, both approaches yield the same answer; therefore we can rely on the linear MMSE approach, which is easier to derive.

Now we consider two examples in which X has a non-Gaussian density.

Example 6.9

In this case we assume that X has a Rayleigh density function:

$$f_X(u) = \frac{u \exp(-\frac{u^2}{2\alpha^2})}{\alpha^2}, \qquad u > 0 \tag{6.81}$$

If we substitute this density into the expression (6.78), we find that the estimate of X is the value of u that results by maximizing the expression

$$\max_u \left\{ \ln(u) - \frac{u^2}{2\alpha^2} - \frac{(Y - u)^2}{2\sigma_N^2} \right\} \tag{6.82}$$

Again, to find the value of u that maximizes the expression in equation (6.82) we differentiate and equate to zero:

$$0 = \frac{1}{u} - \frac{u}{\alpha^2} + \frac{(Y - u)}{\sigma_N^2} \bigg|_{u = \hat{X}} \tag{6.83}$$

The solution for the estimate is then found to be given by the solution of the following quadratic equation:

$$(\alpha^2 + \sigma_N^2)u^2 - \alpha^2 Y u - (\sigma_N \alpha)^2 \bigg|_{u = \hat{X}} = 0 \tag{6.84}$$

We can solve the equation, but we obtain a messy expression, which is given here just to show that we do not always obtain simple results:

$$\hat{X} = \frac{0.5Y}{[1 + (\sigma_N/\alpha)^2]} \left\{ 1 + \sqrt{1 + (2\sigma_N/Y)^2 [1 + (\sigma_N/\alpha)^2]} \right\} \tag{6.85}$$

It is difficult to visualize the solution in the general case, but when the noise variance is small the solution becomes

$$\hat{X} = Y$$

The answer is to be expected, since when the noise is low we just ignore the observation.

Example 6.8

In this example we assume that X has an exponential density function:

$$f_X(u) = \lambda e^{-\lambda u}, \qquad u > 0 \tag{6.86}$$

If we substitute the density into the expression (6.78) to find the estimate of X as the value of u that maximizes the expression, we have

$$\max_u \left\{ -\lambda u - \frac{(Y - u)^2}{2\sigma_N^2} \right\} \tag{6.87}$$

Again, we differentiate and equate to zero to obtain the value that yields the maximum:

$$0 = -\lambda + \left. \frac{(Y - u)}{\sigma_N^2} \right|_{u = \hat{X}} \tag{6.88}$$

After solving equation (6.88) for u, the resulting estimate becomes

$$\hat{X} = Y - \lambda \sigma_N^2 \tag{6.89}$$

The answer is valid as long as the result is positive, since X takes only positive values. It is left as an exercise to find the linear MMSE estimate for this case, because we know that the mean and standard deviation of X are both equal to $1/\lambda$. In this case we can show that the result is

$$\hat{X} = \frac{1}{(1 + \lambda^2 \sigma_N^2)} Y + \lambda \frac{\sigma_N^2}{(1 + \lambda^2 \sigma_N^2)} \tag{6.90}$$

The answers will be the same only when the noise variance tends to zero or λ tends to zero. The resulting minimum MSE for the linear estimation case becomes

$$\text{MSE} = \frac{\sigma_N^2}{1 + \lambda^2 \sigma_N^2} \tag{6.91}$$

Again we see that as the noise variance tends to zero, the MSE tends also to zero, while as the noise variance tends to infinity, the MSE tends to the variance of X, which is equal to $1/\lambda^2$.

In summary, the objective of this section was twofold. First, we wished to show that there is more than one approach to the estimation of signal properties from observed data. Second, we wished to demonstrate that the linear MMSE estimate is the simplest to derive and is equivalent to the MAP and conditional mean estimate for the jointly Gaussian case.

6.7 SUMMARY

Expectations of functions of two random variables:

$$E\{g(X, Y)\} = \sum_j \sum_i g(a_i, b_j)P\{X = a_i, Y = b_j\}, \text{ for discrete cases}$$

$$E\{g(X, Y)\} = \int_{-\infty}^{\infty} \int_{-\infty}^{\infty} g(u, v)f_{XY}(u, v) \, dudv, \text{ for continuous cases}$$

Properties:

Property 1: $E\{C\} = C$
Property 2: $E\{ag(X, Y)\} = aE\{g(X, Y)\}$
Property 3: $E\{g(X, Y) + h(X, Y)\} = E\{g(X, Y)\} + E\{h(X, Y)\}$
Property 4: If $g(X, Y) \geq 0$, then $E\{g(X, Y)\} \geq 0$.
Property 5: If X and Y are independent, then $E\{g(X)h(Y)\} = E\{g(X)\}E\{h(Y)\}$.

Correlation and covariance:

Correlation between X and Y: $R_{XY} = E\{X Y\}$
Covariance of X and Y: $\text{Cov}(X, Y) = C_{XY} = E\{(X - m_X)(Y - m_Y)\}$
$$= R_{XY} - m_X m_Y$$
Correlation Coefficient: $\rho_{XY} = C_{XY}/(\sigma_X\sigma_Y) - 1 \leq \rho_{XY} \leq 1$
If $\rho_{XY} = \pm1$, then X and Y are perfectly correlated.
If $\rho_{XY} = 0$, then X and Y are uncorrelated.

Linear approximation:

Estimating X from the values of Y: $\hat{X} = m_X + (\rho_{XY}\sigma_X/\sigma_Y)(Y - m_Y)$
Mean-Squared Error: $E\{[\hat{X} - X]^2\} = \sigma_X^2(1 - \rho_{XY}^2)$
Gaussian random variables:
    If X and Y are Gaussian and uncorrelated, then they are independent.
    The linear transformation of Gaussian random variables is also Gaussian.

Functions of two random variables:

$$Z = g(X, Y)$$
$$F_Z(w) = P\{g(X, Y) \leq w\}$$

Sums of two variables:

$$Z = X + Y, \text{ then } f_Z(w) = \int_{-\infty}^{\infty} f_{XY}(u, w - u) \, du.$$

If X and Y are independent: $f_Z(w) = \int_{-\infty}^{\infty} f_Y(w - u)f_X(u) \, du$

Mean and variance of a sum:

$$E\{Z\} = E\{X\} + E\{Y\}$$

$$\text{Var}(Z) = \text{Var}(X) + \text{Var}(Y) + 2\text{Cov}(X, Y)$$

For uncorrelated random variables: Variance of a sum is the sum of the variances.

Rayleigh density:

Z = Envelope of a sinusoidal signal, when each component is Gaussian:

$$f_Z(w) = \frac{w}{\sigma^2}\exp\left(-\frac{w^2}{2\sigma^2}\right)$$

Estimation:

Conditional density of X given Y:

$$f_{X|Y}(u|v) = \frac{f_{Y|X}(v|u)f_X(u)}{f_Y(v)}, f_Y(v) = \int_{-\infty}^{\infty} f_{Y|X}(v|u)f_X(u)\,du$$

Maximum a-posteriori probability (MAP) estimate of X given Y:

Maximize $f_{X|Y}(u|v)$ with respect to the value of $X = u$.

Minimum mean-squared-error estimate:

Find the mean of $f_{X|Y}(u|v)$.

Linear estimate:

Use the linear approximation.

For Gaussian random variables, all three estimates are identical.

6.8 PROBLEMS

MATLAB Problems:

1. Generate 5000 random numbers $\{X_i\}$ with normal (Gaussian) distribution with mean zero and unit standard deviation. Generate another 5000 numbers $\{Y_i\}$ with the same distribution. Now use the formula $Z_i = \sqrt{(X_i^2 + Y_i^2)}$ to obtain 5000 new random variables $\{Z\}$. Draw a histogram of $\{Z\}$ using a bin size of 0.1 and show that it is approximately a Rayleigh density. Plot the Rayleigh density obtained in the textbook to illustrate this fact.

2. Repeat Problem 1, but instead of $\{Z\}$, define a random variable $\{V\}$ such that $V_i = (Z_i)^2$. Plot a histogram of $\{V\}$ and compare it with the analytical exponential density function.

3. Generate 2000 random numbers $\{X_i\}$ with normal (Gaussian) distribution with mean zero and unit standard deviation. Generate another 2000 numbers $\{Y_i\}$ with the same

distribution. Use the linear transformation discussed in Section 6.5.2 to convert these random variables to two correlated Gaussian variables $\{U_i\}$ and $\{V_i\}$, such that the mean and variance of U are 1 and 4 and the mean and variance of V are -1 and 9. Consider two cases: one in which the correlation coefficient between U and V is 0.8 and the other in which the correlation coefficient is -0.8. Compute sample values of the parameters and compare them with the values you selected in generating the random variables. Plot scatter diagrams for the pairs $\{U_i, V_i\}$ that you generated in both cases.

4. Generate 5000 independent random variable pairs $\{U_i$ and $V_i\}$ having an exponential density function with parameter $\lambda = 2$. In order to simulate two random variables X and Y representing the time to first and second arrival in a Poisson problem, we use the following transformation from (U_i, V_i) to (X_i, Y_i): $X_i = U_i$ and $Y_i = U_i + V_i$. Generate the conditional densities of X given Y and Y given X, and compare with the mathematical model. Also compare the marginal densities, means, variances, and correlation coefficients with the mathematical results.

Regular Problems

5. Using another approach to the transformation of uncorrelated random variables to obtain a desired correlation coefficient ρ, we start with two uncorrelated random variables, X and Y, with zero means and unit variances. We wish to obtain two new random variables U and V with means μ_U and μ_V and standard deviations σ_U and σ_V, respectively, and correlation coefficient ρ. We first solve for an angle θ in the range $-0.5\pi < \theta < 0.5\pi$ satisfying the relation $\rho = \sin(\theta)$. Show that if we select U and V using the following relations, then they do have the means, variances, and correlation coefficients that we desired:

$$U = \mu_U + \sigma_U[X \sin(\theta/2) + Y \cos(\theta/2)]$$
$$V = \mu_V + \sigma_V[X \cos(\theta/2) + Y \sin(\theta/2)]$$

Next show that if we start with U and V with the same properties, then we can obtain uncorrelated variables X and Y using the inverse transformation:

$$X = [-\sin(\theta/2)(U - \mu_U)/\sigma_U + \cos(\theta/2)(V - \mu_V)/\sigma_V]/\cos(\theta)$$
$$Y = [\cos(\theta/2)(U - \mu_U)/\sigma_U - \sin(\theta/2)(V - \mu_V)/\sigma_V]/\cos(\theta)$$

Repeat MATLAB Problem 3 by using this transformation.

6. The following density function (which is zero outside the specified square below) is a joint probability density function of the random variables X and Y:

$$f_{XY}(u, v) = (u + v), \qquad \text{for } 0 < u < 1, 0 < v < 1,$$
$$\text{and it is zero elsewhere}$$

a. Are X and Y independent?

Find the expected values of the following functions $g(X,Y)$:

b. $g(X, Y) = X + Y$

c. $g(X, Y) = XY$

d. $g(X, Y) = (X + Y)^2$

e. $g(X, Y) = X^2 Y^2$

Find the correlation coefficient between X and Y.

7. The random variables X and Y are uniformly distributed in the following triangle (the density is zero outside the triangle):

$$f_{XY}(u, v) = 0.5, \qquad \text{for } 0 < u, 0 < v, \text{ and } 0 < u + v < 2,$$
$$\text{and it is zero elsewhere}$$

   a. Find the marginal density functions of X and Y.
   b. Are X and Y dependent?
   c. Find the joint distribution function of X and Y.
   Find the expected value of the following functions $g(X,Y)$:
   d. $g(X, Y) = XY$
   e. $g(X, Y) = \exp\{-(X + Y)\}$
   Find the correlation coefficient between X and Y.

8. The random variables X and Y have the following joint density function:

$$f_{XY}(u, v) = 1.5 \exp(-3v), \qquad \text{for } 0 < u < 2, \text{ and } 0 < v < \infty,$$
$$\text{and it is zero elsewhere.}$$

   a. Find the density function of their sum $Z = (X + Y)$.
   b. Find the mean and variance of their sum Z.
   c. Find the expected value of $g(X, Y) = \exp(-XY)$.

9.* Consider Problem 12 in Chapter 5. Find the means, variances, and correlation coefficient between X and Y. Find a linear MMSE estimate of Y from X and find its resulting MSE.

10.* A signal X whose value is a random variable uniformly distributed in the interval $[-a, +a]$ is observed in additive noise N, independent of X, whose density function is given as

$$f_N(v) = 0.5 \exp\{-|v|\}$$

The observation Y is defined by $Y = X + N$.

   a. Find the conditional density of Y given X, and then use Bayes' rule to find the conditional density of X given Y.
   b. Find the estimate of X from observation Y using the value that maximizes the conditional density.
   c. Find the conditional mean estimate of X from observation Y (i.e., find the mean of the density you obtained in part a).
   d. Find the MMSE linear estimate of X from Y.

11.* The arrival rate Λ of calls to a switch is unknown and is therefore assumed to be a random variable with density function

$$f_\Lambda(\lambda) = 0.5 \exp(-0.5\lambda), \text{ for } \lambda > 0.$$

We observe the time to the nth arrival of calls to this switch, and we denote it as a random variable T, which is assumed to have the following density function conditional on the value of Λ:

$$f_{T|\Lambda}(t|\lambda) = \{\lambda(\lambda t)^{n-1} \exp(-\lambda t)\}/(n - 1)!, \text{ for } t > 0$$

    a.   Use Bayes' rule to find the conditional density of the arrival rate Λ given the observation of the nth arrival time T.

    b.   Find the estimate of the arrival rate using the value that maximizes the conditional density.

    c.   Find the conditional mean estimate of the arrival rate.

12.* Assume that the time, Y, to nth arrival of messages to a switch has the following density function:

$$f_Y(y) = \{\lambda(\lambda y)^{n-1} \exp(-\lambda y)\}/(n-1)!, \text{ for } y > 0$$

Suppose the arrival time from the nth arrival to the $(n+1)$th arrival, which may be denoted as a random variable X, has an exponential density with the same parameter λ. Therefore, we can now define the time to $(n+1)$th arrival as a random variable $Z = X + Y$.

Find the density function of Z, and show that it is indeed the same as that of Y but with n replaced by $(n+1)$.

13.* Repeat Problem 17 in Chapter 4, assuming that the value of C is also a random variable uniformly distributed in the interval $10 \pm 5\%\ \mu F$. Assume also that the values of L and C are independent of each other.

14.* Consider Problem 13 and use MATLAB to generate 2000 random numbers representing the values of C and 2000 random numbers representing the values of L. Use the expression for the natural frequency and obtain the resulting natural frequency for each pairs of values of L and C. Plot the histogram and compare it with the one obtained in Problem 13.

7

Characteristic Function

7.1 INTRODUCTION

In previous chapters we considered random variables, their densities and distributions, as well as a variety of averages that allowed us to characterize the behavior of the random variables better and provide us with useful information about engineering problems. We note that in deriving the averages of random variables or functions of random variables, we defined them in terms of integrals using the density functions. While the definitions in terms of integrals over the density functions are simple, the task of carrying out the integration can be quite messy and would not always lead to closed-form results. In order to simplify many of the problems involved in deriving averages of random variables or their functions, we define the characteristic function of a random variable or its distribution. The characteristic function does not have any physical meaning, as do a variety of the averages we have dealt with (such as the mean and variance). It is simply a mathematically defined function that helps simplify the derivation of averages and of distributions of functions of random variables. It is also helpful in many proofs of results involving random variables.

We shall start by defining the characteristic function of a single random variable and deriving its properties. Then we follow that with the definition of the characteristic function of more than one random variable and its properties. Finally, we use the characteristic function to prove important properties about sums of random variables.

7.2 CHARACTERISTIC FUNCTION OF A SINGLE RANDOM VARIABLE

7.2.1 Basic Definitions

Definition: Given a random variable X with cumulative probability distribution function $F_X(u)$, we define the characteristic function $\Phi_X(v)$ of the random variable by the following expectation:

$$\Phi_X(v) = E\{\exp(jvX)\} \tag{7.1}$$

In equation (7.1) the j is the imaginary square root of -1, and v is a real variable. We therefore have to define what we mean by an expectation of a complex quantity. In order to do so we use the expression of the exponential function of imaginary variables:

$$\exp(jvX) = \cos(vX) + j\sin(vX) \tag{7.2}$$

Since the expression inside the expectation is a sum of two terms, we use the linearity property of the expectation to obtain

$$\Phi_X(v) = E\{\exp(jvX)\} = E\{\cos(vX)\} + j\,E\{\sin(vX)\} \tag{7.3}$$

We see therefore that it reduces to a sum of two real expectations, which we know how to deal with. However, in actually performing the expectation, it is easier to use the exponential expression directly.

Hence, the characteristic function is in general a complex function of the variable v, and its real and imaginary parts are shown in equation (7.3). It should be noted that the way equation (7.1) is to be evaluated depends on whether the random variable is discrete, continuous, or mixed, just as it is with any expectation. If the random variable is discrete, we evaluate the characteristic function by using the sum over all values taken by the random variable, weighted by the appropriate probabilities. If the random variable X has a probability mass function $P\{X = a_i\}$, for $i = 1, 2, \ldots, n$, then its characteristic function is derived by the expression

$$\Phi_X(v) = \sum_{i=1}^{n} e^{jva_i} P\{X = a_i\} \tag{7.4}$$

Similarly, when the random variable is continuous with a probability density function $f_X(u)$, then the characteristic function is derived by using the usual integral of the expectation:

$$\Phi_X(v) = \int_{-\infty}^{\infty} e^{jvu} f_X(u)\, du \tag{7.5}$$

Finally, for a mixed random variable we use a mixture of both expressions: We use the density over the continuous range of values taken by the random variable and use the summation for discrete values taken by the random variable. We could also use delta functions to represent mixed density functions.

Before we consider examples, we first need to show why we use the characteristic function at all. We first consider the properties of the characteristic function.

7.2.2 Properties of the Characteristic Function

The properties of the characteristic function can be derived from its definition by using the properties of expectations that we already considered.

> **Property 1:** $\Phi_X(0) = 1$ (7.6)

This property is obtained directly by using $v = 0$ in equation (7.1) and taking note of the fact that $\exp(0) = 1$. Hence the expectation is also equal to 1.

> **Property 2:** $|\Phi_X(v)| \le 1$ (7.7)

This property follows from the fact that $|\exp(jvX)| \le 1$, together with Property 4 of the expectation in Section 4.2.

Since the characteristic function is a Fourier transform of the density function (for continuous random variables), we can use the inverse Fourier transform to obtain the density function from the characteristic function. (See Appendix B for a short review of Fourier transform.) The problem of discrete or mixed random variables will not be addressed in this text, but we can show that the distribution function is uniquely obtained from the characteristic function in these cases as well. (We can use delta functions in such cases, but we must be very careful in carrying out the integrations involved.) We summarize the expression for the density function, as obtained from the characteristic function for continuous random variables, as Property 3:

> **Property 3:** For continuous random variables we have

$$f_X(u) = \frac{1}{2\pi} \int_{-\infty}^{\infty} \Phi_X(v)e^{-jvu} \, dv \qquad (7.8)$$

One key application of the characteristic function is its use in simplifying the derivation of densities of functions of random variables. We summarize this property in property 4.

> **Property 4:** If $Y = g(X)$, then the characteristic function of Y is obtained by the following expression:

$$\Phi_Y(v) = E\{\exp(jvY)\} = E\{\exp[jvg(X)]\} \qquad (7.9)$$

Equation (7.9) means that we do not need to find the probability density or mass function of Y, and we can perform the expectation in equation (7.9) directly from the distribution of X. For example, for continuous random variables the expression for the characteristic function of Y becomes

$$\Phi_Y(v) = \int_{-\infty}^{\infty} e^{jvg(u)} f_X(u) \, du \qquad (7.10)$$

As a matter of fact, equations (7.10) and (7.8) allow us to find the density function of Y without using the complicated method derived in Chapter 4, which can be tedious for non-monotonic functions. We shall illustrate this property with an example.

Example 7.1

Consider the manner in which we defined the Cauchy distributed random variable in Section 3.3.6 as shown in Figure 3.11. We have a pointer that spins in a semicircle, thus moving between the angles of $-\pi/2$ and $\pi/2$. We shall define the resulting angle as a random variable X, which is uniformly distributed in the range $[-\pi/2, \pi/2]$. We now place a screen a distance α away from the center of the semicircle and observe the point at which the continuation of the pointer hits the screen. We define that distance as Y. The relationship between X and Y is obtained from the figure as

$$Y = \alpha \tan(X) \tag{7.11}$$

We now can derive the characteristic function of the random variable Y directly by using equation (7.10) as follows:

$$\Phi_Y(v) = \int_{-\infty}^{\infty} e^{jv\alpha \tan(u)} f_X(u)\, du = \int_{-\pi/2}^{\pi/2} e^{jv\alpha \tan(u)} \frac{1}{\pi}\, du$$

We change the variable of integration $x = \tan(u)$, so that $dx = \{1 + [\tan(u)]^2\}du$, which results in

$$du = \frac{dx}{1 + x^2}$$

When the substitution is performed, we obtain

$$\Phi_Y(v) = \int_{-\infty}^{\infty} e^{jv\alpha x} \frac{1}{\pi(1 + x^2)}\, dx = \exp\{-\alpha|v|\} \tag{7.12}$$

The last expression follows from using tables of integrals or Fourier transforms. We can check and see that the characteristic function satisfies the first two properties we discussed previously. We may now use equation (7.8) to show that the density function is indeed the same one we derived in Chapter 3:

$$f_Y(u) = \frac{1}{2\pi} \int_{-\infty}^{\infty} e^{-\alpha|v|} e^{-jvu}\, dv = \frac{1}{2\pi} \int_{-\infty}^{0} e^{-jvu+\alpha v}\, dv + \frac{1}{2\pi} \int_{0}^{\infty} e^{-jvu-\alpha v}\, dv$$

$$= \frac{e^{(-ju+\alpha)v}}{2\pi(\alpha - ju)}\bigg|_{-\infty}^{0} + \frac{e^{(-ju-\alpha)v}}{2\pi(-\alpha - ju)}\bigg|_{0}^{\infty} = \frac{1}{2\pi(\alpha - ju)} + \frac{1}{2\pi(+\alpha + ju)}$$

$$= \frac{\alpha}{\pi(\alpha^2 + u^2)} \tag{7.13}$$

The result is identical to the Cauchy density function we derived in equation (3.31).

As a special case of a transformation of a random variable, let us consider a linear function of a random variable. Consider the random variable X, with characteristic function $\Phi_X(v)$. We now consider a random variable Y defined as

$$Y = aX + b \qquad (7.14)$$

Then, by using the linearity property of the expectation, we can show that the characteristic function of Y can be expressed as

$$\Phi_Y(v) = E\{\exp(jvY)\} = E\{\exp[jv(aX + b)]\} = E\{\exp(jvb)$$
$$\exp[j(va)X]\} = \exp(jvb)\,E\{\exp[j(va)X]\} = \exp(jbv)\Phi_X(av) \qquad (7.15)$$

We can summarize the result as Property 5.

Property 5: If

$$Y = aX + b, \text{ then } \Phi_Y(v) = \exp(jbv)\,\Phi_X(av) \qquad (7.16)$$

In particular, if we have a random variable with mean m and standard deviation σ and we wish to transform it to a random variable with the same density but having a mean of 0 and variance of 1, we may use the following linear transformation:

$$Y = \frac{(X - m)}{\sigma} \qquad (7.17)$$

The characteristic function of Y in this case becomes

$$\Phi_Y(v) = e^{-jmv/\sigma}\Phi_X\!\left(\frac{v}{\sigma}\right) \qquad (7.18)$$

Similarly, the relationship between X and Y can also be expressed in the opposite direction as

$$X = m + \sigma Y, \qquad \Phi_X(v) = e^{jmv}\Phi_Y(\sigma v) \qquad (7.19)$$

The next example illustrates the linear transformation.

Example 7.2

Let X be a uniformly distributed random variable in the range $[0, 1]$. First we wish to find the characteristic function of X. The density function is simply equal to 1 for all values between 0 and 1. Hence we have

$$\Phi_X(v) = \int_0^1 e^{jvu} f_X(u)\, du = \int_0^1 e^{jvu}\, du = \frac{e^{jv1} - e^{jv0}}{jv} = \frac{e^{jv} - 1}{jv}$$

$$= e^{jv/2}\frac{e^{jv/2} - e^{-jv/2}}{jv}$$

$$= e^{jv/2}\frac{j\sin(v/2) - [-j\sin(v/2)]}{jv} = e^{jv/2}\frac{\sin(v/2)}{(v/2)} = e^{jv/2}\,\mathrm{sinc}(v/2)$$

$$(7.20)$$

Note that we defined the function sinc(x) as

$$\text{sinc}(x) = \sin(x)/x$$

Its value at 0 is indeed equal to 1 if we use limit rules.

Now suppose we wish to find the characteristic function of a random variable Y that is uniformly distributed in the range $[a, b]$. We do not have to do additional work other than transform the random variable X using the transformation

$$Y = a + (b - a)X$$

From equation (7.16) the characteristic function of Y then becomes

$$\Phi_Y(v) = e^{jva}\Phi_X[v(b - a)] = e^{jva}\, e^{jv(b-a)/2} \text{sinc}[(b - a)v/2]$$
$$= e^{jv(b+a)/2} \text{sinc}[(b - a)v/2]$$

As a special case, consider a random variable uniformly distributed between -1 and $+1$, where we obtain the following expression for $a = -1$ and $b = +1$:

$$\Phi_Y(v) = \text{sinc}(v)$$

We now turn to the derivation of the moments of the distributions of random variables by using the characteristic function.

7.2.3 Derivation of Moments from the Characteristic Function

One of the primary uses of the characteristic function is the derivation of moments of distributions of random variables, without having to perform tedious integrations or summations. We have defined moments in equation (4.30) and central moments in equation (4.32). Now we shall show how the moments can be derived from the characteristic function. Let us start by using the definition (7.1) of the characteristic function and differentiating it once with respect to (jv). This means that, we differentiate with respect to v and divide by j. Since the expectation is linear and does not involve the variable v, we can interchange the expectation with the derivative to obtain

$$\frac{d}{d(jv)}\Phi_X(v) = \frac{d}{d(jv)}E\{e^{jvX}\} = E\left\{\frac{d}{d(jv)}e^{jvX}\right\} = E\{Xe^{jvX}\} \qquad (7.21)$$

The preceding expression is valid provided the resulting expectation exists, and we shall see the condition for such existence a little later. Now if, after taking the derivative, we substitute $v = 0$ in equation (7.21), then what we obtain on the right side of equation (7.21) is simply $E\{X\}$.

Hence we summarize the result as

$$m_X = E\{X\} = \frac{d}{d(jv)}\Phi_X(v)\big|_{v=0} \qquad (7.22)$$

Note that we must differentiate with respect to v before substituting $v = 0$ into equation (7.22). If the characteristic function is not differentiable at $v = 0$, then the corresponding expectation does not exist. We can generalize equation (7.22) to higher order moments by differentiating n times with respect to (jv) to obtain the following equation instead of equation (7.21):

$$\frac{d^n}{d(jv)^n}\Phi_X(v) = E\left\{\frac{d^n}{d(jv)^n}e^{jvX}\right\} = E\{X^n e^{jvX}\} \tag{7.23}$$

Hence, if we again evaluate the result at $v = 0$, we obtain the nth moment of X:

$$m_n = E\{X^n\} = \frac{d^n}{d(jv)^n}\Phi_X(v)\Big|_{v=0} \tag{7.24}$$

In order to obtain central moments (i.e., moments about the mean of the random variable), we use the characteristic equation after subtracting the mean of X (which we shall denote by just m) from X. This means that we could use the transformation discussed in the previous section to obtain the characteristic function of the variable $(X - m)$ as

$$e^{-jmv}\Phi_X(v)$$

We therefore use the preceding characteristic equation to evaluate the nth central moment in the same manner that we derive the nth moments from the original characteristic function. On the basis of equation (4.32), the result becomes

$$\mu_n = E\{[X - m]^n\} = \frac{d^n}{d(jv)^n}\{e^{-jmv}\Phi_X(v)\}\Big|_{v=0} \tag{7.25}$$

In particular, we have the following explicit expressions for the mean and variance:

$$m = \frac{d}{d(jv)}\Phi_X(v)\Big|_{v=0}$$

$$\sigma^2 = \frac{d^2}{d(jv)^2}\{e^{-jmv}\Phi_X(v)\}\Big|_{v=0} \tag{7.26}$$

We now consider the various examples of distributions and derive their characteristic functions and their means and variances. This will be helpful in the several cases for which the expressions for the means and variances were not derived in detail in Chapter 4.

7.2.4 Examples of Characteristic Functions

We shall consider most of the examples we discussed in Chapters 3 and 4 involving the various key distributions.

Binomial Random Variable

If X is a random variable with binomial distribution with parameters p and n, then the characteristic function is obtained from equation (7.4) as

$$\Phi_X(v) = \sum_{k=0}^{n} e^{jvk} P\{X = k\} = \sum_{k=0}^{n} e^{jvk} \binom{n}{k} p^k (1 - p)^{n-k}$$

$$= \sum_{k=0}^{n} \binom{n}{k} (pe^{jv})^k (1 - p)^{n-k}$$

We now use the binomial expansion formula for $(a + b)^n$ with $a = [p \exp(jv)]$ and $b = (1 - p)$, to obtain a closed-form expression for the characteristic function:

$$\Phi_X(v) = [pe^{jv} + 1 - p]^n = [p(e^{jv} - 1) + 1]^n \tag{7.27}$$

It is easy to see that at $v = 0$ we have, as expected, $\Phi_X(0) = 1$. For the case of $n = 1$, equation (7.27) is the characteristic function of the Bernoulli random variable. We now derive the mean by using equation (7.26):

$$m = \frac{d}{d(jv)} [p(e^{jv} - 1) + 1]^n \big|_{v=0} = n[p(e^{jv} - 1) + 1]^{n-1} pe^{jv} \big|_{v=0} = np \tag{7.28}$$

In this case the derivation of the variance is easier to perform by obtaining the regular second moment first, and then using the standard method of finding the variance:

$$E\{X^2\} = \frac{d^2}{d(jv)^2} \{[p(e^{jv} - 1) + 1]^n\} \big|_{v=0} = \frac{d}{d(jv)} \{npe^{jv} [p(e^{jv} - 1) + 1]^{n-1}\} \big|_{v=0}$$

$$= np\{(n - 1)pe^{jv}e^{jv}[p(e^{jv} - 1) + 1]^{n-2} + e^{jv}[p(e^{jv} - 1) + 1]^{n-1}\} \big|_{v=0}$$

$$= np\{(n - 1)p + 1\} = (np)^2 + np - np^2$$

The variance then becomes

$$\sigma^2 = E\{X^2\} - (np)^2 = np - np^2 = np(1 - p) \tag{7.29}$$

Geometric Random Variable

Let X be a geometric random variable with parameter p. Then the characteristic function is obtained directly from the definition as

$$\Phi_X(v) = \sum_{k=1}^{\infty} e^{jvk} P\{X = k\} = \sum_{k=1}^{\infty} e^{jvk} p(1 - p)^{k-1} = pe^{jv} \sum_{k=1}^{\infty} [e^{jv}(1 - p)]^{k-1}$$

We now use the formula for the sum of a geometric series to obtain

$$\Phi_X(v) = \frac{pe^{jv}}{1 - e^{jv}(1 - p)} = \frac{p}{e^{-jv} - (1 - p)} \tag{7.30}$$

Again we can verify that at $v = 0$ it takes the value 1. Next we find the mean by using equation (7.26) as follows:

$$m = \frac{d}{d(jv)}\left\{\frac{p}{e^{-jv} - (1 - p)}\right\}\bigg|_{v=0} = \frac{pe^{-jv}}{[e^{-jv} - (1 - p)]^2}\bigg|_{v=0}$$

$$= \frac{p}{[1 - (1 - p)]^2} = \frac{1}{p} \tag{7.31}$$

Here again it is easier to derive the second moment first before evaluating the variance:

$$E\{X^2\} = \frac{d}{d(jv)}\left\{\frac{pe^{-jv}}{[e^{-jv} - (1 - p)]^2}\right\}\bigg|_{v=0}$$

$$= \left\{\frac{2pe^{-2jv}}{[e^{-jv} - (1 - p)]^3} - \frac{pe^{-jv}}{[e^{-jv} - (1 - p)]^2}\right\}\bigg|_{v=0}$$

$$= \frac{2p}{p^3} - \frac{p}{p^2} = \frac{2}{p^2} - \frac{1}{p}$$

The expression for the variance is again obtained directly from the definition as

$$\sigma^2 = E\{X^2\} - \frac{1}{p^2} = \frac{1}{p^2} - \frac{1}{p} = \frac{1 - p}{p^2} \tag{7.32}$$

Poisson Random Variable

In this case we assume that X has a Poisson distribution with parameter α (which is related to the arrival rate λ and the time interval of interest t by $\alpha = \lambda t$). Again the basic definition of the characteristic function yields the equation

$$\Phi_X(v) = \sum_{k=0}^{\infty} e^{jvk}P\{X = k\} = \sum_{k=0}^{\infty} e^{jvk}\frac{\alpha^k}{k!}e^{-\alpha} = e^{-\alpha}\sum_{k=0}^{\infty}\frac{(\alpha e^{jv})^k}{k!} = e^{-\alpha}\exp(\alpha e^{jv})$$

$$= \exp[\alpha(e^{jv} - 1)] \tag{7.33}$$

We used the Taylor series expansion of the exponential function to obtain the answer in equation (7.33). Again, it is easy to verify its value at $v = 0$. Now we obtain the mean and variance as in the earlier examples:

$$m = \frac{d}{d(jv)} \exp[\alpha(e^{jv} - 1)]\big|_{v=0} = \alpha e^{jv} \exp[\alpha(e^{jv} - 1)]\big|_{v=0} = \alpha$$

$$E\{X^2\} = \frac{d}{d(jv)} \alpha \exp[\alpha(e^{jv} - 1) + jv]\big|_{v=0}$$

$$= \alpha(\alpha e^{jv} + 1) \exp[\alpha(e^{jv} - 1) + jv]\big|_{v=0} = \alpha(\alpha + 1) \qquad (7.34)$$

The variance then becomes

$$\sigma^2 = E\{X^2\} - \alpha^2 = \alpha \qquad (7.35)$$

Exponential Random Variable

The exponential random variable was derived to model a variety of interarrival times (such as failures, calls, messages, and packets, among others). In this case the arrival or failure rate is λ and the random variable X has the density function $f_X(u) = \lambda \exp(-\lambda u)$, for $u > 0$. The characteristic function then becomes

$$\Phi_X(v) = \int_0^\infty e^{jvu} f_X(u)\, du = \int_0^\infty e^{jvu} \lambda e^{-\lambda u}\, du = \frac{\lambda e^{(jv-\lambda)u}}{jv - \lambda}\bigg|_0^\infty = \frac{\lambda}{\lambda - jv} \qquad (7.36)$$

Again, it is easy to see that its value at $v = 0$ is indeed 1, and that it satisfies the other properties as well. We now can find the moments of this distribution by using the characteristic function. We use equation (7.24) to obtain

$$m_n = E\{X^n\} = \frac{d^n}{d(jv)^n} \frac{\lambda}{\lambda - jv}\bigg|_{v=0} = \frac{\lambda n!}{(\lambda - jv)^{n+1}}\bigg|_{v=0} = \frac{n!}{\lambda^n} \qquad (7.37)$$

The mean and variance can be obtained for $n = 1$ and $n = 2$ as

$$m = \frac{1}{\lambda}, \qquad m_2 = \frac{2}{\lambda^2}, \qquad \sigma^2 = E\{X^2\} - m^2 = \frac{1}{\lambda^2} \qquad (7.38)$$

Laplace Random Variable

This distribution was not discussed in the earlier chapters, but it is simply a double-sided exponential density, which is used to model noise signals that may have higher probability of taking large values (unlike the Gaussian density, whose tails decay very fast). The random variable X has the Laplace density function if its density is given by

$$f_X(u) = 0.5\alpha \exp(-\alpha|u|) \tag{7.39}$$

The characteristic function is given by

$$\Phi_X(v) = \int_{-\infty}^{\infty} e^{jvu} f_X(u)\, du = 0.5\int_{-\infty}^{0} e^{jvu}\alpha e^{\alpha u}\, du + 0.5\int_{0}^{\infty} e^{jvu}\alpha e^{-\alpha u}\, du$$

$$= \frac{\alpha e^{(jv+\alpha)u}}{2(jv+\alpha)}\Big|_{-\infty}^{0} + \frac{\alpha e^{(jv-\alpha)u}}{2(jv-\alpha)}\Big|_{0}^{\infty} = \frac{\alpha^2}{\alpha^2 + v^2} \tag{7.40}$$

The mean is obviously zero (as you can check directly), and the variance is therefore equal to the second moment and is obtained from

$$\sigma^2 = E\{X^2\} = \frac{d^2}{d(jv)^2}\frac{\alpha^2}{(\alpha^2 + v^2)}\Big|_{v=0} = \frac{2}{\alpha^2} \tag{7.41}$$

The last example of the characteristic function is also the most important one, since it involves the Gaussian random variable.

Gaussian Random Variable

In this case, the random variable X is assumed to have the Gaussian density function with mean m and variance σ^2. We first show the characteristic function for the unit Gaussian random variable Y, which has a mean of zero and a variance of 1. The characteristic function can be derived after complicated mathematical manipulations, so it will not be shown here, but is shown in Appendix A. The result for the unit Gaussian case is

$$\Phi_Y(v) = \int_{-\infty}^{\infty} e^{jvu}\frac{e^{-\frac{u^2}{2}}}{\sqrt{2\pi}}du = e^{-\frac{v^2}{2}} \tag{7.42}$$

You can check that by differentiating the characteristic function twice, you obtain, after the first derivative, a mean of zero, and after the second derivative, a variance of 1. Now we transform the unit random variable Y to obtain the random variable X, using the linear transformation given in equation (7.19), so that from equations (7.19) and (7.42), the characteristic function of X becomes

$$\Phi_X(v) = e^{jmv}\Phi_Y(\sigma v) = e^{jmv}e^{-\frac{\sigma^2 v^2}{2}} \tag{7.43}$$

It is interesting to note that the shape of the characteristic function for the Gaussian case, as a function of v, is the same shape as the density function itself when the mean is zero.

7.3 JOINT CHARACTERISTIC FUNCTION

7.3.1 Basic Definitions

When we have two random variables, their joint cumulative distribution and probability density functions are given by functions of two variables. Therefore, we define the joint characteristic function involving two random variables by using two complex variables as well. For simplicity we shall address the continuous case in this book to avoid complications. Given two random variables, X and Y with joint probability density function $f_{XY}(x, y)$, we define their joint characteristic function by the following expectation:

$$\Phi_{XY}(v, w) = E\{e^{j(vX+wY)}\} = \int_{-\infty}^{\infty} \int_{-\infty}^{\infty} e^{j(vx+wy)} f_{XY}(x, y)\, dx\, dy \quad (7.44)$$

It can be shown (beyond the scope of this text) that the characteristic function uniquely determines the density function using the following integral:

$$f_{XY}(x, y) = \frac{1}{4\pi^2} \int_{-\infty}^{\infty} \int_{-\infty}^{\infty} e^{-j(vx+wy)} \Phi_{XY}(v, w)\, dv\, dw \quad (7.45)$$

The characteristic function is most useful in obtaining moments of two random variables and deriving properties of functions of two random variables without actually finding the density function.

Properties of the Joint Characteristic Function

   Property 1: $\Phi_{XY}(0, 0) = 1$ $\qquad\qquad\qquad\qquad\qquad\qquad$ (7.46)

   Property 2: $\Phi_{XY}(v, 0) = \Phi_X(v), \qquad \Phi_{XY}(0, w) = \Phi_Y(w)$ $\qquad$ (7.47)

   Property 3: $|\Phi_{XY}(v, w)| \le 1$ $\qquad\qquad\qquad\qquad\qquad\qquad$ (7.48)

   Property 4: If X and Y are independent, then
$$\Phi_{XY}(v, w) = \Phi_X(v)\Phi_Y(w) \quad (7.49)$$

   Property 5: If we have two new random variables U and Z given as functions of X and Y, namely,
$$U = g(X, Y) \quad Z = h(X, Y) \quad (7.50)$$

then the characteristic function of U and Z is given directly as

$$\Phi_{UZ}(v, w) = E\{e^{j(vU+wZ)}\} = E\{e^{j[vg(X,Y)+wh(X,Y)]}\}$$

$$= \int_{-\infty}^{\infty} \int_{-\infty}^{\infty} e^{j[vg(x, y)+wh(x, y)]} f_{XY}(x, y)\, dx\, dy \quad (7.51)$$

What this property implies is that we do not need to find the density function of U and Z before finding their characteristic function. The special case of a linear function relating the two variables becomes even simpler for this property, and we shall derive it as Property 6.

Property 6: Let U and Z be given as the linear transformation of the two random variables X and Y as follows:

$$U = aX + bY + c, \quad Z = \alpha X + \beta Y + \gamma \tag{7.52}$$

Then the characteristic function of U and Z is given by

$$\begin{aligned}
\Phi_{UZ}(v, w) &= E\{e^{j(vU+wZ)}\} = E\{e^{j[v(aX+bY+c)+w(\alpha X+\beta Y+\gamma)]}\} \\
&= E\{e^{j[(av+\alpha w)X+(bv+\beta w)Y]}e^{j(cv+\gamma w)}\} \\
&= e^{j(cv+\gamma w)}E\{e^{j[(av+\alpha w)X+(bv+\beta w)Y]}\} \\
&= e^{j(cv+\gamma w)}\Phi_{XY}(av + \alpha w, bv + \beta w)
\end{aligned} \tag{7.53}$$

We now apply Property 6 to the Gaussian case. Suppose X and Y are independent unit Gaussian random variables, with zero means and unit variance. We now define U and V as in equation (7.52). Then, after using equation (7.42) for the unit Gaussian characteristic function, we have the following expression for the joint characteristic function of U and Z:

$$\begin{aligned}
\Phi_{UZ}(v, w) &= e^{j(cv+\gamma w)}\Phi_{XY}(av + \alpha w, bv + \beta w) \\
&= e^{j(cv+\gamma w)}\Phi_X(av + \alpha w)\Phi_Y(bv + \beta w) \\
&= e^{j(cv+\gamma w)}e^{-\frac{(av+\alpha w)^2}{2}}e^{-\frac{(bv+\beta w)^2}{2}} \\
&= e^{j(cv+\gamma w)}e^{-\frac{v^2(a^2+b^2)+2vw(a\alpha+b\beta)+w^2(\alpha^2+\beta^2)}{2}}
\end{aligned} \tag{7.54}$$

In order to relate the result to the means, variances, and covariance of U and Z, we derive these parameters first and then substitute into equation (7.54):

$$\begin{aligned}
m_U &= E\{U\} = E\{aX + bY + c\} = c \\
m_Z &= E\{Z\} = E\{\alpha X + \beta Y + \gamma\} = \gamma \\
\sigma_U^2 &= E\{[U - c]^2\} = E\{[aX + bY]^2\} = a^2 + b^2 \\
\sigma_Z^2 &= E\{[Z - \gamma]^2\} = E\{[\alpha X + \beta Y]^2\} = \alpha^2 + \beta^2 \\
C_{UZ} &= E\{(U - c)(Z - \gamma)\} = E\{[aX + bY][\alpha X + \beta Y]\} = a\alpha + b\beta
\end{aligned} \tag{7.55}$$

We can compare the parameters in equation (7.55) with those in equation (7.54) and note that we could write equation (7.54) for the joint characteristic function of the variables U and Z as

$$\Phi_{UZ}(v, w) = e^{j(m_U v + m_Z w)}\exp\left\{-\frac{v^2\sigma_U^2 + 2vwC_{UZ} + w^2\sigma_Z^2}{2}\right\} \tag{7.56}$$

It should be noted that equation (7.56) is indeed the joint characteristic function of two correlated Gaussian random variables whose parameters are given in equation (7.55). It has been presented indirectly by transforming independent Gaussian random variables, rather than trying to derive it from the definition involving the double integral.

We can summarize this property as Property 7.

Property 7: The joint characteristic function of two Gaussian random variables is given by equation (7.56).

7.3.2 Moments

As in the one random variable case, we can derive the moments directly from the characteristic function. In this case the moments involving just one random variable can be obtained by first setting the other variable in the characteristic function to zero and using the one random variable case. Hence, we shall discuss only joint moments here.

Suppose X and Y are two random variables with joint characteristic function $\Phi_{XY}(v, w)$. Then we can show that the joint $(m + n)$th moment of their distribution is given by

$$M_{mn} = E\{X^m Y^n\} = \frac{\partial^{m+n}}{\partial(jv)^m \partial(jw)^n} \Phi_{XY}(v, w)|_{v=0,w=0} \qquad (7.57)$$

The result can be shown in the same manner as was done for the one-dimensional case, by using the basic definition of the characteristic function and differentiating inside the expectation operation.

If we now wish to consider joint central moments after the means of X and Y have been subtracted first, we use the linear transformation in Property 6 to obtain

$$\mu_{mn} = E\{(X - m_X)^m (Y - m_Y)^n\}$$

$$= \frac{\partial^{m+n}}{\partial(jv)^m \partial(jw)^n} \{e^{-j(vm_X + wm_Y)} \Phi_{XY}(v, w)\}|_{v=0,w=0} \qquad (7.58)$$

If we wish to find the covariance between X and Y, we use the case $m = n = 1$ to obtain

$$C_{XY} = E\{(X - m_X)(Y - m_Y)\} = \frac{\partial^2}{\partial(jv)\partial(jw)} \{e^{-j(vm_X + wm_Y)} \Phi_{XY}(v, w)\}|_{v=0,w=0}$$

$$(7.59)$$

If we apply equation (7.59) to equation (7.56), the expression for the Gaussian case, we should indeed obtain the covariance that appears in the expression of the characteristic function, as expected.

Example 7.3

As an example, consider the two random variables X and Y representing the time to first arrival and the time to second arrival in a Poisson model. In this case the joint probability density function is obtained as in Example 6.3:

$$f_{XY}(x, y) = \lambda^2 \exp(-\lambda y), \qquad 0 < x < y < \infty \tag{7.60}$$

The joint characteristic function is obtained from the definition as follows;

$$\Phi_{XY}(v, w) = \int_0^\infty \int_x^\infty e^{j(vx+wy)} \lambda^2 e^{-\lambda y} \, dy \, dx = \int_0^\infty e^{jvx} \lambda^2 \frac{e^{-(\lambda-jw)x}}{\lambda - jw} dx$$

$$= \frac{\lambda^2}{[\lambda - j(v + w)](\lambda - jw)} \tag{7.61}$$

By setting $w = 0$ we obtain the characteristic function of the time to first arrival:

$$\Phi_X(v) = \frac{\lambda}{(\lambda - jv)} \tag{7.62}$$

That is indeed the characteristic function of the exponential density function. Now if we set $v = 0$, we obtain the characteristic function for the time to the second arrival:

$$\Phi_Y(w) = \frac{\lambda^2}{(\lambda - jw)^2} \tag{7.63}$$

This again can be verified by finding the characteristic function from the density function derived in Example 6.3.
We now find the moments of the joint random variables. We have already found the moments for the exponential random variable, so we shall just find the moments of Y and the covariance between X and Y:

$$m_Y = \frac{d}{d(jw)} \frac{\lambda^2}{(\lambda - jw)^2}\bigg|_{w=0} = \frac{2\lambda^2}{(\lambda - jw)^3}\bigg|_{w=0} = \frac{2}{\lambda}$$

$$E\{Y^2\} = \frac{d^2}{d(jw)^2} \frac{\lambda^2}{(\lambda - jw)^2}\bigg|_{w=0} = \frac{6\lambda^2}{(\lambda - jw)^4}\bigg|_{w=0} = \frac{6}{\lambda^2}$$

$$\sigma_Y^2 = E\{Y^2\} - m_Y^2 = \frac{2}{\lambda^2}$$

$$E\{XY\} = \frac{\partial^2}{\partial(jv)\partial(jw)} \frac{\lambda^2}{[\lambda - j(v + w)](\lambda - jw)}\bigg|_{v=0,w=0}$$

$$= \frac{\partial}{\partial(jw)} \frac{\lambda^2}{[\lambda - j(v + w)]^2(\lambda - jw)}\bigg|_{v=0,w=0}$$

$$= \frac{2\lambda^2}{[\lambda - j(v + w)]^3(\lambda - jw)}\bigg|_{v=0,w=0}$$

$$+ \left.\frac{\lambda^2}{[\lambda - j(v + w)]^2(\lambda - jw)^2}\right|_{v=0,w=0} = \frac{3}{\lambda^2}$$

$$C_{XY} = E\{XY\} - m_X m_Y = \frac{1}{\lambda^2}$$

The resulting correlation coefficient is 0.707. You can verify that all the results agree with those derived in Example 6.3.

7.4 SUMS OF RANDOM VARIABLES

The characteristic function is a very powerful tool that helps find properties of sums of random variables. We have observed the linear transformation in equations (7.52) and (7.53) that allowed us to find the joint characteristic function of the new variables after linear transformation. Here we shall discuss the general problem of the distribution of a sum of two random variables. In Chapter 8 we shall generalize the results to more than two random variables.

Given two random variables X and Y with a known joint characteristic function $\Phi_{XY}(v, w)$, we are interested in finding the properties of the sum of these two variables:

$$Z = X + Y \tag{7.64}$$

First we find the characteristic function of Z using the definition directly:

$$\Phi_Z(v) = E\{e^{jvZ}\} = E\{e^{jv(X+Y)}\} = \Phi_{XY}(v, v) \tag{7.65}$$

In particular, if the two random variables are independent, then if we use equation (7.49), the expression for the characteristic function of the sum Z becomes

$$\Phi_Z(v) = \Phi_X(v)\Phi_Y(v) \tag{7.66}$$

The result for the characteristic function is much simpler than the one in Chapter 6 using the density function, since the earlier function involved a complicated convolution integral.

Example 7.4

Consider two jointly Gaussian random variables X and Y with means m_X and m_Y, variances σ_X^2 and σ_Y^2, and covariance C_{XY}. We shall use equation (7.65) to find the characteristic function of their sum $Z = X + Y$. We know from equation (7.56) that the joint characteristic function of X and Y is given by

$$\Phi_{XY}(v, w) = e^{j(m_X v + m_Y w)} e^{-\frac{v^2\sigma_X^2 + 2vwC_{XY} + w^2\sigma_Y^2}{2}} \tag{7.67}$$

Now we use equation (7.65) to obtain for the characteristic function of Z:

$$\Phi_Z(v) = e^{j(m_X v + m_Y v)} \exp\left\{-\frac{v^2\sigma_X^2 + 2vC_{XY} + v^2\sigma_Y^2}{2}\right\} = e^{j(m_X + m_Y)v} \exp\left\{-\frac{v^2(\sigma_X^2 + 2C_{XY} + \sigma_Y^2)}{2}\right\}$$

$$= e^{jm_Z v} e^{-\frac{v^2\sigma_Z^2}{2}} \tag{7.68}$$

The resulting characteristic function is indeed a Gaussian one corresponding to the mean and variance of Z, as was obtained in Chapter 6 in equations (6.18) and (6.19).

Example 7.5

Let us consider the Poisson arrival problem again from a different perspective. Assume that X is the time to the first arrival, and let Y be the time between the first and second arrival. We also define Z as the time to the second arrival, so that $Z = X + Y$. We know from our definition of the problem that X and Y have identical exponential density functions and that they are independent, so that we have

$$f_X(u) = f_Y(u) = \lambda e^{-\lambda u}, \quad \text{for } u > 0 \tag{7.69}$$

The characteristic functions of X and Y are also the same and are given by

$$\Phi_X(v) = \Phi_Y(v) = \frac{\lambda}{(\lambda - jv)} \tag{7.70}$$

Since they are independent, we may use equation (7.66) to obtain the characteristic function of the sum Z:

$$\Phi_Z(v) = \frac{\lambda^2}{(\lambda - jv)^2} \tag{7.71}$$

This is obviously the same expression we obtained in equation (7.63) for the time to the second arrival, since by adding X and Y here, the new random variable Z is indeed the time to the second arrival.

Example 7.6

Let us consider the case of adding two uniformly distributed random variables, such as the combining in series of two resistors with uniform density in the range $(9, 11)$ that we considered in earlier chapters. We consider a more general case here by using two random variables X and Y that are independent and have identical uniform density function in the interval $(-a, +a)$. If we wish later to have random variables with nonzero means, we can use the property of the effect of the mean on the characteristic function. In this case we have

$$f_X(u) = f_Y(u) = \frac{1}{2a}, \quad \text{for } -a < u < a \tag{7.72}$$

The characteristic function of X and Y is then obtained as in equation (7.20):

$$\Phi_X(v) = \Phi_Y(v) = \int_{-a}^{a} e^{jvu} \frac{1}{2a} du = \frac{\sin(av)}{av} = \text{sinc}(av) \tag{7.73}$$

We now find the characteristic function of $Z = X + Y$ by using equation (7.66):

$$\Phi_Z(v) = [\text{sinc}(av)]^2 \tag{7.74}$$

If, on the other hand, the density of X and Y were uniformly distributed in the interval $(m - a, m + a)$, then all we would have to do is multiply the characteristic function of each by $\exp(jvm)$ so that the characteristic function of Z becomes

$$\Phi_Z(v) = \exp(j2vm)[\mathrm{sinc}(av)]^2 \tag{7.74}$$

The inverse transform may be obtained from Fourier transform tables as the density function of Z:

$$f_Z(u) = \frac{1}{2a}\left\{1 - \frac{|u - 2m|}{2a}\right\}, \qquad \text{for } |u - 2m| < 2a \tag{7.75}$$

This is the triangular density function discussed in earlier chapters.

We shall discuss more general cases of sums of multiple random variables by using the characteristic functions, rather than the density function in the next chapter.

7.5 SUMMARY

Definition and properties of the characteristic function:

$$\Phi_X(v) = E\{\exp(jvX)\}$$

Property 1: $\Phi_X(0) = 1$

Property 2: $|\Phi_X(v)| \le 1$

Property 3: For continuous random variables, $f_X(u) = \dfrac{1}{2\pi}\displaystyle\int_{-\infty}^{\infty} \Phi_X(v)e^{-jvu}\, dv$

Property 4: If $Y = g(X)$, then $\Phi_Y(v) = E\{\exp(jvY)\} = E\{\exp[jvg(X)]\}$.

Property 5: If $Y = aX + b$, then $\Phi_Y(v) = \exp(jbv)\Phi_X(av)$.

Moments:

$$m_n = E\{X^n\} = \frac{d^n}{d(jv)^n}\Phi_X(v)\Big|_{v=0}$$

Joint characteristic function:

$$\Phi_{XY}(v, w) = E\{e^{j(vX+wY)}\} = \int_{-\infty}^{\infty}\int_{-\infty}^{\infty} e^{j(vx+wy)}f_{XY}(x, y)\, dx\, dy$$

$$f_{XY}(x, y) = \frac{1}{4\pi^2}\int_{-\infty}^{\infty}\int_{-\infty}^{\infty} e^{-j(vx+wy)}\Phi_{XY}(v, w)\, dv\, dw$$

Property 1: $\Phi_{XY}(0, 0) = 1$

Property 2: $\Phi_{XY}(v, 0) = \Phi_X(v), \qquad \Phi_{XY}(0, w) = \Phi_Y(w)$

Property 3: $|\Phi_{XY}(v, w)| \le 1$

Property 4: If X and Y are independent, then $\Phi_{XY}(v, w) = \Phi_X(v)\Phi_Y(w)$.

Property 5: If $U = g(X, Y)\quad Z = h(X, Y)$, then

$$\Phi_{UZ}(v, w) = E\{e^{j(vU+wZ)}\} = E\{e^{j[vg(X,Y)+wh(X,Y)]}\}.$$

Property 6: If $U = aX + bY + c$, $Z = \alpha X + \beta Y + \gamma$, then

$$\Phi_{UZ}(v, w) = e^{j(cv + \gamma w)}\Phi_{XY}(av + \alpha w, bv + \beta w).$$

Moments:

$$M_{mn} = E\{X^m Y^n\} = \frac{\partial^{m+n}}{\partial(jv)^m \partial(jw)^n}\Phi_{XY}(v, w)\big|_{v=0, \; w=0}$$

Gaussian random variables:

$$\Phi_{XY}(v, w) = e^{j(m_X v + m_Y w)}e^{-\frac{v^2\sigma_x^2 + 2vwC_{XY} + w^2\sigma_y^2}{2}}$$

Sum of independent random variables:

If $Z = X + Y$, and X and Y are independent, then $\Phi_Z(v) = \Phi_X(v)\Phi_Y(v)$

7.6 PROBLEMS

1. Let X and Y be independent random variables with Cauchy distributions having parameters α and β, respectively. Use the characteristic function to find the density of their sum Z.

2. Let X have a uniform distribution in the interval $[a, b]$ and let Y have a triangular density function in the interval $[2a, 2b]$. If X and Y are independent, find the characteristic function of their sum Z. Use the characteristic function to find the mean and variance of Z.

3. The interarrival times of a Poisson arrival process are independent and exponentially distributed, with parameter λ. Let X_1 and X_2 be the first and second interarrival times. Let Y be the time to second arrival, so that $Y = X_1 + X_2$. Find the characteristic function and density of Y.

4. Let X and Y be jointly Gaussian random variables with means m_X and m_Y, standard deviations σ_X and σ_Y, and correlation coefficient ρ. Define new random variables U_1 and U_2 by the transformation

    $$U_1 = (X - m_X)/\sigma_X + (Y - m_Y)/\sigma_Y \text{ and } U_2 = (X - m_X)/\sigma_X - (Y - m_Y)/\sigma_Y$$

    Use the characteristic function to show that U_1 and U_2 are Gaussian with zero means and zero correlation coefficient. How would you modify the transformation to obtain two new independent Gaussian random variables V_1 and V_2 with zero means and unit variances?

5. Use the result of Problem 4 to obtain a transformation from unit Gaussian variables V_1 and V_2 to generate two arbitrary Gaussian random variables X and Y with properties as in Problem 4.

6. Use the characteristic function of the binomial distribution to show that as n becomes large, it approaches the Gaussian distribution.

7. Use the characteristic function of the Poisson random variable with arrival rate λ to show that it also tends to Gaussian as the time interval in question T becomes large.

8

Multiple Random Variables

8.1 INTRODUCTION

When dealing with two or more random variables, the problems involving densities and distribution functions become very complicated and rather unwieldy mathematically. Hence, in many of these cases we have to rely on expectations on the one hand, involving means, variances, and correlation. On the other hand, we can do more if we assume that the random variables are independent. We shall consider these two cases, discuss some limits involving them, and consider two major applications in the next three chapters: applications to statistics (including inference), hypothesis testing, and applications to reliability.

Since we are dealing with simplified cases, we shall concentrate only on a few applications involving functions of multiple random variables. We shall first consider simple functions, such as the sum of multiple random variables, and then address the cases of other functions of interest. However, we shall start with a brief introduction to the more general way of handling multiple random variables. The general approach will concentrate on a brief description of how to characterize the statistical properties of more than two random variables, as we shall see in the next section.

8.2 DISTRIBUTIONS AND DENSITIES OF MULTIPLE RANDOM VARIABLES

Several random variables occur in many problems, such as in a system with multiple components whose properties (e.g., lifetime, resistance, capacitance, or inductance) are modeled as random variables. We may also consider currents, voltages, or power in various branches of these circuits or systems, to be modeled as random variables. If we take 10 measurements of an unknown quantity such as voltage or current, we may assume that the errors in each measurement are modeled as a different random variable, since we may have 10 different values. We have already defined what a random variable is, namely a transformation from the sample space to the real line. In the same manner, we have defined two random variables as two such transformations. However, mathematical difficulties occurred when we tried to find the probability that these two random variables take values together. That led us to the definition of the two-dimensional distribution and density functions. Obviously, we can generalize this definition to multiple random variables, and we can then speak of n-dimensional distribution and density functions, except that such functions are quite complex to work with. The difficulty stems from the fact that we cannot clearly visualize the values in n-dimensional space that the n random variables may take. As we shall see in the following sections of this chapter, the definitions provided here are strictly for completeness of the coverage of the topic, and in practice we shall not do too much involving n-dimensional distribution and density functions.

8.2.1 Distributions and Densities

Given n random variables $X_1, X_2, \ldots, X_n$, which are defined in the usual manners as assignments of n real numbers to every outcome in a sample space, we define their cumulative probability distribution function by the following expression:

$$F_{X_1, X_2, \ldots X_n}(a_1, a_2, \ldots, a_n) = P\{X_1 \le a_1, X_2 \le a_2, \ldots, X_n \le a_n\} \quad (8.1)$$

Here the variables $a_1, a_2, \ldots, a_n$, can take as values any real number. For continuous random variables, instead of dealing with the distribution function, we prefer to deal with the probability density function, which for the n random variables case is defined as

$$f_{X_1, X_2, \ldots X_n}(a_1, a_2, \ldots, a_n) = \frac{\partial^n F_{X_1 X_2 \ldots X_n}(a_1, a_2, \ldots, a_n)}{\partial a_1 \partial a_2 \ldots \partial a_n} \quad (8.2)$$

We see that the definition is exactly analogous to the two-dimensional case, except that it is not easy to visualize. We can provide an interpretation of the density function, relating it to the probability that the random variables take values in a small n-dimensional cube around a point in the n-dimensional space:

$$P\{a_1 < X_1 \le a_1 + \Delta_1, a_2 < X_2 \le a_2 + \Delta_2, \ldots, a_n < X_n \le a_n + \Delta_n\}$$
$$\approx f_{X_1, X_2, \ldots X_n}(a_1, a_2, \ldots, a_n)\,\Delta_1 \Delta_2 \ldots \Delta_n \quad (8.3)$$

Finally, we present the relation between the probability that the random variables take values in a region A of the n-dimensional space and the probability density function, which is the n-fold integral of the density function over the region in question:

$$P\{(X_1, X_2, \ldots, X_n) \in A\} = \iiint_A f_{X_1 X_2 \ldots X_n}(x_1, x_2, \ldots, x_n)\, dx_1 dx_2 \ldots dx_n \qquad (8.4)$$

In particular, if the region involved is an n-dimensional cube, then the expression is simply the integral of the density function with limits given by the lower and upper values defining the cube:

$$P\{a_1 < X_1 \leq b_1, a_2 < X_2 \leq b_2, \ldots, a_n < X_n \leq b_n\}$$
$$= \int_{a_n}^{b_n} \cdots \int_{a_2}^{b_2} \int_{a_1}^{b_1} f_{X_1 X_2 \ldots X_n}(x_1, x_2, \ldots, x_n)\, dx_1 dx_2 \ldots dx_n \qquad (8.5)$$

Any nth dimensional probability density function has to satisfy the following rules, which follow directly from the case of one and two random variables:

$$\int_{-\infty}^{\infty} \int_{-\infty}^{\infty} \cdots \int_{-\infty}^{\infty} f_{X_1 X_2 \ldots X_n}(x_1, x_2, \ldots, x_n)\, dx_1 dx_2 \ldots dx_n = 1 \qquad (8.6)$$

$$f_{X_1 X_2 \ldots X_n}(x_1, x_2, \ldots x_n) \geq 0 \qquad (8.7)$$

For example, if we have three random variables X, Y, and Z that are uniformly distributed in a region

$$0 < X < a, 0 < Y < b, \text{ and } 0 < Z < c,$$

then the joint three-dimensional density function has the value $1/(abc)$ in the region described above, and is zero outside that region:

$$f_{X, Y, Z}(u, v, w) = 1/(abc), \qquad \text{for } 0 < u < a, 0 < v < b, 0 < w < c$$

The general definitions of the distributions and densities are provided here only for completeness, and we shall move on to the case that is more manageable: that of independent random variables.

8.2.2 Independent Random Variables

Since independence of events is defined by the fact that the probabilities involving these events jointly are the product of the individual probabilities, we can apply that definition to the case of n random variables. The random variables $X_1, X_2, \ldots, X_n$ are independent if the probability that they take values in any arbitrary intervals is given by the product of the individual probabilities:

$$P\{a_1 < X_1 \leq b_1, a_2 < X_2 \leq b_2, \ldots, a_n < X_n \leq b_n\}$$
$$= P\{a_1 < X_1 \leq b_1\} P\{a_2 < X_2 \leq b_2\} \ldots P\{a_n < X_n \leq b_n\} \qquad (8.8)$$

It follows therefore that n random variables are independent if and only if their distribution function is the product of the individual distribution functions. This property extends to the probability density function as well, in view of the relation between distributions and densities. We can therefore state that n random variables are independent if and only if their joint density function is the product of the individual density functions:

$$f_{X_1 X_2 \ldots X_n}(x_1, x_2, \ldots x_n) = f_{X_1}(x_1) f_{X_2}(x_2) \ldots f_{X_n}(x_n) \qquad (8.9)$$

Example 8.1

Consider two cases in which three random variables are uniformly distributed in a region of the three-dimensional space, where in one case the region is a cube, and in the other case the region is a cylinder. Are the three random variables independent in both cases?

Case a: We have three random variables $X, Y,$ and $Z,$ and they are uniformly distributed in a cubic region as follows:

$$0 < X, Y, Z < 2$$

Clearly the density function is just 1/8 in the region defined by the cube and zero outside, since the volume of the cube is 8. If we wish to find the density function of each random variable individually, we have to integrate the other two variables out. This means that the density function of each variable is $\frac{1}{2}$ in the interval $[0, 2]$, and we therefore see that the three-dimensional density function is just the product of the three individual densities.

Case b: We have three random variables $X, Y,$ and Z and they are uniformly distributed in the cylinder defined by

$$(X^2 + Y^2) < 1, \text{ and } 0 < Z < 2$$

The volume of the cylinder is 2π, so that the density function of the three variables is given by

$$f_{XYZ}(u, v, w) = \frac{1}{2\pi}, \text{ for } (u^2 + v^2) < 1, \text{ and } 0 < w < 2$$

If we now try to find the density function of Z, we do so by integrating the values that X and Y take (possibly having to use polar coordinates to do the integration) and find that the density of Z is uniform in the interval $[0, 2]$ and is zero outside the interval. However, if we wish to find the density of X or Y, we have to integrate the values taken by Z and Y or Z and X, respectively. In this case, when we integrate over the values that X or Y takes, the limits of the integral depend on the value of the variable whose density we wish to find. In this manner, the density of X becomes

$$f_X(u) = \int_0^2 \int_{-\sqrt{1-u^2}}^{\sqrt{1-u^2}} \frac{1}{2\pi} dy\, dz = \frac{2\sqrt{1-u^2}}{\pi}, \text{ for } -1 < u < 1$$

We obtain a similar expression for the density of Y; hence the three-dimensional density function does not reduce to the product of the individual densities of each random variable. We conclude from this case that X, Y, and Z are not independent. Now, if instead of X, Y, and Z, we used three random variables representing the radius R and the angle Θ of a point inside the cylinder and its height Z, we can easily see that the distribution of these three attributes of a point in the cylinder is the product of the individual distribution. In this case, for the density of these three variables, we have

$$f_{R\Theta Z}(r, \theta, z) = \frac{1}{4\pi}, \text{ for } 0 < r < 1, 0 < \theta < 2\pi, \text{ and } 0 < z < 2$$

It can be verified that it is indeed the product of the individual densities of the three random variables.

We can utilize the joint density function of multiple random variables to find the probability that they take values in some region. We can also use it to obtain the density or distribution of functions of the random variables. In the next section, we shall address the problem of functions of multiple random variables. Here, we shall illustrate the case of deriving the probability that the random variables take values in a region of interest.

Example 8.2

Consider three components that fail independently of each other, and assume that the lifetime density of each component is exponential but that they have different parameters. Let the random variables X, Y, and Z represent the lifetimes of the three components. Let the individual densities of these random variables be given by

$$f_X(u) = \exp(-u), \quad \text{for } u > 0, \quad f_Y(v) = 2\exp(-2v), \quad \text{for } v > 0,$$
$$f_Z(w) = 3\exp(-3w), \quad \text{for } w > 0$$

Since they are independent, the three-dimensional density of the three random variables is given by the product of the individual densities:

$$f_{XYZ}(u, v, w) = 6\exp(-u - 2v - 3w), \text{ for } 0 < u, v, w$$

We wish to find the probability that the third component fails first, then the second component, and then the first component. Mathematically, we wish to find the probability that Z is less than Y and that Y is less than X. The event so described is $\{Z < Y < X\}$, and its probability can be found by integrating the density function. First we integrate the values taken by Z from 0 to v, where v represents the values taken by Y. Then we integrate the values taken by Y from 0 to u, where u represents the values taken by X. Finally we integrate X over all possible values from zero to infinity:

$$P\{Z < Y < X\} = \int_0^\infty \int_0^u \int_0^v f_{XYZ}(u, v, w)\, dw\, dv\, du$$

$$= \int_0^\infty \int_0^u \int_0^v 6e^{-(u+2v+3w)}\, dw\, dv\, du$$

$$= \int_0^\infty \int_0^u 2e^{-(u+2v)}(1 - e^{-3v})\, dv\, du = \int_0^\infty e^{-u}[(1 - e^{-2u}) - 0.4(1 - e^{-5u})]\, du$$

$$= 1 - (1/3) - 0.4(1 - 1/6) = (1/3)$$

If the density functions of the individual random variables were identical, the result would have been (1/4). It is left as an exercise to verify that this is indeed the correct result.

Similarly, for the preceding case, we can find the probability that $\{X < Y < Z\}$ is equal to 0.067. The result is intuitively satisfying since the average lifetimes of the three components are 1 for the X variable, 0.5 for the Y variable, and 1/3 for the Z variable. So it is more likely that Z will fail first and X will fail last.

In the sequel, we shall consider the case of Gaussian random variables as well. In the following sections, we shall consider functions of multiple random variables, and we start with the simple function of a sum.

8.3 SUMS OF RANDOM VARIABLES

8.3.1 Probability Density Function of a Sum

When do we encounter sums involving several random variables? Such a case occurs whenever we wish to estimate some value and our measurements are noisy. What we do in such a case is take several measurements, add them, and divide by the number of measurements. Our objective is to eventually show why such an approach works. In addition, we shall address the issue of the resulting accuracy of such an approach based on the number of measurements. Here we shall just discuss the probability density function of a sum of multiple random variables, and some of its properties.

We considered the sum of two independent random variables in Chapter 6. We shall extend the result here to two random variables that are not independent and then to more than two random variables. In this case we have two random variables X and Y with a known joint density function $f_{X,Y}(u, v)$. We are considering the new random variable Z defined as

$$Z = X + Y \tag{8.10}$$

We derive the density of the sum directly by using the definition of the distribution function. In this case we want to find the probability that the sum is less than an arbitrary value we denote by w:

$$F_Z(w) = P\{Z \leq w\} = P\{X + Y \leq w\} \tag{8.11}$$

The probability defined in equation (8.11) is the volume under the joint density function of X and Y, bounded by the area in the X–Y plane shown cross-hatched in Figure 8.1. The area over which the density needs to be integrated is cross-hatched in the figure (both vertical and horizontal cross-hatching). The distribution function is obtained as follows:

$$F_Z(w) = P\{X + Y \leq w\} = \int_{-\infty}^{\infty} \int_{-\infty}^{w-u} f_{X,Y}(u, v)\, dv\, du \tag{8.12}$$

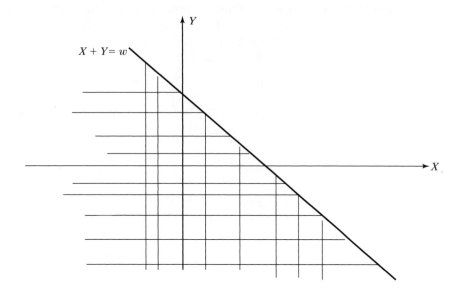

Figure 8.1   Cross-hatched area represents the relation $(X + Y) \leq w$

If we now take the derivative with respect to w, we obtain the density function of the sum:

$$f_Z(w) = \frac{dF_Z(w)}{dw} = \int_{-\infty}^{\infty} f_{X,Y}(u, w - u)\, du \qquad (8.13)$$

It should be noted that differentiating with respect to w, which appears in the limit of the integral of the variable v, means that we have to replace v, the argument of the density of Y inside the integral, with $(w - u)$.

How do we handle sums of more than two random variables? If the random variables are dependent, then we have to repeat what we just did for two random variables with more than two. The expressions tend to become rather complicated to deal with and will not be presented here. However, if the random variables are independent, then we only have to evaluate the density using two random variables at a time. Let us first look again at the case of two random variables that are independent. In this case equation (8.13) reduces to

$$f_Z(w) = \int_{-\infty}^{\infty} f_X(u)\, f_Y(w - u)\, du \qquad (8.14)$$

The operation defined by equation (8.14) is called a convolution of f_X and f_Y. This means that if we have more than two random variables, we just keep repeating the process, by convolving the density of the third random variable with the density of the sum of the first two. We continue the process until we find the density of the sum of all variables. We shall illustrate this with the sum of three random variables, and then just provide the expression for the general case. Consider the sum of the three independent random variables X, Y, and V:

$$W = X + Y + V = Z + V \tag{8.15}$$

Here Z is as defined in equation (8.10). We now use equation (8.14) for the density of W in terms of the densities of Z and V:

$$f_W(\alpha) = \int_{-\infty}^{\infty} f_Z(v)\, f_V(\alpha - v)\, dv \tag{8.16}$$

Then, we substitute the expression of the density of Z from equation (8.14) into equation (8.16) to obtain the final result for the density of W:

$$f_W(\alpha) = \int_{-\infty}^{\infty} \int_{-\infty}^{\infty} f_X(u)f_Y(v - u)f_V(\alpha - v)\, du\, dv \tag{8.17}$$

This result can be generalized to the case of n independent random variables, but is not very useful in its most general case, since it is much easier to do the convolution by adding two random variables one at a time, as we have done for the case $n = 3$.

As an example, consider the Poisson arrival times we discussed in Chapter 6. In that case we found (by adding the interarrival times of the first two arrivals) the density of the time to the second arrival, which we denoted by Z:

$$f_Z(w) = \lambda^2 w \exp(-\lambda w), \qquad \text{for } 0 < w \tag{8.18}$$

The random variables are as defined in Figure 8.2, where X, Y, and U are the first three interarrival times, while Z is the time to the second arrival, and V is the time to third arrival.

If we now convolve this density with the interarrival time of the third arrival U, we obtain the density of the time V to the third arrival:

$$f_V(\alpha) = \int_{-\infty}^{\infty} f_Z(v)f_U(\alpha - v)\, dv = \int_{0}^{\alpha} \lambda^2 v \exp(-\lambda v)\lambda \exp[-\lambda(\alpha - v)]\, dv$$

$$= \frac{\lambda^3}{2}\alpha^2 \exp(-\lambda\alpha), \qquad \text{for } 0 < \alpha \tag{8.19}$$

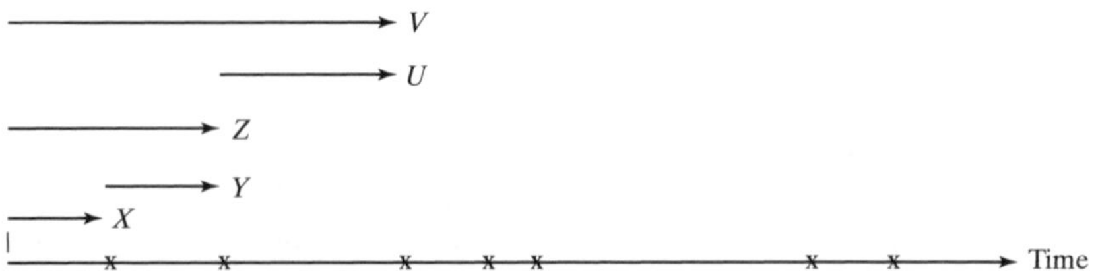

Figure 8.2   Arrival times X, Y, U, V, and Z

In the derivation of [equation (8.19)] the limits of the integral are determined by the regions in which the densities involved are not zero, as $f_Z(v)$ is not zero for values of $v > 0$, while $f_U(\alpha - v)$ is not zero for $(\alpha - v) > 0$, so that v must be less than α. The approach works for any other cases we wish to consider. The major difficulty in such problems is in evaluating the results using multiple integrations, which can be very tedious if the limits are finite, such as when we add a third resistor to the two resistors in series we considered earlier.

Due to the fact that such problems become tedious and may not provide any useful information beyond what we could obtain from the mean and variance, we tend to be satisfied in many cases with just the mean and variance of sums of random variables.

8.3.2 Mean and Variance of a Sum

Suppose we have two random variables and we wish to find the mean and variance of their sum Z. In this case we have

$$m_Z = E\{Z\} = E\{X + Y\} = m_X + m_Y, \tag{8.20}$$

The preceding expression is always true no matter what the density or the dependence of the two random variables. The same holds for more than two random variables: If we have n random variables $\{X_k\}$, for $k = 1, 2, 3, \ldots, n$, with means $m_k = E\{X_k\}$, we define their sum Y as

$$Y = \sum_{k=1}^{n} X_k \tag{8.21}$$

If we now use the linearity property of expectations, we obtain for the mean of Y

$$m_Y = E\{Y\} = \sum_{k=1}^{n} E\{X_k\} = \sum_{k=1}^{n} m_k \tag{8.22}$$

The problem is a little more complex when we look for the variance of a sum of n random variables. Let us look at the case of two random variables first. In this case we have $Z = X + Y$, so that the variance of Z is obtained as

$$\begin{aligned}
\sigma_Z^2 &= E\{[Z - m_Z]^2\} = E\{[X + Y - m_X - m_Y]^2\} \\
&= E\{[(X - m_X) + (Y - m_Y)]^2\} \\
&= E\{(X - m_X)^2\} + E\{(Y - m_Y)^2\} + 2E\{(X - m_X)(Y - m_Y)\} \\
&= \sigma_X^2 + \sigma_Y^2 + 2\rho_{XY}\sigma_X\sigma_Y \tag{8.23}
\end{aligned}$$

We see that the variance of a sum of two variables involves three terms, where the most interesting part appears in the term with the correlation coefficient. This means that if the random variables are correlated, then the variance of their sum may be larger or smaller than the sum of their variances, depending on whether they are positively or negatively correlated. On the other hand, we come to the very important result that if two random variables are uncorrelated, then the variance of their sum is equal to the sum of their variances.

This result of the variance of a sum can be generalized to the case of n variables. As we shall see, even though we are considering n variables, if we are concerned only with the mean and variance of the sum, then we need only know their correlation, which means that we need only know how they behave two at a time. Suppose we consider the same n variables $\{X_k\}$ as before, and suppose we know their means $\{m_k\}$ and denote their variances and correlation coefficients as follows:

$$\sigma_k^2 = E\{(X_k - m_k)^2\}$$

$$\rho_{ki}\sigma_k\sigma_i = E\{(X_k - m_k)(X_i - m_i)\}, \qquad k \neq i \qquad (8.24)$$

If they are uncorrelated, then all the correlation coefficients are zero. We are now ready to find the variance of the sum Y as defined in equation (8.21):

$$\sigma_Y^2 = E\{(Y - m_Y)^2\} = E\left\{ \left(\sum_{k=1}^{n} X_k - \sum_{k=1}^{n} m_k \right)^2 \right\} = E\left\{ \left[\sum_{k=1}^{n} (X_k - m_k) \right]^2 \right\}$$

$$= E\left\{ \sum_{k=1}^{n} (X_k - m_k) \sum_{i=1}^{n} (X_i - m_i) \right\} = E\left\{ \sum_{k=1}^{n} \sum_{i=1}^{n} (X_k - m_k)(X_i - m_i) \right\}$$

$$= \sum_{k=1}^{n} \sigma_k^2 + \sum_{k=1}^{n} \sum_{i \neq k} \rho_{ki}\sigma_k\sigma_i \qquad (8.25)$$

In the preceding derivation we used the rules of linearity of the expectation and the definition of the variance and correlation coefficient. Again we see that if the random variables are correlated, the correlation affects the variance of their sum. If the random variables are uncorrelated, then the variance of the sum is equal to the sum of the variances. This property is very important in inference and in recovering useful data from noisy measurements.. The result given in equation (8.25) can be simplified if we use the fact that $\rho_{ik} = \rho_{ki}$, where we obtain the following:

$$\sigma_Y^2 = \sum_{k=1}^{n} \sigma_k^2 + 2\sum_{k=1}^{n} \sum_{i=k+1}^{n} \rho_{ki}\sigma_k\sigma_i = \sum_{k=1}^{n} \sigma_k^2 + 2\sum_{k=1}^{n} \sum_{i=1}^{k-1} \rho_{ki}\sigma_k\sigma_i \qquad (8.25a)$$

In order to illustrate the usefulness of such expressions, we consider a simple problem of estimating the value of an unknown constant. We wish to estimate the value of an unknown constant c, and we take n independent measurements $\{X_k\}$, for $k = 1, 2, 3, \ldots, n$. Suppose we assume that the measurement errors are additive and have zero mean, so that the actual measurements are equal to the unknown constant c plus the errors. If we also assume that the errors have the same variance σ^2, then the measurements $\{X_k\}$ will be uncorrelated (since the errors are assumed to be independent) and will have means c (the unknown constant) and variances σ^2.

Now suppose that we estimate the value of c by simply adding the measurements and dividing by n:

$$\hat{c} = \frac{1}{n} \sum_{k=1}^{n} X_k \qquad (8.26)$$

The estimate of the unknown c will have the following mean and variance:

$$E\{\hat{c}\} = \frac{1}{n} \sum_{k=1}^{n} E\{X_k\} = \frac{1}{n} \sum_{k=1}^{n} c = c \qquad (8.27)$$

$$\text{Var}(\hat{c}) = \text{Var}\left(\frac{1}{n} \sum_{k=1}^{n} X_k\right) = \frac{1}{n^2} Var\left(\sum_{k=1}^{n} X_k\right) = \frac{n\sigma^2}{n^2} = \frac{\sigma^2}{n} \qquad (8.28)$$

The result means that our estimate has a mean that is equal to the value we wish to find, and a variance that becomes smaller as n becomes large. For example, if we assume that the measurement errors are Gaussian, then we can (on the basis of the variance of the estimate) determine the margin of error in our estimate of c, using the 3-sigma rule, with probability 99.7%. For example, if we are measuring a voltage and the error in each measurement has a standard deviation of 2 mV, then with 9 measurements the 3-sigma error in the measured signal is 2 mV, while if we take 16 measurements the 3-sigma error will be 1.5 mV. Finally, if we take 100 measurements, the 3-sigma error becomes 0.6 mV.

The expression used in equation (8.26) is appropriately defined as the sample mean of the random variables X_k, which are assumed to form an independent sample of an unknown variable. We shall address this concept further in Chapter 9, where we discuss inference.

8.3.3 Characteristic Function of a Sum

In this section we shall consider just the special case of the sum of n independent random variables. The more general case is beyond the scope of this text. Consider the sum Y of n random variables $\{X_k\}$ for $k = 1, 2, \ldots, n$, as given in equation (8.21). The characteristic function of the random variable Y is obtained by using the definition in equation (7.1) as follows:

$$\Phi_Y(v) = E\{\exp(jvY)\} = E\left\{\exp\left[jv\left(\sum_{k=1}^{n} X_k\right)\right]\right\} = E\left\{\prod_{k=1}^{n} \exp(jvX_k)\right\} \quad (8.29)$$

The product in equation (8.29) inside the expectation can be expressed as the product of the expectation because the random variables are independent:

$$\Phi_Y(v) = \prod_{k=1}^{n} E\{\exp(jvX_k)\} = \prod_{k=1}^{n} \Phi_k(v) \qquad (8.30)$$

In equation (8.30) we denoted the characteristic function of the random variable X_k by $\Phi_k(v)$. In the special case when all the random variable X_k have the same distribution and hence the same characteristic function, which we shall denote by $\Phi_X(v)$, equation (8.30) reduces to

$$\Phi_Y(v) = [\Phi_X(v)]^n \tag{8.31}$$

We can use the characteristic function of Y to derive expectations and other properties of Y in much simpler expressions than the convolution we introduced earlier.

We shall not address this question further in this text, but we shall use it to prove important theorems for large values of n.

8.4 THE LAW OF LARGE NUMBERS AND THE CENTRAL LIMIT THEOREM

8.4.1 The Weak Law of Large Numbers

The results obtained in the previous section on the sum of uncorrelated random variables can be summarized by what is called the **weak law of large numbers**. If we have n uncorrelated random variables with mean m and standard deviation σ, then as n tends to infinity, the probability that the arithmetic average is outside a fixed interval around the mean tends to zero. The result can be stated formally by the expression

$$\lim_{n \to \infty} \text{Prob.} \left\{ \left| \frac{1}{n} \sum_{k=1}^{n} X_k - m \right| > \alpha \right\} = 0 \tag{8.32}$$

Here the number α is any arbitrary number defining a fixed interval around the mean. The result follows from the fact that the variance of the expression shown tends to zero as n tends to infinity, and if we apply Chebyshev's inequality as given by equation (4.53), we obtain the result shown in equation (8.32) concerning the probability of being away from the mean by any arbitrary amount:

$$\lim_{n \to \infty} \text{Prob.} \left\{ \left| \frac{1}{n} \sum_{k=1}^{n} X_k - m \right| > \alpha \right\} \leq \lim_{n \to \infty} \left\{ \text{Var} \left[\frac{1}{n} \sum_{k=1}^{n} X_k \right] / \alpha^2 \right\}$$

$$= \lim_{n \to \infty} [\sigma^2/(n\alpha^2)] = 0$$

Another important rule governing the analysis of a sum of many random variables is called the **central limit theorem**. Again we are dealing with a sum of n independent random variables, which have the same distribution and have finite means and variances.

8.4.2 The Central Limit Theorem

A simple version of the central limit theorem can be stated as follows:

Given n independent, identically distributed random variables with finite means and variances, their sum has a distribution that tends to a Gaussian distribution as n tends to infinity.

If we define our random variables $\{X_k\}$ for $k = 1, 2, \ldots, n$, as we have done previously, having means m and standard deviation σ, then we define the following sum:

$$Y_n = \sum_{k=1}^{n} X_k \tag{8.33}$$

The central limit theorem (CLT) implies that the sum Y_n (which, as shown earlier, has mean mn and variance $n\sigma^2$) will have a Gaussian density function with mean mn and variance $n\sigma^2$ as n tends to infinity.

We can define a new random variable Z_n as follows:

$$Z_n = \frac{1}{\sigma\sqrt{n}} \sum_{k=1}^{n} (X_k - m) = \frac{1}{\sqrt{n}} \sum_{k=1}^{n} W_k \tag{8.34}$$

This new random variable has mean zero and variance 1, and is a linear transformation of the random variable Y_n. Hence, we expect the random variable Z_n to have a density function that is approximately Gaussian with mean zero and variance 1 as n becomes large. In equation (8.34), we defined the random variables $W_k = (X_k - m)/\sigma$ so that they have mean zero and variance 1 as well. The CLT states that we can approximate the density of Z_n as follows for n sufficiently large:

$$f_{Zn}(u) \approx \frac{\exp\left(-\dfrac{u^2}{2}\right)}{\sqrt{2\pi}} \tag{8.35}$$

The relationship between the sums shown in equations (8.33) and (8.34) is obtained as

$$Y_n = \sum_{k=1}^{n} X_k = \sqrt{n}\sigma Z_n + nm \tag{8.36}$$

The random variable Y_n is just a linear transformation of Z_n, with mean nm and variance $n\sigma^2$. Hence, we can show that if Z_n is approximately Gaussian, then Y_n will also be approximately Gaussian.

In order to prove the central limit theorem, we find the characteristic function of Z_n, as we did in Section 8.3.3 when we considered the sum of n independent random variables:

$$\Phi_{Zn}(v) = E\left\{ \exp\left[jv \frac{1}{\sigma\sqrt{n}} \sum_{k=1}^{n} (X_k - m) \right] \right\}$$

$$= E\left\{ \prod_{k=1}^{n} \exp\{j(v/\sqrt{n})[(X_k - m)/\sigma]\} \right\}$$

$$= \prod_{k=1}^{n} E\{\exp\{j(v/\sqrt{n})[(X_k - m)/\sigma]\}\} = \prod_{k=1}^{n} E\{\exp[j(v/\sqrt{n})W_k]\}$$

$$= \prod_{k=1}^{n} \Phi_k(v/\sqrt{n})$$

$$= [\Phi_0(v/\sqrt{n})]^n \tag{8.37}$$

In equation (8.37) we denoted the characteristic function of W_k by $\Phi_k(v)$, and since they are identically distributed, all the characteristic functions are identical and are denoted by $\Phi_0(v)$. For large n we see that the argument of the function in equation (8.37) will be small for finite v. Hence we may use a Taylor series expansion of the characteristic function $\Phi_0(v)$ to yield (since each W_k has zero mean and unit variance)

$$\Phi_0(v/\sqrt{n}) = 1 - \frac{1}{2}(v/\sqrt{n})^2 + o(1/n) = 1 - (1/2)(v^2/n) + o(1/n) \tag{8.38}$$

We use the notation $o(1/n)$ to denote terms that tend to zero faster than $(1/n)$ as n tends to infinity. If we substitute the equation (8.38) into equation (8.37) and find the limit as n approaches infinity, we obtain the exponential function

$$\lim_{n\to\infty} [\Phi_{Zn}(v)] = \lim_{n\to\infty} [\Phi_0(v/\sqrt{n})]^n = \lim_{n\to\infty} [1 - (1/2)(v^2/n) + o(1/n)]^n$$
$$= \exp[-(1/2)v^2] \tag{8.39}$$

In getting the final expression in equation (8.39) we used the standard result of the limit of the following expression:

$$\lim_{n\to\infty} [1 + a/n]^n = \exp(a)$$

The result of equation (8.39) proves the central limit theorem for the distribution of the random variable Z_n, and hence it applies to Y_n as well.

How large should n be before we can use the Gaussian approximation for a sum of n random variables? In many cases values of n as small as 15 or 20 are sufficient to yield a good enough answer. The binomial distribution behavior for large n, which allows it to be approximated by a Gaussian distribution, is the result of the central limit theorem. In such a case we consider the outcome of each trial as a Bernoulli random variable, which takes two values: either 0 (for failure) or 1 (for success). If we denote the outcome so defined for the kth trial by X_k, then the number of successes in n trials is simply the sum of the $\{X_k\}$. Since each variable has mean p and variance $p(1 - p)$, the number of successes in n trials, which is equal to the sum, will have mean np and variance $np(1 - p)$, and we can approximate the binomial distribution by the Gaussian distribution.

Example 8.3

As an example, suppose we connect in series 27 resistors selected at random from a group of resistors with values uniformly distributed in the range $(9, 11)$. We need to find the approximate probability density function of the resulting resistance. The mean of each resistance is 10 and its variance is $(2)^2/12 = 1/3$. Since the total resistance Y is the sum of the 27 individual ones, we have for the mean and the variance of the sum the following:

$$m_Y = 27 \times 10 = 270$$
$$\sigma_Y^2 = 27 \times (1/3) = 9$$

Hence the resistance Y is approximately Gaussian with mean 270 and standard deviation of 3. We started with resistors whose value was in the range $10 \pm 10\%$. Let us find the probability that the series combination results in $\pm 2\%$ accuracy. In this case we wish to find the probability that the value of the resistance is within $\pm 2\%$ of 270 (i.e., in the range 270 ± 5.4):

$$P\{|Y - 270| < 5.4\}$$

We find this probability by using the unit Gaussian table, so we need to find what fraction of sigma the tolerance 5.4 represents. If we define Z as a unit Gaussian variable such that

$$Z = (Y - 270)/3$$

then we have

$$P\{|Y - 270| < 5.4\} = P\{|Z| < 5.4/3\} = P\{-1.8 < Z < 1.8\}$$
$$= \Phi(1.8) - \Phi(-1.8)$$
$$= 0.9641 - 0.0359 = 0.9282$$

We see here an illustration of the use of the central limit theorem and also the effect of the law of large numbers. We started with resistance values with $\pm 10\%$ accuracy, and by combining 27 such elements, we ended up with an accuracy of $\pm 2\%$ with a probability of almost 93%. This means that if we actually combined such elements in series, we exceed the 2% tolerance only about 7% of the time.

We shall see a demonstration of both of these concepts when we deal with the basic elements of statistics and inference.

Finally, as an example to illustrate the central limit theorem, we consider the distribution of the nth arrival time in a Poisson arrival problem.

Example 8.4

Consider the Poisson arrival problem shown in Figure 8.2. In equation (8.19) we derived the density function for the time to the third arrival, by performing the convolution twice on the exponential density of the interarrival times. We now extend this to the nth arrival time. If we continue the convolution successively, we can assume the final result. We prove the result by performing the convolution for the derivation of the formula from $(n - 1)$ to n. We have shown the density for the third arrival time, which we denote by $f_3(w)$

$$f_3(w) = \frac{\lambda^3 w^2}{2!} \exp(-\lambda w), \qquad 0 < w$$

Suppose we now assume that the $(n - 1)$ arrival time satisfies

$$f_{n-1}(w) = \frac{\lambda^{n-1}w^{n-2}}{(n-2)!}\exp(-\lambda w), \qquad 0 < w$$

Then, if we convolve this density with the exponential density, we should obtain the same expression for the density of the nth arrival time with $n - 1$ replaced by n:

$$f_n(w) = \int_0^w \lambda \exp[-\lambda(w - u)]\frac{\lambda^{n-1}u^{n-2}}{(n-2)!}\exp(-\lambda u)\ du$$

$$= \frac{\lambda^n w^{n-1}}{(n-1)!}\exp(-\lambda w), \qquad 0 < w$$

The result proves that our assumption on the expression is indeed a valid one. It is easy to show that the mean of the density and its variance are given by the expressions (where we are denoting by Z_n the time to the nth arrival)

$$E\{Z_n\} = n/\lambda, \qquad \text{Var}(Z_n) = n/\lambda^2$$

Since the time to the nth arrival involves the sum of independent random variables, does the density also tend to Gaussian in this case? In Figure 8.3 we show the densities of the times to the nth arrival for $n = 1, 2, 10,$ and 20, and we compare the case of $n = 10$ and $n = 20$ with Gaussian densities (N10 and N20) with the same mean and variance. The densities in the figure were normalized so that they all have the same mean of 5.

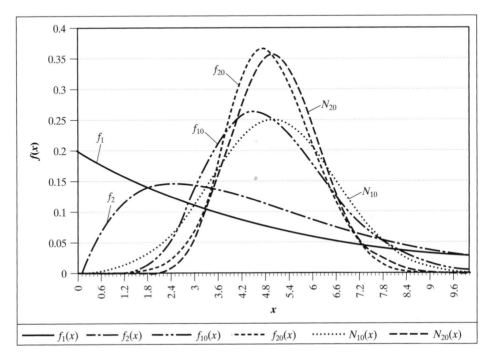

Figure 8.3 Density function for arrival times (for $n = $ **1, 2, 10, 20** and denoted $f_n(x)$) and compared with the Gaussian density for $n = $ **10, 20** (denoted by $N10(x)$ and $N20(x)$)

8.5 FUNCTIONS OF INDEPENDENT RANDOM VARIABLES

The concept of independence of multiple random variables was briefly described in Section 8.2.3, and it follows from the basic definition of independence. In such a case the probability of any of the variables taking values in a given interval is independent of whatever happens to the other random variables. Rather than dealing with the multi-dimensional density or distribution functions, in this section we shall just multiply the probability of any intersection of events involving more than one random variable. To that end we shall concentrate only on a few functions of random variables that have applications in engineering. In Section 8.3.3 we considered the sum of independent random variables, and here we consider other functions of engineering interest.

8.5.1 Maximum Function

This function occurs when we try to define a random variable as the largest of several random variables. As an example of such a case consider a parallel connection of elements in a system, with each having a known lifetime distribution or density. We shall assume that the elements fail independently of each other, which means that the lifetime variables are independent. At the beginning we shall assume any arbitrary distribution of the lifetime, and then we can look at a special case of identical distributions and in particular at exponential distributions.

Consider the system in Figure 8.4, which shows n components in parallel, each of which has a lifetime denoted by X_k, which are assumed to be independent.

Since the components are connected in parallel, the lifetime Y of the entire system is the largest of the lifetime of each component. We can express that relation as follows:

$$Y = \text{Max}\{X_1, X_2, \ldots, X_n\} \tag{8.40}$$

The problem is to find the density or distribution functions of the system lifetime Y if we know the distributions $F_k(u)$ of the individual X_k and if we assume that they fail independently of each other. In order to do so, we start by using the definition of the distribution function of the random variable Y:

$$F_Y(v) = P\{Y \le v\} = P\{\text{Max}(X_1, X_2, \ldots, X_n) \le v\} = P\left\{\bigcap_{k=1}^{n}(X_k \le v)\right\} \tag{8.41}$$

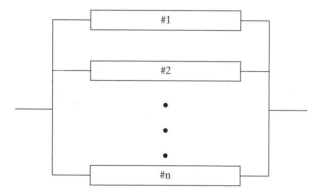

Figure 8.4 A Parallel Connection of Components

Here we used the fact that for the maximum X_k to be smaller than some value v, all of the variables must be smaller than that value as well. Now we use the fact that since the random variables are independent, the probability of the intersection is the product of the probabilities of each event. We obtain

$$F_Y(v) = \prod_{k=1}^{n} P\{X_k \le v\} = \prod_{k=1}^{n} F_k(v) \tag{8.42}$$

If we now assume that all the distributions are the same, and are equal to $F_X(v)$, then the distribution function of Y is given by

$$F_Y(v) = [F_X(v)]^n \tag{8.43}$$

Let us consider two special cases for this type of problem.

Case 1: Lifetime distribution is exponential, with failure rate λ. In this case the density and distribution of the individual lifetime is given by

$$f_X(u) = \lambda \exp(-\lambda u), \quad \text{for } u > 0$$
$$F_X(u) = 1 - \exp(-\lambda u), \quad \text{for } u > 0 \tag{8.44}$$

From equation (8.43) the distribution function of Y is given as

$$F_Y(v) = [1 - \exp(-\lambda v)]^n, \quad \text{for } u > 0 \tag{8.45}$$

The corresponding density function is obtained by taking the derivative, which results in

$$f_Y(v) = n\lambda[1 - \exp(-\lambda v)]^{n-1} \exp(-\lambda v), \quad \text{for } u > 0 \tag{8.46}$$

The distribution and density functions are plotted for $n = 1, 2,$ and 3 in Figure 8.5. What happens to the average lifetime in this case? We can compute the average lifetime directly from the density function as follows:

$$E\{Y\} = \int_0^\infty vn\lambda[1 - \exp(-\lambda v)]^{n-1} \exp(-\lambda v) \, dv$$

$$= \int_0^\infty vn\lambda \sum_{k=0}^{n-1} \binom{n-1}{k}[-\exp(-\lambda v)]^k \exp(-\lambda v) \, dv$$

$$= \sum_{k=0}^{n-1} \frac{n!(n-1-k)!}{(k+1)!\lambda(k+1)}(-1)^k$$

$$= \sum_{k=1}^{n} \binom{n}{k}\frac{(-1)^{k-1}}{\lambda k} = \sum_{k=1}^{n} \frac{1}{\lambda k} \tag{8.47}$$

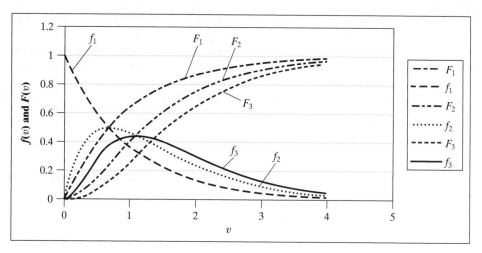

Figure 8.5   Distributions and Densities of Lifetimes for a Parallel Connection for $n = 1, 2,$ and **3**

Note that for $n = 1$, we obtain the usual average lifetime of $1/\lambda$, and for $n = 2$, we obtain an average lifetime of $1.5/\lambda$, which is 50% larger than for a single component. Finally, for $n = 3$, we obtain an average lifetime of $1.833/\lambda$. We see here the benefit of a parallel combination for improved reliability. In the past we were able to find only the probability of failure in a fixed interval, while this case shows the importance of dealing with random variables.

Case 2: Another example that has exactly the same type of function is the timing delay occurring in an AND gate in a logical device or circuit. Suppose we have a gate with incoming signals $S_k(t - X_k)$, where the $S_k(t)$ are unit step inputs to an AND gate and the X_k are timing delays in the start of each step. Since the output of the AND gate is 1 only when all n signals are present, the output will be a step whose delay time is the largest of the values taken by the random variables X_k. This is illustrated for $n = 3$ in Figure 8.6. In order to show the signals in the figure, their amplitude was drawn with levels other than 1. It should also be noted that the subscripts of the timing delays do not denote

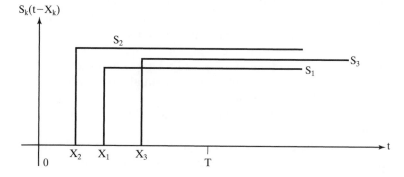

Figure 8.6   Three inputs to a logic gate device

their sizes. For the example, as shown in the figure, the output will be starting at X_3 since it is then that all signals are present.

Suppose that the X_k are uniformly distributed in $(0, T)$. Then what is the distribution of the timing delay of the output step signal? The output will have the form $S(t - Y)$, where Y is the maximum value of the X_k, as was the case for the lifetime of the parallel components. The distribution functions of the X_k are the same and are given by the usual uniform distribution:

$$F_X(u) = u/T, \quad \text{for } 0 < u < T, \text{ and is equal to 1 for } u > T \qquad (8.48)$$

The distribution of Y is obtained from equation (8.35) and therefore becomes

$$F_Y(v) = \begin{cases} 0, & v < 0 \\ (v/T)^n, & 0 < v < T \\ 1, & T < v \end{cases} \qquad (8.49)$$

The corresponding density function is obtained by differentiating the distribution function to yield

$$f_Y(v) = (n/T)(v/T)^{n-1}, \text{ for } 0 < v < T, \text{ and is zero elsewhere} \qquad (8.50)$$

The average delay for a single signal is $T/2$. What is the average delay for the output of the AND gate with n inputs? It is easy to find that it should be larger, and it is derived as the average of Y:

$$E\{Y\} = \int_0^T v(n/T)\left(\frac{v}{T}\right)^{n-1} dv = \frac{nT}{(n+1)} \qquad (8.51)$$

For $n = 2$, the delay is $(2/3)T$, and for $n = 3$, it is $0.75T$. As n becomes large, the average delay approaches T.

8.5.2 Minimum Function

This function occurs when we try to define a random variable as the smallest of several random variables. As an example of such a case consider a series connection of elements in a system, with each having a known lifetime distribution or density. We shall assume that the elements fail independently of each other, which means that the lifetime variables are independent. At the beginning we shall assume any arbitrary distribution of the lifetime, and then we can look at a special case of identical distributions and in particular an exponential distribution.

Consider the system shown in Figure 8.7, where there are n components in series, each of which has a lifetime denoted by X_k, which are assumed to be independent.

Since the components are connected in series, the lifetime Y of the entire system is the smallest of the lifetimes X_k and may be expressed as

$$Y = \text{Min}\{X_1, X_2, \ldots, X_n\} \qquad (8.52)$$

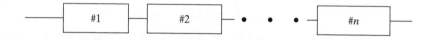

Figure 8.7   A series connection of components

We shall assume that the distributions and densities of the X_k are as defined in Section 8.5.1. Hence, if we try to use the definition of the distribution function to find the distribution function of Y, we obtain

$$F_Y(v) = P\{Y \le v\} = P\{\text{Min}(X_1, X_2, \ldots, X_n) \le v\} = P\left\{\bigcup_{k=1}^{n}(X_k \le v)\right\} \quad (8.53)$$

The reason for using the union in the expression in equation (8.53) is that for the smallest X_k to be less than some arbitrary time v, either one of them may be smaller than v to satisfy the relation (by **or** we mean here **inclusive or**). However, we know from the rules of probability that finding the probability of a union is more complex than finding the probability of an intersection when the events are independent. Hence, instead of the preceding equation, we obtain the complement of the distribution function:

$$1 - F_Y(v) = P\{Y > v\} = P\{\text{Min}(X_1, X_2, \ldots, X_n) > v\} = P\left\{\bigcap_{k=1}^{n}(X_k > v)\right\}$$
$$(8.54)$$

Now we use the fact that the probability of the intersection is the product of the probabilities (since the random variables are independent), and we identify the probability that $(X_k > v)$ as $1 - F_X(v)$ to obtain the final result:

$$F_Y(v) = 1 - P\left\{\bigcap_{k=1}^{n}(X_k > v)\right\} = 1 - \prod_{k=1}^{n}P\{X_k > v\} = 1 - \prod_{k=1}^{n}[1 - F_k(v)]$$
$$(8.55)$$

If the distributions of the random variables of the components lifetimes are identical, then we have the special case

$$F_Y(v) = 1 - [1 - F_X(v)]^n \quad (8.56)$$

We again consider two special cases, the first involved with exponential lifetime density for each component, and the second involving OR gates in digital circuits.

  Case 1: If the distributions of the lifetimes of the components satisfy the exponential distribution as given in equation (8.44), then from equation (8.56), the lifetime distribution of the system becomes

$$F_Y(v) = 1 - [1 - (1 - \exp(-\lambda v))]^n = 1 - \exp(-\lambda n v), \quad \text{for } v > 0 \quad (8.57)$$

The corresponding density can be found by differentiating the distribution:

$$f_Y(v) = \lambda n v \exp(-\lambda n v), \qquad \text{for } v > 0 \tag{8.58}$$

It is easy to see that the result is as if we have one component with n times the failure rate of a single component. Also, the average lifetime is $1/(n\lambda)$, which is $1/n$ times the average lifetime of a single component. We do not need to plot this density or distribution, as it is still exponential with a larger failure rate.

Case 2: Another example that has exactly the same type of function is the timing delay occurring in an OR gate in a logical device or circuit. Suppose we have a gate with incoming signals $S_k(t - X_k)$, where the $S_k(t)$ are unit step inputs to an

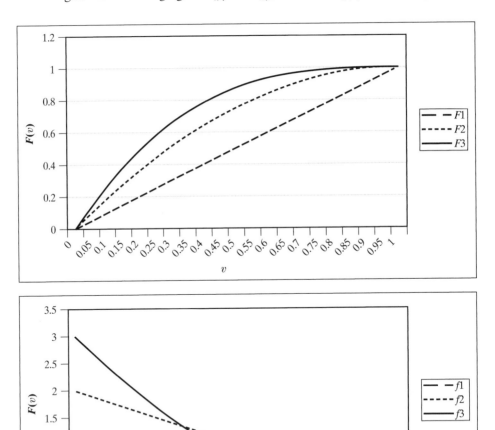

Figure 8.8 The distributions and densities of timing delays in an OR gate for $n = 1, 2,$ and 3

OR gate and the X_k are timing delays in the start of each step. Since the output of the OR gate is 1 when any of the n signals are present, the output will be a step whose delay time is the smallest of the X_k. This is illustrated for $n = 3$ in Figure 8.6 where we previously considered the AND gate case. For the example shown in the figure the output will be starting at X_2, since that signal arrives first at the gate.

We assume that the distribution of the timing delay of each signal is uniform in the interval $(0, T)$ and is given by equation (8.48), so that the distribution of the output delay Y is expressed as

$$F_Y(v) = 1 - [1 - (v/T)]^n, \qquad \text{for } 0 < v < T \tag{8.59}$$

The resulting density function is of course given by

$$f_Y(v) = (n/T)[1 - (v/T)]^{n-1}, \qquad \text{for } 0 < v < T \tag{8.60}$$

The distribution and density functions are shown for $n = 1, 2$, and 3 in Figure 8.8. As seen from the figure, we expect the average delay time to become smaller as the number n increases. We can actually find the average time by directly using the density function:

$$E\{Y\} = \int_0^T v(n/T)[1 - (v/T)]^{n-1} \, dv = T/(n + 1) \tag{8.61}$$

We see that indeed the average delay decreases inversely to n and becomes zero in the limit as n becomes very large. These two examples illustrate the way we use multiple random variables in problems involving reliability or tolerance issues. We shall address the applications of random variables to general reliability problems in Chapter 11.

In the rest of this chapter we shall consider the characteristic function of n random variables as well as the case of n jointly Gaussian random variables.

8.6 CHARACTERISTIC FUNCTION

8.6.1 Basic Definitions

If we wish to do more with n random variables, we need first to define the characteristic function for n random variables. The characteristic function is an important tool in handling functions of random variables, as well as in dealing with Gaussian random variables. Before we define the characteristic function, we should introduce vector notations for n random variables. We define in this case a random vector of dimension n by the boldface letter X, to represent a set of n random variables:

$$X^T = [X_1, X_2, \ldots, X_n] \tag{8.62}$$

Here we use the superscript letter T to denote a transpose, so that X is indeed a column vector. If we now define the lowercase vector x to denote a column vector of real variables $x_1, x_2, \ldots, x_n$, we can write the n-dimensional density function of n random variables denoted by X as

$$f_X(x) = f_{X_1, X_2, \ldots X_n}(x_1, x_2, \ldots, x_n) \tag{8.63}$$

We now define the characteristic function of the n random variables represented by X as follows:

$$\Phi_X(v) = \Phi_X(v_1, v_2, \ldots, v_n) = E\{\exp(jv^T X)\} = E\left\{\exp\left(j\sum_{i=1}^{n} v_i X_i\right)\right\} \tag{8.64}$$

Here we are using the notation $v^T = [v_1, v_2, \ldots, v_n]$ for the vector v. The expectation defined in equation (8.64) is to be evaluated as any other expectation; that is, we have to multiply by the probability density function and integrate over all values of the random variables:

$$
\begin{aligned}
\Phi_X(v) &= \int_{-\infty}^{\infty} \int_{-\infty}^{\infty} \cdots \int_{-\infty}^{\infty} \exp(jv^T x) f_X(x)\, dx \\
&= \int_{-\infty}^{\infty} \int_{-\infty}^{\infty} \cdots \int_{-\infty}^{\infty} \exp\left(j\sum_{i=1}^{n} v_i X_i\right) f_{X_1 X_2 \ldots X_n}(x_1, x_2, \ldots, x_n)\, dx_1 dx_2 \ldots dx_n
\end{aligned}
$$
$$\tag{8.65}$$

We can obtain the density function from the characteristic function in the same manner as with the two random variables case, and we can use the characteristic function to derive moments involving n random variables. This will not be addressed further here, as we shall use the function to derive linear transformation of n random variables, and to consider the Gaussian case.

An important property of the characteristic function of n independent random variables is that it reduces to a product of the individual characteristic functions, since in that case equation (8.65) reduces to the product of n integrals. We summarize this property with the following expression, where we define $\Phi_{X_i}(v_i)$ as the characteristic function of the random variable X_i. If the n random variables $\{X_i\}$ are independent, then their characteristic function can be expressed by the following product:

$$\Phi_X(v) = \prod_{i=1}^{n} \Phi_{X_i}(v_i) \tag{8.66}$$

We shall next consider linear transformation involving n random variables.

8.6.2 Linear Transformation of n Random Variables

Let n-dimensional vector X represent n random variables $\{X_i\}$, and let an m-dimensional random vector Y (whose elements are $\{Y_k\}, k = 1, 2, \ldots, m$) be defined by the following linear transformation of X, where the matrix A is a constant (nonrandom) m-by-n matrix with $m \leq n$:

$$Y = AX \tag{8.67}$$

In order to find the density function of Y, we utilize the characteristic function:

$$\Phi_Y(\boldsymbol{v}) = E\{\exp(j\boldsymbol{v}^T Y)\} = E\{\exp(j\boldsymbol{v}^T A X)\} = E\{\exp[j(A^T\boldsymbol{v})^T X]\}$$

$$= \Phi_X(A^T\boldsymbol{v}) \tag{8.68}$$

It is now possible to derive the density function of the random vector Y by using the inverse transformation from the characteristic function. We shall address this only for two cases: $m = 1$ and $m = n$. The case $m = 1$ reduces to sums of random variables, with some scaling factors, which we shall not consider here. The case $m = n$ is of interest only if the matrix A is nonsingular (i.e., it has an inverse). We shall consider this case first.

Suppose that $m = n$ and the matrix A in equation (8.67) has an inverse. We shall use equation (8.68) to explicitly derive the characteristic function of Y:

$$\Phi_Y(v) = \int_{-\infty}^{\infty} \int_{-\infty}^{\infty} \cdots \int_{-\infty}^{\infty} \exp(j\boldsymbol{v}^T A \boldsymbol{x}) \, f_X(\boldsymbol{x}) \, d\boldsymbol{x} \tag{8.69}$$

We now make a change of variables of integration from $\boldsymbol{x}$ to $\boldsymbol{y} = A\boldsymbol{x}$, so that instead of $\boldsymbol{x}$, we have $\boldsymbol{x} = A^{-1}\boldsymbol{y}$, and instead of $d\boldsymbol{x}$ we should have

$$d\boldsymbol{x} = dx_1 dx_2 \ldots dx_n = (1/|\det A|) \, dy_1 dy_2 \ldots dy_n = (1/|\det A|) \, d\boldsymbol{y} \tag{8.70}$$

Equation (8.69) then becomes

$$\Phi_Y(v) = \int_{-\infty}^{\infty} \int_{-\infty}^{\infty} \cdots \int_{-\infty}^{\infty} \exp(j\boldsymbol{v}^T\boldsymbol{y}) \, f_X(A^{-1}\boldsymbol{y})(1/|\det A|) \, d\boldsymbol{y} \tag{8.71}$$

If we now compare equation (8.71) with the definition of the characteristic function of Y, as expressed in equation (8.65) with changing X for Y, we see that the density function of Y is given by the expression

$$f_Y(\boldsymbol{y}) = f_X(A^{-1}\boldsymbol{y})(1/|\det A|) \tag{8.72}$$

We now consider an important example dealing with n Poisson arrivals that we discussed earlier in a different context.

Example 8.5

Consider a Poisson arrival problem with arrival rate λ, where we are looking at the first n arrivals. Define the random variables $\{X_i\}$ as the n interarrival times; that is, X_i is the time between the $(i - 1)$th and the ith arrivals, for i between 1 and n. We now define the random variables $\{Y_i\}$ as the time to the ith arrival, which means that the Y_i are given as the following transformation of the X_k:

$$Y_i = \sum_{k=1}^{i} X_k \tag{8.73}$$

If we represent equation (8.73) as in equation (8.67), the matrix A in this case has the following form:

$$A = \begin{bmatrix} 1 & 0 & 0 & \cdots & & 0 \\ 1 & 1 & 0 & \cdots & & 0 \\ 1 & 1 & 1 & 0 & \cdots & 0 \\ \cdots & \cdots & \cdots & \cdots & \cdots & \cdots \\ 1 & 1 & \cdots & \cdots & \cdots & 1 \end{bmatrix} \qquad (8.74)$$

We can therefore compute the determinant of A to be equal to 1, and the inverse is then shown to yield

$$X_i = Y_i - Y_{i-1}, \qquad \text{for } i = 1, 2, \ldots n, \text{ with } Y_0 = 0 \qquad (8.75)$$

The expression for the joint density functions of the interarrival times is given as a product of the exponential density:

$$f_X(x) = \prod_{i=1}^{n} [\lambda \exp(-\lambda x_i)] = \lambda^n \exp\left(-\lambda \sum_{i=1}^{n} x_i\right), \text{ for } x_i > 0 \qquad (8.76)$$

Now if we substitute the values of the x_i from the inverse transformation in equation (8.75) and use equation (8.72), we find that the joint density function of the arrival time Y_i results in

$$f_Y(y) = \lambda^n \exp(-\lambda y_n), \quad \text{for } 0 < y_1 < y_2 < \cdots < y_{n-1} < y_n < \infty \qquad (8.77)$$

If we now integrate the joint density over the variables $y_1, y_2, \ldots, y_{n-1}$, we obtain the same density function for the time to the nth arrival we obtained in Example 8.4.

We now consider the case $m = 1$, and we shall consider only the case in which all the entries of A are unity, so that Y is a single variable given by

$$Y = \sum_{k=1}^{n} X_k \qquad (8.78)$$

The expression for the characteristic function of Y is obtained by using equation (8.68) and replacing of all the v_i in the characteristic function of the $\{X_i\}$ by a single variable v:

$$\Phi_Y(v) = \Phi_X(v, v, \ldots, v) \qquad (8.79)$$

In particular, we considered the special case of independent random variables $\{X_i\}$ in Section 8.3.3, where we obtained the following characteristic function for independent and identically distributed random variables $\{X_i\}$:

$$\Phi_Y(v) = [\Phi_X(v)]^n \qquad (8.80)$$

We can check that the characteristic function for the nth arrival time we considered earlier is given by

$$\Phi_Y(v) = \left(\frac{\lambda}{\lambda - jv}\right)^n \qquad (8.81)$$

The preceding equation can then be used to find the moments as well as the density of the n-th arrival time. Further study of this case will not be carried out here.

8.7 GAUSSIAN RANDOM VARIABLES

In this section we consider the general density function of n jointly Gaussian random variables. Only the means, variances, and correlation coefficients are needed to completely determine the density function for Gaussian random variables. Suppose the n-dimensional vector X represents n Gaussian random variables $\{X_i\}$. Let us also assume that the means, variances, and correlation coefficients of the random variables are known and that we shall also represent them in vector and matrix form. We use the n-dimensional vector m to denote the means of the random variables:

$$m^T = [m_1, m_2, \ldots, m_n] = [E\{X_1\}, E\{X_2\}, \ldots, E\{X_n\}] \tag{8.82}$$

We shall also denote the covariance (and variance when $i = k$) between X_i and X_k by C_{ik}:

$$C_{ik} = E\{[X_i - m_i][X_k - m_k]\} = \rho_{ik}\sigma_i\sigma_k \tag{8.83}$$

Here we use the notation ρ_{ik} as the correlation coefficient between X_i and X_k, and it is understood that $\rho_{ii} = 1$. If we now denote the $n \times n$ matrix whose elements are C_{ik} by C_X, then the general expression for the n-dimensional probability density function of the n Gaussian random variables can be given as

$$f_X(x) = \frac{\exp\{-0.5(x - m)^T C_X^{-1}(x - m)\}}{\sqrt{(2\pi)^n \det(C_X)}} \tag{8.84}$$

A very interesting observation follows from the preceding expression: If the variables are uncorrelated, then $\rho_{ik} = 0$, for $i \neq k$, so that C_X becomes a diagonal matrix. In that case equation (8.84) reduces to a product of the n individual Gaussian densities of the $\{X_i\}$.

The expression for the n-dimensional Gaussian characteristic function is much simpler, as it does not require the matrix inversion of C_X. The expression for the characteristic function can be given as

$$\Phi_X(v) = \exp(jv^T m)\exp\{-0.5 v^T C_X v\}$$

$$= \exp\left\{ j\sum_{i=1}^{n} v_i m_i \right\} \exp\left\{ -0.5\sum_{i=1}^{n}\sum_{k=1}^{n} C_{ik} v_i v_k \right\} \tag{8.85}$$

A very important property resulting from this expression is that if we use a linear transformation of the random variables $\{X_i\}$ into the m random variables $\{Y_i\}$ as in equation (8.67), we obtain the following expression for the characteristic function of the vector Y:

$$\Phi_Y(v) = \Phi_X(A^T v) = \exp(jv^T Am)\exp\{-0.5 v^T AC_X A^T v\} \tag{8.86}$$

Equation (8.86) is identical to the characteristic function of an m-dimensional Gaussian random vector whose mean is given by $\boldsymbol{m}_Y$ and whose matrix of covariance elements is given by C_Y, such that

$$\boldsymbol{m}_Y = A\boldsymbol{m}, \quad C_Y = AC_XA^T \tag{8.87}$$

The conclusion we draw from this observation is that linear transformation of Gaussian random variables is always Gaussian. Hence, in order to obtain the resulting density functions in such cases, we need only find the means, variances, and covariances of the variables involved, and we do not need to execute any convolution of the original densities.

As a special case, we conclude then that a sum of Gaussian random variables is always Gaussian. We learned earlier that a sum of a large number of independent random variables is approximately Gaussian. For the Gaussian case the result is exact rather than an approximation based on a large number of variables, and the variables need not be independent.

8.8 SUMMARY

Distribution and density functions of n random variables:

$$F_{X_1, X_2, \ldots X_n}(a_1, a_2, \ldots, a_n) = P\{X_1 \le a_1, X_2 \le a_2, \ldots, X_n \le a_n\}$$

$$f_{X_1, X_2, \ldots X_n}(a_1, a_2, \ldots, a_n) = \frac{\partial^n F_{X_1 X_2 \ldots X_n}(a_1, a_2, \ldots, a_n)}{\partial a_1 \partial a_2 \ldots \partial a_n}$$

$$P\{a_1 < X_1 \le a_1 + \Delta_1, a_2 < X_2 \le a_2 + \Delta_2, \ldots, a_n < X_n \le a_n + \Delta_n\} \approx$$
$$f_{X_1, X_2, \ldots X_n}(a_1, a_2, \ldots, a_n)\, \Delta_1 \Delta_2 \ldots \Delta_n$$

Independent random variables:

$$f_{X_1, X_2, \ldots X_n}(a_1, a_2, \ldots, a_n) = \prod_{i=1}^{n} f_{X_i}(a_i)$$

Sums of two random variables:

$$Z = X + Y$$

$$f_Z(w) = \int_{-\infty}^{\infty} f_{X,Y}(u, w - u)\, du$$

If X and Y are independent:

$$f_Z(w) = \int_{-\infty}^{\infty} f_X(u)\, f_Y(w - u)\, du = f_X(w)*f_Y(w)$$
$$= \text{convolution of the two densities}$$

The density of a sum of n independent random variables is equal to the convolution of the n densities.

The mean of a sum of n random variables is equal to the sum of the means of the random variables

The variance of a sum of uncorrelated random variables is equal to the sum of the variances of the random variables.

The variance of the sum of n random variables with means m_k, variances σ_k^2 and correlation coefficients ρ_{ki}:

$$\sigma_Y^2 = \sum_{k=1}^{n} \sum_{i=1}^{n} \rho_{ki} \sigma_k \sigma_i, \text{ where } \rho_{kk} = 1$$

Law of large numbers:

The arithmetic average of n uncorrelated random variables with equal means m and equal variance σ^2 approaches the mean as n tends to infinity.

Central limit theorem:

The density of a sum of n independent random variables with identical distribution with finite mean and variance approaches the Gaussian density as n tends to infinity.

Max function of n independent identically distributed random variables:

$Y = \text{Max}\{X_1, X_2, \ldots, X_n\}$

$F_Y(v) = [F_X(v)]^n$

Min function of n independent identically distributed random variables:

$Y = \text{Min}\{X_1, X_2, \ldots, X_n\}$

$F_Y(v) = 1 - [1 - F_X(v)]^n$

Characteristic function of n random variables:

$$\Phi_X(\boldsymbol{v}) = \Phi_X(v_1, v_2, \ldots, v_n) = E\{\exp(j\boldsymbol{v}^T \boldsymbol{X})\} = E\left\{\exp\left(j\sum_{i=1}^{n} v_i X_i\right)\right\}$$

Linear transformation of n random variables:

$Y = AX$

$\Phi_Y(\boldsymbol{v}) = \Phi_X(A^T \boldsymbol{v})$

Gaussian random variables:

Uncorrelated Gaussian variables are independent.

A linear transformation of Gaussian random variables is also Gaussian.

8.9 PROBLEMS

MATLAB Problems:

1. Generate $n = 50$ uniformly distributed random numbers $\{X_i\}$ in the interval $[2, 6]$, and add them to obtain just a single number Y. Repeat 1000 times and thus generate 1000 values $\{Y_j\}$.

   a. Find the sample mean and sample standard deviation of Y and compare it with the analytical result.
   b. Plot a histogram of the variables Y and compare it with a Gaussian density with the appropriate mean and variance.
   c. Repeat for $n = 100$ and $n = 200$ and show that the Gaussian approximation becomes better.

2. Repeat Problem 1, but instead of uniformly distributed $\{X_i\}$, generate random variables with exponential density $2 \exp(-2x)$.

3. Generate 500 pairs of Gaussian random variables $\{X_i\}$ and $\{Y_i\}$ by using the MATLAB function *randn*, with zero mean and unit variance. Transform the (X, Y) pairs that you generated to generate two new pairs (Z, W) of variables $\{Z_i\}$ and $\{W_i\}$ as follows:

   $Z_i = aX_i - bY_i$ and $W_i = aX_i + bY_i$, where $a = [0.5(1 + r)]^{1/2}$ and $b = [0.5(1 - r)]^{1/2}$, where r is a correlation coefficient. Use three cases for values of $r = 0.7, 0.9, -0.9$.

   a. Generate a scatter plot of Z versus W and show that the two variables are indeed correlated, corresponding to the value of the correlation coefficient r. Compare this plot with the scatter plot of X and Y.
   b. Plot histograms of Z and W and show that the two variables are indeed Gaussian.
   c. Find the sample correlation coefficient from the data you generated, and compare it with the value of r. Compare it with the correlation coefficient of X and Y.

4. Generate $n = 400$ random numbers $\{X_i\}$ uniformly distributed in the interval $[a, b]$ for $a = 5 - 4\sqrt{3}$ and $b = 5 + 4\sqrt{3}$ (so that the mean is 5 and the variance is 16).

   a. Find the sample average and compare it with the mean. Repeat 1000 times, and find the fraction of times out of these 1000 that the sample average is outside the intervals $(4.8, 5.2), (4.6, 5.4)$, and $(4.4, 5.6)$. Compare the result with the Gaussian distribution being outside the interval of $\pm\sigma, \pm2\sigma$, and $\pm3\sigma$ around the mean.
   b. Repeat for $n = 900$ and $n = 1600$, and appropriately adjust the intervals around the mean to illustrate how the law of large number is "verified" in that the interval around the mean becomes smaller for the same fraction of the values being outside the interval as the number of samples increases.

Regular Problems:

5. Let X and Y be independent random variables, with means $m_X = 2$ and $m_Y = 5$, and variances $\mathrm{Var}(X) = 9$ and $\mathrm{Var}(Y) = 4$, respectively. Define new random variables Z and W as follows:

$$Z = 2X + 1.5Y - 2.5$$
$$W = X - 3Y + 3$$

Find the means, variances and covariance of Z and W. Find the covariance and correlation coefficient between: X and Z, Y and Z, X and W, Z and W.

6. The AND and OR gates shown have inputs $S_i(t) = u(t - T_i)$, where $u(t)$ is a unit step function and the delays in the timing of the steps $\{T_i\}$ are independent random variables with the following identical density function:

$$f_{Ti}(t) = [\pi/(2T)]\sin(t\pi/T), \quad \text{for } 0 < t < T, \text{ and is zero elsewhere.}$$

a.

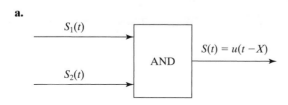

b.

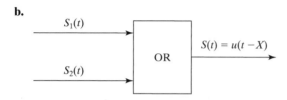

c.

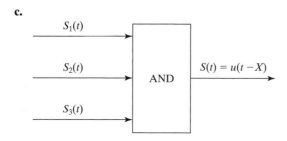

d.

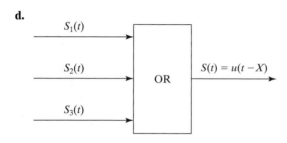

For each of the preceding four cases, find the distribution and density functions of the random delay X at the output of the gate. Find the average delay as well.

7. Repeat Problem 6 for the following probability density functions of the delays:

    a. $f_{Ti}(t) = 2t/T^2$, for $0 < t < T$

    b. $f_{Ti}(t) = 2\dfrac{(T - t)}{T^2}$, for $0 < t < T$

8.* The AND and OR gates combinations shown have inputs $S_i(t) = u(t - T_i)$, where $u(t)$ is a unit step function, and the delays in the timing of the steps $\{T_i\}$ are independent random variables with the following identical density function:

$$f_{Ti}(t) = 1/T, \quad \text{for } 0 < t < T, \text{ and is zero elsewhere.}$$

a.

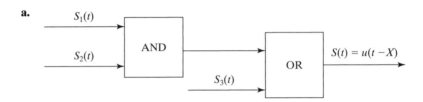

b.

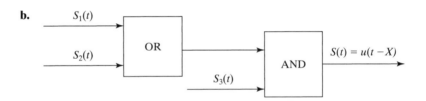

c.

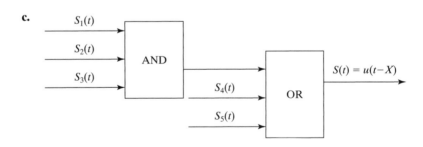

d.

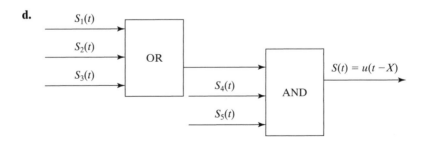

For each of the preceding four cases, find the distribution and density functions of the random delay X at the output of the circuit. Find the average delay as well.

9.[*] Use the two cases of delay densities defined in Problem 7 to find the probability density, distribution functions, and expectation of total delay X, if n such signals are used as inputs to an OR gate. Calculate and plot the results for $n = 2, 3, 4, 5$.

10.[*] Use the two cases of delay densities defined in Problem 7 to find the probability density, distribution functions, and expectation of total delay X, if n such signals are used as inputs to an AND gate. Calculate and plot the results for $n = 2, 3, 4, 5$.

11. Three resistors R_1, R_2, and R_3 are randomly selected from resistors with nominal value of $100 \pm 10\%$ ohms. They are assumed to have a uniform density function within the tolerance interval. They are combined in series to obtain a single resistor R whose value is $300 \pm 10\%$ ohms but whose density function is obviously not uniform.

   a. Find the density function of the resistance R of the series combination.
   b. Find the probability that the resistance R falls outside the $\pm 5\%$ region around the nominal value of 300 ohms.
   c. Find the mean and variance of the resistance R.

12. Two signals X and Y are independent and have identical density functions:

$$f_X(u) = f_Y(u) = \exp(-2|u|)$$

   a. Find the density function of their sum $Z = X + Y$.
   b. Find the mean and variance of their sum.

13. Three random variables X, Y, and Z are jointly Gaussian with equal means of 2 and equal variances of 9. Their correlation coefficients are given by $\rho_{XY} = \rho_{YZ} = 0.5$ and $\rho_{XZ} = 0$. Two new random variables U and V are defined as follows:

$$U = X + 2Y + Z - 8$$
$$V = X - 2Y + Z$$

   a. Find the means, variances, and correlation coefficient of U and V.
   b. Write the joint density function of U and V.

14. Let X and Y be correlated random variables with means $m_X = 2$ and $m_Y = 5$, and variances $\mathrm{Var}(X) = 9$ and $\mathrm{Var}(Y) = 4$, respectively, and covariance $C_{XY} = 5$. Two new random variables are defined as follows:

$$U = aX + bY + m_1, \qquad V = cX + dY + m_2$$

   a. For values of $a = 2, b = 1.5, c = 2, d = -2.5, m_1 = m_2 = 0$, find the means, variances, covariance, and correlation coefficient of U and V.
   b. Let $c = 0$. Find values of a, b, d, m_1, and m_2 so that U and V will have zero means, variances of 1, and covariance of 0.
   c. If X and Y are jointly Gaussian, write the joint probability density function of U and V you obtained in part (b).

15.[*] Suppose we are considering the arrivals of packets at a node in a network, and we assume that the number of arrivals satisfies the Poisson model with arrival rate λ. Let the number of arrivals in an interval of length t (starting at $t = 0$) be denoted by N.

Suppose that each packet that arrives can be a packet from a voice message with probability p or from a data message with probability $(1 - p)$. In this way, we may define, at the kth arrival time t_k, a random variable X_k that takes the value 1 if the message is a voice message and 0 if it is a data message. We assume that the random variables X_k are independent of each other and of N. We then define a random variable Y as follows:

$$Y = \sum_{k=1}^{N} X_k$$

This way, the random variable Y counts the number of packets from voice messages that arrive in time t. Note that N is also random, having a Poisson distribution, while for a given value of $N = n$, the number of voice messages is binomial.

Find the distribution of the random variable Y, and show that it is Poisson with average arrival rate of $p\lambda$. Find the mean and variance of the random variable Y.

16.* Consider the Poisson arrivals system discussed in Problem 15. We now define the random variables X_k as taking the value $+1$ with probability p and the value -1 with probability $(1 - p)$. Let Y be as defined in Problem 15. Find the mean and variance of Y. Compute the answer for the case $p = 0.5$.

17. Let X be a binomially distributed random variable with $n = 30$ and $p = 0.5$. Find the following probabilities by using the central limit theorem and comparing the results with the exact value. $P\{10 \le X \le 20\}, P\{10 \le X < 20\}, P\{10 < X \le 20\}, P\{10 < X < 20\}$.
Simulate using MATLAB (by repeating the experiment generating the binomial random variables 1000 times) and compare the calculated results with the simulated results.

18.* In a voice communication system there are n calls in progress. The length of a voice call is assumed to be exponential, with average length of $1/\mu$. A new call arrives and can be accommodated only if one of the n calls in progress is completed in a time period of T (the period during which the call can be delayed without causing difficulties). If no call is completed during the period T, then the new call will be blocked. Find the probability that the call will be blocked. Calculate for $T = 2$ sec, $n = 64$, and $1/\mu = 30$ sec. (Hint: First find the probability that any of the existing calls will terminate before time T. Then use the binomial to compute the desired result.)

19.* In a network node there are n digital messages awaiting transmission in a queue. We assume that the message length is exponentially distributed with average length of $1/\mu$.

a. If a new message arrives at the node, what is the average time until the transmission of the message is completed? Solve for general n, and then compute for $n = 20$ and $\mu = 2(\text{min})^{-1}$.
b. What is the variance of this total transmission time? Again, provide the general case and compute for the values provided in (a).
c. If we denote the average time for transmission by T, what is the probability that the actual time exceeds $1.05T$? What is the probability that the transmission time exceeds $1.10T$?

9

Basic Statistics

9.1 INTRODUCTION

So far we have considered a variety of probabilistic models to approximate various applications, involving reliability, noisy observations, and estimation, among others. However, these models require knowledge of the values of some parameters such as the mean, variance, correlation coefficient, and sometimes even the shape of the distribution if it is not assumed in advance. Statistics deal with the subject of confirming the validity of a probabilistic model by using empirical data. We have alluded to this in the introduction to the textbook in Chapter 1. This chapter deals with the basic problem of obtaining the parameters of simple probabilistic models from experimental data. It is not intended as a comprehensive coverage of statistics, which in itself can take an extensive textbook to cover adequately. First we address the issue of how to obtain various statistical parameters from empirical data. Then we consider the accuracy of such results for a few important cases.

9.2 HISTOGRAMS AS APPROXIMATIONS TO DISTRIBUTIONS

Suppose we wish to obtain complete statistical information about a variable, which we are modeling as a random variable, such as the time to failure of a component or the amplitude of a signal or noise. In this case we collect a number of sample values of the variable in question. For the result to make sense, we have to assume that the data collected in this manner are independent of each other, else the result may not be reliable. Once we collect such data, we can plot a histogram, which provides the relative frequency of each range of values of the random variable in question. If the relative frequency is plotted in such a manner that the area under the curve is equal to the relative frequency, we obtain an empirical density function of the random variable. If we find the relative frequency of the values obtained in ranges less than some value u, as u extends over the entire range of values collected, then we actually obtain an approximation of the cumulative distribution function of the random variable. In practice, we do not usually obtain the cumulative distribution function empirically, since the graph of the histogram is much more informative pictorially, and it is customary to derive it as an approximation to the density or probability mass function.

In Figures 9.1 and 9.2 we display an empirical cumulative distribution function and its histogram for an empirically generated 1000 values of an exponentially distributed random variable with parameter $\lambda = 0.5$. Figure 9.1 displays the cumulative distribution function only. The histogram is shown in Figure 9.2. Figure 9.2 has three parts. The first (Figure 9.2(a)) shows the raw histogram, which just provides the number of occurrences of the values in each range between 0 and 12 using a range width of 0.5. If we convert this figure by using relative frequency and then plotting the relative frequency so that the area in each bar is equal to the relative frequency, we obtain an approximation of the density function shown in Figure 9.2(b). This indeed seems to be the case when we compare the empirical density with the corresponding mathematical version, $0.5 \exp(-0.5u)$, of the exponential density function shown in Figure 9.2(c).

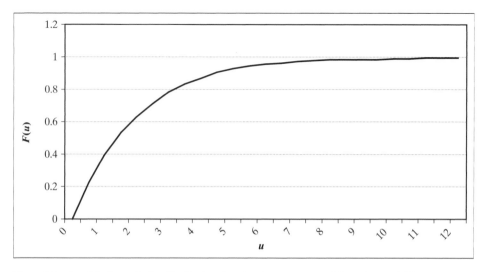

Figure 9.1 Empirical cumulative distribution function for an exponential random variable

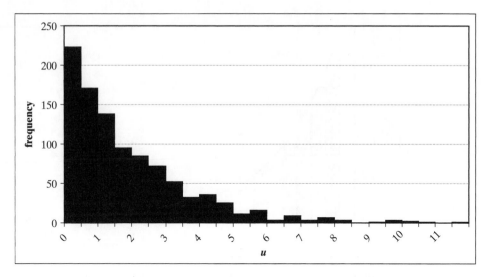

Figure 9.2(a)   The raw histogram of 1000 outcomes of an exponentially distributed random variable

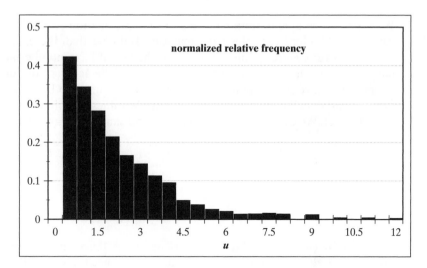

Figure 9.2(b)   The normalized histogram so that the relative frequency equals the value of the function times the range width

Of course we expect our approximation of the density to improve as we collect more data. The granularity in the distribution or the density functions disappears with more data as well. We see that the result becomes less accurate when the probabilities are small, as we observe for larger values of the argument in the preceding density function. Clearly, we need a large amount of data to obtain density or distribution information from data. In the next section we discuss how to obtain information about the mean, variance, and correlation coefficient from data.

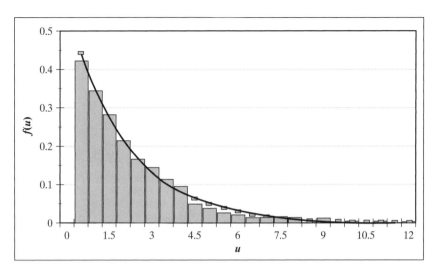

Figure 9.2(c)   The empirical and mathematical densities for the exponential example

9.3 SAMPLE MEAN, VARIANCE, AND CORRELATION

We expect to be able to obtain more accurate information about the mean and the variance of random variables from experimental data than the exact shape of the density function. Here we also expect that the law of large number and the central limit theorem will help us determine a measure of the accuracy of our information. Suppose we have n data points $\{x_i\}$, which are assumed to be sample values of a random variable. We assume that these sample values are obtained independently of each other. We define the sample mean $\bar{x}$ and sample variance as:

$$\bar{x} = \frac{1}{n}\sum_{i=1}^{n} x_i \tag{9.1}$$

$$s_x^2 = \frac{1}{n-1}\sum_{i=1}^{n}(x_i - \bar{x})^2 = \frac{1}{n-1}\left[\sum_{i=1}^{n} x_i^2 - \frac{1}{n}\left(\sum_{i=1}^{n} x_i\right)^2\right] \tag{9.2}$$

We divide by $(n-1)$ to obtain the variance, since the sample mean we use in the expression is already obtained from the data and hence the sum of the differences in the expression used for the variance is equal to zero. Therefore we do not have n independent observations for estimating the variance. The sample standard deviation is of course the square root of the sample variance. It should be noted that when we are dealing with the values obtained in the experiment, we use lower case notations for these values. When we wish to obtain the properties of such sample values if we were to repeat the experiment, with different sample values, then we have to use the notation of the random variables, as the values may be different every time we repeat the experiment. In such a case we use the notation $\{X_i\}$ to indicate the set of random variables representing all the values that may be taken by the n samples, with X_i representing the random variable taking the values of the ith sample.

Finally, we define the sample correlation and sample correlation coefficient by using n pairs $\{x_i, y_i\}$ of data points representing sample outcomes of two random variables. First, we define the **sample covariance** of the pair of data sets:

$$c_{xy} = \frac{1}{n-1} \sum_{i=1}^{n} (x_i - \bar{x})(y_i - \bar{y}) = \frac{1}{n-1} \left[\sum_{i=1}^{n} x_i y_i - \frac{1}{n} \left(\sum_{i=1}^{n} x_i \right) \left(\sum_{i=1}^{n} y_i \right) \right] \quad (9.3)$$

In order to obtain the **sample correlation coefficient** r_{xy}, we simply have to divide by the sample standard deviations:

$$r_{xy} = \frac{c_{xy}}{s_x s_y} \quad (9.4)$$

It is possible to verify that the sample correlation coefficient takes values in the interval $(-1, +1)$. As with the correlation coefficient we defined in Chapter 6, the sample correlation coefficient figures prominently in linear curve fitting, or as it is called in statistics, **linear regression**, involving the sets of data pairs. Here again we say that the sets of two data are uncorrelated when the coefficient is equal to zero, and they are perfectly correlated when it is either $+1$ or -1. In order to see what the linear regression means, let us plot a scatter diagram of 100 sample pairs $\{x_i, y_i\}$ as shown in Figure 9.3.

We show three different examples in the figure. As can be seen, the first two appear not to be suitable for a good linear regression, while the third one seems to

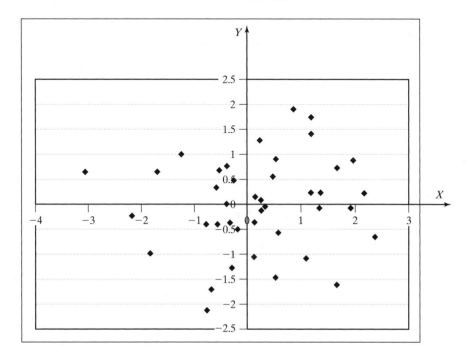

Figure 9.3(a)   Scatter plot for data with $r_{xy} = 0.0936$

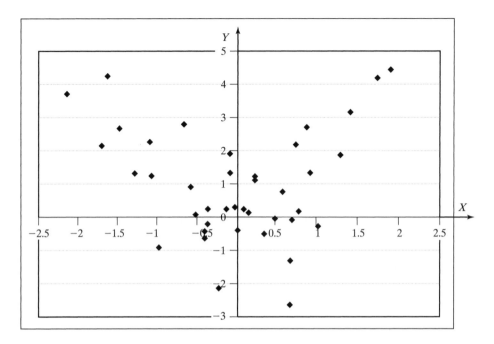

Figure 9.3(b)   Scatter plot for data with $r_{xy} = -0.0364$ (with possible nonlinear relation)

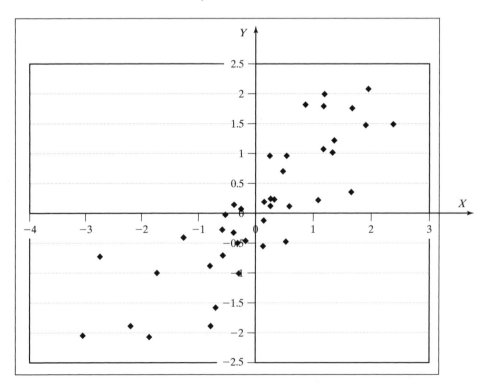

Figure 9.3(c)   Scatter plot for data with $r_{xy} = 0.8714$

be appropriate for a linear approximation or regression. Indeed, if we compute the correlation coefficient, we obtain the following respective values for the three figures: $r_{xy} = 0.0936$, $r_{xy} = -0.0364$, and $r_{xy} = 0.8714$.

How can we utilize this for linear regression (also known as linear curve fitting)? We are trying to fit a straight line to the data pair, so that we approximate y_i by $\hat{y}_i$ using a straight line:

$$\hat{y}_i = ax_i + b \tag{9.5}$$

The errors e_i in this approximation (also called the residuals) are given by

$$e_i = y_i - \hat{y}_i = y_i - ax_i - b \tag{9.6}$$

We would like then to choose the slope a and the intercept b of the line so as to minimize the sample variance of the error:

$$s_e^2 = \frac{1}{n-1}\sum_{i=1}^{n} e_i^2 \tag{9.7}$$

Note that we are not subtracting the sample mean in equation (9.7), since the minimization of equation (9.7) will yield a residual with zero sample mean. If we take the partial derivatives with respect to the parameters a and b and set them equal to zero, than as in the probabilistic case, we obtain the following equations to be satisfied by a and b:

$$\sum_{i=1}^{n} 2e_i x_i = 0 \tag{9.7a}$$

$$\sum_{i=1}^{n} 2e_i = 0 \tag{9.7b}$$

The solution of equation (9.7b) yields the following value for b:

$$b = \bar{y} - a\bar{x} \tag{9.8}$$

Since the sum of the residuals is zero as required by equation (9.7b), we can subtract the constant $\bar{x}$ from x_i in equation (9.7a). We now substitute equation (9.8) into the resulting equation (9.7a) to obtain the following (where we divided by the factor 2):

$$\sum_{i=1}^{n} [(y_i - \bar{y}) - a(x_i - \bar{x})](x_i - \bar{x}) = 0 \tag{9.8a}$$

We now solve equation (9.8a) for the value of a to obtain

$$a = \frac{\sum_{i=1}^{n}(y_i - \bar{y})(x_i - \bar{x})}{\sum_{i=1}^{n}(x_i - \bar{x})^2} = \frac{r_{xy}s_x s_y}{s_x^2} = r_{xy}\frac{s_y}{s_x} \tag{9.9}$$

After a and b are substituted from equation (9.8) and (9.9) into equation (9.7), the resulting residual becomes

$$s_e^2 = s_y^2(1 - r_{xy}^2) \tag{9.10}$$

We can also write the regression line directly as

$$\hat{y}_i = \bar{y} + r_{xy}\frac{s_y}{s_x}(x_i - \bar{x}) \tag{9.11}$$

The regression line for the example in Figure 9.3(c) is shown together with the data in Figure 9.4.

It should be noted that while the data in Figure 9.3(b) appear to be uncorrelated, this does not mean the data points are independent, as there maybe two such lines with two different slopes that together may fit the data. Hence, the correlation measures only the possibility of a linear relationship.

We shall not discuss the problem of how accurate the correlation coefficient is if we have only n data pairs. In later sections we shall discuss the accuracy problem for the sample mean. First, we shall discuss some MATLAB statistical functions in the next subsection.

9.3.1 MATLAB Statistical Functions

Before we move on to the next topic, we provide here the functions used to compute some of the parameters described in Section 9.3. Suppose we generated two vectors

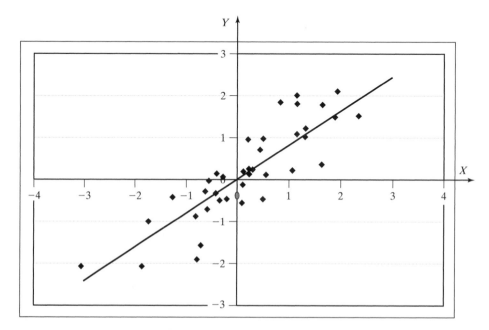

Figure 9.4   Scatter plot for the data of Fig. 9.3(c) with a regression line

X and Y involving n random numbers each. We list below the MATLAB commands that we can use to analyze the data provided by X and Y. These MATLAB commands are available only in the statistical toolbox of the program.

The mean, variance, and standard deviations of the vectors can be obtained by the following commands:

$$\text{Sample mean of } X = \textit{mean}(X)$$
$$\text{Sample standard deviation of } X = \textit{std}(X)$$
$$\text{Sample variance of } X = \textit{var}(X)$$
$$V = \text{Sample covariance matrix of } X \text{ and } Y = \textit{cov}(X, Y)$$

The sample covariance provided by the preceding command yields a matrix V whose elements are the variances of X and Y and the covariance between X and Y. The matrix V has the following elements:

$$V(1, 1) = \text{sample variance of } X$$
$$V(2, 2) = \text{sample variance of } Y$$
$$V(1, 2) = V(2, 1) = \text{sample covariance between } X \text{ and } Y.$$

Similarly, the correlation coefficient is obtained with the following command:

$$W(1, 2) = \text{Sample correlation coefficient between } X \text{ and } Y = \textit{corrcoef}(X, Y)$$

These commands were used to generate the parameters used in Figure 9.4 to obtain the regression.

9.4 CONFIDENCE INTERVAL FOR THE SAMPLE MEAN

Suppose that we have a sample $\{x_i\}$ of size n from a population that we assume has the same distribution. We also assume that we know the variance σ^2 but we do not know the mean μ of the distribution. We shall also assume that the sample was generated in such a way that each sample is independent of the others. If we take the sample average as the estimate of the mean, we know by the law of large numbers that the estimate approaches the mean as the number of samples approaches infinity. The question is how to derive a measure of the accuracy of the estimate if n is finite? In order to answer this question, we must ensure that the samples obtained are independent. An example illustrating the assumption where we know the variance (or know some bound on the variance) is the case in which we are measuring a variable and our measurement device is calibrated so that we know its error variance. In the binomial case, for which we do not know the probability of success p, we know that the variance for each trial is $p(1 - p)$, but since $0 < p < 1$, we can show that the variance is less than 0.25, so that the standard deviation is less than 0.5. (See Figure 9.5, which shows that the variance achieves its maximum value at $p = 0.5$.) Hence we obtain a conservative result if we assume that the variance in such a case is equal to 0.25.

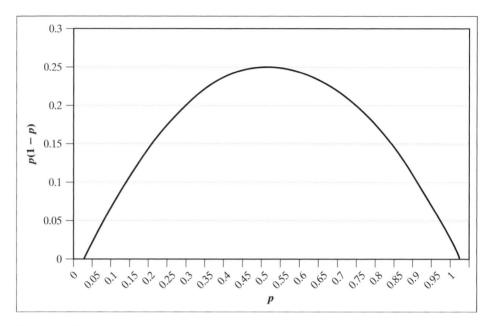

Figure 9.5   Variance of the binomial random variable

In order to analyze the quality of our estimate, we assume that each sample x_i collected is one possible value taken by a random variable X_i (representing the ith data point in the sample), since, were we to repeat the experiment, we could possibly obtain another value for variable X_i. We know that we are using the sample average as our estimate of the mean. Because the n data points are assumed to be outcomes of the random variables $\{X_i\}$ whose mean we are trying to estimate, we also know that the sample average has a mean that can be obtained by the rule of the mean of sums of random variables as

$$E\{\overline{X}\} = \frac{1}{n}\sum_{i=1}^{n}E\{X_i\} = \mu \tag{9.12}$$

The reason we are using the random variables instead of their outcomes to analyze the result of the sample mean is that we wish to find what would happen to our estimate, if we were to repeat the experiment with several different data sets. How big is the spread of the sample average from the true mean μ we are trying to estimate? We also use the notation $\overline{X}$ for the sample mean, as we wish to emphasize that this is a random quantity, which may take a different value for different samples. When we perform the experiment once, we obtain only one instance of the quantity, which we denoted by $\overline{x}$. The analysis is therefore based on the properties of the random variable represented by the sample average as a random variable $\overline{X}$. Since the mean of the sample average is indeed equal to μ, we next need to find its variance, so as to know the spread of our estimate about the true mean. This spread represents the variation from sample to sample were we to repeat the experiment. The variance of the sample average is found by using the fact that the variance of a sum of independent random variables is equal to the sum of the variances:

$$\text{Var}\{\overline{X}\} = \frac{1}{n^2}Var\left(\sum_{i=1}^{n} X_i\right) = \frac{1}{n^2}\sum_{i=1}^{n} Var(X_i) = \frac{1}{n^2}\sum_{i=1}^{n}\sigma^2 = \frac{\sigma^2}{n} \qquad (9.13)$$

We now apply the central limit theorem to approximate the probability density of the sample average. In such a case, we know for example that the estimate will be within 3 standard deviations of the mean with probability 99.7%, and within 2 standard deviations with probability 95%. In general, if we are to pick a confidence level C (say 98%), what is the margin of error of our estimate about the true mean μ with that confidence level? We call this margin of error a **confidence interval** and we denote it by m. In this case we wish to have

$$P\{|\overline{X} - \mu| \le m\} = C \qquad (9.14)$$

By using the central limit theorem, we find that this probability is equal to

$$C = P\{|\overline{X} - \mu| \le m\} = P\left\{-\frac{m\sqrt{n}}{\sigma} \le Z \le \frac{m\sqrt{n}}{\sigma}\right\} \qquad (9.15)$$

Here Z represents the unit Gaussian random variable with zero mean and unit variance, which is obtained from $\overline{X}$ via the relation $Z = \left[(\overline{X} - \mu)\sqrt{n}\right]/\sigma$. We therefore can evaluate the expression in equation (9.15) by using the Gaussian table as

$$C = P\{|\overline{X} - \mu| \le m\} = \Phi\left(\frac{m\sqrt{n}}{\sigma}\right) - \Phi\left(-\frac{m\sqrt{n}}{\sigma}\right) = 2\Phi\left(\frac{m\sqrt{n}}{\sigma}\right) - 1 \quad (9.16)$$

What does the margin of error and confidence level tell us? Suppose we have a confidence level of $C = 98\%$ and a margin of error of $m = 5$ in the measurement of some unknown quantity μ. Then we carry out the experiment one time to obtain the value $\overline{x}$ as an estimate of μ. If we repeat this experiment 100 times, we may obtain different values of $\overline{x}$, but 98 of these values will be within the interval $(\mu - m, \mu + m) = (\mu - 5, \mu + 5)$ and only 2 of these 100 will be outside the range. That relation of the value of $\overline{x}$ to the interval $(\mu - 5, \mu + 5)$ implies that the unknown constant μ will fall in the interval $(\overline{x} - 5, \overline{x} + 5)$ 98 times and only 2 times will the true value be outside this interval, which we call the confidence interval. A pictorial illustration of this observation for the case of $C = 90\%$ is shown in Figure 9.6. In this figure we assumed that the unknown value was indeed $\mu = 3$, and we obtained $m = 2$ for the assumed measurement standard deviation and number of measurements. Of 10 times that the experiment was repeated, only once was the true value outside the confidence interval.

In the figure we repeated the estimation 10 times, and we obtained the following quantities for $\overline{x}$: [1.56, 0.32, 4.20, 2.37, 3.40, 3.03, 1.78, 1.85, 2.55, 3.28]. We marked the values with an $\times$ in 10 separate lines that show the true value as well as the confidence interval limits. We see that only for the value of $\overline{x} = 0.32$ does the true

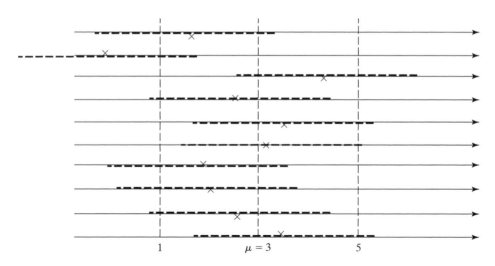

1                      $\mu = 3$ 5

Figure 9.6   Graphical illustration of the confidence interval

value of the mean (in this case 3) fall outside the range 0.32 ± 2 obtained by the estimate. In the other 9 experiments the true value falls within ± 2 of the estimate $\bar{x}$. A dashed line of length $2m$ is shown centered around each result for $\bar{x}$, which illustrates the fact stated in the last sentence.

Another way to illustrate this fact is to show the probability density function of the random variable $\overline{X}$ and draw an interval of $\pm m$ around the true mean μ of the resulting density. The probability of being outside this range is shown in the figure and it is equal to $[1 - C]$, so that if a sample $\bar{x}$ of $\overline{X}$ is obtained inside the marked range of values, it will have a probability C. In this case the true mean will be within the same margin of error $\pm m$ around the sample value so obtained. This observation is shown in Figure 9.7. In the figure two values, namely, $\bar{x} = \alpha$, which is larger than the true mean, and $\bar{x} = \beta$, which is smaller than the true mean, are also shown to illustrate that if these values fall within the margin of $\pm m$ from the true mean, then the true mean falls within the same margin from the resulting sample mean value. This last fact is shown by the margin of error displayed around these two values by dashed lines of length $2m$. (The $2m$ value of the length is not noted in the figure in order not to clutter the picture).

We see that the result of the estimate has three parameters: the confidence level C, the margin of error m, and the number of samples used n. These parameters are related by equation (9.16). We now have three choices:

1. If we fix m and n, then using equation (9.16), we can find the confidence level C.
2. If we fix C and n, we can then find the confidence interval m as follows: From C we obtain the critical value Z_c that satisfies the expression

$$2\Phi(Z_c) - 1 = C, \quad \text{or} \quad 1 - \Phi(Z_c) = \frac{1 - C}{2} \tag{9.17}$$

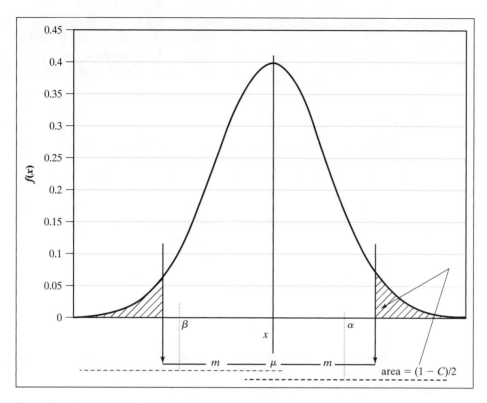

Figure 9.7   Illustration of the confidence interval for inference of the mean

The value of Z_c can be found directly from the unit Gaussian table or from special tables that provide the value of Z_c for every value of $(1 - C)/2$. The expression for m then becomes

$$m = \frac{Z_c \sigma}{\sqrt{n}} \tag{9.18}$$

3. Finally, if we desire both a specific C and a specific confidence interval m, then the only way we can satisfy both is to change the number of samples n. First we have to find the value of Z_c from C as we did previously. Then we evaluate n from equation (9.18) to yield the expression

$$n = \left(\frac{Z_c \sigma}{m} \right)^2 \tag{9.19}$$

We shall consider an example that illustrates all three possible choices. The first example is a simple one of measuring an unknown voltage when the instrument has measurement errors with zero means and known standard deviation. The second example deals with a binomial random variable: We need to find the probability p of the preference in a poll of n persons. The latter case can also apply to finding the error rate in a binary channel, or the probability of Heads in the toss of a coin, or in the probability of failures of components, or the probably of packet loss in a network.

Example 9.1

Consider the case of taking n measurements of an unknown voltage μ when the measurement errors are independent and have mean zero and standard deviation of 5 mV. In order to see how the three choices are used, we shall consider each case.

1. We fix n at 100, and we would like a confidence level of $C = 98\%$. Suppose that the sample average of these 100 measurements gives us an answer of $\bar{x} = 8.5$ mV. What is the confidence interval in the estimate of the value of μ?
   From the table of the Gaussian distribution, for $C = 0.98$, by using equation (9.17) we find the value of $Z_c = 2.326$. We therefore have the expression for the confidence interval as

$$m = \frac{Z_c\sigma}{\sqrt{n}} = \frac{2.326 \times 5}{\sqrt{100}} = 1.163$$

   We now can state that the value of the unknown voltage is 8.5 ± 1.163 mV with 98% confidence.

2. We fix n at 100 again, but we would like a margin of error of ± 1.0 mV. What should be our confidence in this estimate? Again suppose that we obtain $\bar{x} = 8.5$ mV as the sample average. In order to find the confidence level in our choice of error margin $m = 1.0$ mV we have to find its fraction of the standard deviation:

$$Z_c = \frac{m\sqrt{n}}{\sigma} = \frac{1.0\sqrt{100}}{5} = 2.0$$

   Hence, by using the Gaussian table we find that

$$C = 2\Phi(Z_c) - 1 = 2\Phi(2) - 1 = 2(0.97725) - 1 = 0.9545 = 95.45\%$$

   In this case we can state that the value of the unknown voltage is equal to 8.5 ± 1.0 mV with 95.45% confidence.

3. Finally, we would like a margin of error of ± 1.0 mV and a confidence level of 98%. How many samples should we use? Here, since we require a confidence level $C = 98\%$, the inverse of the Gaussian distribution provides us with the same value of $Z_c = 2.326$ that we obtained in part 1. We now apply equation (9.19) relating n to the margin of error m and the value of Z_c to obtain the number n required:

$$n = \left(\frac{Z_c\sigma}{m}\right)^2 = \left(\frac{2.326 \times 5}{1.0}\right)^2 = 135.3$$

This means that if we wish to have the value of the measurement be 8.5 ± 1.0 mV with a 98% confidence level, we need 136 samples.

Example 9.2

In this example, we wish to evaluate the probability p of failures of components. We test n components and we count the number of failures. We use the ratio as the estimate for p. We know that in this case the sample average (which is the number of failures divided by n) would have mean p and variance $p(1-p)/n$ that is bounded by $1/(4n)$, as discussed earlier with the help of Figure 9.5. Hence the standard deviation is bounded by $\frac{1}{2\sqrt{n}}$, which means that if we use this value, our results will be on the conservative side. Again we have three possible choices in formulating the problem, depending on what we wish our estimate properties to be. Suppose we sample n components and we obtain an answer of $p = 0.32$ as the failure probability.

1. If we set $n = 100$ as before, and we would like a confidence level of 98%, what should be the margin of error in our estimate? Here we have, as we have done in the previous example, $Z_c = 2.326$, which is obtained from $C = 0.98$ and the Gaussian tables. As a result, m will be given by

$$m = \frac{Z_c \sigma}{\sqrt{n}} = \frac{2.326 \times 0.5}{\sqrt{100}} = 0.1163$$

This means that we can state our answer as $p = 0.32 \pm 0.1163$ with 98% confidence. We see that we have a very large margin of error, and that is due to the small number of samples and the high confidence level we required.

2. If we now require a margin of error of 0.08 in the estimate of p, then what should be our confidence if n remains at 100? Again we first find the value of Z_c so that we can use the Gaussian table for C:

$$Z_c = \frac{m\sqrt{n}}{\sigma} = \frac{0.08\sqrt{100}}{0.5} = 1.6$$

That results in a value of C as follows:

$$C = 2\Phi(1.6) - 1 = 2(0.9452) - 1 = 0.8904$$

We can now state that the failure probability is equal to $p = 0.32 \pm 0.08$ with 89% confidence. Since we did not increase n, we only traded confidence level with margin of error.

3. If we now would like to keep the same margin of error $m = \pm 0.08$ we wanted in part 2, but we wish C to be 98% again, how many samples should we use? In this case we have the same C as in part 1, and hence we have the same value of $Z_c = 2.326$. We now use this value together with the margin of error $m = 0.08$ to find n, as we did in the previous example:

$$n = \left(\frac{Z_c \sigma}{m}\right)^2 = \left(\frac{2.326 \times 0.5}{0.08}\right)^2 = 211.4$$

We therefore can state that the value of $p = 0.32 \pm 0.08$ with 98% confidence, provided that we obtained the 0.32 value using $n = 212$ samples.

Finally, let us consider polls. Usually polls try to determine the fraction of a population that is for one issue or against it (or for one candidate or another). This is the same as finding the probability p that a person picked at random is for or against the issue. Therefore, in a sense we are again trying to estimate the value of p in Bernoulli trials, as we pick n samples from the population and test their opinion. The confidence level is fixed in this case to 99.74%, since the 3-sigma rule is implicitly assumed. For this confidence level we have the 3 standard deviation rule for the margin of error. The pollsters set the margin of error at ±0.04 (4 percentage points in the result). We can therefore apply the results of Example 9.2, using part 3 to obtain

$$n = \left(\frac{Z_c\sigma}{m}\right)^2 = \left(\frac{3 \times 0.5}{0.04}\right)^2 = 1406$$

You may notice that when poll results are shown in the news, they do mention the ±4-percentage point margin of error and they also mention that about 1400 persons were polled. They assume that the 99.7% confidence is a certainty. If we needed a confidence level of only 99%, then we would have to poll a sample size of only

$$n = \left(\frac{Z_c\sigma}{m}\right)^2 = \left(\frac{2.58 \times 0.5}{0.04}\right)^2 = 1040$$

The answer would have to be slightly different when we have more than two possible choices in the polls, but it will not be addressed here.

9.5 OTHER STATISTICAL PARAMETERS

We have looked at how we can obtain an estimate for the mean of a random variable model from collected data. We have considered the known variance case. What happens if the variance is unknown as well, and we are using the data to estimate both the mean and the variance? In such a case we still obtain similar results for the mean, except that now we do not use the cumulative unit Gaussian distribution to obtain the value of Z_c from the confidence level C, but we have to use different data tables. The principle remains the same; just which table to use becomes different. In the unknown variance case the table is called the student t-distribution.

Similar results can be obtained for the confidence interval in estimating the variance from data samples, or estimating the correlation coefficient from data samples. In each case, we can derive an expression for the density of the parameter we are estimating and then use tables for that density to obtain the confidence level for a given error margin, or an error margin for a given confidence level. We shall leave detailed study of this subject to a course in statistics. Again, for estimating the variance of a population, we use the chi-square distribution with n degrees of freedom. The result can also be extended to cover the accuracy in estimating distributions, but the amount of data required for such cases is very large. In the following two subsections we shall address the estimate of the mean when the variance is unknown and the estimate of the variance when the mean is known or unknown.

9.5.1 Unknown Variance Case

In this section we are concerned with the estimate of the mean of a random model from data when the variance is also unknown. We have already discussed the sample mean and the sample variance as shown in equations (9.1) and (9.2). Obviously, these estimates will serve as the estimates of the actual mean and variance of the model. Since we are interested in the estimate of the mean, and we wish to provide an error margin and confidence level, we can still use the mean as the desired estimate, but we run into difficulties in finding the density function of the error so that we can obtain the margin of error as a fraction of the estimated standard deviation. Clearly, the sample average still has a mean that is equal to the mean of the model. If we assume that the sample variance is a reasonable estimate of the variance, we need to find the density function of the following variable:

$$Z = \frac{(\bar{x} - \mu)}{(s/\sqrt{n})} \tag{9.20}$$

The reason we are looking at this variable is that we observe equations (9.12) and (9.13), which show the mean and variance of the sample average, and we see that its mean is μ and its standard deviation is $(\sigma/\sqrt{n})$. Therefore the variable defined in equation (9.20) should have zero mean and a standard deviation of 1 if we were to substitute σ for s. As a matter of fact, due to the central limit theorem, the resulting variable will have a unit Gaussian distribution. However, the use of the sample standard deviation instead of the true standard deviation will not result in a Gaussian distribution for Z. The distribution depends on the original distribution function of the variables we are using to calculate the sample average and sample variance. We can derive the model for the distribution of Z in equation (9.20) only if we assume that the original model of the variables used is Gaussian. In that case the density function of Z is what is called the student t-distribution with $(n - 1)$ degrees of freedom. Such a distribution tends to a Gaussian distribution as n becomes large. Obviously, it can be seen that the smaller the value of n, the greater is the discrepancy from the Gaussian distribution. Clearly, the smallest value of n must be 2, since we are estimating two parameters. This means that the t-distribution is tabulated as a function of its argument with degrees of freedom 1, 2, 3, ... as a parameter. Since it is primarily used to obtain confidence intervals, the tables usually provide the threshold t_c as a function of the probability α of exceeding it. The t-distribution is also symmetric. Hence we may have one-sided or two-sided confidence intervals, so that the threshold is obtained from $\alpha = (1 - C)$ for a one-sided confidence interval and from $\alpha = (1 - C)/2$ if we interested in a two-sided confidence interval:

$$\alpha = (1 - C) = P\{Z > t_c\} = P\{Z < -t_c\} \tag{9.21a}$$

$$2\alpha = (1 - C) = P\{|Z| > t_c\} = 2P\{Z > t_c\} \tag{9.21b}$$

The relationship between the confidence interval and error margin is exactly the same as in the known variance case, except that we use the t-distribution to find the threshold t_c instead of the Gaussian distribution to find Z_c, and we use the sample standard deviation in place of the actual standard deviation. In this case equation (9.18) becomes

$$m = \frac{t_c s}{\sqrt{n}} \tag{9.22}$$

We can see then that the probability of being within $\pm m$ of the estimate, in the two-sided case, is given by:

$$P\{|\overline{X} - \mu| \leq m\} = P\{|\overline{X} - \mu| \leq t_c s/\sqrt{n}\} = P\{|Z| \leq t_c\}$$
$$= 1 - P\{|Z| > t_c\} = C \tag{9.23}$$

Here we used the definition of the threshold from equation (9.21b). Similarly, we can show that the same holds true for one-sided estimates. It is easy to find the t-distribution and its critical values using any standard spreadsheet program. For example, in Microsoft Excel, the value of the distribution is found by the function TDIST, and the critical values for two-sided confidence level are found by the TINV function.

For the sake of completeness, the actual density function of the t-distribution with n degrees of freedom is given by

$$f_Z(t) = \frac{\Gamma\{(n + 1)/2\}}{\sqrt{n\pi}\,\Gamma(0.5n)\{(t^2/n) + 1\}^{(n+1)/2}} \tag{9.24}$$

Here $\Gamma(x)$ is the Gamma function, which becomes the factorial function for integer values of x, $\Gamma(n + 1) = n!$ It can be shown that for $n > 2$, the t-distribution has a mean of zero and a variance of $[n/(n - 2)]$, which we see tends to unity as n becomes large. Note that here n is not the number of samples but the number of degrees of freedom, which is one less than the number of samples.

Example 9.3

Consider the problem posed in Example 9.1, but assume that the standard deviation of 5 used in the example is obtained from the data as a sample standard deviation. If we wish to have a confidence level of, say, $C = 98\%$ and the number of samples is still $n = 100$, then the critical value obtained from the tables is $t_c = 2.364$ instead of 2.326 obtained for the known variance case. Hence the margin of error at this confidence level is

$$m = \frac{s t_c}{\sqrt{n}} = \frac{5 \times 2.364}{10} = 1.182$$

We may wish to compare this result with the result of 1.163 obtained in the previous case. Note that as the number of degrees of freedom becomes smaller, the results become less accurate (i.e., we obtain a larger margin of error). For example, at the same confidence level with 41 samples (40 degrees of freedom) we have a critical value of $t_c = 2.423$, and at 21 samples (20 degrees of freedom) we have $t_c = 2.528$.

The next example illustrates the mean estimation problem using a sampling of the population, which obviously implies that the variance is unknown.

Example 9.4

In a random sample of $n = 36$ schools throughout the country, the average number of pupils per school in the sample is found to be equal to 379.2 (i.e., $\overline{X} = 379.2$) with a sample standard deviation s_X of 124. We wish to use the sample to construct a 95% confidence interval for the mean number of pupils per school, μ_X, for all schools in the country.

We are given $n = 36$ and confidence level C = 95%. We first find the 95% confidence interval (i.e., the margin of error m) using the t-distribution with $n = 35$. In this case we find a critical value of 2.03. Note that for the Gaussian table we would have obtained a critical value of 1.96.

We wish to stress the difference between the sample standard deviation s_X and the standard deviation of the estimate of the sample mean. It should be noted that the number $s_X = 124$ given to us means that for any school (assuming a normal distribution), the **number of students** in a school is in the range

$$\mu_X \pm 3s_X$$

with a probability of 99.7%. Here we are asking for a more accurate value for the **average number** of students μ_X, since the 379.2 was obtained by measuring the average of only $n = 36$ schools. We are looking for the standard deviation $\sigma_{\overline{X}}$ in the measured value of μ_X:

$$\sigma_{\overline{X}} = \frac{s_X}{\sqrt{n}} = \frac{s_X}{\sqrt{36}}$$

The critical value was obtained as $t_c = 2.03$, so that with 95% confidence level, the average number of students per school μ_X is in the range

$$\mu_X = \overline{X} \pm 2.03\,\sigma_{\overline{X}} = 379.2 \pm 2.03(124/6) = 379.2 \pm 41.95$$

The interval from 337.25 to 421.15 forms a 95% confidence interval for the mean μ_X. Note that if the 124 was a known standard deviation σ_X rather than a sample standard deviation, we could have used the normalized unit Gaussian table to obtain a critical value of $Z_c = 1.96$.

It follows that the 95% confidence interval for the true value of μ_X for this case is given by

$$\mu_X = \overline{X} \pm 1.96\,\sigma_{\overline{X}}$$

$$m = 1.96\,\sigma_{\overline{X}} = 1.96\frac{\sigma_X}{\sqrt{n}} = 1.96 \times \frac{124}{\sqrt{36}} = \frac{1.96 \times 124}{6} = 40.51$$

The interval from 338.69 to 419.71 forms a 95% confidence interval for μ_X. We are 95% sure that the **average number** of students per school throughout the country lies between 338.69 and 419.71.

On the other hand, the **number of students** in each school lies in the interval

$$\mu_X \pm 1.96 \times 124 \text{ with 95% confidence.}$$

The preceding illustrates the difference between the variance of the estimate of the sample mean and the sample variance of the population.

9.5.2 Estimation of the Variance

In the previous section we considered the estimation of the mean when both the mean and the variance of the model are unknown. In this section we consider the case of estimation of the variance, when we are interested in obtaining a confidence interval for such an estimate.

In this case the estimates of the mean and variance are still obtained by the sample mean and sample variance given in equations (9.1) and (9.2). In order to find the distribution of the sample variance, we have to assume that the population or the data model satisfies a Gaussian distribution. In order to normalize the distribution, we divide the estimate defined in equation (9.2) by $\sigma^2/(n-1)$:

$$Z = \frac{s^2(n-1)}{\sigma^2} \tag{9.25}$$

It can be shown that the distribution of Z under the Gaussian assumption is the chi-square distribution with $(n-1)$ degrees of freedom. The density of the chi-square distribution with n degrees of freedom is given by

$$f_Z(x) = \frac{x^{(n/2)-1}e^{-(x/2)}}{2^{(n/2)}\Gamma(n/2)}, \qquad x > 0 \tag{9.26}$$

This density is provided here just for completeness, as it is not possible to obtain the value of the cumulative distribution function analytically. Tables of the tails of the chi-square distribution are provided in statistics reference books to allow us to find the critical values for a given confidence level and with the degree of freedom as a parameter. For simplicity we shall consider only a one-sided confidence interval in the estimate of the variance. If our confidence level is C, then we wish to find the upper bound on the value that the sample variance falls below with probability C:

$$C = P\{Z < \chi_c\} = 1 - P\{Z > \chi_c\} \tag{9.27}$$

We can obtain the critical value χ_c from the tails of the chi-square distribution table as a function of $\alpha = (1-C)$. If we use the resulting critical value in the expression for the estimate, we find that

$$\frac{s^2(n-1)}{\sigma^2} > \chi_c \tag{9.28}$$

The resulting value of the standard deviation satisfies

$$\sigma^2 < \frac{s^2(n-1)}{\chi_c} \tag{9.29}$$

We can similarly derive a lower bound on the estimate of the true variance with appropriate confidence level.

The subject of this section is more thoroughly covered in texts on statistics and inference. The results can also be applied to the inference of correlation as well, but this will not be discussed in this book.

9.5.3 General Approach to Inference

In this section we briefly introduce the general approach to deriving an inference for values of parameters of known distributions or densities. More detailed study is available in textbooks on statistics and signal estimation. Suppose we observe n independent samples of a random variable X whose density function is known to be $f_X(u; \theta_1, \theta_2, \ldots, \theta_m)$ but has m unknown parameters, which we shall denote by a vector $\boldsymbol{\theta} = [\theta_1, \theta_2, \ldots, \theta_m]^T$. The observations in general are represented by the independent random variables $\{X_i\}$, for $i = 1, 2, \ldots, n$, which are assumed to be independent but have the same distribution. These last assumptions stem from the fact that these are independent observations of samples from the same random variable. We can therefore write the density of the observations $\{X_i\}$ as a conditional density given the value of the parameter vector $\boldsymbol{\theta}$, and we call such a conditional density the likelihood function and denote it by Λ:

$$\Lambda = \prod_{i=1}^{n} f_X(x_i | \boldsymbol{\theta}) \qquad (9.30)$$

As an estimate of the parameter vector $\boldsymbol{\theta}$, the maximum likelihood approach to estimation and inference uses the value of such a vector that maximizes the likelihood function. It really means that our estimate is the one that makes the actual observation $\{x_i\}$ the most likely to have occurred. Since the logarithmic function is monotonic, instead of maximizing the likelihood function, we can maximize its logarithm to obtain

$$\ln \Lambda = \sum_{i=1}^{n} \ln f_X(x_i | \boldsymbol{\theta}) \qquad (9.31)$$

Hence, for the inference of the parameter vector $\boldsymbol{\theta}$, we use the values of $\boldsymbol{\theta}$ that maximize the expression in equation (9.31). The evaluation of the estimate and confidence interval still requires the use of a variety of analysis and approximations based on the relations between the estimate and the observed values $\{x_i\}$. It will not be addressed further in this text. As an example, we shall consider the problem of estimating the mean and variance of a Gaussian random variable from n independent observations.

In this case we have only two parameters: the mean μ and the variance σ^2. After using the Gaussian density, the log-likelihood function of equation (9.31) becomes

$$\ln \Lambda = \sum_{i=1}^{n} \left\{ -\ln\left(\sqrt{2\pi\sigma^2}\right) - \frac{(x_i - \mu)^2}{2\sigma^2} \right\} \qquad (9.32)$$

If we now select those values which maximize equation (9.32), as the estimate of μ and σ^2, we obtain for the estimate of the mean

$$\frac{\partial \ln \Lambda}{\partial \mu} = \sum_{i=1}^{n} \left\{ \frac{2(x_i - \mu)}{2\sigma^2} \right\} = 0 \tag{9.33}$$

$$\hat{\mu} = \frac{1}{n}\sum_{i=1}^{n} x_i = \bar{x} \tag{9.34}$$

The result is identical for the estimate using the sample average we have considered throughout this chapter. Now we shall find the estimate for the variance, which we shall denote by V:

$$\frac{\partial \ln \Lambda}{\partial V} = \frac{-n}{2V} + \sum_{i=1}^{n} \frac{(x_i - \mu)^2}{2V^2} = 0 \tag{9.35}$$

This equation should be solved simultaneously with equation (9.33) for the mean, so that the result we obtain for the estimate of the variance is

$$\hat{V} = \frac{1}{n}\sum_{i=1}^{n} (x_i - \bar{x})^2 \tag{9.36}$$

We see that this result differs by a factor of $[n/(n-1)]$ from the usually defined sample variance of n independent observations.

9.6 SUMMARY

Sample mean:

$$\bar{x} = \frac{1}{n}\sum_{i=1}^{n} x_i$$

Sample variance:

$$s_x^2 = \frac{1}{n-1}\sum_{i=1}^{n} (x_i - \bar{x})^2 = \frac{1}{n-1}\left[\sum_{i=1}^{n} x_i^2 - \frac{1}{n}\left(\sum_{i=1}^{n} x_i \right)^2 \right]$$

Sample correlation coefficient:

$$r_{xy} = \frac{1}{(n-1)s_x s_y}\sum_{i=1}^{n} (x_i - \bar{x})(y_i - \bar{y})$$

Regression line:

$$\hat{y}_i = \bar{y} + r_{xy}\frac{s_y}{s_x}(x_i - \bar{x})$$

Residual error:

$$s_e^2 = \frac{1}{n-1}\sum_{i=1}^{n} e_i^2 = \frac{1}{n-1}\sum_{i=1}^{n} (y_i - \hat{y}_i)^2 = s_y^2(1 - r_{xy}^2)$$

Estimation of the mean:

Mean = $\bar{x} \pm m$ with probability C, where

C = confidence level,

m = margin of error or confidence interval,

n = number of samples.

$$Z_c = \frac{m\sqrt{n}}{\sigma} = \text{critical value}$$

$$C = 2\Phi(Z_c) - 1$$

9.7 PROBLEMS

MATLAB Problems

1. In order to illustrate the law of large numbers and the central limit theorem as it relates to inference of the mean, generate 64 random numbers uniformly distributed in the interval [0,1] and find their sample average. Repeat the process 100 times. (This means that you will have generated 6400 numbers in batches of 64 each, and thus will have generated 100 sample averages.)

   a.   Plot a histogram of the sample means (the 100 sample means you generated) and compare it with the Gaussian probability density function you will find in Problem 4(b). (Plot both on the same graph.)

   b.   What fraction of the 100 sample averages fall within 15% of the true mean of 0.5? Compare the result with that you will obtain in Problem 4(c).

2. Generate $n = 100$ samples of a binary random variable taking the value 1 with probability $p = 0.5$ and the value zero with probability $(1 - p)$. Obtain the sample average as an inference of the probability of success p with-confidence level of 95%.

   a.   Find the relevant margin of error. Repeat 200 times and show that indeed, in about 5% (10 times) of the experiments the inference for p so obtained will fall outside the margin of error.

   b.   Repeat part (a) for the six combinations of $n = 900$ and $p = 0.2$ and $p = 0.4$.

   c.   Repeat part (b) for $C = 99.7\%$.

3. Generate 1000 pairs of Gaussian random variables using the method of Problem 8-3, with correlation coefficients 0.7, 0.9, and −0.9. For each case, generate the regression line and compute the variance of the residuals. Compare this with the mathematical results.

Regular Problems

4. Let $\{X_i\}$ for $i = 1, 2, 3, \ldots, n$ be independent random variables uniformly distributed in the interval [0,1]. We derive a sample average Y (which we use as an estimate of the true mean of X_i, which we know is 0.5) as follows:

$$Y = (X_1 + X_2 + \cdots + X_n)/n$$

   a. Find the mean and variance of Y. Compute for $n = 64$.

   b. Use the central limit theorem to write the approximate probability density function of Y. Compute for $n = 64$.

   c. For $n = 64$, find the probability that $P(|Y - 0.5| < 0.075)$. (This is a 15% error margin in our estimate of the mean, which in this case we know is 0.5.)

   d. What should be the number of samples n if we wish the error margin to be 5% of the mean with the same confidence level we arrived at in (c).

5. In order to estimate the probability of error p in a binary channel, $n = 10,000$ bits are used as a test. It was found that during the test 12 bits were in error. The errors in the test bits are assumed to occur independently of each other.

   a. Assuming a confidence level of $C = 0.95$, find the estimate of p and the margin of error in the estimate.

   b. If we wish for a margin of error of 0.0001, what should be our confidence level C in the estimate?

TABLE P1   Data for Problem #6

X
0.66
1.02
0.02
0.54
0.73
1.66
0.49
1.59
0.42
0.66
0.65
1.43
0.5
0.71
1.27
1.08
0.69
1.57
1.11
1.9

    c.   If we wish a margin of error of 0.0001 and require a confidence level of $C = 0.997$, what should be the number n of test bits?

6. Consider the data samples shown in Table P1 from a random variable X containing 20 data points:

    a.   Find the sample mean and sample variance of the sample.

    b.   Assuming that the standard deviation of the distribution is known and is given to you as 0.5, estimate the mean of the distribution of X and provide a margin of error m for a confidence level of 0.85 (85%).

    c.   How large should the number of samples be if we were to wish for the same margin of error you obtained in (b) but we want a confidence level of 0.95?

    d.   What is the confidence level in estimating the mean if we want a margin of error of 0.05 and $n = 100$ (instead of 20)?

7. Consider the three data samples shown in Table P2 from three variables X, Y and Z, each containing 20 data points:

TABLE P2   Data for Problem #7

X	Y	Z
0.66	0.81	0.72
1.02	0.32	0.74
0.02	0.95	0.39
0.54	0.15	0.38
0.73	0.1	0.47
1.66	1.79	1.71
0.49	1.68	0.96
1.59	0.42	1.12
0.42	1.44	0.82
0.66	0.99	0.79
0.65	0.95	0.77
1.43	1.29	1.37
0.5	1.23	0.79
0.71	0.07	0.45
1.27	0.76	1.06
1.08	0.66	0.91
0.69	0.27	0.52
1.57	1.28	1.45
1.11	0.43	0.83
1.9	0.52	1.34

Find the sample mean, sample variance of all three, and find the sample correlation coefficient between X and Y and between X and Z. Which pair is correlated or uncorrelated? Draw a regression line for the correlated pair, if any, and compute the residual sample variance.

8. We are interested in estimating the average failure rate λ of a component for which we assume that the number of failures in a given time interval satisfies the Poisson probability model. We fix an interval of time, which we shall denote by T, and count the number of failures N during that time. Our estimate of λ is obtained as

$$\bar{\lambda} = N/T$$

   a. We fix $T = 1000$ hours, and count $N = 25$ failures. Find the estimate of λ and its margin of error at confidence level 95%. (Note that the variance of the random variable N is known from the Poisson distribution.)

   b. What is the confidence level if we keep T as in (a) and we assume that we counted 25 failures, but we wish for a margin of error $m = 0.005$ in our estimate of the failure rate?

   c. What should the value of T be (assuming that we count proportional number of failures) so that $m = 0.005$ with confidence level $C = 95\%$?

   d. Repeat parts (a), (b), and (c), assuming that we are interested only in an upper margin of error (i.e., we wish to have confidence C that the estimate of the failure rate is less than $\bar{\lambda} + m$).

9. We are interested in estimating the average message length in a communication system for which the length T is assumed to satisfy the exponential density model with parameter λ. We measure the lengths of n such messages and obtain our estimate of the average length by the expression

$$\bar{T} = \frac{1}{n}\sum_{k=1}^{n} T_k$$

   a. Suppose we measure $n = 10,000$ messages and we obtain an estimate of 40 seconds. Find the margin of error m in the estimate if we wish a confidence level of 95%.

   b. If we wish a margin of error of 0.5 seconds, what would C be in this case?

   c. If we wish a margin of error of 0.5 seconds and a confidence level of 95%, what should be the number of messages n we need to measure? Assume that we obtain the same value of 40 seconds for the estimate.

10. We wish to estimate the probability p of dropped packets in a packet-switched network. We send n packets and count the number N of packets that are dropped. We evaluate the probability of dropped packets by

$$\bar{p} = N/n$$

   a. Suppose we sent 100 packets and observed that 20 were dropped. Find the estimate and its margin of error if we wish a confidence level of 95%.

   b. If we wish a margin of error of $m = 0.06$, what is our confidence in the estimate?

   c. If we wish a margin of error of $m = 0.04$ at a confidence level of 95%, what should be the number n of test packets we send?

   d. Repeat parts (a), (b), and (c), assuming that we are interested only in a one-sided margin of error (i.e., we wish our true value to be less than $\bar{p} + m$ with confidence level C).

10

Introduction to Hypothesis Testing

10.1 INTRODUCTION

In Chapter 9, when we dealt with basic statistics, we considered the matter of inference, namely the estimation of some parameters (such as the mean of a density) from observed data. Other examples of estimation were considered in other chapters as well, where the primary interest was the estimation of the amplitude of a signal from noisy observations. We now address a problem that is similar in that it extracts useful information from data, but the information desired is in some sense binary. Examples of such problems, involve the transmission of binary digits by using a different signal to denote "zero" or "one." At the receiver, we wish to determine which digit was sent rather than estimating the amplitude of the signals used. Another classical example occurs in radar, where a signal is transmitted and the receiver checks whether a reflection from an airplane is included in the received signal. In that case, we are trying to decide whether a received signal contains a return from a target or just noise alone. Our objective is therefore to determine whether a target is present or not present on the basis of the waveforms we received. As another example, we toss a coin and wish to determine whether it is fair or not, rather than find the exact value of the probability of Heads.

All these problems are characterized by the need of a **yes** or **no** answer, rather than a numerical value. We are not requesting the result in the form of a number with a confidence interval around it, as we did in Chapter 9. We need a crisp answer as to the validity of an assumption or hypothesis. We call this topic by a variety of names. In probability it is called hypotheses testing, while statisticians call it significance testing. In telecommunication and radar it is called signal detection or just detection.

Before formulating the problem let us look at a simple example. We want to test whether a coin is fair, and we toss it 20 times. We obtained 12 Heads and 8 Tails. Is the coin fair? We know that a fair coin implies that $p = 0.5$, while here (before we applied the confidence interval) we obtained the value 0.6. How do we answer such a question? Our answer depends on the impact or the cost of our decision. There are two kinds of errors we could make in this case. One possibility is that the coin is fair but because the estimate of p was 0.6, we said it was not. (It is obviously higher than 0.5.) We can then use the same techniques as in our study of inference to find the probability that we made such an error. The coin could also be unfair, but we declared it as fair. (The outcome was 0.6, after all, and too close to 0.5 to claim that the coin is unfair.) Here it is more difficult to obtain the probability of making such an error, since the "coin is unfair" is not a very simple hypothesis. A coin could be unfair with $p = 0.9$, or unfair with $p = 0.7$, or unfair with $p = 0.3$. There is a vast difference between just these simple cases. In order to make the answer to such a problem more systematic, we have to identify the errors and have a way to characterize them.

There are two basic approaches to the formulation and solution of such problems. The Bayesian approach assumes certain costs associated with each type of error. For example, in radar we may assign some cost to false alarms and a different cost to a miss. Then we make the decision rule in such a way as to minimize the average cost. However, it is difficult in many situations to assign such costs to begin with. The problem may also be asymmetric, as seen in the testing of a coin to determine whether it is fair or not. That is the rationale for using an alternative approach that is not based on some form of average cost. In detection theory, the approach is called Neyman–Pearson detection. In the remainder of this chapter, we shall discuss only the second approach, since the Bayesian approach can be derived in a similar fashion.

10.2 HYPOTHESIS TESTING PROBLEM FORMULATION

We start by stating the problem as one in which we are collecting data (samples that are assumed to be independent, since we know that dependent samples are not very reliable), and we wish to determine whether the data satisfy one hypothesis, which we denote as H_0, and call it the **null hypothesis**. The name implies that the situation is normal, no change: a fair coin, no target present, no malignancy, etc. The second hypothesis is called the **alternative**, and we denote it by H_1. It implies that a change is present: The coin is unfair, the target is present, a tumor is malignant, etc. We use the data to make a decision to either **accept** or **reject** H_0, so we have two possible errors.

Type I error: We decide in favor of the alternative (we accept H_1) and we reject the null hypothesis (H_0), while the true hypothesis is indeed H_0. We also call this error a false alarm or false positive. We denote the conditional probability of such an error by α, which is the probability that we accept H_1 when H_0 is true:

$$\alpha = P\{\text{accept } H_1|H_0 \text{ is true}\} = P\{\text{reject } H_0|H_0 \text{ is true}\} \qquad (10.1)$$

Type II error: We decide in favor of the null hypothesis (we say that the hypothesis $\boldsymbol{H_0}$ is true), and we reject the alternative (H_1) when the true hypothesis is indeed H_1. This is also called a **miss**, since it means we miss a correct diagnosis, or miss detecting the presence of a target. We denote the conditional probability of this error by β, the conditional probability that we say that the target is not present when it is indeed present:

$$\beta = P\{\text{accept } H_0|H_1 \text{ is true}\} = P\{\text{reject } H_1|H_1 \text{ is true}\} \qquad (10.2)$$

We can also define the probability of correctly detecting the alternative hypothesis H_1 when it is indeed present. In medical terms, it is the probability of correctly diagnosing an abnormal behavior; in radar terms, it is the probability of correctly detecting the presence of a target. This probability is sometimes called the **power** of the test and is defined by

$$\text{Power} = 1 - \beta = P\{\text{accept } H_1|H_1 \text{ is true}\} \qquad (10.3)$$

Before we determine how we perform the test and under what criteria, we shall again consider the example of testing a coin.

Example 10.1

We toss a coin 20 times and count the number of Heads. Suppose we decide that it is fair if the number of Heads is between 9 and 11 (inclusive) and it is unfair if the number of Heads is outside that range. What are the expressions of the two error probabilities in this case?

Suppose the probability of Heads for the coin being tested is p. It is fair if $p = 0.5$ and it is unfair if $p \neq 0.5$. Since the number of Heads in 20 tosses is binomially distributed, we can actually find the probabilities α and β as follows:

$$\alpha = P\{\text{less than 9 Heads or more than 11 Heads in 20 tosses}|p = 0.5\}$$

$$= \sum_{k=0}^{8} \binom{20}{k}(0.5)^{20} + \sum_{k=12}^{20} \binom{20}{k}(0.5)^{20}$$

$$\beta = P\{\text{between 9 and 11 Heads in 20 tosses}|p \neq 0.5\}$$

$$= \sum_{k=9}^{11} \binom{20}{k}p^k(1-p)^{20-k}$$

It is easy to observe that while the value of α can be obtained exactly, the value of β depends on the value of p, which reflects the relative unfairness of the coin we are testing.

  A second example involves the detection of a constant signal in noise observed in an interval of length T. Such an example may represent the transmission of a binary digit, using the signal when we wish to send "1" and using no signal when we wish to send "0." It also may represent the detection of the presence or absence of a radar return from a target.

Example 10.2

We make n independent observations $X_k, k = 1, 2, \ldots, n$, to decide the presence or absence of a constant signal of magnitude A. The observations contain errors, which are assumed to be independent random variables. Under the hypothesis H_0 the observations contain the random errors N_k only, while under the hypothesis H_1 the observations contain the constant signal A in addition to the random errors. We assume that the random errors are Gaussian with mean zero and variance σ^2. For simplicity, we shall assume that the magnitude of the constant signal is positive (i.e., $A > 0$). Then we have

$$\begin{aligned} &\text{If } H_0 \text{ is true } X_k = N_k, &&k = 1, 2, \ldots, n \\ &\text{If } H_1 \text{ is true } X_k = A + N_k, &&k = 1, 2, \ldots, n \end{aligned}$$

  A simple solution is to estimate the value of A using a sample average of the observations, and we shall denote this estimate by Y:

$$Y = \frac{1}{n} \sum_{k=1}^{n} X_k$$

We then make our decision by comparing the estimate Y with a threshold η and deciding in favor of H_1 if the output is larger than the threshold and in favor of H_0 if the output is smaller than the threshold. The resulting detector may be implemented as shown in Figure 10.1.

  Now we shall evaluate the two error probabilities for this case. If hypothesis H_0 is true, then the estimate Y contains just the observation errors:

$$Y = \frac{1}{n} \sum_{k=1}^{n} N_k$$

It is therefore a Gaussian random variable with mean zero and variance

$$\sigma_Y^2 = E\{Y^2 | H_0\} = \sigma^2/n$$

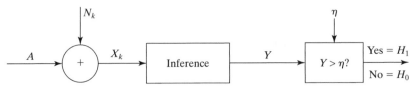

Figure 10.1 Block diagram of the detection problem of Example 10.2

Thus a probability of false alarm (or type I error) is equal to the probability that a Gaussian random variable with mean zero and variance σ_Y^2 exceeds the threshold η:

$$\alpha = P\{Y > \eta | H_0\} = \int_\eta^\infty \frac{\exp\{-y^2/(2\sigma_Y^2)\}}{\sqrt{2\pi}\sigma_Y} dy = \int_\eta^\infty \frac{\exp\{-y^2 n/(2\sigma^2)\}}{\sqrt{2\pi}(\sigma/\sqrt{n})} dy$$

$$= 1 - \Phi(\eta\sqrt{n}/\sigma)$$

Now if the hypothesis H_1 is true, then the output Y would contain two terms. The first contains the average of the observation errors, and the second term is the signal component, which is equal to A and is also equal to the conditional mean of Y given the hypothesis H_1.

The variance of Y is the same variance as that under H_0 and is therefore equal to σ^2/n. The power of the test—that is, the probability of correctly deciding that H_1 is true—is therefore given by

$$1 - \beta = P\{Y > \eta | H_1\} = \int_\eta^\infty \frac{\exp\{-(y - A)^2 n/(2\sigma^2)\}}{\sqrt{2\pi}(\sigma/\sqrt{n})} dy$$

$$= 1 - \Phi[(\eta - A)\sqrt{n}/\sigma]$$

We again see that if we fix the acceptable value of α, we can determine the threshold by

$$\eta = (\sigma/\sqrt{n})\Phi^{-1}(1 - \alpha)$$

We see that the threshold does not depend on the value of the amplitude A. On the other hand, we can check to verify that β does indeed depend on the value of A, so that stronger signals will have higher probability of being correctly detected.

A more general case of the signal detection problem we briefly explored in Example 10.2 will be considered in more detail in Chapter 14.

Now that we have looked at two different examples, we are ready to discuss the general principle of hypothesis testing. We shall concentrate on testing changes in the mean value of the variables observed, as was the case in the two examples previously considered.

The simplest case again uses the variation of the mean as a definition of the two hypotheses we are considering. Such a case is indeed valid for the fair coin case, as the mean is either equal to 0.5 or not equal to 0.5 for the probability of Heads in a fair coin toss. In detecting the presence of a target, again we either have a random return, which may be assumed to have zero mean, or we have a real target with mean that is not zero. In all such examples, we assume that we have n independent data samples of random variables from the same distribution. We assume that the variance σ^2 of such a distribution is known, but that the mean μ is unknown and is assumed to be from one of the two models. Under the null hypothesis, the mean is assumed to be a known value μ_0:

$$\text{If } H_0 \text{ is true: } \mu = \mu_0 \tag{10.4}$$

However, under the alternative hypothesis, we may have one of the three possible scenarios or cases:

a. If H_1 is true:
$$\mu = \mu_1 > \mu_0 \tag{10.5a}$$

b. If H_1 is true:
$$\mu = \mu_1 < \mu_0 \tag{10.5b}$$
c. If H_1 is true:
$$\mu = \mu_1 \neq \mu_0 \tag{10.5c}$$

Clearly each of these scenarios would lead to a slightly different answer to the problem. We shall start with case (a) at first and then consider the other two cases. Note that the problem could be complicated further if we defined the null hypothesis in the form of an inequality as well (i.e., the mean is less than some value, while under the alternative it is larger than some value). In the three scenarios, we assume that the value of the mean under the alternative hypothesis is not known, as was the case in the examples we previously considered.

10.3 ONE-SIDED HYPOTHESIS TESTING

First we consider the case in which the mean under the alternative is greater than μ_0—that is, scenario (a) represented by equation (10.5a). We have n independent samples $\{x_i\}$ of the random variables $\{X_i\}$, as we had in the case of inference. Clearly, one way to check which of the hypotheses is true is to estimate the mean of the distribution by using the sample mean of the data:

$$\overline{X} = \frac{1}{n}\sum_{i=1}^{n} X_i \tag{10.6}$$

Now we can use the central limit theorem to find the sampling distribution of the sample mean. However, recall that we have two distributions here, depending on which hypothesis is the true one. Let us assume that the null hypothesis is true and find the sampling distribution of the sample mean. In this case we simply have an average of n independent sample points of a distribution with mean μ_0 and variance σ^2. The distribution of $\overline{X}$ in this case is approximately Gaussian with mean μ_0 and standard deviation $\frac{\sigma}{\sqrt{n}}$, as we found in Chapter 9 about inference. The obvious decision in rejecting the null hypothesis for this case is to do so when the sample average is larger than some threshold or critical value, which we call $\eta = x_c$.

In Figure 10.2 we show the distribution of the sample mean and we also indicate the critical value on which we base our decision to accept or reject the null hypothesis. We can easily see from the figure that we make a Type I error (false alarm) if we reject H_0 (meaning our sample mean is larger than η) while the true mean is still μ_0. This probability can be obtained from the distribution of the sample mean when the true hypothesis is the null one. The distribution is Gaussian with mean μ_0 and variance σ^2/n, so that the false alarm probability becomes

$$\alpha = P\{\overline{X} > \eta | H_0\} = \int_{\eta}^{\infty} \frac{\exp\{-(y-\mu_0)^2/(2\sigma^2/n)\}}{\sqrt{2\pi}(\sigma/\sqrt{n})} dy$$
$$= 1 - \Phi\left[\frac{(\eta - \mu_0)\sqrt{n}}{\sigma}\right] \tag{10.7}$$

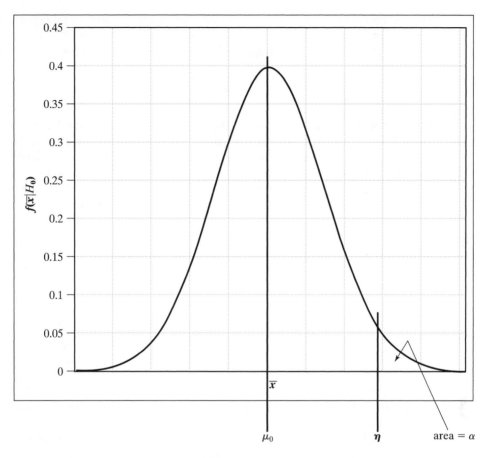

Figure 10.2   Conditional density of the sample average given the null hypothesis

The preceding expressions indicate that if we know the critical value η that we base our decision upon, we can find the false alarm probability α. In general, decisions such as this one are based on how large a false alarm rate (or Type I errors) we can tolerate. Hence the value of α is determined in advance and the decision rule is based on that value. The value of α is also called the **significance level of the test**. If we know α, we can find the critical value Z_α of a unit Gaussian random variable Z that yields the same false alarm rate:

$$\alpha = P\{Z > Z_\alpha\} = \int_{Z_\alpha}^{\infty} \frac{\exp\{-y^2/2\}}{\sqrt{2\pi}} dy = 1 - \Phi(Z_\alpha) \qquad (10.8)$$

Here we defined Z by the transformation

$$Z = \frac{(\overline{X} - \mu_0)\sqrt{n}}{\sigma} \qquad (10.9)$$

The critical value Z_α can be obtained from the standard Gaussian tables or from the confidence level tables discussed in Chapter 9. Once we have found the critical value for Z, we can find the threshold or the critical value for the sample mean:

$$\eta = x_c = \frac{\sigma Z_\alpha}{\sqrt{n}} + \mu_0 \qquad (10.10)$$

What the significance level means is that if we reject the null hypothesis at a significance level α, the data support this rejection with confidence $(1 - \alpha)$. In other words, if $\alpha = 0.05$, then we may be wrong in rejecting the null hypothesis only 5% of the time. What is even more important is that although we design the test with a particular significance level (otherwise we could not come up with a firm algorithm for the decision), when we actually perform the test we may obtain a specific value of the sample mean on which we are basing our test. In such a case we can actually compute the probability of the tail of the distribution under the null hypothesis, and we should have a number smaller than α if our sample mean is larger than the critical value. We call the probability we obtain in such a manner the P-value of the test.

The P-value is formally defined as the probability that the sample mean exceeds the specific value obtained in a given test, under the condition that the null hypothesis is true:

$$P\{\text{data is against rejecting } H_0 | H_0 \text{ is true}\} = P\left\{Z > \frac{(\bar{x} - \mu_0)\sqrt{n}}{\sigma}\right\} \qquad (10.11)$$

The sample mean in the preceding expression (lowercase $\bar{x}$) is for a specific value or realization of the data, unlike earlier when we dealt with its more generic form as a random quantity $\overline{X}$.

If the P-value is less or equal to α, we say that the test is **significant at level α**.

The P-value provides evidence against rejecting the null hypothesis when it is true. This means that the smaller the P-value, the **weaker** is the evidence **against** rejecting the null hypothesis and the **stronger** is the evidence **for** rejecting it if it is indeed true.

We now consider the probability of Type II error (which we may also call a miss), β. This probability is equal to the probability that the sample mean is lower than the threshold, even though the true mean $\mu = \mu_1 > \mu_0$. It should be noted that the result depends on the actual value of μ_1 and its relative distance from the mean under the null hypothesis. Since under H_1 the conditional mean of the sample average is equal to μ_1 while the standard deviation does not change, the conditional density of the sample mean is also Gaussian with mean μ_1 and variance (σ^2/n). Therefore, the probability of error is obtained by the expression

$$\beta = P\{\overline{X} < \eta | H_1\} = P\left\{Z < \frac{(\eta - \mu_1)\sqrt{n}}{\sigma}\right\} = \Phi\left(\frac{(\eta - \mu_1)\sqrt{n}}{\sigma}\right) \qquad (10.12)$$

Here we defined Z as a unit Gaussian random variable obtained by the transformation

$$Z = \frac{(\overline{X} - \mu_1)\sqrt{n}}{\sigma} \qquad (10.13)$$

Instead of the error probability, we sometimes use the power of the test as the probability that we correctly decide in favor of accepting the alternative hypothesis, in which case we obtain

$$1 - \beta = P\{\text{correctly accepting } H_1|H_1\} = P\left\{ Z > \frac{(\eta - \mu_1)\sqrt{n}}{\sigma} \right\} \quad (10.14)$$

Since the critical value η is derived from the null hypothesis and the false alarm rate, we can substitute its value for the one in the preceding probability to obtain

$$\beta = P\left\{ Z < \frac{(\mu_0 - \mu_1)\sqrt{n}}{\sigma} + Z_\alpha \right\} = \Phi\left(\frac{(\mu_0 - \mu_1)\sqrt{n}}{\sigma} + Z_\alpha \right) \quad (10.15)$$

The relationship between these error probabilities is illustrated in Figure 10.3.

The two densities for the sample mean under either hypothesis are shown in two different attributes. Under the null hypothesis it has mean μ_0, and under the alternative it has mean μ_1. The threshold η that determines the decision resulting from the test is shown between the two means. The false alarm rate (probability of Type I error) α is equal to the area under the solid density centered at μ_0 to the right

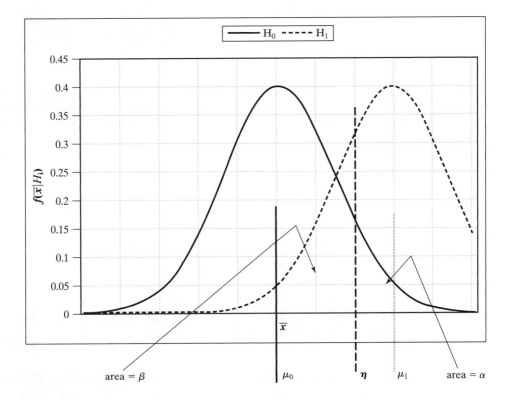

Figure 10.3   The conditional densities under both hypotheses illustrating the probabilities of Type I ($\boldsymbol{\alpha}$) and Type II ($\boldsymbol{\beta}$) errors

of the threshold. The probability of an error of Type II β is the area under the dashed density centered at μ_1 to the left of the threshold. We see therefore that as the means of the alternative and the null hypothesis become close, one of the probabilities (either α or β) will become large. As the distance between these two means becomes greater, the probabilities of the errors become small. This is also evident from the expression for the probability of the Type II error β shown in the figure. If we want to distinguish between two close hypotheses while keeping the decision errors small, we need to increase the number of samples n, as it appears explicitly in the expression for β.

Example 10.3

Consider a coin-testing example in which we toss a coin n times to test whether it is fair or is weighted in favor of Heads. Let us suppose that $\alpha = 0.05$. The hypotheses are the following:

$$H_0\text{: } p = 0.5$$
$$H_1\text{: } p = p_1 > 0.5 \qquad\qquad (10.16)$$

We count the number of Heads and divide by n to obtain an estimate of p, which we shall denote by $\bar{p}$. We know that $\bar{p}$ under the null hypothesis is approximately Gaussian with mean 0.5 and standard deviation $\frac{1}{2\sqrt{n}}$. First we need to compute the critical value of Z for this test from Gaussian or confidence level tables (for $\alpha = 0.05$):

$$Z_\alpha = 1.645 \qquad\qquad (10.17)$$

The test for rejecting or accepting the null hypothesis is based on whether the estimate of p is larger or smaller than the critical value or threshold obtained for $\bar{p}$ from equation (10.10). If we assume 100 tosses, we obtain a threshold of

$$\eta = 0.5 + \frac{Z_\alpha}{2\sqrt{n}} = 0.5 + \frac{1.645}{2\sqrt{100}} = 0.58225 \qquad\qquad (10.18)$$

The threshold value means that if the estimate of p is larger than 0.58225, then we reject the fair coin hypothesis, and otherwise we accept it. If we actually obtained exactly 60 Heads in the 100 tosses, then the estimate of p is 0.6, which is indeed greater than the critical value. The P-value in this case is found by considering the probability that the unit Gaussian variable is larger than $(0.6 - 0.5)2\sqrt{n}$:

$$P\{Z > (0.6 - 0.5)2\sqrt{n}\} = P\{Z > 2\} = 0.0228 \qquad\qquad (10.19)$$

This means that for the case in which we obtained 60 Heads in 100 tosses, the evidence against rejecting the null hypothesis is 0.0228, which is less than 2.3%. It means that for this exact value of the data, the test is significant at level 0.05, or 0.04 or 0.03, but is not significant at level 0.02.

We now evaluate the probability of a Type II error β. Obviously, the Type II error probability depends on the actual value of p if the coin is unfair. Suppose that the unfair coin has a probability $p = p_1 = 0.6$. What is the probability of Type II error in this case? To find the value of β, we assume that the coin is unfair and find the probability

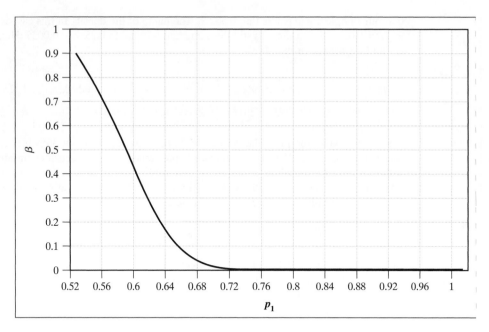

Figure 10.4(a)   Wide range of p_1

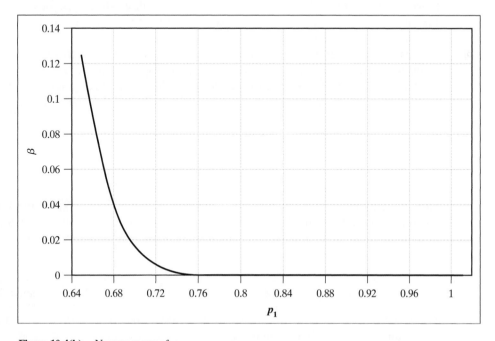

Figure 10.4(b)   Narrow range of p_1

Figure 10.4   Probability of Type II error as a function of the probability p_1

that our sample mean is less that 0.58225. The mean of the density in this case is equal to $p_1 = 0.6$, but its variance is still the same and is equal to $0.25/n = 0.0025$. Hence we are looking for the probability

$$\beta = P\{\bar{p} < \eta | H_1\} = P\left\{Z < \frac{(\eta - \mu_1)\sqrt{n}}{\sigma}\right\} = P\{Z < (0.58225 - 0.6)2\sqrt{100}\}$$
$$= P\{Z < -0.01775 \times 20\} = P\{Z < -0.355\} = 0.361 \qquad (10.20)$$

We see that while the false alarm rate is 5%, the miss rate is about 36% if the unfair coin is not too unfair. We obtain an even higher miss rate if we consider unfair coins with even smaller probability of Heads, for example, $p_1 = 0.51$.

Just as an illustration of how the value of the Type II error behaves as a function of the alternative, we can see that if $p_1 = 0.9$, the value of β becomes

$$\beta = P\{Z < (0.58225 - 0.9)20\} = P\{Z < -6.355\} = 0 \qquad (10.21)$$

In Figures 10.4(a) and 10.4(b), we show the probability of Type II error as a function of p_1, where in Figure 10.4(a), we use a wide range of the value for p_1, while a narrower range of values is shown in Figure 10.4(b). Figure 10.4(b) would have been better shown in a logarithmic scale, as the probability becomes very small.

We see therefore that the probability β of Type II error is a function of the distance of the mean of the distribution μ_1 under the alternative hypothesis H_1 from the mean under the null hypothesis. It is not possible to specify both α and β unless we increase the distance between the means of the two hypotheses, $\mu_1 - \mu_0$, or increase the number of data points n. Let us consider the possibility of setting fixed levels for both α and β, but it has to be done for a specific mean of the alternative, since we could not specify it for every possible value of the mean under the alternative. In this case we have two critical values obtained from the tails of the Gaussian distribution:

$$\alpha = P\{Z > Z_\alpha\} = P\{Z < -Z_\alpha\}$$
$$\beta = P\{Z > Z_\beta\} = P\{Z < -Z_\beta\} \qquad (10.22)$$

Here we are using the upper tail, where the critical values are both positive, but we could have used the lower tail as well. We now check the equation for β from the distributions of the sample means, which relates β to the critical value for α as in equation (10.15):

$$\beta = P\{Z < -Z_\beta\} = P\left\{Z < \frac{(\mu_0 - \mu_1)\sqrt{n}}{\sigma} + Z_\alpha\right\} \qquad (10.23)$$

When comparing these two values, we obtain a relationship between the distance of the mean and the number of samples and the two critical values:

$$-Z_\beta = \frac{(\mu_0 - \mu_1)\sqrt{n}}{\sigma} + Z_\alpha \qquad (10.24)$$

The resulting relationship becomes

$$\frac{(\mu_1 - \mu_0)\sqrt{n}}{\sigma} = Z_\alpha + Z_\beta \tag{10.25}$$

The final expression for the choice of n if the means are fixed becomes

$$n = \left(\frac{(Z_\alpha + Z_\beta)\sigma}{(\mu_1 - \mu_0)}\right)^2 \tag{10.26}$$

Similarly the choice of the distance between the means that will determine the value of β for fixed n becomes

$$\mu_1 - \mu_0 = \frac{(Z_\alpha + Z_\beta)\sigma}{\sqrt{n}} \tag{10.27}$$

In many symmetric applications in which we are trying to distinguish between two fixed means, which may be assumed to be equally likely to be present, we can specify that the probabilities of both types of error be equal (i.e., $\alpha = \beta$). In this case the threshold will fall exactly in the middle between the two means, and the probability of error in the decision process will become equal to the resulting $\alpha = \beta$.

As mentioned earlier, in many instances, instead of the error of Type II, we prefer to consider the probability of correctly detecting the presence of the alternative. We then obtain as a probability the value $(1 - \beta)$, which we defined as the **power** of the test. We shall illustrate this for the case in which the mean of the alternative is larger than the mean of the null hypothesis.

In this case, from equations (10.14) and (10.15) and the fact that $\Phi(Z_\alpha) = (1 - \alpha)$, we have

$$1 - \beta = P\left\{Z > -\frac{(\mu_1 - \mu_0)\sqrt{n}}{\sigma} + Z_\alpha\right\}$$

$$= P\left\{Z > -\frac{(\mu_1 - \mu_0)\sqrt{n}}{\sigma} + \Phi^{-1}(1 - \alpha)\right\}$$

$$= 1 - \Phi\left[-\frac{(\mu_1 - \mu_0)\sqrt{n}}{\sigma} + \Phi^{-1}(1 - \alpha)\right] \tag{10.28}$$

We can therefore create graphs of the power of the test as a function of the false alarm probability α. Such graphs will be parameterized by the value of the distance of the means normalized by the standard deviation of the sample mean, which we shall denote by d:

$$d = \frac{(\mu_1 - \mu_0)\sqrt{n}}{\sigma}$$

$$1 - \beta = P\{Z > -d + \Phi^{-1}(1 - \alpha)\} = 1 - \Phi[-d + \Phi^{-1}(1 - \alpha)] \tag{10.29}$$

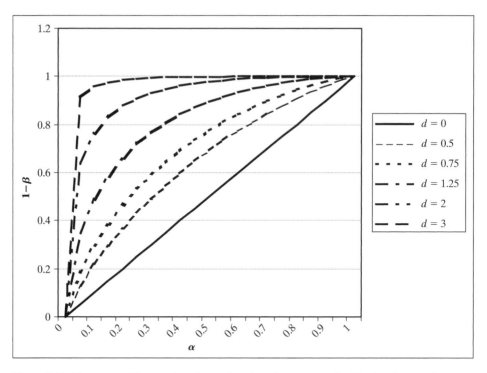

Figure 10.5   The power of the test, $1 - \beta$, as a function of α parameterized by the distance d

A set of such curves is shown in the Figure 10.5 for various values of d as a function of the false alarm rate. We call such curves **receiver operating characteristic**, since they allow us to select various values of α and $(1 - \beta)$, and if we are unhappy with one set, we can determine what value of d will yield the desired results. The curves allow us to find the value of $(1 - \beta)$ when we fix α for a variety of values of d, which is determined by the relative difference between the means normalized by the sample standard deviation. All we have to do in each case is just evaluate the parameter d for the problem at hand.

Example 10.3 (Continued):

As an example, consider the coin-tossing problem again with $p_1 = 0.6$, and assume that we wish both errors to have probability $\alpha = \beta = 0.05$. In this case the critical values are the same and are equal to

$$Z_\beta = Z_\alpha = 1.645$$

The decision in this case is based on the number of Heads in the n tosses. If the number exceeds 55% we decide in favor of the unfair coin, and if it is less than 55% we decide in favor of the fair coin. The number of samples required to achieve this is obtained from equation (10.26), where we replaced the means by the values of p under the two hypotheses:

$$n = \left(\frac{(Z_\alpha + Z_\beta)\sigma}{(p_1 - p_0)}\right)^2 = \left(\frac{(1.645 + 1.645)0.5}{(0.6 - 0.5)}\right)^2 = 270.6$$

This means that we need 271 samples if we wish to also fix the value of both α and β. Obviously, if the difference between the alternatives is smaller, we shall need an even larger sample. For example, in order to distinguish between a fair coin and one with probability of Heads of 0.51, we need many more samples if the error probabilities are fixed.

10.3.1 Case (b) for Hypothesis H_1

We now consider scenario (b), represented by equation (10.5b) for the value of the mean under the hypothesis H_1. In this case the alternative is testing whether the mean is smaller than the null hypothesis. The results we have seen so far are derived in exactly the same way, but we use the lower tail of the Gaussian distribution. In this case we are testing whether the mean is equal to μ_0 or smaller than μ_0. The derivations and the analysis are exactly the same except that all inequality signs are reversed. Here again we assume n independent samples having the same mean and the same known variance. We compute the sample average $\overline{X}$ and compare it with a threshold or critical value. The critical value Z_α is derived from the unit Gaussian variable Z and is based on the false alarm rate (or significance level) α:

$$\alpha = P\{Z < -Z_\alpha\} = \Phi(-Z_\alpha) = 1 - \Phi(Z_\alpha) \qquad (10.30)$$

Since we are dealing with the lower tails of the density, the critical value of the sample mean is obtained from the following expression:

$$\eta = x_c = -\frac{\sigma Z_\alpha}{\sqrt{n}} + \mu_0 \qquad (10.31)$$

The decision becomes in favor of rejecting the null hypothesis if the sample mean is smaller than the critical value or threshold and for accepting the null hypothesis if the sample mean is larger than the threshold. If we reject the null hypothesis, the P-value is obtained from the probability that the unit Gaussian variable Z is smaller than the relative sample average obtained for that specific data set:

$$P\text{-value} = P\left\{Z < \frac{(\overline{x} - \mu_0)\sqrt{n}}{\sigma}\right\} \qquad (10.32)$$

Here again the value of the sample mean in equation (10.32) is the specific value obtained from the data and not its generic form.

In a manner similar to the procedure used for case (a), we can also derive the probability of Type II error (a miss) or the power of the test as follows:

$$\beta = P\{\overline{X} > \eta|H_1\} = P\left\{Z > \frac{(\eta - \mu_1)\sqrt{n}}{\sigma}\right\} = 1 - \Phi\left(\frac{(\eta - \mu_1)\sqrt{n}}{\sigma}\right) \qquad (10.33)$$

Here we defined Z as a unit Gaussian random variable obtained by the transformation

$$Z = \frac{(\overline{X} - \mu_1)\sqrt{n}}{\sigma} \qquad (10.34)$$

The expression for the power of the test becomes

$$1 - \beta = P\left\{Z < \frac{(\eta - \mu_1)\sqrt{n}}{\sigma}\right\} = \Phi\left(\frac{(\eta - \mu_1)\sqrt{n}}{\sigma}\right) \qquad (10.35)$$

Since the critical value η is derived from the null hypothesis and the false alarm rate, we can substitute its value for the one in the preceding probability to obtain

$$\beta = P\left\{Z > \frac{(\mu_0 - \mu_1)\sqrt{n}}{\sigma} - Z_\alpha\right\} = \Phi\left(-\frac{(\mu_0 - \mu_1)\sqrt{n}}{\sigma} + Z_\alpha\right) \qquad (10.36)$$

We can then derive equations similar to equations (10.27) to (10.29) that relate the two error probabilities to the distance between the means under the two hypotheses. We arrive at the same equations, except that the role of the means is reversed in the three expressions and the distance d used in equation (10.29) is now defined as

$$d = \frac{(\mu_0 - \mu_1)\sqrt{n}}{\sigma} \qquad (10.37)$$

We now consider the coin-tossing example for this case.

Example 10.4

Let us illustrate this approach with the same coin example used previously, except that we are testing whether it is weighted in favor of Tails. Let us suppose again that $\alpha = 0.05$.

In this case we have the following hypotheses:

$$\begin{aligned} H_0 &: p = 0.5 \\ H_1 &: p = p_1 < 0.5 \end{aligned} \qquad (10.38)$$

We count the number of Heads and divide by n to obtain an estimate of p, which we shall denote by $\bar{p}$. We know that under the null hypothesis $\bar{p}$ is approximately Gaussian with mean 0.5 and standard deviation $\frac{1}{2\sqrt{n}}$. First we need to compute the critical value of Z for this test from tables ($\alpha = 0.05$):

$$Z_\alpha = 1.645 \qquad (10.39)$$

The test for rejecting or accepting the null hypothesis is based on whether the estimate of p is larger or smaller than the threshold (or critical value) obtained for $\bar{p}$ from equation (10.31), where we again assume 100 tosses:

$$\eta = 0.5 - \frac{Z_\alpha}{2\sqrt{n}} = 0.5 - \frac{1.645}{2\sqrt{100}} = 0.41775 \qquad (10.40)$$

The critical value means that if the estimate of p is smaller than 0.41775, then we reject the fair coin hypothesis, and otherwise we accept it. If we actually obtained exactly 40 Heads in the $n = 100$ tosses, then the estimate of p is 0.4, which is indeed smaller than the critical value. The P-value in this case is found by considering the probability that the unit Gaussian variable is smaller than $(0.4 - 0.5)2\sqrt{n}$:

$$P\{Z < (0.4 - 0.5)2\sqrt{n}\} = P\{Z < -2\} = 0.0228 \qquad (10.41)$$

This means that for the case in which we obtained 40 Heads in 100 tosses, the evidence against rejecting the null hypothesis is 0.0228, which is less than 2.3%. It also means that for this exact value of the data, the test is significant at level 0.05, or 0.04 or 0.03 but is not significant at level 0.02.

Now we wish to find the probability of a Type II error when the true value of $p = 0.4$. In this case we are looking for the probability that the sample mean of p is higher than η when the true mean is $p_1 = 0.4$. The expression for β then becomes

$$\beta = P\{\overline{X} > \eta | H_1\} = P\left\{Z > \frac{(\eta - p_1)\sqrt{n}}{\sigma}\right\} = P\{Z > (0.41775 - 0.4)2\sqrt{100}\}$$

$$= P\{Z > 0.01775 \times 20\} = P\{Z > 0.355\} = 0.361 \qquad (10.42)$$

Again we can ask what would be the probability of error if the true value for p under the alternative was $p_1 = 0.1$. In this case we obtain

$$\beta = P\{Z > (0.41775 - 0.1)20\} = P\{Z > 6.355\} = 0 \qquad . \qquad (10.43)$$

We can obtain a figure like the one we obtained for the previous case, but it would be exactly the same as a function of the distance from 0.5, which represents the null hypothesis.

10.4 TWO-SIDED HYPOTHESIS TESTING

Finally, how we do we treat the case in which the alternative is simply testing that the mean is **not equal** to the regular mean of the null hypothesis? This is scenario (c) described in equation (10.5c), where, under the hypothesis H_1, the mean is $\mu_1 \neq \mu_0$. In this case, since the distribution of the sample mean is symmetric about the mean of the null hypothesis, we have to reject the null hypothesis if our sample mean is either larger or smaller than a critical distance or threshold from the mean under the null hypothesis.

Figure 10.6 shows the false alarm probability and the appropriate thresholds (or critical values) and indicates that we need to have 0.5α as the probability in each tail so that the total false alarm rate is indeed α. In this case we have, for the false alarm probability, the following expression:

$$\alpha = P\{|Z| > Z_{\alpha/2}\} \qquad (10.44)$$

Here we can obtain the critical value of Z from the Gaussian tables by using 0.5α. Then we relate the critical value of Z to the two thresholds of the sample mean x_1 and x_2. These values are obtained from the linear relation between Z and the sample mean:

$$x_1 = -\frac{\sigma Z_{\alpha/2}}{\sqrt{n}} + \mu_0$$

$$x_2 = \frac{\sigma Z_{\alpha/2}}{\sqrt{n}} + \mu_0 \qquad (10.45)$$

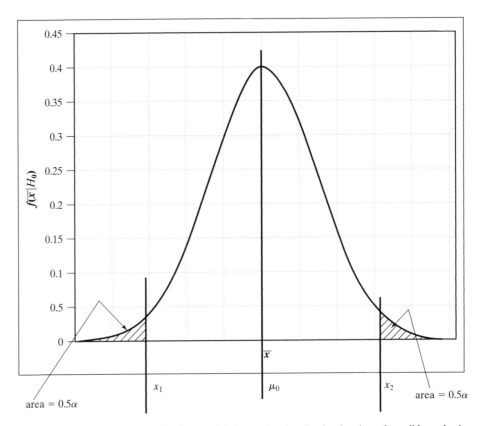

Figure 10.6   Hypothesis testing for the two-sided case, showing the density given the null hypothesis

The test in this case is to reject the null hypothesis whenever the sample mean falls outside the interval (x_1, x_2). It may be expressed in more simplified form as rejection of the null hypothesis if the sample mean satisfies

$$|\overline{X} - \mu_0| > \frac{\sigma Z_{\alpha/2}}{\sqrt{n}} \qquad (10.46)$$

The P-value obtained for a specific case of data points is obtained in the same manner as in the previous two cases.

We now consider the probability of Type II error as well. Since the test is two sided, the decision to accept H_0 is made when the sample mean satisfies

$$|\overline{X} - \mu_0| < \frac{\sigma Z_{\alpha/2}}{\sqrt{n}} \qquad (10.47)$$

Consequently, when the alternative is true with mean μ_1, an error is made when the mean is indeed μ_1 but the sample mean is within the interval previously shown:

$$\beta = P\left\{|\overline{X} - \mu_0| < \frac{\sigma Z_{\alpha/2}}{\sqrt{n}} \,\middle|\, H_1 \text{ is true}\right\} \qquad (10.48)$$

Since we assume that the mean is μ_1, which we shall assume is larger than the mean under the null hypothesis, in this case the unit normal random variable Z satisfies

$$\overline{X} = \mu_1 + \frac{Z\sigma}{\sqrt{n}} \tag{10.49}$$

The result for the expression for the error becomes

$$\beta = P\left\{\left|\frac{Z\sigma}{\sqrt{n}} + \mu_1 - \mu_0\right| < \frac{\sigma Z_{\alpha/2}}{\sqrt{n}}\right\} = P\{-Z_{\alpha/2} - d < Z < Z_{\alpha/2} - d\}$$
$$= \Phi(Z_{\alpha/2} - d) - \Phi(-Z_{\alpha/2} - d) \tag{10.50}$$

Here we have defined the relative distance as we did earlier:

$$d = \frac{(\mu_1 - \mu_0)\sqrt{n}}{\sigma} \tag{10.51}$$

It is important to relate these results to the estimation with two-sided confidence interval that we considered in Chapter 9. Since the confidence interval determines the range around the mean in which the sample mean falls with probability C, it means that if we define $\alpha = (1 - C)$, then if our estimate falls within the confidence

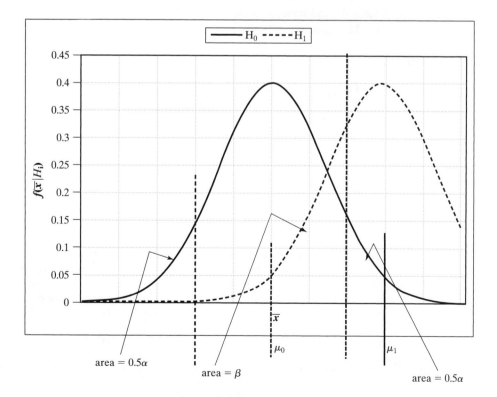

Figure 10.7   The probability of both types of errors for the two-sided test

interval for a given C the null hypothesis is accepted, and if it falls outside the confidence interval the null hypothesis is rejected with significance level α.

Figure 10.7 illustrates how the probability of Type II error is obtained. The dashed vertical lines represent the region where the null hypothesis is accepted. The false alarm rate is obtained from the tails of the sample distribution under the null hypothesis. The probability of a Type II error is obtained from the area under the density given that H_1 is true (shown as a dashed curve) between the two dashed lines.

We revisit the coin-tossing example for this case as well.

Example 10.5

We conclude this with the coin example, in which we assume that the alternative is just that the coin is unfair. Let us suppose again that $\alpha = 0.05$, which means that for each Tail, we have 0.025 probability.

The hypotheses in this case are the following:

$$H_0: p = 0.5$$
$$H_1: p = p_1 \neq 0.5 \tag{10.52}$$

We count the number of Heads and divide by n to obtain an estimate of p, which we shall denote by $\bar{p}$. We know that under the null hypothesis $\bar{p}$ is approximately Gaussian with mean 0.5 and standard deviation $\frac{1}{2\sqrt{n}}$. First we need to compute the critical value of Z for this test from tables:

$$Z_{\alpha/2} = 1.96 \tag{10.53}$$

The test for rejecting or accepting the null hypothesis is based on whether the difference between the estimate of p and 0.5 is greater than or less than the following expression, obtained from the critical value for Z:

$$|\bar{p} - 0.5| > \frac{Z_{\alpha/2}}{2\sqrt{n}} = \frac{1.96}{2\sqrt{100}} = 0.098 \tag{10.54}$$

The result is that we accept the hypothesis that the coin is fair if

$$0.598 > \bar{p} > 0.402 \tag{10.55}$$

The critical value means that if the estimate of p is smaller than 0.402 or larger than 0.598, we reject the fair coin hypothesis; otherwise we accept it. If we actually obtained exactly 40 Heads in the $n = 100$ tosses, then the estimate of p is 0.4, which is indeed smaller than the lower critical value. The P-value in this case is found by considering the probability that the unit Gaussian variable is smaller than $(0.4 - 0.5)2\sqrt{n}$.

$$P\{Z < (0.4 - 0.5)2\sqrt{n}\} = P\{Z < -2\} = 0.0228 \tag{10.56}$$

This means that for the case in which we obtained 40 Heads in 100 tosses, the evidence against rejecting the null hypothesis is 0.0228, which is less than 2.3%. We would get the same P-value if we counted exactly 60 Heads.

We now consider the probability of Type II error for this example if the true value of $p_1 = 0.6$. We can use the expression derived for β directly, where the value of d in this case is

$$d = \frac{(p_1 - p_0)\sqrt{n}}{0.5} = \frac{(0.6 - 0.5)\sqrt{100}}{0.5} = 2 \qquad (10.57)$$

The result becomes

$$\beta = P\{-1.96 - 2 < Z < 1.96 - 2\} = P\{-3.96 < Z < -0.04\} = 0.484 \quad (10.58)$$

If we increase the value of p_1 under the Hypothesis H_1 to 0.7, we obtain

$$d = 4$$
$$\beta = P\{-1.96 - 4 < Z < 1.96 - 4\} = P\{-5.96 < Z < -2.04\} = 0.0207 \quad (10.59)$$

Example 10.2 (Continued):

We can also revisit Example 10.2 if the hypothesis H_1 implies that $A \neq 0$. In this case we also have a two-sided test, so the critical value of Z is obtained on the basis of the value 0.5α, and the decision is made to accept H_1 if $|Y| > \eta$, where the threshold η is given by

$$\eta = Z_{\alpha/2}(\sigma/\sqrt{n}) = \Phi^{-1}(1 - 0.5\alpha)(\sigma/\sqrt{n}) \qquad (10.60)$$

We now consider the probability of Type II error (a miss) when the signal present has amplitude A. In this case Y has mean A and variance $\sigma/\sqrt{n}$, and a miss occurs when its values does not exceed the threshold:

$$\beta = P\{|Y| < \eta | H_1\} = \Phi[(\eta - |A|)\sqrt{n}/\sigma] - \Phi[(-\eta - |A|)(\sqrt{n}/\sigma)] \quad (10.61)$$

The absolute value of A is used in equation (10.61) since it can be either positive or negative. The symmetry of the Gaussian density was exploited in deriving the equation.

We conclude with a comment about more general hypothesis testing cases. Just as in the case of inference, we have to deal with cases of unknown variances, so in such cases we use the sample variance and the t-distribution. We can also test for different variances, or correlated versus uncorrelated data, and many other situations. The basic principle is the same. Just the tables we have to use, as well as the derivation of the tests and their statistical parameters, are more complex.

10.5 GENERAL HYPOTHESIS TESTING PROBLEM

In this section we address a more general formulation of the hypothesis testing problem and mention a few of the approaches that are used to solve such problems. This is not intended to serve as a comprehensive treatment of the subject, so only a brief introductory overview is included here.

Suppose we collect n samples (or observations) $\{X_i\}$ of a random variable whose statistical properties satisfy one of two hypotheses, H_0 or H_1. We shall denote by $\mathbf{X}$ the n-dimensional vector whose elements are X_i. Suppose that we know the conditional density functions of $\mathbf{X}$ given H_i. Then we can show that the decision to accept or reject H_1 is based on whether the following ratio Λ (which is called the likelihood ratio) is greater or smaller than a threshold η:

$$\Lambda = f_X(\boldsymbol{x}|H_1)/f_X(\boldsymbol{x}|H_0) \tag{10.62}$$

The decision is therefore given as in the following:

$$\text{If } \Lambda > \eta, \text{ accept } H_1 \tag{10.63}$$

It is sometimes easier to use the logarithm of the likelihood ratio, so that instead of Λ we use $\ln(\Lambda)$, and the decision is based on whether $\ln(\Lambda)$ is larger or smaller than a different threshold η', which is the logarithm of the original threshold η. The value of the threshold is obtained by the desired false alarm rate α, which depends only of the conditional density of $\mathbf{X}$ given the null hypothesis H_0. As an illustration, consider the case in which the samples X_i are independent and identically distributed. Then the log likelihood ratio becomes

$$\ln(\Lambda) = \sum_{i=1}^{n}\ln[f_X(x_i|H_1)] - \sum_{i=1}^{n}\ln[f_X(x_i|H_0)] \tag{10.64}$$

If we now assume that our samples have a Gaussian density with the same variance σ^2, but different means μ_k that depend on the hypotheses H_k, we obtain the simple expression for the log likelihood ratio:

$$\ln(\Lambda) = \sum_{i=1}^{n} -[(x_i - \mu_1)^2/(2\sigma^2)] - \sum_{i=1}^{n} -[(x_i - \mu_0)^2/(2\sigma^2)]$$

$$= \sum_{i=1}^{n}x_i(\mu_1 - \mu_0)/\sigma^2 + n(\mu_0^2 - \mu_1^2)/(2\sigma^2) \tag{10.65}$$

If we now assume that $\mu_1 > \mu_0$, we can divide by $n(\mu_1 - \mu_0)$ and multiply by σ^2 to obtain the following decision rule:

$$\text{If } \frac{1}{n}\sum_{i=1}^{n}x_i > \{\eta'\sigma^2/[n(\mu_1 - \mu_0)] + (\mu_1 + \mu_0)/2\} = \eta'', \text{ then accept } H_1. \tag{10.66}$$

We denoted the new threshold in equation (10.66) by η'', and we see that the decision is the same one we considered when we discussed testing with respect to the mean in the previous sections. The decision is indeed based on the sample average of the samples, and hence the derivation of the threshold and evaluation of Type II errors will be the same as we have done in that section. The general formulation allows more complex decision rules if the conditional densities of the samples given H_i are not Gaussian and if the hypotheses are represented by different variances or parameters other than just the means.

10.5.1 Testing for Variance

We shall not pursue this general approach further in this section, but we shall consider the case of testing whether the variance is larger than a nominal variance, which we consider as the null hypothesis. We shall assume in this case that the samples are

independent and identically distributed Gaussian variables with zero mean and variances that depend on the hypotheses H_i. We shall denote the standard deviations of
the conditional densities given the hypotheses H_i by σ_i. In this case the log likelihood
ratio becomes

$$\ln(\Lambda) = \sum_{i=1}^{n}\left\{- x_i^2/(2\sigma_1^2)\right\} - \sum_{i=1}^{n}\left\{- x_i^2/(2\sigma_0^2)\right\} + n[\ln(\sigma_0) - \ln(\sigma_1)]$$

$$= \sum_{i=1}^{n}x_i^2\left[\frac{1}{2\sigma_0^2} - \frac{1}{2\sigma_1^2}\right] + n[\ln(\sigma_0) - \ln(\sigma_1)] \qquad (10.67)$$

If we now assume that $\sigma_1 > \sigma_0$, divide the expression in equation (10.67) by n and
by the coefficient multiplying the summation, and compare the result with a threshold, we obtain

$$\text{If } \frac{1}{n}\sum_{i=1}^{n}x_i^2 > \{[\ln(\sigma_1) - \ln(\sigma_0)] + \eta'/n\}\frac{2\sigma_1^2\sigma_0^2}{(\sigma_1^2 - \sigma_0^2)} = \eta'', \text{ accept } H_1.(10.68)$$

We see that the decision is based on comparing the sample variance with a threshold. (When the mean is known, we just divide by n.) If we assume that the variance
under the null hypothesis is known, then the threshold will depend only of the variance σ_0^2 and the desired false alarm rate α. It should be noted that the sample variance used for the test has the chi-square density with n degrees of freedom, since we
assumed that the random variables are Gaussian with known mean (zero). The
process is similar to the case in which we tested for the mean, except that instead of
using the cumulative Gaussian distribution tables, we have to use the chi-square distribution tables, as was the case when we discussed the estimation of the variance in
Chapter 9. The details will not be pursued further in this brief introduction to the
subject.

Similar results can be obtained if we were to test whether two samples of random variables are correlated or uncorrelated, and many other features of the distributions of random variables. The more general approach is best left to texts on
statistics or detection theory.

10.6 SUMMARY

Hypothesis testing definitions:

Null hypothesis: H_0,

Alternative hypothesis: H_1,

Error types and probabilities:

Type I error (false alarm): $\alpha = P\{\text{accept } H_1|H_0\}$

Type II error (miss): $\beta = P\{\text{accept } H_0|H_1\}$

Power of the test: $1 - \beta = P\{\text{accept } H_1|H_1\}$

Testing for the mean:

H_0: mean $= \mu_0$

(a) H_1: mean $= \mu_1 > \mu_0$

(b) H_1: mean $= \mu_1 < \mu_0$

(c) H_1: mean $= \mu_1 \neq \mu_0$

Decision rules based on n independent samples $\{x_i\}$:

Compute sample average: $\bar{x} = \dfrac{1}{n}\displaystyle\sum_{i=1}^{n} x_i$

For case (a):

Accept H_1 if $\overline{X} > X_c = \mu_0 + Z_\alpha \sigma / \sqrt{n}$

Critical value: $\Phi(Z_\alpha) = 1 - \alpha$

Type II error rate: $\beta = \Phi\left[-\dfrac{(\mu_1 - \mu_0)\sqrt{n}}{\sigma} + Z_\alpha \right]$

Power of the test: $1 - \beta = 1 - \Phi[-d + \Phi^{-1}(1 - \alpha)]$

Distance: $d = \dfrac{(\mu_1 - \mu_0)\sqrt{n}}{\sigma}$

For case (b):

Accept H_1 if $\overline{X} < X_c = \mu_0 - Z_\alpha \sigma / \sqrt{n}$

Critical value: $\Phi(Z_\alpha) = 1 - \alpha$

Type II error rate: $\beta = \Phi\left[-\dfrac{(\mu_0 - \mu_1)\sqrt{n}}{\sigma} + Z_\alpha \right]$

Power of the test: $1 - \beta = 1 - \Phi[-d + \Phi^{-1}(1 - \alpha)]$

Distance: $d = \dfrac{(\mu_0 - \mu_1)\sqrt{n}}{\sigma}$

For case (c):

Accept H_1 if $|\overline{X} - \mu_0| < \dfrac{\sigma Z_{\alpha/2}}{\sqrt{n}}$

Critical value: $\Phi(Z_{\alpha/2}) = 1 - \alpha/2$

Type II error rate: $\beta = \Phi(Z_{\alpha/2} - d) - \Phi(-Z_{\alpha/2} - d)$

Distance: $d = \dfrac{|\mu_1 - \mu_0|\sqrt{n}}{\sigma}$

10.7 PROBLEMS

1. We wish to test packet losses in a communications network. We send 100 test packets and measure the number of lost packets.

   a. Design a test to determine whether the loss rate p is larger than 0.4 with desired Type I error rate of 0.05.
   b. If $p = 0.6$, what is the probability of Type II error?
   c. What should n be if we wish the Type II error probability to be equal to 0.05 as well?

2. In order to determine whether a noise disturbance interfering with a channel reception is too high to allow effective use of the channel, we measure 100 samples of the disturbance amplitude, and we obtain sample values $\{x_i\}$. Assume that the standard deviation of the noise is known and is equal to 5 and the acceptable mean is $\mu_0 = 2$.

   a. Design a test to determine whether the mean of the interference is higher than 2 at a desired false alarm rate of 0.1.
   b. If the actual interference mean is 3, what is the probability of Type II error?
   c. What should n be if we wish a Type II error of 0.05?

3. A binary channel uses square pulses of duration T and amplitude A to send a "1" and uses zero during the period T to send a "0". We observe the signal at n sample times during the interval, and we obtain n measurements X_k that are equal to the value of the signal and measurement errors N_k, which are assumed to be independent Gaussian random variables with zero means and variances σ^2. We assume that A is known and positive. Design a hypothesis testing rule for this problem.

   a. Find the threshold, if we require a false alarm rate of α.
   b. Find the probability of Type II error if we assume we know the value A.
   c. Determine the threshold if we wish the two error rates to be the same for a given value of A.

4. Repeat Problem 1, assuming that we wish to determine whether the loss rate is less than 0.4, while in part (b) assume that $p = 0.2$.

5. Repeat Problem 3(a) and (b), assuming that the amplitude A can be either positive or negative.

6. Use MATLAB to simulate the results of Problem 1. Generate 100 random variables satisfying the null hypothesis, and perform the test using the false alarm rate defined in the problem. Repeat the test 1000 times, and then count the number of times the decision was made to accept the alternative hypothesis, resulting in a false alarm. Compare these results with the value of the false alarm rate used in the design.

7. Repeat Problem 6 by generating 100 samples of random numbers satisfying the alternative hypothesis ($p = 0.6$). Now repeat 1000 times, and verify that the Type II error found in Problem 1 is confirmed by your 1000 samples.

11

Basic Concepts of Reliability

11.1 INTRODUCTION

In previous chapters we discussed many examples involving failures and probability of failures in a given interval of time, or the distribution of the time to first failure of a system or a component. In this chapter we plan to address some basic concepts of reliability, which in some cases repeat what we have already described. However, the coverage of the topic here is more systematic and consistent, rather than just illustrative examples of the theory of probability and random variables.

If we study the probability of failure of a system in a fixed interval of time, we obtain a probability function (or a discrete distribution function), which may depend on the time interval in question. On the other hand, we may define a new random variable that describes the time to the first failure or the time between failures, and this random variable is sometimes called either time to failure or lifetime of the system or its components. It is obviously a continuous random variable. Finally, we may wish to define the probability that the system does not fail during that time interval, which we can then call the reliability of the system.

11.2 RELIABILITY FUNCTIONS

In past chapters we described the arrival of failures by a Poisson model. This way we found that if the arrival rate (which we may also call failure rate, since it defines failures per unit time) is constant and is given as λ, then the probability of k failures in t time units is given by equation (3.34):

$$P\{k \text{ failures in time } t\} = \frac{(\lambda t)^k}{k!} \exp(-\lambda t), \quad k = 0, 1, 2, \ldots \tag{11.1}$$

If, as we did in earlier chapters, we define a random variable T as the time to the first failure (or the time between failures), then we find that the distribution function of this random variable (if the average failure rate is constant) is as given in equation (3.36):

$$F_T(t) = P\{T \le t\} = 1 - \exp(-\lambda t), \text{ for } t > 0 \tag{11.2}$$

The meaning of the distribution function is that it defines the probability that the system or component fails **before** time t. If, on the other hand, we are interested in the probability that the system fails **after** time t, then we are looking at the probability that the random variable representing the time to failure T is larger than some arbitrary time interval of length t. The resulting probability is defined as the **reliability** of the system and is denoted by $R(t)$:

$$R(t) = P\{T > t\} = 1 - F_T(t), \tag{11.3}$$

For the case of Poisson arrival of failures with constant failure rate, the resulting reliability function is given by

$$R(t) = \exp(-\lambda t), \text{ for } t > 0 \tag{11.4}$$

So far we have considered only a constant failure rate. However, we know that as a system becomes older, it may fail more frequently than before. How then do we define the failure rate in more general ways, so that it can be used when it is not always a constant? For example, the failure rate for any system may be higher toward the end of its useful life. In some cases we may also have higher failure rates during the breaking-in period of the life of a system. One way of defining failure rate is to find the conditional probability, assuming that the system lasts until time t that it fails during the interval $(t, t + \Delta t)$ and then to divide that probability by the length of the interval Δt. Let us first define this quantity properly, and then find that its value indeed coincides with the constant failure rate λ we defined earlier for the Poisson arrival case. In terms of the random variable T, the formal definition of the failure rate $\lambda(t)$ is as follows:

$$\lambda(t) = \lim_{\Delta t \to 0} \frac{P\{t < T \le t + \Delta t | T > t\}}{\Delta t} = \lim_{\Delta t \to 0} \frac{P\{(t < T \le t + \Delta t) \cap (T > t)\}}{P\{T > t\} \, \Delta t}$$

$$\tag{11.5}$$

Equation (11.5) is precisely equal to the probability that the system fails during the small interval $(t, t + \Delta t)$ divided by the length of the time interval in question, given that it survived until time t. We used the definition of conditional probability to obtain the rightmost expression in equation (11.5). We now need to use the distribution function or its complementary reliability function to simplify the expression for the failure rate. We first note that the event in the numerator of equation (11.5) is exactly equal to

$$\{(t < T \le t + \Delta t) \cap (T > t)\} = \{t < T \le t + \Delta t\}.$$

Equation (11.5) then becomes

$$\lambda(t) = \lim_{\Delta t \to 0} \frac{P\{t < T \le t + \Delta t\}}{P\{T > t\}\,\Delta t} = \lim_{\Delta t \to 0} \frac{F_T(t + \Delta t) - F_T(t)}{[1 - F_T(t)]\,\Delta t}$$

$$= \frac{1}{R(t)} \frac{dF_T(t)}{dt} = \frac{f_T(t)}{R(t)} \tag{11.6a}$$

or alternatively,

$$\lambda(t) = \lim_{\Delta t \to 0} \frac{R(t) - R(t + \Delta t)}{R(t)\,\Delta t} = -\frac{1}{R(t)} \frac{dR(t)}{dt} \tag{11.6b}$$

Equation (11.6b) can be further simplified by using the derivative of the log function to yield

$$\lambda(t) = -\frac{d\,ln[R(t)]}{dt} \tag{11.7}$$

First, let us see what we obtain for the case of the exponential reliability function that we considered in the Poisson arrival case. In that case, from equation (11.4) we obtain

$$\lambda(t) = -\frac{d\,ln[\exp(-\lambda t)]}{dt} = -\frac{d(-\lambda t)}{dt} = \lambda \tag{11.8}$$

We see that our definition of failure rate is consistent with the case of a constant failure rate during the entire life of the system. If we know the failure rate of a system as a function of its age, we can use equation (11.7) to derive the reliability function from the failure rate. If we integrate both sides of equation (11.7) with the added information that at $t = 0$ the reliability function is equal to 1 (the system at time zero is 100% reliable), then after moving the minus sign to the other side of the equation, we obtain

$$-\int_0^t \lambda(u)\,du = ln[R(t)] - ln[R(0)] \tag{11.9}$$

Since $R(0) = 1$, as a final result we obtain the following expression for the reliability when the failure rate is not constant:

$$R(t) = \exp\left\{ -\int_0^t \lambda(u)\, du \right\} \qquad (11.10)$$

What are the cumulative distribution and the density function of the time to failure in this case? It is easy to find the distribution function, since it complements the reliability function. Then all we have to do to find the density function is differentiate the distribution function. The resulting functions are given as follows:

$$F_T(t) = 1 - R(t) = 1 - \exp\left\{ -\int_0^t \lambda(u)\, du \right\} \qquad (11.11)$$

$$f_T(t) = \lambda(t) \exp\left[-\int_0^t \lambda(u)\, du \right] = \lambda(t)[1 - F_T(t)] = \lambda(t)R(t) \quad (11.12)$$

We see that equation (11.12) agrees with the results obtained earlier in equation (11.6a). Again, we can easily check to see that the results reduce to the formerly derived expressions for the constant failure rate case.

Now, we need to find the average time to failure, which is sometimes also defined as the mean time between failures (MTBF) and is denoted by $E\{T\}$. We can obtain the average time to failure by using the standard definitions of expectations. In this case we can find a direct relationship between $E\{T\}$ and the reliability function. Consider the definition of $E\{T\}$ and replace the density as a derivative of the distribution function, which in turn becomes the negative of the derivative of the reliability function:

$$E\{T\} = \int_0^\infty t f_T(t)\, dt = \int_0^\infty t \frac{dF_T(t)}{dt}\, dt = -\int_0^\infty t \frac{dR(t)}{dt}\, dt \qquad (11.13)$$

We now perform integration by parts of the integral in equation (11.13) to obtain

$$E\{T\} = -tR(t)\big|_0^\infty + \int_0^\infty 1 R(t)\, dt = \int_0^\infty R(t)\, dt \qquad (11.14)$$

The limits at both zero and infinity of $[t\, R\,(t)]$ tend to zero, since $R(\infty) = 0$ and it approaches zero exponentially fast, so that even after multiplying by t we obtain zero. For a time-varying failure rate, the MTBF can be expressed as

$$E\{T\} = \int_0^\infty \exp\left[-\int_0^t \lambda(u)\, du \right] dt \qquad (11.15)$$

It is easy to verify that if the failure rate λ is a constant, then equation (11.15) results in an MTBF of $1/\lambda$, as we derived earlier in equation (4.49).

Example 11.1

Consider a system whose failure rate increases linearly with time. What is the reliability function, the distribution and density functions of the time to failure, and the mean time between failures?

Suppose that the failure rate is given as

$$\lambda(t) = a + bt$$

In this case the reliability function is immediately determined by

$$R(t) = \exp[-(at + 0.5bt^2)]$$

The distribution and density functions can then be derived as we did previously:

$$F_T(t) = 1 - \exp[-(at + 0.5bt^2)], \qquad 0 < t$$
$$f_T(t) = (a + bt) \exp[-(at + 0.5bt^2)], \qquad 0 < t$$

Note that if $a = 0$, then the density and distribution function are just a Rayleigh distribution and density functions given in equations (6.49) and (6.48), respectively. The MTBF in this case (when $a = 0$) is given by

$$E\{T\} = \int_0^\infty \exp(-0.5bt^2)\, dt = \sqrt{\frac{\pi}{2b}}$$

The last expression is obtained from the fact that the Gaussian density integrates to unity, and the preceding expression differs from the Gaussian density by only a multiplicative factor.

Example 11.2

Consider a system with failure rate that is given by the following expression:

$$\lambda(t) = 0.2, \qquad \text{for } 0 < t < 10, \text{ and} \qquad \lambda(t) = 20, \qquad \text{for } 10 < t$$

We now would like to find the same functions we found in the previous example. In this case we have

$$R(t) = \exp(-0.2t), \qquad\qquad 0 < t < 10$$
$$R(t) = \exp(-2) \exp[-20(t - 10)], \qquad 10 < t$$

The distribution and density are also given in two segments as well:

$$F_T(t) = 1 - \exp(-0.2t), \qquad\qquad 0 < t < 10$$
$$F_T(t) = 1 - \exp(-2) \exp[-20(t - 10)], \quad 10 < t$$
$$f_T(t) = 0.2 \exp(-0.2t), \qquad\qquad 0 < t < 10$$
$$f_T(t) = 20 \exp(-2) \exp[-20(t - 10)], \qquad 10 < t$$

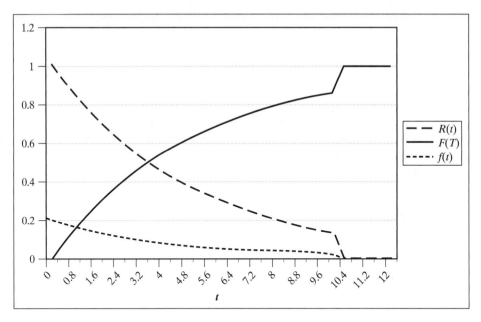

Figure 11.1   The reliability, distribution, and density functions for Example 11.2

The average time to failure is then obtained as

$$E\{T\} = \int_0^{10} \exp(-0.2t)\, dt + \int_{10}^{\infty} \exp(-2) \exp[-20(t-10)]\, dt$$

$$= 5[1 - \exp(-2)] + 0.05 \exp(-2) = 4.33$$

The functions are shown in Figure 11.1. As expected, it is as if the system fails immediately after reaching the age of 11.

Before we leave the subject, an important property of the constant failure rate is that in such a case the conditional distribution of the time to failure given that the system did not fail at time T_0 is still exponential with the same parameter. Let us define $A = \{$the system did not fail by time $T_0\}$. Then we are looking for the conditional distribution of T given A. To prove this assertion, we use the definition of the conditional distribution:

$$F_{T|A}(t|T > T_0) = P\{T \le t | T > T_0\} = \frac{P\{(T \le t) \cap (T > T_0)\}}{P\{T > T_0\}}$$

$$= \frac{P\{T_0 < T \le t\}}{R(T_0)}$$

$$= \frac{R(T_0) - R(t)}{R(T_0)} = 1 - \exp[-\lambda(t - T_0)], \qquad t > T_0 \qquad (11.16)$$

The corresponding density function is also the same, except that it starts after the time T_0, as expected:

$$f_{T|A}(t|T > T_0) = \lambda \exp[-\lambda(t - T_0)], \quad t > T_0 \tag{11.17}$$

This implies that the average life after T_0 is still $1/\lambda$, no matter how long the system has lived already. This memoryless property of the exponential distribution was discussed in Example 5.5 as well. We repeat it here, as it is important to recall the limitation of the reliance on the exponential density model in practical situations. One must allow for the time-varying failure rate, even if it is in the form of the piecewise constant example shown in Example 11.2.

We now turn to the reliability of systems composed of various components in parallel, in series, and in standby mode. We have discussed the lifetime distributions of these cases in Chapter 8 (Section 8.5) for the constant failure rate case. Here we shall just establish the expressions for the failure rate and reliability and address the time-varying failure rate as well.

11.3 RELIABILITY OF INTERCONNECTED SYSTEMS

We shall consider systems composed of n components in various connections. If we label the lifetime of the components as T_i, then we shall denote the corresponding distribution, density, and reliability functions as $F_i(t)$, $f_i(t)$, and $R_i(t)$, respectively. The failure rates are denoted by $\lambda_i(t)$. In this case we are not limiting the results to the exponential distribution case. We have the standard relations we defined in the previous section:

$$R_i(t) = 1 - F_i(t) \tag{11.18}$$

$$\lambda_i(t) = -\frac{d \ln R_i(t)}{dt} \tag{11.19}$$

As we discussed in Chapter 8, we shall first consider parallel connections of components whose failures are independent of each other. We shall follow that by the series connection and then by the standby mode. For simplicity, we shall avoid any subscript to denote the distribution, density, and reliability functions of the system.

11.3.1 Parallel Connection

The parallel connection case is shown in Chapter 8, Figure 8.4. In that case we found that the lifetime is the "max" function as described by equation (8.40), in that it is the largest of all the component lifetimes:

$$T = \text{Max}\{T_1, T_2, \ldots, T_n\}$$

We found then that the distribution function of the system lifetime is given by equation (8.42) and is expressed as (after we use the notations for the distribution functions of the T_i)

$$F(t) = \prod_{i=1}^{n} F_i(t) = \prod_{i=1}^{n} [1 - R_i(t)] \tag{11.20}$$

The corresponding reliability is obtained directly as the complement of the distribution function (11.3) and is expressed as

$$R(t) = 1 - F(t) = 1 - \prod_{i=1}^{n} [1 - R_i(t)] \tag{11.21}$$

The failure rate of the system is then obtained from equation (11.7) as

$$\lambda(t) = -\frac{d \ln R(t)}{dt} = \frac{F(t)}{R(t)} \sum_{i=1}^{n} \lambda_i(t) \frac{R_i(t)}{F_i(t)} \tag{11.22}$$

We also can differentiate the expression for $F(t)$ to obtain the density function for the time to failure:

$$f(t) = F(t) \sum_{i=1}^{n} \frac{f_i(t)}{F_i(t)} = F(t) \sum_{i=1}^{n} \lambda_i(t) \frac{R_i(t)}{F_i(t)} \tag{11.23}$$

In general, we cannot simplify the preceding expressions any more. For the case in which all of the distributions of the components are identical and equal to $F_1(t)$, we obtain

$$F(t) = [F_1(t)]^n \tag{11.24}$$

$$R(t) = 1 - [F_1(t)]^n \tag{11.25}$$

$$\lambda(t) = n\lambda_1(t) \frac{[F_1(t)]^{n-1}[1 - F_1(t)]}{1 - [F_1(t)]^n} = nf_1(t) \frac{[F_1(t)]^{n-1}}{1 - [F_1(t)]^n} \tag{11.26}$$

$$f(t) = nf_1(t)[F_1(t)]^{n-1} \tag{11.27}$$

As an example, consider the case of constant failure rates, which we discussed in Chapter 8. The results are as shown in Section 8.5.1:

$$F(t) = [1 - \exp(-\lambda t)]^n \tag{11.28}$$

$$R(t) = 1 - [1 - \exp(-\lambda t)]^n \tag{11.29}$$

$$f(t) = n\lambda \exp(-\lambda t)[1 - \exp(-\lambda t)]^{n-1} \tag{11.30}$$

$$\lambda(t) = n\lambda \exp(-\lambda t) \frac{[1 - \exp(-\lambda t)]^{n-1}}{1 - [1 - \exp(-\lambda t)]^n} \tag{11.31}$$

Example 11.3

Consider the case of constant failure rates with two components $n = 2$ with rates of λ_1 and λ_2. We wish to find the reliability, failure rates, distribution and density functions, as well as the expected time to failure. The results for this case are as follows:

$$F(t) = [1 - \exp(-\lambda_1 t)][1 - \exp(-\lambda_2 t)]$$

$$R(t) = 1 - F(t) = \exp(-\lambda_1 t) + \exp(-\lambda_2 t) - \exp[-(\lambda_1 + \lambda_2)t]$$

$$f(t) = \lambda_1 \exp(-\lambda_1 t) + \lambda_2 \exp(-\lambda_2 t) - (\lambda_1 + \lambda_2) \exp[-(\lambda_1 + \lambda_2)t]$$

$$\lambda(t) = f(t)/R(t)$$

The expected time to failure is obtained by taking the average of the density function or the integral of the reliability function, and results in

$$E\{T\} = \frac{1}{\lambda_1} + \frac{1}{\lambda_2} - \frac{1}{(\lambda_1 + \lambda_2)}$$

When both rates are equal, the average lifetime is 50% larger than for a single component.

11.3.2 Series Connection

The series connection of several components is considered in Chapter 8, Figure 8.7. In that case we found that the lifetime of the system satisfies the "min" function as given by equation (8.53), in that it is the smallest lifetime of all the components' lifetimes:

$$T = \text{Min}\{T_1, T_2, \ldots, T_n\}$$

This is the case because the system fails as soon as the first component fails, and hence its lifetime is equal to the smallest of the lifetimes of the components. The distribution is then given by equation (8.55):

$$F(t) = 1 - \prod_{i=1}^{n}[1 - F_i(t)] = 1 - \prod_{i=1}^{n} R_i(t) \tag{11.32}$$

For the reliability function, we therefore have the very simple expression

$$R(t) = 1 - F(t) = \prod_{i=1}^{n} R_i(t) \tag{11.33}$$

If we now use equation (11.7) to consider the failure rate of the system, we also obtain a simplified expression, since the log function becomes a sum of the logs in the product in equation (11.33), resulting in

$$\lambda(t) = -\frac{d \ln R(t)}{dt} = -\frac{d}{dt}\sum_{i=1}^{n} \ln[R_i(t)] = \sum_{i=1}^{n} \lambda_i(t) \tag{11.34}$$

It is quite interesting to note that in a series connection (even with time-varying failure rates) the failure rate of the system is equal to the sum of the failure rates of the components. The density function is similarly derived from equation (11.12), resulting in

$$f(t) = R(t)\,\lambda(t) = R(t)\sum_{i=1}^{n}\frac{f_i(t)}{R_i(t)} = R(t)\sum_{i=1}^{n}\lambda_i(t) \qquad (11.35)$$

For the constant failure rate case, we find that the system failure rate is also constant (unlike the parallel connection), and the density function becomes

$$f(t) = R(t)\sum_{i=1}^{n}\lambda_i = \left\{\sum_{i=1}^{n}\lambda_i\right\}\left\{\exp\left[-\left(\sum_{i=1}^{n}\lambda_i\right)t\right]\right\} = \lambda\exp(-\lambda t) \quad (11.36)$$

The failure rate of the system λ is also constant and is given as the sum of the failure rates of the n components:

$$\lambda = \sum_{i=1}^{n}\lambda_i \qquad (11.37)$$

The average lifetime therefore becomes the inverse of the average of the inverse lifetimes:

$$E\{T\} = \frac{1}{\lambda} = \frac{1}{\displaystyle\sum_{i=1}^{n}\lambda_i} \qquad (11.38)$$

If all the rates are the same, then the average lifetime is n times smaller than the lifetime of a single component, since the failure rate is n times larger than that of a single component.

11.3.3 Standby Connection

In the standby connection the components are not operating together at the same time. They operate in tandem, and hence the time to failure of the system is the sum of the times to failure of the components. In this case we have

$$T = \sum_{i=1}^{n}T_i$$

As we have seen in Chapter 8, Example 8.4, we simplify the expressions for the density or the distribution function only for the case of constant failure rates of the components. In that chapter we observed that when we add n independent random variables, the density of the sum is obtained as a convolution of the individual densities, which in general yields complicated expressions. We can derive a simple expression for the expected value of the time to failure of the system by using equation (8.22):

$$E\{T\} = \sum_{i=1}^{n} E\{T_i\} \tag{11.39}$$

The expressions for the reliability, the distribution, failure rate, and density functions are not easy to derive. The case of constant failure rate with identical components was already considered in Chapter 8, and we then obtained the density function for the lifetime from Example 8.4 as

$$f(t) = \frac{\lambda^n t^{n-1}}{(n-1)!} \exp(-\lambda t), \qquad 0 \le t \tag{11.40}$$

We can derive the expression for the distribution, but it involves a sum of n elements and would not provide any additional insight into the problem. It is important to remember that if n is large, then the density function approaches a Gaussian density function, since then we can apply the central limit theorem.

11.4 PERIODIC FAILURE RATE

In this section we consider the case for which the failure rate is periodic. This may represent the situation in which the system undergoes periodic maintenance that brings the failure rate back to a new starting time, following the same rate until the next maintenance. As an example, an engine that undergoes complete overhaul periodically every fixed number of working hours. We shall first consider the general case and then provide an example. Consider the case for which the failure rate $\lambda(t)$ is periodic with period H (since we already use the letter T for the random variable defined as the time to first failure or lifetime). In order not to worry about dimensions, we define the shape of the failure rate by a function $r(t)$ which is nonzero in the interval $[0, 1]$. An example of such a function is given in Figure 11.2.

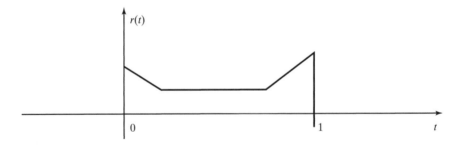

Figure 11.2   General failure rate shape during a period

In this case the failure rate $\lambda(t)$ maybe expressed as a scaled periodic version of $r(t)$ as follows:

$$\lambda(t) = \frac{1}{H}r\left(\frac{t - nH}{H}\right) = \frac{1}{H}r\left(\frac{t}{H} - n\right), \text{ for } nH < t < (n + 1)H \quad (11.41)$$

Here the integer n defines the period and takes the values $n = 0, 1, 2, \ldots$

We shall also need to define a function representing the integral of $r(t)$ over the interval $(0, 1)$, and we shall denote such a function by

$$g(t) = \int_0^t r(u) \, du \qquad \text{for } 0 < t \le 1 \quad (11.42)$$

First we find the reliability function over the interval $(0, H]$, and then we find the general form for any period. For the first period, we have equation (11.10), which defines $R(t)$ in terms of the failure rate as

$$R(t) = \exp\left\{-\int_0^t \lambda(u) \, du\right\} = \exp\left\{-\int_0^t \frac{1}{H}r\left(\frac{u}{H}\right) du\right\}$$

$$= \exp\left\{-\int_0^{t/H} r(v) \, dv\right\}$$

$$= \exp\left\{-g\left(\frac{t}{H}\right)\right\}, \qquad \text{for } 0 < t \le H \quad (11.43)$$

In particular, the reliability at the end of one period, before the overhaul becomes

$$R(H) = \exp\{-g(1)\} = \exp\left\{-\int_0^1 r(v) \, dv\right\} \quad (11.44)$$

We now derive the reliability function for any arbitrary period between nH and $(n + 1)H$. In this case we need to break the integral over the failure rate into a sum of the integrals over the different periods in view of equation (11.41). Let us first derive the integral of the failure rate and then substitute in the reliability function for $nH < t < (n + 1)H$:

$$\int_0^t \lambda(u) \, du = \sum_{k=0}^{n-1}\left\{\int_{kH}^{(k+1)H} \lambda(u) \, du\right\} + \int_{nH}^t \lambda(u) \, du$$

$$= \sum_{k=0}^{n-1}\left\{\int_{kH}^{(k+1)H} \frac{1}{H}r\left(\frac{u - kH}{H}\right) du\right\} + \int_{nH}^t \frac{1}{H}r\left(\frac{u - nH}{H}\right) du$$

$$= \sum_{k=0}^{n-1}\left\{\int_0^1 r(v)\,dv\right\} + \int_0^{(t-nH)/H} r(v)\,dv = \sum_{k=0}^{n-1}g(1) + g\left(\frac{t-nH}{H}\right)$$

$$= ng(1) + g\left(\frac{t-nH}{H}\right), \qquad \text{for } nH < t < (n+1)H \qquad (11.45)$$

We now use equation (11.45) in the general expression for the reliability function $R(t)$ to obtain

$$R(t) = \exp\left\{-ng(1) - g\left(\frac{t-nH}{H}\right)\right\} = \{\exp[-g(1)]\}^n \exp\left\{-g\left(\frac{t-nH}{H}\right)\right\}$$

$$= [R(H)]^n R(t-nH), \qquad \text{for } nH < t < (n+1)H \qquad (11.46)$$

Note that the second term in the product given by equation (11.46) has already been derived, since it represents the reliability function in the interval $(0, H)$ as shown in equation (11.43). We see that the reliability function has a periodic component, but that periodic component is multiplied by a decreasing factor $[R(H)]^n$ for the nth period. We also see that the reliability at the end of the nth period is given by

$$R(nH) = [R(H)]^n \qquad (11.47)$$

Before we derive other statistical functions, it is interesting to note that if we observe the system only at the end of each period, then the reliability decays exponentially. It should be noted that within the periods, the reliability is higher than the standard constant failure rate with exponential decay. However, for the purpose of the ends of the periods, the reliability behaves as if it has an equivalent constant failure rate, which we shall denote by λ_0, which can be derived by considering the exponential decay at the end of periods and comparing that with a system with a constant failure rate:

$$R(nH) = \exp\{-ng(1)\} = \exp\{-n\lambda_0 H\} \qquad (11.48)$$

We can now solve for the equivalent failure rate to obtain

$$\lambda_0 = \frac{1}{H}g(1) = \frac{1}{H}\int_0^1 r(u)\,du = \frac{1}{H}\int_0^1 H\lambda(uH)\,du = \frac{1}{H}\int_0^H \lambda(v)\,dv \qquad (11.49)$$

We see that it is indeed equal to the time average of the failure rate over one period.
    We now derive the other statistical properties of the system in this periodic case. The lifetime distribution function becomes

$$F_T(t) = 1 - R(t) = 1 - [R(H)]^n R(t-nH)$$

$$= 1 - \exp[-ng(1)]\exp\left\{-g\left(\frac{t-nH}{H}\right)\right\}, \qquad \text{for } nH < t < (n+1)H$$

$$(11.50)$$

The probability density function of the lifetime is obtained by taking the derivative of equation (11.50) to yield

$$f_T(t) = \frac{1}{H} r\left(\frac{t - nH}{H}\right) \exp[-ng(1)] \exp\left\{-g\left(\frac{t - nh}{H}\right)\right\} \qquad (11.51)$$

It also exhibits a periodic term that is multiplied by an exponentially decreasing multiplier after each period. Finally, we derive the average time to failure by using the expression for the expectation of T. Here we also have to perform the integrals separately for each period as follows:

$$E\{T\} = \int_0^\infty R(t)\, dt = \sum_{n=0}^\infty \int_{nH}^{(n+1)H} R(t)\, dt$$

$$= \sum_{n=0}^\infty \int_{nH}^{(n+1)H} [R(H)]^n \exp\left\{-g\left(\frac{t - nH}{H}\right)\right\} dt$$

$$= \sum_{n=0}^\infty \{[R(H)]^n \int_0^1 H \exp\{-g(u)\}\, du \qquad (11.52)$$

The term inside the integral is the same for each of the summation terms; hence it can be taken outside the summation. The summation is over a geometric series with a quotient of $R(H)$, so that after the result of the summation is performed, we obtain

$$E\{T\} = H\frac{\int_0^1 \exp[-g(u)]\, du}{1 - R(H)} = H\frac{\int_0^1 \exp[-g(u)]\, du}{1 - \exp\{-g(1)\}} \qquad (11.53)$$

We shall now consider an example to illustrate the type of answers we obtain for the periodic case.

Example 11.4

Consider a linearly increasing failure rate during the period with slope b and period H starting at zero:

$$\lambda(t) = bt, \qquad \text{for } 0 < t < H \qquad (11.54)$$

The failure rate during a period increases from 0 to a maximum of bH. We can see that the normalized failure rate is obtained from equation (11.41) by using the first period only, to yield

$$r(t) = H\lambda(tH) = bH^2 t = \alpha^2 t, \qquad \text{for } 0 < t < 1 \qquad (11.55)$$

Here we defined a dimensionless parameter α given by

$$\alpha = H\sqrt{b} \qquad (11.56)$$

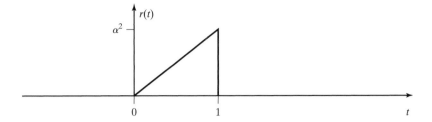

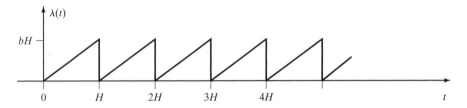

Figure 11.3   Failure rate for the periodic example

The failure rate and the function $r(t)$ are shown in Figure 11.3. In this case the function $g(t)$ is given by the expression

$$g(t) = 0.5\alpha^2 t^2, \qquad \text{for } 0 < t < 1 \tag{11.57}$$

We now use the results obtained in the general case to find the four statistical parameters of interest. First we find the reliability function:

$$R(H) = \exp\{-g(1)\} = \exp\{-0.5\alpha^2\} \tag{11.58}$$

$$R(t) = \exp\{-0.5\alpha^2 n\} \exp\left\{-0.5\alpha^2\left(\frac{t - nH}{H}\right)^2\right\}, \qquad \text{for } nH < t < (n + 1)H \tag{11.59}$$

In this case the distribution function becomes

$$F_T(t) = 1 - \exp\{-0.5\alpha^2 n\} \exp\left\{-0.5\alpha^2\left(\frac{t - nH}{H}\right)^2\right\}, \qquad \text{for } nH < t < (n + 1)H \tag{11.60}$$

Similarly, the density function of the lifetime is expressed as

$$f_T(t) = 0.5\alpha^2\left(\frac{t - nH}{H^2}\right)\exp\{-0.5\alpha^2 n\} \exp\left\{-0.5\alpha^2\left(\frac{t - nH}{H}\right)^2\right\},$$

$$\text{for } nH < t < (n + 1)H \tag{11.61}$$

In order to find the average lifetime, we need to perform the integral in the numerator of equation (11.53):

$$\int_0^1 \exp[-g(u)]\, du = \int_0^1 \exp(-0.5\alpha^2 u^2)\, du = \frac{1}{\alpha}\int_0^\alpha \exp(-0.5v^2)\, dv$$

$$= \frac{\sqrt{2\pi}}{\alpha}\{\Phi(\alpha) - \Phi(0)\} = \frac{\sqrt{2\pi}}{\alpha}\{\Phi(\alpha) - 0.5\} \qquad (11.62)$$

Here the function Φ is the unit cumulative Gaussian distribution. We now can obtain the average lifetime, expressed as

$$E\{T\} = \frac{H\sqrt{2\pi}\{\Phi(\alpha) - 0.5\}}{\alpha\{1 - \exp(-0.5\alpha^2)\}} \qquad (11.63)$$

We can show that for small α the average lifetime approaches infinity:

$$\frac{E\{T\}}{H} \approx 2/\alpha^2$$

For large α the average lifetime approaches zero:

$$\frac{E\{T\}}{H} \approx \frac{\sqrt{\pi}}{\alpha}$$

It is interesting to find the equivalent failure rate (or the time-average failure rate) for this case:

$$\lambda_0 = \frac{1}{H}g(1) = \frac{0.5\alpha^2}{H} = 0.5bH \qquad (11.64)$$

This is exactly half the maximum failure rate that occurs at the end of each period. We see then that the reliability at the end of each period is given by

$$R(nH) = \exp\{-0.5\alpha^2 n\} = \exp\{-(0.5bH)nH\} = \exp\{-\lambda_0 nH\} \qquad (11.65)$$

The average lifetime, normalized relative to the period H, is shown in Figure 11.4 as a function of the parameter α.

The statistical functions, the reliability $R(t)$, the distribution function $F(t)$, the normalized density function $Hf(t)$, and the normalized failure rate $H\lambda(t)$, are shown in Figure 11.5 for the value of $\alpha^2 = 0.8$. For example, if the period is 2 and the slope is 0.2, then the maximum failure rate is 0.4 for the selected value of α.

In the figure we could not get a sharp transition for the failure rate and the density function at the beginning of each period due to the plotting program used.

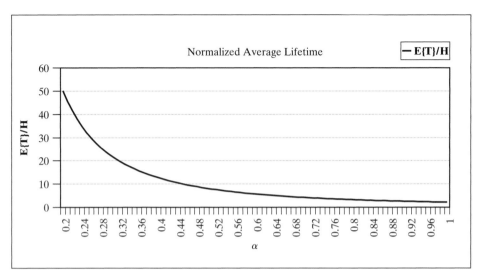

Figure 11.4   Normalized average lifetime as a function of the normalized maximum failure rate

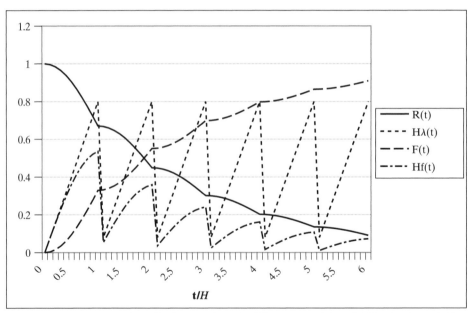

Figure 11.5   The density and distribution functions, the failure rate, and the reliability for the periodic example for $\alpha^2 = 0.8$

11.5 SUMMARY

T = Time to failure or lifetime

$F_T(t)$ and $f_T(t)$ = Distribution and density function of T

Reliability function:

$$R(t) = P\{T > t\} = 1 - F_T(t)$$

Failure rate:

$$\lambda(t) = \frac{P\{t < T \leq t + \Delta t | T > t\}}{\Delta t} = \frac{f_T(t)}{R(t)} = -\frac{d \, ln[R(t)]}{dt}$$

$$R(t) = \exp\left\{-\int_0^t \lambda(u) \, du\right\}$$

Average lifetime or mean time between failures:

$$E\{T\} = \int_0^\infty R(t) \, dt$$

Parallel connection:

$$F(t) = \prod_{i=1}^n F_i(t) = \prod_{i=1}^n [1 - R_i(t)]$$

$$R(t) = 1 - F(t) = 1 - \prod_{i=1}^n [1 - R_i(t)]$$

Series connection:

$$F(t) = 1 - \prod_{i=1}^n [1 - F_i(t)] = 1 - \prod_{i=1}^n R_i(t)$$

$$R(t) = \prod_{i=1}^n R_i(t)$$

$$\lambda(t) = \sum_{i=1}^n \lambda_i(t)$$

Standby connection:

$$E\{T\} = \sum_{i=1}^n E\{T_i\}$$

11.6 PROBLEMS

MATLAB Problems:

1. Write a MATLAB program to simulate the failure probability of a system composed of two components in parallel, and compare the reliability function obtained this way with the one obtained analytically. Use the 2000 random numbers you generated in Problem

1 from Chapter 4 so that the failure rate is equal to 2 for each component. In order to simulate two in parallel, you have to generate 2000 more numbers for the second component. Then, for each pair, you select the larger value to represent the time to failure of the parallel connection. Generate the following plots from the data you generated:

a. The reliability functions of one component (fraction of components surviving after time t) and of the system, and compare the results with the analytical result.
b. A histogram of the time to failure of the system, and compare it with the theoretical one.
c. The sample average of the time to failure of each component and of the system.

2. Repeat Problem 1 for the case of two components connected in series. This means that you take the smaller of the values of the pair of random numbers to represent the time to failure of the system.

Regular Problems:

3. A component has a probability density function for the time to failure X of

$$f_X(t) = 2t/T^2, \quad \text{for } 0 < t < T, \text{ and is zero elsewhere}$$

a. Find its reliability function and its failure rate. Plot for $T = 1$.
b. Find the mean time to failure.

4. For the two systems shown in the diagrams that follow, suppose that the components fail independently of each other and that the reliability function of each component is given by

$$R(t) = \exp(-\lambda t)$$

a. For each system, find the reliability function $R(t)$, the failure probability $F(t)$, the failure probability density function, and the failure rate. Plot for $\lambda = 1$.
b. Find the mean time to failure for each system.

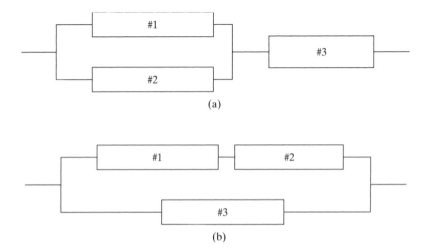

5.* Repeat Problem 4 for the case in which each component has a different failure rate, such that component i has failure rate λ_i.

    a.   Evaluate for the system in (a) for the case $\lambda_1 = \lambda_2 = 2$ and $\lambda_3 = 1$.
    b.   Evaluate for the system in (b) for the case $\lambda_1 = \lambda_2 = 0.75$ and $\lambda_3 = 1$.

6.* Repeat Problem 4 for the two systems shown in the accompanying diagram, but assume failure rates of component i to be equal to $\lambda_i(t)$. First find the answer for variable failure rates. Then consider the case for which the failure rates are constant and not a function of t.

    Finally, for system (a), consider the case for which $\lambda_1 = \lambda_2 = 2$, $\lambda_3 = 1$, and $\lambda_4 = 1.5$.

    For system (b), consider the case of $\lambda_1 = \lambda_2 = 0.5$, $\lambda_3 = 1.5$, and $\lambda_4 = 1$.

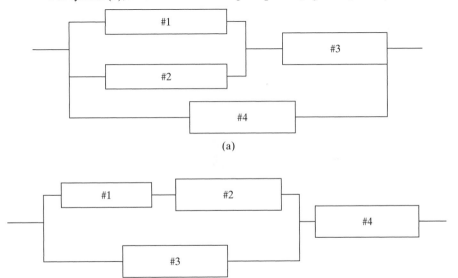

(a)

(b)

7. Suppose we have a system with a failure rate having the following form as a function of time:

$$\lambda(t) = \begin{cases} 5, & \text{for } 0 < t < 0.2 \\ 0.1, & \text{for } 0.2 < t < 10 \\ 10, & \text{for } 10 < t \end{cases}$$

    a.   Find the reliability, distribution, and density function of the system.
    b.   Find the average lifetime of the system.

8.* Consider a system having a periodic failure rate with period of $H = 4$. Suppose the failure rate changes as a function of time during the first period by the following expression:

$$\lambda(t) = 0.25\sqrt{t}, \quad \text{for } 0 < t < 4$$

Find the reliability function, the distribution function, and the density function of the time to failure of the system. Find the mean time to failure of the system.

9.* Two systems are used in standby mode. The systems have failure rates of $\lambda_1(t)$ and $\lambda_2(t)$. We are interested in the reliability of the two systems together.

    a. Find expressions for the failure rate, reliability function, distribution, and density functions of the entire system. Find also the mean time to failure.

    b. Evaluate the result for the case $\lambda_1(t) = \lambda_2(t) = \lambda t$.

    c. Evaluate the result for the case $\lambda_1 = \lambda$ and $\lambda_2(t) = \lambda t$.

12

Introduction to Random Processes

12.1 BASIC CONCEPTS

Random processes occur a great deal in electrical engineering problems. So far we have dealt with random variables, which can take values in some range. Random variables alone cannot represent phenomena that change with time. In many electrical engineering problems, we encounter signals, which are usually functions of time. However, when these functions are not known exactly, we have to resort to random descriptions and modeling of these signals. We call such signals random processes. Examples of random processes include the signal carrying information between two points on a cable or a telephone wire, the signal carrying radio or TV information on cable or the "airwaves." The current or voltage generated by the random motion of electrons in a conductor. The load in a network link in terms of number and length of messages as time moves along. All of the preceding examples can be represented with random process models. First, we have to define such processes so that we can learn to analyze their properties and eventually be able to make decisions based on these so-called random signals.

12.1.1 Definition of a Random Process

We are all familiar with the picture of a function that looks like it has no specific shape and really fits what we conceive to be a random signal, as shown in Figure 12.1.

Figure 12.1   This function is not a random process

Unfortunately, the function shown in the figure is not necessarily a random process. A single time function, no matter how unpredictable its shape, is not a random process. In order to define a random process, let us go back to the definition of a random variable. For every outcome ζ of a sample space with a given probability assignment $P(.)$, we assign a real number, and we call the function that assigns these numbers a random variable and denote it by $X(\zeta)$. In general, we do not bother to keep the argument of X when we work with random variables. This means that a random variable defines a variable that may take different values if a random experiment is conducted, and we do not know in advance which value will occur. This leads us to the definition of a random process in exactly the same manner. The definition will have to assign a time function for every outcome of the sample space of the random experiment. It means that a random process is such that it may take the shape of different time functions every time a random experiment is performed. We do not know in advance which of the possible functions it takes when we conduct the experiment.

Definition: Given a sample space S with events and a probability P defined for each event, a **random process** $X(t, \zeta)$ is a function assigned to each outcome ζ of the sample space.

From the definition, it is clear that a random process is not one function, just as a random variable is not one number. A random process is a collection of functions. Using the basic definition, we can define a random process by providing all such possible functions for each outcome of a probability space. However, this is difficult to do if the number of outcomes is large, let alone infinite. First let us consider a few examples to illustrate what a random process is. Before we go to the examples, it should be noted that a random process is **not** one function, but a collection of functions with some probability assigned to each. Furthermore, when we actually perform the random experiment, we get to observe exactly only one of the functions, which we call a **realization** or a **sample function** of the process in such a case. We get to observe more than one function only if we are to repeat the experiment. Armed with these cautionary notes, let us consider a few simple examples.

Example 12.1

Suppose we toss a coin twice and, for each of the four outcomes, we assign one of the following functions:

$$X(t, HH) = 3 \sin t$$

$$X(t, TT) = 3 \cos t$$

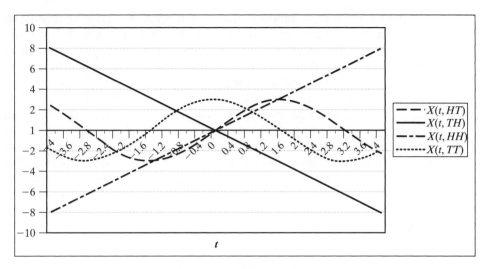

Figure 12.2   The sample functions of the process of Example 12.1

$$X(t, HT) = 2t$$

$$X(t, TH) = -2t$$

We can actually plot all four functions and each will be a sample function of the process, as shown in Figure 12.2.

Furthermore, we can state that each function occurs with probability 0.25 (assuming that the coin is fair). In practice, we tend to forget about the underlying sample space and we write $X(t)$ to denote a random process. Also, in this simple example, we can just draw all the sample functions and show their probabilities, without having to mention the coin tosses. In such a case we define the random process as in Figure 12.2, but instead of stating the outcomes for each sample function, we should just show their probabilities, which in this case is equal to 0.25 for each one.

We see that a random process is a time function when we actually perform the random experiment. This means that if we consider only a single outcome, we obtain just one function, or as we previously called it, a realization or a sample function. In general, we may be able to plot only a few of the realizations of a random process, since the number of such realizations may be infinitely large. We are able to draw all sample functions in the simple case of Example 12.1. Hence, in general, we may plot only a few sample functions, which we hope represent the random process as a whole.

What happens if we sample the random process at given points in time, such as the three time instants $t = t_1$, $t = t_2$, and $t = t_3$? In such a case we obtain the three random variables defined by $X(t_1, \zeta)$, $X(t_2, \zeta)$, and $X(t_3, \zeta)$. If we consider the process in Example 12.1 and we look at $t_1 = 0.5\pi$, then the random variable we obtain, $X(0.5\pi, \zeta)$, takes four possible values with a probability of 0.25 each. These values are π, $-\pi$, 3, and 0. If we use a different time instant, we obtain a different random variable.

In summary, a random process has a dual personality: If we fix the time instant(s), we obtain random variable(s), but if we perform the experiment once, we get a single time function.

Before we discuss random processes further, we have to classify random processes as to whether we consider all points in time (continuous time) or only a discrete number of time instants (used, for example, in processing by a computer). Similarly, we can speak about continuous-amplitude cases, in which the value of the sample functions can be arbitrary, and about the discrete-amplitude case, in which only discrete levels of amplitudes can be taken by the sample functions of the random process. In the next two figures we show an example of continuous-time processes with continuous amplitude in Figure 12.3 and with discrete amplitude in Figure 12.4. It should be noted that the discrete-amplitude random process may be obtained from a continuous-amplitude random process by quantization—that is, by using only discrete approximations of the continuous amplitudes of the process. While we do not show the examples of discrete-time processes here, it is easy to visualize them by simply considering the two examples of continuous-time processes and showing only the values at discrete points in time, which in most cases are assumed equally spaced, namely, at $t = kT$, where k is an integer (both negative and positive) and T is considered to be the sampling period. It follows that while discrete-amplitude processes are obtained from continuous-amplitude processes by quantization, the discrete-time processes may be obtained from continuous-time processes by sampling.

As previously mentioned, when we perform only one experiment, we obtain just one sample function (or realization) of the random process. Only if we repeat

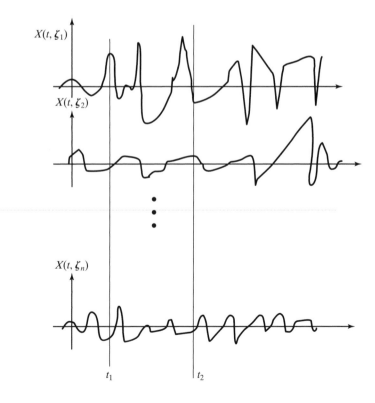

Figure 12.3 Three sample functions of a continuous-time and continuous-amplitude random process

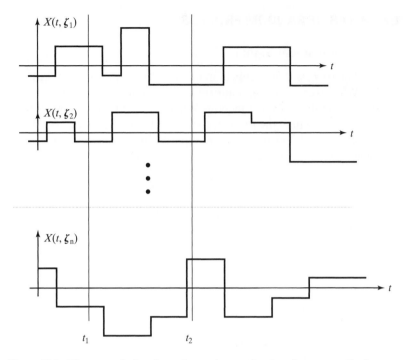

Figure 12.4 Three sample functions of a continuous-time but discrete-amplitude random process

the experiment do we obtain more sample functions, just as only if we repeat an experiment with random variables do we obtain another outcome out of all possible outcomes. Now what happens if we take the value of the process at one time instant $t = t_1$ as shown in Figure 12.3 (where two time instants are shown). At that instant we obtain one random variable $X(t_1, \zeta)$, which we usually write as $X(t_1)$, since we usually do not bother to explicitly show the outcome ζ of the sample space. We can now discuss the probabilistic property of this random variable and consider, for example, its distribution and density functions, its mean, and its variance, among other properties. In most cases we expect that such properties to be different if we take a different instant of time. Hence these properties will be dependent on time. Similarly, if we take two time instants, $t = t_1$ and $t = t_2$ as shown in the figure, we obtain the two random variables $X(t_1)$ and $X(t_2)$. Here again we did not show the outcome of the sample space in writing $X(t)$. These two random variables may then be described by their joint distribution function, which in general depends on both time instants t_1 and t_2. In such a case we can speak of joint density functions as well as the correlation or covariance of the two random variables. In the next section we shall define some of these functions and describe what they tell us about the random process. Before we do so, however, we wish to consider other examples of important random processes.

12.2 EXAMPLES OF RANDOM PROCESSES

12.2.1 Sinusoidal Signal

One key process that occurs in many telecommunications applications is the sine function. Whenever we transmit information via radio, TV, or wireless, we send it using a sine or a combination of sine functions. When we receive a sinusoidal signal with known frequency, we can tune the receiver to that particular frequency, but we can usually assume that we do not know its phase or amplitude in advance, and hence we may model it by a sine function with known frequency but with random amplitude and phase:

$$X(t) = A \cos(\omega_0 t + \Theta) \qquad (12.1)$$

Here we assume that the frequency ω_0 is known but that the amplitude A and the phase Θ are random variables with known joint distribution. For simplicity, we may assume that the phase and amplitude are independent variables. Depending on the number of values taken by the amplitude and phase, we may have infinitely many sample functions. They all will look the same in the sense that they are all sine functions with the same frequency, but they will have different amplitudes and different phase shifts. We shall discuss the properties of this signal in later sections.

12.2.2 Random Linear Trajectories

If we consider a radar which is tracking an airplane that is moving at constant speed, then the trajectory (in one dimension) of the plane is simply a straight line, but with random slope (representing the velocity) and random intercept, as we may not know the speed and starting point of the trajectory. In this case we can say that the trajectory in one of the coordinates is given by

$$X(t) = A + Bt \qquad (12.2)$$

Here again we assume that we know the statistical properties of the two random variables A and B. All sample functions will look like straight lines but with arbitrary slopes and intercepts. Obviously, if we know, for example, that A and B each can take only two values with given probabilities, we obtain exactly four sample functions. We can then assign these probabilities to the sample functions in question.

12.2.3 Random Telegraph Signal

This example represents a signal that switches between two values at random points in time. Starting at some arbitrary time instant t_0 as either $+a$ or $-a$, the process switches between these two values at the points of arrival of a Poisson random model with arrival rate λ. Suppose that at time $t = t_0$ the process takes a value $-a$ (as in Figure 12.5). Then, after the first arrival it switches to $+a$, and after the second arrival it switches to $-a$ again, and so on. We can explicitly show its value at some arbitrary time t if we know its value at time $t = t_0$. Since it requires $1, 3, 5, \ldots$ arrivals in the interval (t_0, t) for the value to be $+a$ if it started at $-a$ at $t = t_0$, then an odd number of arrivals causes the process to have the value opposite to its value at

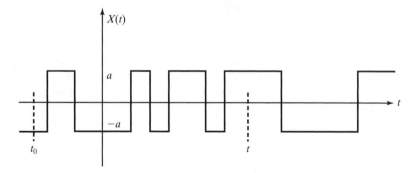

Figure 12.5 One sample function of the random telegraph signal

$t = t_0$. We can utilize this fact in deriving the probability that at time t $X(t)$ takes the value $+a$, given that it started at $-a$ at $t = t_0$:

$$P\{X(t) = +a | X(t_0) = -a\} = P\{\text{odd number of arrivals in } (t_0, t)\}$$

$$= \sum_{k=0}^{\infty} \frac{[\lambda(t - t_0)]^{2k+1}}{(2k + 1)!} \exp[-\lambda(t - t_0)] = 0.5\{1 - \exp[-2\lambda(t - t_0)]\} \quad (12.3)$$

The preceding probability is also equal to the probability that it takes the value $-a$ at time t, given that it started at $+a$ at time $t = t_0$, by using the same argument:

$$P\{X(t) = -a | X(t_0) = +a\} = P\{X(t) = +a | X(t_0) = -a\} \quad (12.4)$$

Similarly, we can find the probability that it takes the value of $-a$ at time t if it has the value of $-a$ at $t = t_0$, and this will occur only if there are an even number of arrivals in the interval (t_0, t), so we have

$$P\{X(t) = -a | X(t_0) = -a\} = P\{\text{even number of arrivals in } (t_0, t)\}$$

$$= \sum_{k=0}^{\infty} \frac{[\lambda(t - t_0)]^{2k}}{(2k)!} \exp[-\lambda(t - t_0)] = 0.5\{1 + \exp[-2\lambda(t - t_0)]\} \quad (12.5)$$

The preceding is also equal to the probability that it takes the value $+a$, at time t, given that it started at $+a$ at time $t = t_0$, by using the same argument:

$$P\{X(t) = +a | X(t_0) = +a\} = P\{X(t) = -a | X(t_0) = -a\} \quad (12.6)$$

Since the process takes only two values, we could also obtain the probabilities in equations (12.6) and (12.5) by taking the complement of the probabilities derived in equations (12.4) and (12.3), since the total probability should add to 1.

We therefore see that if the starting time $t = t_0$ is some long time in the past, say at some large negative time, the probability that the process takes the value $+a$ at some arbitrary time t is equal to 0.5 as the limiting value obtained from equations (12.3) or (12.5) as t_0 tends to negative infinity. Similarly, the probability that the process take the value $-a$ also approaches the limit of 0.5 from equations (12.3) or (12.5). The preceding expressions also allow us to find the joint probability mass function of the process if we consider its value at two time instants t_1 and t_2. In such a case we obtain the following four probabilities, where, for simplicity, we assume that $t_1 < t_2$:

$$P\{X(t_1) = +a, X(t_2) = +a\} = P\{X(t_1) = -a, X(t_2) = -a\}$$
$$= 0.5 \times 0.5\{1 + \exp[-2\lambda(t_2 - t_1)]\} = 0.25\{1 + \exp[-2\lambda(t_2 - t_1)]\} \quad (12.7)$$

$$P\{X(t_1) = +a, X(t_2) = -a\} = P\{X(t_1) = -a, X(t_2) = +a\}$$
$$= 0.5 \times 0.5\{1 - \exp[-2\lambda(t_2 - t_1)]\} = 0.25\{1 - \exp[-2\lambda(t_2 - t_1)]\} \quad (12.8)$$

We see that the value of the arrival rate (in this case the switching rate) affects how the probability of the values taken at the two time instants changes with time. For the same value of time difference, the probability changes rapidly and the random variables become independent as the probability becomes the product of 0.5×0.5 if the arrival rate is high, and it changes very slowly if the arrival rate is low. We shall study more about this process in the next section as well.

12.2.4 Random Binary Signal

This process represents one way of transmitting binary information over a telecommunication channel. If we are to send one bit every T seconds, we encode every bit by a waveform so that we can send it over the channel. As an example, when we want to send a "1" we may send a pulse of magnitude $+a$ and width T, while if we wish to send a "0" we send a pulse of the same width but with magnitude $-a$. Since, for simplicity, we shall assume that the bits are independent of each other and also that their two values are equally likely, it follows that the sample function of the process will look like an arbitrary number of pulses of the same width but whose amplitude is in each period T are either $+a$ or $-a$ with equal probability. Also, since we may assume that the receiver does not know precisely when the beginning of a bit occurred, we have a random starting point of the period T. A sample function of the process $X(t)$ defined in the preceding is shown in Figure 12.6.

We can define the probability that the signal takes the values $+a$ or $-a$, since it follows from the definition that

$$P\{X(t) = +a\} = P\{X(t) = -a\} = 0.5 \qquad (12.9)$$

Furthermore, here again we can try to see how the joint probability of the two random variables $X(t_1)$ and $X(t_2)$ behaves. If the difference $|t_1 - t_2| > T$, we can state for sure that since the values depend on the values of two bits, which we assumed are independent, then the random variables $X(t_1)$ and $X(t_2)$ are independent when $|t_1 - t_2| > T$. We shall see how they behave when $|t_1 - t_2| < T$ in the next section.

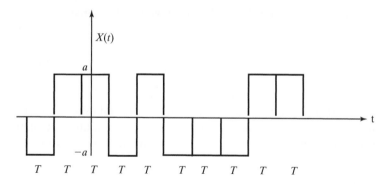

Figure 12.6   One sample function of the random binary signal

12.3 DISTRIBUTIONS OF RANDOM PROCESSES

We noted in the previous section that when random processes are sampled at specific instants of time, they simply define random variables. Since we know that random variables may be described by their distributions or density functions, then we can describe random processes by their distributions or density functions. One key difference is that as we sample the process at some time t, the resulting distribution may in general depend on that time instant as well. Similarly, if we take two sample times to define a joint distribution, the resulting joint distribution will in general depend on the two time instants selected. Here again we can describe the distribution function for all types of processes, but we can describe densities only for continuous-amplitude processes, while we need probability mass functions for discrete-amplitude processes. If we are very careful, we may use the impulse function in such cases to represent the density function of discrete-amplitude processes.

12.3.1 First-Order Distributions

We start by considering the random variable obtained when we fix the time at instant t, which we shall consider a constant for the time being. In such a case we obtain a random variable $X(t, \zeta)$, which we shall denote by $X(t)$. We therefore can define its distribution function in the usual manner, but since the resulting distribution may in general depend on t, we also list this dependence as a parameter of the distribution function:

$$F_{X(t)}(x; t) = P\{X(t) \leq x\} \tag{12.10}$$

We call the resulting distribution function the first-order distribution of the random process $X(t)$. If the process is continuous, we may then be able to define its first-order density function as the derivative of the distribution function with respect to x. Note that since the distribution depends on the time t, it is a function of two variables; therefore, when we take the derivative, it has to be a partial derivative, since the time element t is just a parameter of the distribution:

$$f_{X(t)}(x;t) = \frac{\partial}{\partial x} F_{X(t)}(x;t) \tag{12.11}$$

If the process is not continuous or if at any time t it takes only a finite number of values, then the density will not exist unless we use impulse functions. In such a case we use probability mass functions instead of the density functions.

Example 12.1(a)

As an example, consider the distribution of the process defined in Example 12.1 at $t = 0.5\pi$. The process at that instant takes the values of 0, 3, π, and $-\pi$ with equal probabilities. It is easier to show its probability mass function rather than its distribution. As a matter of fact, we can write its probability mass function for any time t we wish simply by considering the way it was defined, and in this case we obtain

$$P\{X(t) = 3 \sin t\} = 0.25$$
$$P\{X(t) = 3 \cos t\} = 0.25$$
$$P\{X(t) = 2t\} = 0.25$$
$$P\{X(t) = -2t\} = 0.25$$

Example 12.2

Consider the random linear trajectory process we discussed in Section 12.2.2:

$$X(t) = A + Bt \tag{12.12}$$

Suppose that A and B are Gaussian random variables with zero means and variances σ_A^2 and σ_B^2, respectively. Suppose also that the random variables A and B are uncorrelated. We see then that at any instant t, the "random variable" $X(t)$ is just a sum of two Gaussian random variables (multiplied by a "constant" t), so that $X(t)$ will also have a Gaussian density function with mean zero and variance

$$\sigma_{X(t)}^2 = E\{[X t)]^2\} = E\{(A + Bt)^2\} = \sigma_A^2 + \sigma_B^2 t^2 \tag{12.13}$$

Note that when we try to find the variance in equation (12.13), we assume that t is a constant (not random), and we take expectations only over the random variables A and B. We can therefore write the density of $X(t)$ at any instant t as

$$f_{X(t)}(x;t) = \frac{\exp\left\{-\frac{x^2}{2(\sigma_A^2 + \sigma_B^2 t^2)}\right\}}{\sqrt{2\pi(\sigma_A^2 + \sigma_B^2 t^2)}} \tag{12.14}$$

It should be noted that the first-order density is a density function with respect to the variable x (which determines the values to be taken by the random process), but its variance depends on t as a parameter. Hence, as stated previously, t serves as a parameter of the density function, which is a function of the variable x.

This example (as well as the previous one) illustrates the important fact that when considering the statistical properties of random processes, we consider the time as a "constant," (i.e., the time is not one of the random elements to be assigned probabilistic values).

We shall address some of the other examples we considered in Section 12.2 later in this section.

12.3.2 Second-Order Distributions

If we are now to take two time instants, $t = t_1$ and $t = t_2$, we obtain two random variables $X(t_1)$ and $X(t_2)$. We therefore can define their joint distribution function in the usual manner, except that in this case the distribution depends on the time instants t_1 and t_2 as parameters. We call the resulting distribution function the second-order distribution function of the process $X(t)$, and the parameters of time identify which sample times are involved in the variables considered by the distribution function. The definition of the second-order distribution function is then given as

$$F_{X(t)}(x_1, x_2; t_1, t_2) = P\{X(t_1) \le x_1 \text{ and } X(t_2) \le x_2\} \qquad (12.15)$$

The dependence on time of the distribution function is very critical, because it shows how the process changes with time. For example, as t_1 approaches t_2, the probability that $X(t_1)$ is equal to $X(t_2)$ approaches 1. In such a case the distribution becomes just a first-order distribution, with the added probability that $P\{X(t_1) = X(t_2)\} = 1$. Here again we may consider joint density functions defined in the usual manner, or a joint probability mass function if the variables are discrete. We have seen an illustration of the joint probability mass function in the example of the random telegraph signal when we found the probability of the values taken at two time instants.

The definition of the second-order density function of a continuous-amplitude random process is given as follows for completeness:

$$f_{X(t)}(x_1, x_2; t_1, t_2) = \frac{\partial^2}{\partial x_1 \partial x_2} F_{X(t)}(x_1, x_2; t_1, t_2) \qquad (12.16)$$

In general, it is rather difficult to obtain density functions of random processes, except for special cases. We shall mention just two in this section, and we shall consider a few others in future sections.

Case 1: When the process is Gaussian, it is easy to derive its second-order density function, for then all we need are the means, variances, and covariance of the two variables $X(t_1)$ and $X(t_2)$. Example 12.2 is a simple illustration of such a case because, if we also find the covariance between $X(t_1)$ and $X(t_2)$, we can write its joint density function. It is left as an exercise to find the joint density for that case.

Case 2: When the time instants are such that the random variables $X(t_1)$ and $X(t_2)$ are independent, then the joint density function becomes just the product of the first-order density functions taken at the two time instants. We have seen that the binary random signal behaves that way when the difference between the time instants is greater than T.

12.3.3 Stationary Processes

We noticed that in some examples we considered in the previous sections, the first-order distribution sometimes depended on the time instant and sometimes it did not. We also noted that the second-order distribution sometimes depended on the values of both time instants and sometimes it depended only on their difference (the random telegraph signal, for example). This leads us to the concept of stationarity. We noticed that in the random telegraph signal and the random binary signal, the position of the origin does not matter to the description of the process. This property defines a stationary process in the strict sense.

A **strictly stationary** process is one whose statistical properties do not change if we change the origin in time. Another way of presenting this concept is to state that all of its statistical properties depend only on time *differences* rather than on the absolute values of the time instants.

We may also define more limited concepts, such as first-order stationary and second-order stationary processes, to mean that the first-order distribution does not depend on time or that the second-order distribution depends only on the time difference of the two time instants. We can define these mathematically as follows:

For a first-order stationary process, we have a first-order distribution that is not a function of the time t:

$$F_{X(t)}(x; t) = P\{X(t) \le x\} = F_{X(t)}(x) \tag{12.17}$$

For a second-order stationary process, we have a joint distribution function whose parameters depend only on the time difference:

$$F_{X(t)}(x_1, x_2; t_1, t_2) = P\{X(t_1) \le x_1 \text{ and } X(t_2) \le x_2\} = F_{X(t)}(x_1, x_2; t_1 - t_2) \tag{12.18}$$

We mentioned previously that the random telegraph signal satisfies these two conditions, but from the way it was defined, it appears to be strictly stationary, as the origin does not play any part in its statistical behavior. We consider another example next.

Example 12.3

Consider the sinusoidal signal we discussed in Section 12.2.1 and here. We assume that the random variable Θ defining the phase is uniformly distributed in the interval $(0, 2\pi)$. We also assume that the amplitude $A = a$, which is just a constant value rather than a random variable:

$$X(t) = a \cos(\omega_0 t + \Theta) \tag{12.19}$$

As we plot several of the sample functions, we see that they all look the same as far as the origin is concerned, since the phase shift will cause all possible positions of the origin to be equally likely, and hence will not affect the statistical properties of the process. We shall derive its first-order distribution. (We describe it only as a function of x, since we observed that the process is stationary.) Its first order distribution is as follows:

$$F_{X(t)}(x) = P\{X(t) \le x\} = P\{a\cos(\omega_0 t + \Theta) \le x\} \tag{12.20}$$

Since the phase is uniformly distributed between 0 and 2π, which is a complete period of the sine function, shifting the region from 0 to 2π, to a different region of length 2π should not affect the distribution. Hence we replace the argument $(\omega_0 t + \Theta)$ by a random variable Y that is uniformly distributed in the interval $(\omega_0 t, \omega_0 t + 2\pi)$. In this case we have a simple function of a random variable Y, which we considered in Example 4.4, and we can state that the answer will be the same for this case as well due to the periodic nature of the sine function. The resulting distribution may be expressed by the formula obtained in equation (4.24) to yield

$$F_{X(t)}(x) = 1 - \frac{1}{\pi}\arccos(x/a), \quad \text{for } -a < x < a \tag{12.21}$$

Obviously the distribution function will have a value 0 for $x < -a$, and has the value 1 for $x > a$.

In this case we can also derive the first-order density function of the random process, as it is simply the derivative of the distribution function:

$$f_{X(t)}(x) = \frac{1}{\pi\sqrt{a^2 - x^2}}, \quad \text{for } -a < x < a \tag{12.22}$$

As we have seen in the case of random variables, most of the time we prefer to describe statistical properties in terms of averages or expectations, rather than in terms of density functions and distributions. We shall do the same in the case of random processes in the next section.

12.4 MEAN AND AUTOCORRELATION FUNCTION

Since distribution and densities can be quite cumbersome to derive and in many cases provide more information than we need, we usually concentrate on expectations involving the random processes, just as we did for random variables. As with random variables, we shall discuss only the mean and correlation, as they are easy to derive and provide us with sufficient information to process random signals via linear operations.

12.4.1 Mean of a Random Process

We define the mean of the random process $X(t)$ as the expected value of the process—that is, the expected value of the random variable defined by $X(t)$ for a fixed instant of time. Note that when we take expectations, we hold the time as a nonrandom parameter and we average only over the random quantities. We denote the mean of the random process by $m_X(t)$, since in general it may depend on time. The definition of the mean is just the expectation of $X(t)$:

$$m_X(t) = E\{X(t)\} \tag{12.23}$$

Two important notes

a. The first has to do with the fact the averaging is **not** with respect to time, but only with respect to the random outcomes, which are implicit in the definition of $X(t)$.

b. The second has to do with the fact that while we can describe the expectation in terms of the first order density of the process, in general we find the expectation **without** the need to find the first-order density first. If we were to write the mean in terms of the density function, then we would have the relation

$$m_X(t) = \int_{-\infty}^{\infty} x f_{X(t)}(x; t)\, dx \tag{12.24}$$

Warning: Equation (12.24) has to be used very rarely and is given here to formally show that the mean of a random process is nothing but the mean of the random variable defined by $X(t)$ for a given instant of time t. We shall consider examples after we define the autocorrelation function of the random process.

12.4.2 The Autocorrelation Function

When we consider the process at two time instants $t = t_1$ and $t = t_2$, we obtain the two random variables $X(t_1)$ and $X(t_2)$. Since one of the key properties of two random variables is their correlation, because that property describes whether they are linearly related, we would like to find the correlation between $X(t_1)$ and $X(t_2)$. Since such a correlation will obviously depend on the time instants t_1 and t_2 in question, in such a case we obtain a correlation that depends on these two time instants. We therefore call such a correlation, the correlation function; however, since it is a correlation between the values of the same process sampled at two different instants of time, we call it the **autocorrelation function** of the process $X(t)$ and it is denoted by $R_X(t_1, t_2)$. It is defined in the usual way for expectations, as in the following expression:

$$R_X(t_1, t_2) = E\{X(t_1)X(t_2)\} \tag{12.25}$$

Again we could define it in terms of the second-order density function of the process $X(t)$, but we shall not do so to avoid overreliance on the use of the second-order density.

Just as in the two random variables case, we can define the covariance and correlation coefficient, but in this case the name used is slightly different. We define the autocovariance function as

$$C_X(t_1, t_2) = E\{[X(t_1) - m_X(t_1)][X(t_2) - m_X(t_2)]\} = R_X(t_1, t_2) - m_X(t_1)m_X(t_2) \tag{12.26}$$

Note that the variance of the process and its average power (the names used for the average of $[X(t) - m_X(t)]^2$ and $[X(t)]^2$, respectively) can be directly obtained from the autocorrelation and the autocovariance functions, by simply using the same time instants for both t_1 and t_2:

$$E\{[X(t)]^2\} = R_X(t, t) \qquad (12.27)$$

$$\sigma_X^2(t) = E\{[X(t) - m_X(t)]^2\} = C_X(t, t) = R_X(t, t) - [m_X(t)]^2 \quad (12.28)$$

We see therefore that we do not need to find the variance or the average power of the process directly, since it follows from the definition of the autocorrelation and autocovariance functions.

Before we consider examples, we have to define one more key property. Previously we discussed the general stationarity property, and we defined strictly stationary processes. However, what if we are interested only in the mean and the autocorrelation functions? We see here a new and more limited type of stationarity, and we define it next.

12.4.3 Wide Sense Stationary Processes

We noted that when a process is strictly stationary, its distribution and density functions do not depend on the absolute values of the time instants in question, but only on the differences of the time instants. For example, its first-order distribution and density do not depend on time. Similarly, its second-order distribution or density functions do not depend on both time instants, but only on their difference. However, if we are concerned only with the mean and autocorrelation function, then we can restrict our definition of a stationary process to a limited form, and we call such processes wide-sense stationary processes. A **wide-sense stationary (WSS)** process has a constant mean, and its autocorrelation function depends only on the time difference:

$$m_X(t) = E\{X(t)\} = m_X \qquad (12.29)$$

$$R_X(t_1, t_2) = E\{X(t_1)X(t_2)\} = R_X(t_2 - t_1) \qquad (12.30)$$

Since the time does not appear in the mean, we simply write it as a constant mean m_X. Similarly, since the autocorrelation function is a function only of the time difference, we may write it as a function of one variable—the time difference, τ:

$$R_X(\tau) = E\{X(t)X(t + \tau)\} \qquad (12.31)$$

We can obtain similar expressions for the autocovariance function, which in this case is dependent only on the time difference as well:

$$C_X(\tau) = E\{[X(t) - m_X][X(t + \tau) - m_X]\} = R_X(\tau) - [m_X]^2 \quad (12.32)$$

Finally, the variance and average power of the process are obtained for WSS processes by the following expressions:

$$E\{[X(t)]^2\} = R_X(0) \qquad (12.33)$$

$$\sigma_X^2 = C_X(0) = R_X(0) - [m_X]^2 \qquad (12.34)$$

We see that WSS processes have constant average power and constant variance; hence the dependence on t is no longer shown for these attributes.

Before we consider the properties of the autocorrelation function, we shall consider the four important examples we discussed in Section 12.2.

12.4.4 Major Examples

a. Random Linear Trajectories

We defined the process in Section 12.2.2 as follows, where we assumed that A and B are random variables:

$$X(t) = A + Bt \tag{12.35}$$

Suppose that A and B are uncorrelated random variables with means m_A and m_B, and variances σ_A^2 and σ_B^2. We now wish to find the mean and autocorrelation function of the process. We use the properties of expectations without having to resort to any of the densities involved. We obtain the following for the mean and autocorrelation functions, where we use only the linearity property of expectations:

$$m_X(t) = E\{X(t)\} = E\{A + Bt\} = E\{A\} + E\{B\}t = m_A + m_B t$$
$$R_X(t_1, t_2) = E\{X(t_1)X(t_2)\} = E\{[A + Bt_1][A + Bt_2]\}$$
$$= E\{A^2\} + E\{AB\}(t_1 + t_2) + E\{B^2\}t_1 t_2 \tag{12.36}$$
$$= (\sigma_A^2 + m_A^2) + m_A m_B(t_1 + t_2) + (\sigma_B^2 + m_B^2)t_1 t_2 \tag{12.37}$$

Again we used only the fact that the expectation of a sum is equal to the sum of expectations, and that, for uncorrelated random variables, the expectation of the product is equal to the product of the means. We similarly obtain the expression for the auto-covariance function by the following expression:

$$C_X(t_1, t_2) = R_X(t_1, t_2) - m_X(t_1)m_X(t_2) = \sigma_A^2 + \sigma_B^2 t_1 t_2 \tag{12.38}$$

The preceding expression reduces to equation (12.14) for the case of the same time instants, to obtain the variance of the process.

It is obvious from the preceding expressions that the process is not stationary, even in the wide sense. Trajectories that always increase with time cannot reach a steady-state condition, which is one way to measure some sort of stationarity. We hope to be luckier in the next few examples.

b. Random Sinusoidal Signal

We now consider the sinusoidal signal we discussed in Section 12.2.1, where it was defined by the following expression:

$$X(t) = A \cos(\omega_0 t + \Theta) \tag{12.39}$$

We shall assume again that A and Θ are independent random variables with A having mean m_A and variance σ_A^2, while Θ has a density function $f_\Theta(u)$ that is nonzero only in the interval $(0, 2\pi)$. We now find its mean and autocorrelation function. Again, to the extent possible, we use the properties of the expectation, and only as a last resort do we use the definition in terms of the density functions. We start by deriving the mean of $X(t)$:

$$m_X(t) = E\{X(t)\} = E\{A \cos(\omega_0 t + \Theta)\} = E\{A\}E\{\cos(\omega_0 t + \Theta)\} \quad (12.40)$$

We used the fact that when we have independent variables the expectation of the product of functions of these variables becomes the product of the expectations. Equation (12.40) can now be evaluated using the density of the random variable representing the phase:

$$m_X(t) = m_A \int_0^{2\pi} \cos(\omega_0 t + u) f_\Theta(u) \, du \quad (12.41)$$

The expression for the mean cannot be simplified any further unless we know the density function of the phase variable. Suppose we now assume that the density is uniformly distributed in the interval $(0, 2\pi)$:

$$f_\Theta(u) = \frac{1}{2\pi}, \qquad \text{for } 0 < u < 2\pi \quad (12.42)$$

Then the expression for the mean, equation (12.41), reduces to zero, since the integral of a cosine over one period is zero:

$$m_X(t) = m_A \int_0^{2\pi} \cos(\omega_0 t + u) \frac{1}{2\pi} du = 0 = m_X \quad (12.43)$$

The autocorrelation function can similarly be derived, by using the properties of the sine function and the expectation:

$$R_X(t_1, t_2) = E\{X(t_1)X(t_2)\} = E\{A \cos(\omega_0 t_1 + \Theta)A \cos(\omega_0 t_2 + \Theta)\}$$

$$= E\{A^2\}E\{0.5[\cos(\omega_0 t_2 - \omega_0 t_1) + \cos(\omega_0 t_2 + \omega_0 t_1 + 2\Theta)]\}$$

$$= 0.5(\sigma_A^2 + m_A^2)\left\{\cos[\omega_0(t_2 - t_1)] + \int_0^{2\pi} \cos[\omega_0(t_2 + t_1) + 2u]f_\Theta(u) \, du\right\} \quad (12.44)$$

Here we used the property of the expectation of A^2 as the sum of the variance and the square of the mean. We also use the fact that the first term involving the cosine is **not** random, as it is a function of only the time instants and the frequency. We see again that the autocorrelation function may depend on both time instants if the density function of the phase angle is arbitrary. If, on the other hand, the density function is uniformly distributed as in equation (12.42), then the last term in equation (12.44) becomes zero due to the fact that integrating the cosine function over the interval of one period is zero. In such a case we can write the autocorrelation function as a function of only the time difference, and the process becomes WSS:

$$R_X(\tau) = E\{X(t)X(t + \tau)\} = 0.5(\sigma_A^2 + m_A^2) \cos(\omega_0 \tau) \quad (12.45)$$

We see therefore that the average power of the process is equal to

$$E\{[X(t)]^2\} = R_X(0) = 0.5(\sigma_A^2 + m_A^2) \tag{12.46}$$

If $A = a$, which is just a constant and not a random variable, then the term $(\sigma_A^2 + m_A^2)$ becomes just that constant squared (i.e., $E\{[X(t)]^2\} = 0.5a^2$).

We can conclude that the average power of a sinusoidal signal with uniformly distributed random phase is just half the average of the square of its amplitude. We also note that in this case the autocorrelation is just a cosine and the process is WSS.

C. Random Telegraph Signal

We introduced the random telegraph signal in Section 12.2.3, and we also derived the probability mass function of the values it takes at two time instants. The result was shown in equations (12.7) and (12.8), where we have seen that these probabilities depend only on the time difference of the two time instants. We can conclude that the process is stationary and therefore it is also wide-sense stationary. In deriving its mean and its autocorrelation function, we shall use the notation that the mean is constant and the autocorrelation depends on the time difference. We start by finding the mean of the process:

$$m_X = E\{X(t)\} = +a\, P\{X(t) = +a\} + (-a)\, P\{X(t) = -a\}$$
$$= +a\, 0.5 + (-a)\, 0.5 = 0$$

The process has zero mean, as expected. We now derive the autocorrelation function:

$$R_X(\tau) = E\{X(t)X(t + \tau)\} = +a^2\, P\{X(t) = +a, X(t + \tau) = +a\}$$
$$+ a^2\, P\{X(t) = -a, X(t + \tau) = -a\} - a^2\, P\{X(t) = +a, X(t + \tau) = -a\}$$
$$- a^2\, P\{X(t) = -a, X(t + \tau) = +a\}$$
$$= a^2\{0.5[1 + \exp(-2\lambda|\tau|)] - 0.5[1 - \exp(-2\lambda|\tau|)]\}$$
$$= a^2 \exp(-2\lambda|\tau|) \tag{12.47}$$

We used the variable $|\tau|$ in equations (12.7) and (12.8) instead of $t_2 - t_1$, since we assumed there that the difference was positive, namely, $t_1 < t_2$. We plot the autocorrelation function in Figure 12.7 for $a = 2$, and $\lambda = 0.75$. It is important to note that the correlation between the values of the process at two time instants falls off exponentially with the time difference. The correlation drops faster if the switching rate λ is larger, and it drops slower if the rate is smaller. We see that the behavior of the autocorrelation function indicates whether the process changes rapidly or slowly. Since we may use the correlation to estimate the value of one random variable from another, the correlation function determines whether we can predict the value of the process at one instant from its value at another instant. The quality of the prediction depends on the relative value of the autocorrelation as a function of the time difference. These arguments can also be seen directly from the behavior of the process.

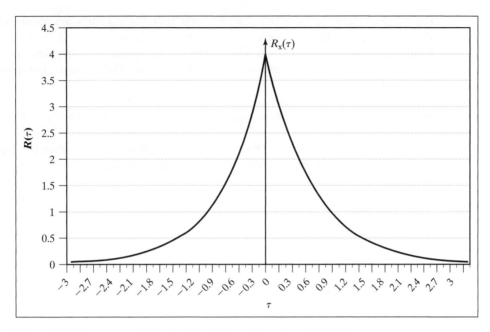

Figure 12.7   The autocorrelation function of the random telegraph signal

If the rate is high, then the switches occur too frequently; hence the process is less predictable. In that case the correlation at the time difference will be too small as well. The opposite argument holds for a small switching rate: The process does not change rapidly; hence if is more predictable, and indeed the autocorrelation stays at a high value as the time difference increases.

d. Random Binary Signal

This process was also defined in Section 12.2.4, and here we find its mean and auto-correlation function. We assumed then that the start of the period where the pulses change between $+a$ and $-a$, with equal probability, is random and could be equally likely anywhere between 0 and T. If we assume that the start of the period is uniformly distributed in the interval $(0, T)$, then we can see that any sample function could be translated by an arbitrary amount and will still yield a sample function. Hence, the origin of the time axis is not important, which implies that the process is stationary. Using this assumption, we shall define the autocorrelation function as a function of only the time difference, as we did in the random telegraph signal example. First we find the mean of the process:

$$m_X = E\{X(t)\} = +a\, P\{X(t) = +a\} + (-a)\, P\{X(t) = -a\}$$
$$= +a\, 0.5 + (-a)\, 0.5 = 0$$

In order to arrive at the expression that resulted in zero mean for the process, we used the probabilities defined in equation (12.9). We also found that if we look at the value of the process at two time instants, then these values are independent if they occur at two different periods, which means they are the result of two bits and hence are independent of each other. They are independent if the time difference $|\tau| = |t_2 - t_1| > T$. In this case we can easily show that the autocorrelation satisfies the equation

$$R_X(\tau) = E\{X(t)X(t + \tau)\} = E\{X(t)\}E\{X(t + \tau)\} = 0, \quad \text{for } |\tau| > T \quad (12.48)$$

The only thing remaining is to find the autocorrelation function when the time difference is less than T. We can have two situations in this case, shown as (a) and (b) in Figure 12.8:

The following provides descriptions of the two situations shown in the figure, where two pulses are drawn as having opposite values for clarity and to highlight the independence assumption:

a. The beginning of the period occurs outside the interval $|\tau|$, so that both time instants $t = t_1$ and $t = t_2$ occur in the same pulse and hence in the same bit.

b. The beginning of the period occurs inside the interval $|\tau|$, so that the two time instants $t = t_1$ and $t = t_2$ occur at two different pulses and hence yield independent values of $X(t)$.

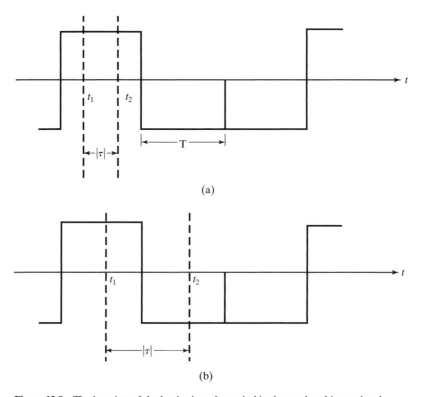

(a)

(b)

Figure 12.8   The location of the beginning of a period in the random binary signal

Since the beginning of the period is uniformly distributed in the interval $(0, T)$, the probability that such a beginning occurs inside the interval of length $|\tau|$ is proportional to the length of the interval and is the ratio of the length of the interval to the length of the period T. Thus we have

$$P\{\text{period begins inside } |\tau|\} = \frac{|\tau|}{T} \qquad (12.49)$$

$$P\{\text{period begins outside} |\tau|\} = 1 - P\{\text{period begins inside } |\tau|\} = 1 - \frac{|\tau|}{T} \qquad (12.50)$$

We are now ready to find the autocorrelation function. Since the autocorrelation function is the expected value of the product $X(t)$ and $X(t + \tau)$, these values are identical (the same pulse) if the period occurs outside the interval of length $|\tau|$, and in that case the product is exactly a^2. On the other hand, the values are independent if the period occurs inside the interval. Because when they are independent the expectation is the product of the expectations, which is zero (as the process has zero mean), we obtain the following expression for the autocorrelation function when $|\tau| < T$:

$$R_X(\tau) = E\{X(t)X(t + \tau)\} = a^2 P\{\text{period begins outside the interval } |\tau|\}$$
$$+ E\{X(t)\}E\{X(t + \tau)\}P\{\text{period begins inside the interval } |\tau|\}$$
$$= a^2\left\{1 - \frac{|\tau|}{T}\right\} + 0 \times \frac{|\tau|}{T} = a^2\left\{1 - \frac{|\tau|}{T}\right\} \qquad (12.51)$$

We show a plot of the autocorrelation function in Figure 12.9 for $T = 2.5$ and $a = 2$.

In this example we see again that as T becomes large the autocorrelation stays high for large values of the time difference, while as T becomes small the autocorrelation drops to zero very rapidly. Here again our intuitive feel about how fast the process changes is confirmed by the behavior of the autocorrelation function.

12.4.5 Properties of the Autocorrelation Function

Now that we have seen how the autocorrelation function behaves for various examples, we are ready to consider the general properties of the autocorrelation function. As we noted earlier, we defined two functions. One was the autocorrelation function and the other was the autocovariance function. These functions are really the same, except for the mean value that appears in the autocorrelation function and is removed from the autocovariance function. For example, if we have a process $X(t)$ with mean m_X, then the relationship between its autocorrelation and autocovariance functions is

$$C_X(\tau) = R_X(\tau) - [m_X]^2 \qquad (12.52)$$

If we subtract the mean from the process to define a new process

$$Y(t) = X(t) - m_X \qquad (12.53)$$

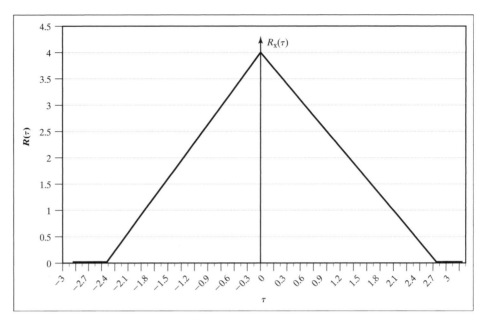

Figure 12.9   The autocorrelation function of the binary random signal

then the autocorrelation of $Y(t)$ is indeed equal to the autocovariance of $X(t)$:

$$R_Y(\tau) = R_X(\tau) - [m_X]^2 = C_X(\tau) \tag{12.54}$$

Hence autocorrelation functions and autocovariance functions will satisfy the same general properties. The difference between the two is reflected in their limiting behavior as τ tends to infinity. As τ tends to infinity, in general (unless the process is periodic) the autocorrelation tends to the squared value of the mean, while the autocovariance function tends to zero. All other properties of the autocorrelation function are also satisfied by the autocovariance function.

1. $R_X(-\tau) = R_X(\tau)$. The autocorrelation function is even. This follows from its definition, as it depends only on the magnitude of the time difference between the two time instants.
2. $|R_X(\tau)| \leq R_X(0)$. It achieves it largest value at the origin.
3. If it reaches a limit as $\tau \rightarrow \infty$, then that limit is equal to $[m_X]^2$.
4. If it achieves its value at the origin at some other point, then it is periodic with that period (i.e., if $R_X(T) = R_X(0)$, then it is periodic with period T).
5. It is a positive semidefinite function. However, we shall not discuss this property at this time, but will return to it in Chapters 13 and 14.

12.4.6 Ergodicity

In many situations we may have only one sample function of a process, and we would like to obtain some statistical information about the random process from that one sample function. Since with one sample function we cannot do any expectations (we do not know what the other sample functions are like), we have to be satisfied with taking time averages instead of expectations. If, as the time interval becomes large, the time averages tend to the expectation, we say that the random process is **ergodic**. This is a very useful property since we do not need the entire collection of sample functions to obtain information about the random process. However, it is a property that is the most difficult to prove or verify. As an example of what the ergodicity property means, consider the case of the random sinusoidal signal:

$$X(t) = A \cos(\omega_0 t + \Theta)$$

If A is a random variable, then one sample function cannot provide us with information about different values of the amplitude A that may occur. Hence, such a signal cannot possibly be ergodic unless $A = a$, a constant nonrandom value. Even then, the process is not ergodic in general unless we can show that the sample mean and the sample autocorrelation obtained by time averages are the same as the mean and the autocorrelation function. For the case of uniformly distributed phase angle, we found that the mean was zero and that the autocorrelation function was

$$R_X(\tau) = 0.5 \, a^2 \cos(\omega_0 \tau)$$

We can easily show that if we take the time average of $X(t)$ by averaging over one period we obtain zero, and if we multiply $X(t)$ by $X(t + \tau)$ and average over time we obtain the same function as the autocorrelation function. In more complex cases it is quite difficult to prove ergodicity. Hence, we shall not address the general ergodic properties of random processes in this text and will consider only a more limited ergodicity property.

We shall just state the ergodic property for the mean and the autocorrelation function of a random process.

A process is ergodic with respect to the mean if the following holds:

$$\lim_{T \to \infty} \frac{1}{2T} \int_{-T}^{T} X(t) \, dt = E\{X(t)\} = m_X \tag{12.55}$$

Similarly, we can define that a process is ergodic with respect to the autocorrelation function if the time average of the product tends to the autocorrelation function:

$$\lim_{T \to \infty} \frac{1}{2T} \int_{-T}^{T} X(t)X(t + \tau) \, dt = E\{X(t)X(t + \tau)\} = R_X(\tau) \tag{12.56}$$

It should be noted that a process must first be stationary before we can even begin to check whether it is ergodic. If it is not stationary, the expectations usually depend on the time instants; therefore the expectations cannot be obtained by time averages, which remove the time element via averaging. We can define more general ergodic properties, such as ergodic with respect to the first-order distribution, for example. However, we defer such coverage to more advanced texts on random processes.

However, as an illustration of ergodicity, a MATLAB problem is assigned to show that the random telegraph signal is ergodic with respect to the autocorrelation function.

12.5 CROSS-CORRELATION FUNCTION

In many applications we encounter at least two random processes. For example, in any communications channel we have two signals: the signal we desire to transmit and receive and the noise inherent in all physical systems. Hence, as in the case of two random variables, we need to consider the statistical properties relating two random signals. This leads us to the definition of the cross-correlation function.

Given two random processes $X(t)$ and $Y(t)$, we define their cross-correlation function as

$$R_{XY}(t_1, t_2) = E\{X(t_1)Y(t_2)\} \tag{12.57}$$

The cross-correlation function is simply the joint second moment of the two random variables, obtained by sampling one random process at time $t = t_1$ and the second random process at time $t = t_2$.

If $X(t)$ and $Y(t)$ are WSS, then we say that the two processes are jointly WSS if the cross-correlation function also depends only on the difference of the two time instants. In such a case, we use the following notation for the cross-correlation function:

$$R_{XY}(\tau) = E\{X(t)Y(t + \tau)\} \tag{12.58}$$

If the two processes are uncorrelated, then we have

$$R_{XY}(\tau) = m_X m_Y \tag{12.59}$$

As an example of two such processes, consider the two random processes defined by

$$X(t) = a\cos(\omega_0 t + \Theta)$$
$$Y(t) = a\sin(\omega_0 t + \Theta) \tag{12.60}$$

Here we assume that the phase Θ is uniformly distributed in $(0, 2\pi)$. We can show that the autocorrelation functions of $X(t)$ and $Y(t)$ are the same; they are given together with the derivation of the cross-correlation function of $X(t)$ and $Y(t)$ as follows:

$$R_X(\tau) = R_Y(\tau) = 0.5\,a^2\cos(\omega_0\tau)$$

$$R_{XY}(\tau) = E\{[a\cos(\omega_0 t + \Theta)][a\sin(\omega_0 t + \omega_0\tau + \Theta)]\}$$

$$= 0.5a^2\,E\{\sin(\omega_0\tau) + \sin(2\omega_0 t + \omega_0\tau + 2\Theta)\} = 0.5a^2\sin(\omega_0\tau) \tag{12.61}$$

In deriving the cross-correlation function in equation (12.61), we used the fact that the expectation with respect to the random phase of the second term in the second line yields zero. Another example of interest is the cross-correlation function between a random process and its derivative, assuming that the derivative exists.

Let $X(t)$ be a random process and let $Y(t)$ be defined formally as its derivative:

$$Y(t) = \lim_{\Delta \to 0} \frac{X(t + \Delta) - X(t)}{\Delta} \qquad (12.62)$$

If we assume that we can interchange the limit operation and the expectation, then we can find the properties of the derivative. Let us start with the mean and the cross-correlation function:

$$m_Y(t) = E\{Y(t)\} = \lim_{\Delta \to 0} \frac{E\{X(t + \Delta)\} - E\{X(t)\}}{\Delta} = \frac{d}{dt} m_X(t) \quad (12.63)$$

The preceding expression for the mean implies that if the process $X(t)$ is WSS, then the mean of the derivative is zero. We now consider the cross-correlation function between $X(t)$ and $Y(t)$:

$$R_{XY}(t_1, t_2) = E\{X(t_1)Y(t_2)\} = \lim_{\Delta \to 0} \frac{E\{X(t_2 + \Delta)X(t_1)\} - E\{X(t_2)X(t_1)\}}{\Delta}$$

$$= \lim_{\Delta \to 0} \frac{R_X(t_1, t_2 + \Delta) - R_X(t_1, t_2)\}}{\Delta} = \frac{\partial}{\partial t_2} R_X(t_1, t_2) \qquad (12.64)$$

If the process is WSS, then the autocorrelation function $R_X(t_1, t_2) = R_X(t_2 - t_1)$, which means that if we use equation (12.64) with $t_1 = t$ and $t_2 = t + \tau$, we obtain

$$R_{XY}(\tau) = E\{X(t)Y(t + \tau)\} = \frac{\partial}{\partial t_2} R_X(t_2 - t_1) = \frac{d}{d\tau} R_X(\tau) \qquad (12.65)$$

Since the autocorrelation function of a WSS random process is an even function, it follows from equation (12.65) that the cross-correlation function of a process and its derivative is an odd function. Hence its value at $\tau = 0$ is zero, so that $X(t)$ and its derivative taken at the same instant are not correlated.

Finally, we wish to find the autocorrelation function of the derivative of $X(t)$, which we defined as $Y(t)$. We shall first derive it for the general case and then show what it reduces to for the WSS case.

$$R_Y(t_1, t_2) = E\{Y(t_1)Y(t_2)\} = \lim_{\Delta \to 0} \frac{E\{X(t_1 + \Delta)Y(t_2)\} - E\{X(t_1)Y(t_2)\}}{\Delta}$$

$$= \lim_{\Delta \to 0} \frac{R_{XY}(t_1 + \Delta, t_2) - R_{XY}(t_1, t_2)}{\Delta} = \frac{\partial}{\partial t_1} R_{XY}(t_1, t_2) = \frac{\partial^2}{\partial t_2\, \partial t_1} R_X(t_1, t_2) \quad (12.66)$$

In deriving equation (12.66), we used the result of the cross-correlation obtained in equation (12.64).

Finally, for the WSS case, we can show that since the original autocorrelation function depends only on the difference of the two time instants, the derivative with respect to the second time instant is equal to minus the derivative with respect to the first instant:

$$R_Y(\tau) = E\{Y(t)Y(t + \tau)\} = \frac{\partial^2}{\partial t_2 \, \partial t_1} R_X(t_2 - t_1) = -R_X''(\tau) \qquad (12.67)$$

In particular, the mean-squared value (i.e., the average power) of the derivative is obtained as

$$E\{Y^2(t)\} = -R_X''(0) \qquad (12.68)$$

Let us consider two examples to illustrate the results.

Example 12.4

Consider the linear trajectory example shown in equation (12.35). In this case we can find $Y(t)$ directly as

$$Y(t) = B \qquad (12.69)$$

We can now obtain the cross-correlation of $X(t)$ and $Y(t)$ directly from equation (12.35) and (12.69) and compare it with the result obtained in equation (12.64):

$$R_{XY}(t_1, t_2) = E\{X(t_1)Y(t_2)\} = E\{(A + Bt_1)B\} = m_A m_B + (\sigma_B^2 + m_B^2)t_1 \quad (12.70)$$

It is easy to see that if we differentiate equation (12.37) with respect to t_2, we should obtain the same expression. We shall not bother with the autocorrelation of $Y(t)$, since it is a constant and does not depend on time.

Example 12.5

Consider the sinusoidal example defined in equation (12.39) with the density of the random phase as defined in equation (12.42). For simplicity we shall assume that the amplitude $A = a$ is a constant and not random. Again, we can obtain a direct expression for $Y(t)$ by simply differentiating equation (12.39):

$$Y(t) = -a \, \omega_0 \sin(\omega_0 t + \Theta) \qquad (12.71)$$

We can now use the result of equation (12.60) to yield

$$R_X(\tau) = 0.5 \, a^2 \cos(\omega_0 \tau) \qquad (12.72a)$$

$$R_{XY}(\tau) = -0.5 \, a^2 \, \omega_0 \sin(\omega_0 \tau) = \frac{d}{d\tau} R_X(\tau) \qquad (12.72b)$$

Finally, we can derive the autocorrelation function of $Y(t)$ directly to obtain

$$R_Y(\tau) = 0.5\, a^2\, \omega_0^2 \cos(\omega_0\tau) = -R_X''(\tau) \qquad (12.73)$$

For completeness, we list below the properties of the cross-correlation function of two WSS random processes $X(t)$ and $Y(t)$:

1. $R_{XY}(-\tau) = R_{YX}(\tau)$. This follows directly from the definition. Note that this property relates the two functions $R_{XY}(\tau)$ and $R_{YX}(\tau)$

2. $|R_{XY}(\tau)|^2 \le R_X(0)R_Y(0)$. This property relates the cross-correlation function to the autocorrelation functions of the two processes.

One interesting observation from equation (12.65) is that since the cross-correlation of $X(t)$ and its derivative $Y(t) = X'(t)$ is an odd function, we obtain

$$R_{XY}(0) = 0 \qquad (12.74)$$

This expression implies that $X(t)$ and its derivative taken at the same time instant are not correlated. It may seem strange, but one should recall that for a given value of $X(t)$, the derivative could equally likely be positive (going up) as negative (going down); hence the product with $X(t)$ averages to zero:

$$E\{X(t)X'(t)\} = 0 \qquad (12.75)$$

This is easily seen for the case of the sinusoidal signal in Example 12.5.

An additional observation about the existence of the derivative of a WSS random process is derived from the average power of the derivative, given by equation (12.68):

$$E\{[X'(t)]^2\} = -R_X''(0) \qquad (12.76)$$

The result implies that the derivative exists (has finite power) if and only if the autocorrelation function is differentiable twice at the origin. It should be noted that the binary random signal and the random telegraph signals have no derivative, which is obvious from their structure, as they include sharp switches between two values.

Now that we have considered the basic functions related to random processes and their properties, we are ready to consider how to process these random processes using linear systems in the next chapter.

12.6 GAUSSIAN RANDOM PROCESS

The Gaussian random process $X(t)$ is defined as follows: If we sample the process at n time instants, then the samples $X(t_k)$ for $k = 1, 2, \ldots, n$, have an nth order Gaussian density function. Since the Gaussian distribution and density are completely determined by the means and covariances of the variables, then a Gaussian random process is completely determined if we know its mean and its autocorrelation or autocovariance functions. An example of a Gaussian random process is the random linear trajectories case that was discussed in Section 12.2.4(a). An important property of the Gaussian random process is that if it is wide-sense stationary, then it is also strictly stationary, since all of its statistical properties are derived from its autocorrelation function. We shall refer to some of its other properties in the next two chapters.

12.7 SUMMARY

First- and second-order distribution of a random process:

$$F_{X(t)}(x;t) = P\{X(t) \le x\}$$

$$F_{X(t)}(x_1, x_2; t_1, t_2) = P\{X(t_1) \le x_1 \text{ and } X(t_2) \le x_2\}$$

Mean, autocorrelation, and autocovariance functions:

$$m_X(t) = E\{X(t)\}$$

$$R_X(t_1, t_2) = E\{X(t_1)X(t_2)\}$$

$$C_X(t_1, t_2) = E\{[X(t_1) - m_X(t_1)][X(t_2) - m_X(t_2)]\} = R_X(t_1, t_2)) - m_X(t_1)m_X(t_2)$$

Wide-sense stationary processes:

$$m_X = E\{X(t)\}$$

$$R_X(\tau) = E\{X(t)X(t + \tau)\}$$

$$C_X(\tau) = E\{[X(t) - m_X][X(t + \tau) - m_X]\} = R_X(\tau) - [m_X]^2$$

Cross-correlation function:

$$R_{XY}(t_1, t_2) = E\{X(t_1)Y(t_2)\}, \text{ for the general case}$$

$$R_{XY}(\tau) = E\{X(t)Y(t + \tau)\}, \text{ for jointly WSS processes}$$

12.8 PROBLEMS

MATLAB Problems:

1.   Generate five sample functions of the random telegraph signal. Start at $t = 0$ with a value for $x(0)$ of either $a = 1$ or $a = -1$ with probability 0.5 each. Use a switching rate λ of 2 per minute, which means that the density of the time T between switches is exponential, with average $1/2 = 0.5$: $f_T(t) = 2\exp(-2t), t > 0$. Note that you derived this in Problem 1 of Chapter 4.

   Plot the five sample functions as a function of t in the interval $[0, 12]$.

Here is what you should do to generate each sample function:

a.   Generate about 30 independent random variables T_i for $i = 1, 2, \ldots, 30$ with the exponential distribution as in Problem 1 of Chapter 4.

b.   Define $t_0 = 0$. Then define $t_i = t_{i-1} + T_i$, for $i = 1, 2, 3, \ldots, 30$.

c.   The sample function of the random process is defined as follows:

The value of $x(t)$ for $t_i < t < t_{i+1}$ is equal to $x(t) = -x(0)$ when $i =$ odd and $x(t) = x(0)$ when $i =$ even.

2.   From Problem 1, generate 500 sample functions of the random telegraph signal. Compute and plot the autocorrelation function in two ways:

a.   Pick any value of t, which we shall denote by t_s (say, $t_s = 2$ or $t_s = 3$), and compute the autocorrelation function as follows:

For values of τ between 0 and 0.75 in increments of 0.025, average the product $X(t_s)X(t_s + \tau)$ over all 500 sample functions you generated. (Note: You must multiply the values in the preceding product from the same sample function, namely,

$$\frac{1}{500} \sum_{k=1}^{500} X_k(t_s) X_k(t_s + \tau),$$

where $X_k(t)$ is the kth sample function.) In the preceding sum t_s is fixed, and for each value of τ, it is fixed as well.

Plot the resulting function.

b.   Compute the time average to derive the time-autocorrelation function by averaging the product over 1100 samples of a single time function.

Here is how you do it: Use the time increments of $\Delta = 0.01$ (so that you need 1200 points for the 12-minute interval).

$$\text{Compute} \ \frac{1}{1100} \sum_{k=1}^{1100} X(k\Delta)X(k\Delta + \tau)$$

c.   Compare your results for both types of autocorrelation functions and compare with the analytical expression $\exp(-4\tau)$ for $0.75 > \tau > 0$.

(You do not need to use negative values of τ, since the function is even).

3.   Generate 500 sample functions of the random sinusoidal signal with fixed amplitude $a = 1$, fixed frequency equal to 2 Hz, and random phase uniformly distributed in the interval $(0, 2\pi)$. Each sample function should be 250 seconds long.

a.   Plot several sample functions.

b.   Derive the time average of the autocorrelation function and compare it with the one obtained by averaging over the 500 samples, as you did in Problems 2(b) and 2(c).

Regular Problems:

4. Consider the random process $X(t)$, defined as follows:

$$X(t) = Yu(t) - Zu(t - 2), t > 0$$

Here $u(t)$ is the unit step function. Y and Z are independent random variables, taking the following values with equal probability:

Y takes the values 1, 2, and 3, with probability 1/3 each, and Z takes the values 2 and 4, with probability 0.5 each.

a.   Sketch and assign probabilities to all six sample functions of the process.
b.   Find the mean of the process as a function of t.

5. Consider the random process $Y(t)$ defined by

$$Y(t) = X(t) \cos(\omega_0 t + \Theta)$$

where $X(t)$ is a stationary random process with autocorrelation function $R_X(\tau)$ $= 4\exp(-3|\tau|)$ and Θ is random variable independent of $X(t)$ and uniformly distributed in the interval $(0, 2\pi)$. Find the autocorrelation function of $Y(t)$.

6. Consider the random processes $X(t)$ and $Y(t)$, which are independent and have the following autocorrelation functions:

$$R_X(\tau) = 4\exp(-2|\tau|), \text{ and } R_Y(\tau) = 9\exp(-|\tau|)$$

a.   Find the autocorrelation function of $Z(t) = X(t) + Y(t)$.
b.   Find the autocorrelation function of $W(t) = X(t) - Y(t)$.
c.   Find the cross-correlation function of $Z(t)$ and $W(t)$.

7. Consider the following random processes, $U(t)$ and $V(t)$, defined in terms of two random processes $X(t)$ and $Y(t)$:

$$U(t) = X(t) \cos(\omega_0 t) + Y(t) \sin(\omega_0 t)$$
$$V(t) = -X(t) \sin(\omega_0 t) + Y(t) \cos(\omega_0 t)$$

Assume that $X(t)$ and $Y(t)$ are jointly wide-sense stationary, have zero means, and have the same autocorrelation function $R_X(\tau) = R_Y(\tau) = \alpha(\tau)$, and odd cross-correlation functions $R_{XY}(\tau) = -R_{YX}(\tau) = \beta(\tau)$. Find the autocorrelation and cross-correlation functions of $U(t)$ and $V(t)$.

8. Consider the binary random signal and derive its mean, autocorrelation function, and autocovariance function if the two signals we send do not have the same amplitude. Assume that we send a signal with amplitude $+a$ with probability p, and $+b$ with probability $(1 - p)$.

9. Consider the random telegraph signal when the signal switches between two levels $+a$ and $+b$ rather than between $+a$ and $-a$. Find the mean, autocorrelation function, and autocovariance function in this case.

10. Suppose we reconsider the random telegraph signal in Problem 9, except that now, at every switching time in the process, there is a switch with probability p and there is no switch with probability $(1 - p)$. Find the mean and autocorrelation function of the process.

11. A random process $X(t)$ is defined as follows:

    $$X(t) = A \exp(-Bt), \text{ for } t > 0, \text{ and is zero for } t < 0.$$

    Assume that A and B are independent random variables having uniform probability density functions, with A distributed in the range $(-a, +a)$ and B distributed in the range $(0.5b, 1.5b)$. Draw several sample functions of the process. Find the mean and autocorrelation function of the process $X(t)$. Note that it is not a stationary process.

12. Repeat Problem 5 with an arbitrary density function of the random variable Θ. Find a condition of the density function of Θ for the process to be WSS.

13. A random process $X(t)$ is defined as

    $$X(t) = g(t - T)$$

    where $g(t)$ is a periodic function with period 2 and T is a random variable that is uniformly distributed in the interval $[0, 2]$. Find the mean and autocorrelation function of $X(t)$ for an arbitrary $g(t)$. Then derive them for the case in which the first period of $g(t)$ is as follows:

    $$g(t) = +a, \text{ for } 0 < t < 1, \text{ and } g(t) = -a, \text{ for } 1 < t < 2.$$

13

Processing of Random Signals

13.1 INTRODUCTION TO LINEAR OPERATIONS

In this section we consider the problem of linear processing of random signals for applications such as the recovery of signals from noise or in the prediction or extrapolation of random signals. We first shall address the problem of prediction and extrapolation, since in such a problem only one random process is under consideration. In the recovery of signals from noise, we need to define the relationship between two signals, which we shall do in a later section.

Before we consider the prediction and extrapolation problem, we shall consider what happens when we process a random signal using linear operations. Suppose we have a WSS process $X(t)$ with mean m_X and autocorrelation function $R_X(\tau)$, and we wish to find the properties of a linear operation on the random signal. For simplicity we shall assume that we are using the value of the process at discrete points in time $\{t_k\}$, which we shall assume are equally spaced (i.e., $t_k = kT$). We now perform a linear operation defined in the following equation to yield a random variable $Y(kT)$:

$$Y(kT) = b + \sum_{i=0}^{N} a_i X(kT - iT) \qquad (13.1)$$

We call such an operation the processing of the random signal with a **digital filter**. We see that the "filter" uses only past values of the signal, assuming that we are at present

354

observing the kth sample. Since the signal is a sample function of a random process, the value of Y is a random variable; hence we can find its mean and variance.

The mean and variance of Y are easily obtained if we recall the basic properties of expectations. We note that the expectation of a sum is the sum of the expectations and that the autocorrelation function of the random process allows us to obtain the following identity:

$$E\{X(\alpha T)X(\beta T)\} = R_X[(\alpha - \beta)T] \qquad (13.2)$$

The mean and variance of Y are obtained directly by using the properties we mentioned. The expression for the mean becomes

$$E\{Y(kT)\} = E\left\{b + \sum_{i=0}^{N}a_iX(kT - iT)\right\} = b + m_X\sum_{i=0}^{N}a_i \qquad (13.3)$$

We can now find the variance by first finding the second moment of Y:

$$E\{[Y(kT)]^2\} = E\left\{\left[b + \sum_{i=0}^{N}a_iX(kT - iT)\right]^2\right\}$$

$$= E\left\{b^2 + 2b\sum_{i=0}^{N}a_iX(kT - iT) + \sum_{j=0}^{N}\sum_{i=0}^{N}a_ia_jX(kT - iT)X(kT - jT)\right\}$$

$$= b^2 + 2bm_X\sum_{i=0}^{N}a_i + \sum_{j=0}^{N}\sum_{i=0}^{N}a_ia_jR_X(jT - iT) \qquad (13.4)$$

We can find the variance by subtracting the square value of the mean, or finding it directly. The expression becomes simpler if we use the covariance function of $X(t)$ instead of the autocorrelation function $R_X(\tau)$:

$$C_X(\tau) = R_X(\tau) - [m_X]^2$$

After some tedious algebra, the result becomes

$$\sigma_Y^2 = \sum_{j=0}^{N}\sum_{i=0}^{N}a_ja_iC_X(jT - iT) \qquad (13.5)$$

Let us consider a simple application in which we are interested in estimating the value of a constant m that is observed with an additive noise $X(t)$, so that we are observing the following N samples of the measurements:

$$Y(kT) = X(kT) + m, \quad k = 1, 2, \ldots, N \qquad (13.6)$$

We assume that the process $X(t)$ is WSS with mean zero and correlation function $R_X(\tau)$. Suppose that we decide to estimate the value of m by adding the N measurements and dividing by N:

$$\hat{m} = \frac{1}{N}\sum_{k=1}^{N}Y(kT) \qquad (13.7)$$

If we just take the expectation of the estimate in equation (13.7), we obtain the value m, since the process $X(t)$ has zero mean. We now need to find the variance of the error of such an estimate, since its mean is indeed equal to m. The mean-squared error (MSE) of the estimate would indeed provide us with the error variance and is obtained as follows:

$$\text{MSE} = E\{(\hat{m} - m)^2\} = E\left\{\left[\frac{1}{N}\sum_{k=1}^{N}X(kT)\right]^2\right\} = \frac{1}{N^2}\sum_{\ell=1}^{N}\sum_{k=1}^{N}R(kT - \ell T) \quad (13.8)$$

In arriving at equation (13.8), we used the same approach as we did in equation (13.4). In order to observe the value of the resulting MSE, we may consider a special case in which the autocorrelation function has the form (as for the binary random signal)

$$R_X(\tau) = \sigma^2\left(1 - \frac{|\tau|}{2T}\right), \text{ for } |\tau| < 2T, \text{ and is zero elsewhere.} \quad (13.9)$$

In this case, in the double sum of equation (13.8) only the values of $k = \ell$ and $k = \ell \pm 1$ will be nonzero, so that the result becomes

$$\text{MSE} = \frac{1}{N^2}\left\{\sum_{k=1}^{N}\sigma^2 + \sum_{k=2}^{N}0.5\sigma^2 + \sum_{k=1}^{N-1}0.5\sigma^2\right\}$$

$$= \frac{N + 0.5(N - 1) + 0.5(N - 1)}{N^2}\sigma^2$$

$$= \frac{2 - \dfrac{1}{N}}{N}\sigma^2 \quad (13.10)$$

If the samples were uncorrelated, then the sample average given in equation (13.7) yields a variance of σ^2/N; and hence it tends to zero as N becomes large. Note that for the correlated samples case the variance of the difference between m and its estimate also approaches zero as N approaches infinity. However, it tends to zero slower by a factor of 2 than it would if the samples were uncorrelated. We would have the same behavior as for a sum of N independent samples if we selected a sampling period of $2T$ or larger.

In the next section we shall apply this type of result to the problem of extrapolation and prediction of random signals.

13.2 EXTRAPOLATION AND PREDICTION OF RANDOM SIGNALS

Suppose we observe a sample function of a WSS random process $X(t)$ at discrete points in time $t_k = kT$. We wish to extrapolate the value of the signals at time $kT < t < (k + 1)T$ from a few neighboring sample values, for example $N + 1$ past samples and M future samples. We shall assume that the process has autocorrelation function $R_X(\tau)$. We shall use linear extrapolation so that the extrapolated value of $X(t)$ will be denoted by $\hat{X}(t)$ and is expressed as

$$\hat{X}(t) = \sum_{i=-M}^{N} a_i X(kT - iT) + b, \quad \text{for } kT < t < (k + 1)T \qquad (13.11)$$

We would like to minimize the expected value of the square of the extrapolation error, which we call the mean-squared error (MSE):

$$\text{MSE} = E\{[\hat{X}(t) - X(t)]^2\} \qquad (13.12)$$

After we find the expression for the expectation, equation (13.12), we minimize it with respect to the parameters b and $\{a_i\}$. We can simplify the expression if we denote the difference between t and kT with αT, where $0 < \alpha < 1$, so that when $\alpha = 0.5$, we wish to extrapolate at a point in the middle of the sampling interval:

$$t = kT + \alpha T \qquad (13.13)$$

The expression for the extrapolated value and the MSE become

$$\hat{X}(\alpha T + kT) = \sum_{i=-M}^{N} a_i X(kT - iT) + b \qquad (13.14)$$

$$\text{MSE} = E\left\{\left[b + \sum_{i=-M}^{N} a_i X(kT - iT) - X(\alpha T + kT)\right]^2\right\} \qquad (13.15)$$

All we have to do now is simply evaluate the expectation using the linearity property and using the fact that equation (13.2) holds, which simply follows from the basic definition of the autocorrelation function of WSS processes. If we now open the squares in equation (13.15) and use the definition of the autocorrelation function, we obtain

$$\begin{aligned}
\text{MSE} = E\Bigg\{ &b^2 + 2b \sum_{i=-M}^{N} [a_i X(kT - iT)] - 2bX(\alpha T + kT) + [X(\alpha T + kT)]^2 \\
&+ \sum_{j=-M}^{N}\sum_{i=-M}^{N} [a_i X(kT - iT)a_j X(kT - jT)] \\
&- 2\sum_{i=-M}^{N} a_i X(kT - iT)X(\alpha T + kT)] \Bigg\} \\
= &\,b^2 + 2bm_X \sum_{i=-M}^{N} a_i - 2bm_X + R_X(0) - 2\sum_{i=-M}^{N} a_i R_X(\alpha T + iT) \\
&+ \sum_{i=-M}^{N}\sum_{j=-M}^{N} a_i a_j R_X(jT - iT) \qquad (13.16)
\end{aligned}$$

All we have to do now is take the derivatives with respect to the constants b and $\{a_i\}$ and set them equal to zero; thus we obtain $M + N + 2$ equations for the same number of unknowns. The equation for b is very simple and results in

$$2b + 2m_X \sum_{i=-M}^{N} a_i - 2m_X = 0 \tag{13.17}$$

The solution for b is therefore

$$b = m_X - m_X \sum_{i=-M}^{N} a_i \tag{13.18}$$

The substitution of equation (13.18) into the original equation for the MSE results in

$$\text{MSE} = C_X(0) - 2 \sum_{i=-M}^{N} a_i C_X(\alpha T + iT) + \sum_{i=-M}^{N} \sum_{j=-M}^{N} a_i a_j C_X(jT - iT) \tag{13.19}$$

The differentiation with respect to the coefficients $\{a_i\}$ of the filter results in the following linear equations for the unknown $(N + M + 1)$ coefficients:

$$-2C_X(\alpha T + iT) + 2 \sum_{j=-M}^{N} a_j C_X(jT - iT) = 0, \qquad \text{for } i = -M, \ldots N \tag{13.20}$$

After we solve these equations, we obtain the optimal extrapolating "filter" and the resulting MSE is

$$\text{MSE} = C_X(0) - \sum_{i=-M}^{N} a_i C_X(\alpha T + iT) \tag{13.21}$$

The expression for second term in equation (13.20) is used in equation (13.19) to obtain the final result.

Consider as an example the special case of using just one past and one future sample for the extrapolation (i.e., $N = 0$ (using the sample immediately past) and $M = 1$). In this case the two equations for a_0 and a_{-1} are

$$a_{-1}C_X(0) + a_0 C_X(-T) = C_X(\alpha T - T)$$
$$a_{-1}C_X(-T) + a_0 C_X(0) = C_X(\alpha T) \tag{13.22}$$

The solution becomes

$$a_{-1} = \frac{C_X(0)C_X(T - \alpha T) - C_X(T)C_X(\alpha T)}{C_X^2(0) - C_X^2(T)}$$

$$a_0 = \frac{C_X(0)C_X(\alpha T) - C_X(T)C_X(T - \alpha T)}{C_X^2(0) - C_X^2(T)} \tag{13.23}$$

We used the fact that the covariance function is even in simplifying the solution, so instead of $C_X(-T)$, we used $C_X(T)$. Suppose we have the same covariance function as that described in equation (13.9), and assume that we use $\alpha = 0.5$, which means we are extrapolating at the mid-point of the sampling interval. The values in this case are

$$a_{-1} = \frac{0.75 - 0.5(0.75)}{1 - 0.25} = 0.5$$

$$a_0 = \frac{0.75 - 0.5(0.75)}{1 - 0.25} = 0.5$$

This means that if the mean of $X(t)$ is zero, then the extrapolation involves just averaging the two neighboring values of the samples. The values will be different if $\alpha = 0.25$ or $\alpha = 0.75$. For these two cases, the roles of the two coefficients are reversed. What is the value of the MSE for $\alpha = 0.5$? We can use equation (13.20) to evaluate the answer:

$$\text{MSE} = C_X(0) - a_{-1}C_X(T - 0.5T) - a_0C_X(0.5T) = \sigma^2(1 - 0.75) = 0.25\sigma^2$$

$$(13.24)$$

Obviously, as we get closer to one of the sample values, the MSE should be smaller. The expression for the coefficients and the MSE as a function of α is given by the following equations:

$$a_{-1} = \frac{[1 - 0.5(1 - \alpha)] - 0.5(1 - 0.5\alpha)}{1 - 0.25} = \alpha$$

$$a_0 = \frac{(1 - 0.5\alpha) - 0.5[1 - 0.5(1 - \alpha)]}{1 - 0.25} = 1 - \alpha$$

$$\text{MSE} = \sigma^2\{1 - \alpha[1 - 0.5(1 - \alpha)] - (1 - \alpha)(1 - 0.5\alpha)\} = \sigma^2\alpha(1 - \alpha)$$

As expected, the error is the smallest (equal to zero) at the ends of the extrapolation interval and largest at the middle. It should be noted that the simple result for the coefficients is due to the specific form of the autocorrelation function we selected for the example. If we had selected the autocorrelation of the random telegraph signal, the results would have been totally different.

The results obtained so far are also applicable to prediction if we use only past samples to predict the value of $X(kT + \alpha T)$, where $\alpha > 0$, and where in the estimator form we use only past samples, which means that $M = 0$. The equations become exactly the same as the one we derived earlier. The difference is in the range of values and the number of equations. Suppose we use two samples to predict a future value of $X(t)$ and we have the same autocorrelation function we considered in the previous example. For simplicity we shall assume zero mean, so we do not have to be concerned with the value of b. Equations (13.20) for $N = 1$ and $M = 0$ become, in general,

$$a_1C_X(0) + a_0C_X(T) = C_X(\alpha T + T)$$

$$a_1C_X(T) + a_0C_X(0) = C_X(\alpha T)$$

$$(13.25)$$

The solution for this general case is

$$a_1 = \frac{C_X(0)C_X(T + \alpha T) - C_X(T)C_X(\alpha T)}{C_X^2(0) - C_X^2(T)}$$

$$a_0 = \frac{C_X(0)C_X(\alpha T) - C_X(T)C_X(T + \alpha T)}{C_X^2(0) - C_X^2(T)} \tag{13.26}$$

The MSE of the prediction is

$$\text{MSE} = C_X(0) - \sum_{i=0}^{1} a_i C_X(\alpha T + iT) \tag{13.27}$$

For the special case of the autocorrelation having the same form as for the random binary signal, we obtain (provided that $\alpha < 1$)

$$a_1 = \frac{[1 - 0.5(1 + \alpha)] - 0.5(1 - 0.5\alpha)}{1 - 0.25} = -\frac{1}{3}\alpha$$

$$a_0 = \frac{(1 - 0.5\alpha) - 0.5[1 - 0.5(1 + \alpha)]}{1 - 0.25} = 1 - \frac{1}{3}\alpha$$

$$\text{MSE} = \sigma^2\left\{1 + \frac{1}{3}\alpha[1 - 0.5(1 + \alpha)] - \left(1 - \frac{1}{3}\alpha\right)(1 - 0.5\alpha)\right\} = \sigma^2\alpha\left(1 - \frac{1}{3}\alpha\right)$$

If we compare this result with the case $N = 0$, meaning that we use only the immediate past sample for prediction, we obtain

$$a_0 = (1 - 0.5\alpha)$$

The MSE in the single sample prediction is

$$\text{MSE} = \sigma^2\alpha\left(1 - \frac{1}{4}\alpha\right)$$

We see that the prediction using two samples is a little bit better than using just a single sample.

If we were to use the random telegraph signal to solve the prediction problem for two or more samples, we would find that there is no difference, since the coefficients are all zero except for a_0. It is left as an exercise to verify that the result for the random telegraph signal is indeed true.

Example 13.1

Numerical Results for Extrapolation and Prediction
The general examples of prediction and extrapolation just discussed were computed for various values of α between 0 and 1. Two cases are considered:

Case a: In this case the autocorrelation of the random binary signal used for the extrapolation and prediction is the same as in equation (13.9). Three curves are

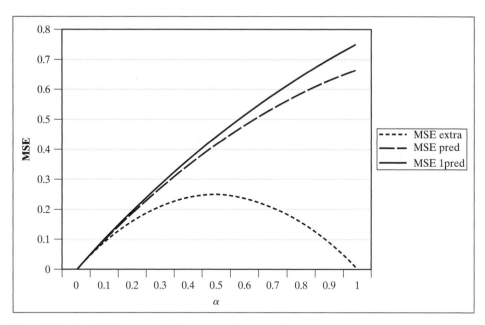

Figure 13.1   The MSE for extrapolation and prediction of the random binary signal

shown in Figure 13.1, displaying the relative MSE (divided by σ^2) as a function of the parameter α. The first curve shows the result for extrapolation and obviously has the smallest MSE. The next curve shows the result for prediction by using two past samples. Finally, the last curve shows the result for prediction using a single past sample, and it has the largest MSE. Since the samples were relatively too far apart (their correlation is about 0.5) the use of an additional sample does not reduce the MSE by very much.

Case b: In order to see how correlation between the samples affects the results, we consider the case of strongly correlated samples to see if the results improve. We considered the case for which the autocorrelation function of $X(t)$ has the following form:

$$R_X(\tau) = \left(1 - \frac{|\tau|}{4T}\right)$$

We have assumed a variance of 1 for simplicity. In this case the correlation between the samples we are using for the extrapolation and prediction is 0.75 (while it was 0.5 in the first case).

In this case, for the extrapolation estimate, we obtain the same value for the coefficients a_{-1} and a_0. The expression for the MSE is exactly 50% of the MSE for the previous case. For the single sample prediction, when we assume $N = 0$, the MSE is

$$\text{MSE} = \frac{\alpha}{2}\left(1 - \frac{\alpha}{8}\right)$$

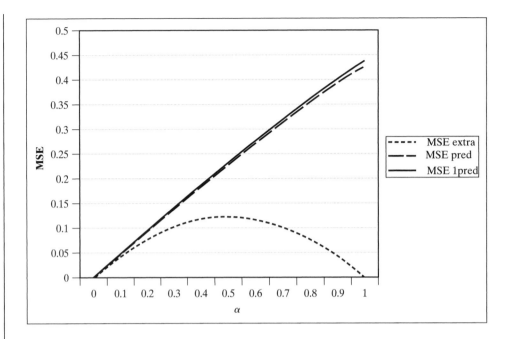

Figure 13.2 The MSE for extrapolation and prediction for the case of a higher correlation between samples

Finally, the prediction using two samples results in

$$a_1 = -\frac{1}{7}\alpha$$

$$a_0 = 1 - \frac{1}{7}\alpha$$

$$\text{MSE} = \frac{\alpha}{2}\left(1 - \frac{\alpha}{7}\right)$$

The results are displayed in Figure 13.2. The results are similar to those we obtained before except that the MSE is smaller by a factor of close to 2 in all three cases.

13.3 CONTINUOUS-TIME PROCESSING

So far we have used just sample values at discrete time points to process the random signal. What happens when we do linear operation as a continuous-time operation? In this case we can weigh the signal with some time-dependent function and integrate the result. In general, we can have an expression such as the following one, which represents a linear time-invariant system:

$$Y(t) = \int_{-\infty}^{\infty} h(\alpha)X(t - \alpha)\, d\alpha \qquad (13.28)$$

We use here the limits from minus infinity to infinity (meaning that we process the data for both past and future values) to allow for as general a case as possible. The function $h(t)$ can take care of processing past-only cases, future-only cases, or finite time interval cases by making the function zero at the appropriate time intervals. Since we allow our result of the processing to depend on time t, $Y(t)$ is also a random process. We see that we have to deal with two random processes $X(t)$ and $Y(t)$; therefore we have to use the cross-correlation function that was defined in Section 12.5.

What we are doing here is passing the random signal through a linear and time-invariant system. In such a case, in equation (13.28) $X(t)$ is the input to the system, the function $h(t)$ is called the impulse response of the system, and the expression for the output, $Y(t)$, is just the convolution of the input with the impulse response.

Input–Output Cross-Correlation Function

Since $Y(t)$ is obtained by processing the random signal $X(t)$, we expect that the two are correlated. Hence, before we find the properties of the output, we first find the cross-correlation function between $X(t)$ and $Y(t)$:

$$R_{XY}(\tau) = E\{X(t)Y(t+\tau)\} = E\left\{X(t)\int_{-\infty}^{\infty}h(\alpha)X(t+\tau-\alpha)\,d\alpha\right\}$$

$$= \int_{-\infty}^{\infty}h(\alpha)E\{X(t+\tau-\alpha)X(t)\}\,d\alpha = \int_{-\infty}^{\infty}h(\alpha)R_X(\tau-\alpha)\,d\alpha \tag{13.29}$$

In deriving equation (13.29), we interchanged the integration with the expectation, since the expectation deals only with the randomness and it is a linear operation, so we can take the expectation inside the integral. We also used equation (13.2) to relate the expectation inside the integral to the autocorrelation function of $X(t)$.

Output Autocorrelation Function

We now find the autocorrelation of the output process $Y(t)$:

$$R_Y(\tau) = E\{Y(t)Y(t+\tau)\} = E\left\{\int_{-\infty}^{\infty}h(\alpha)X(t+\tau-\alpha)\,d\alpha Y(t)\right\}$$

$$= \int_{-\infty}^{\infty}h(\alpha)E\{X(t+\tau-\alpha)Y(t)\}\,d\alpha = \int_{-\infty}^{\infty}h(\alpha)R_{YX}(\tau-\alpha)\,d\alpha \tag{13.30}$$

Again we used the expectation inside the integral and the definition of the cross-correlation function. Finally, we can simplify the resulting expression when we substitute equation (13.29) into equation (13.30) to obtain

$$R_Y(\tau) = \int_{-\infty}^{\infty}\int_{-\infty}^{\infty}h(\alpha)h(\beta)R_X(\tau+\alpha-\beta)\,d\alpha\,d\beta \tag{13.31}$$

We cannot simplify the resulting expression further unless we resort to the frequency domain, which is beyond the scope of this chapter, and will be considered in the next Chapter.

As an example, if we wish to find the second moment of Y, we obtain

$$E\{[Y(t)]^2\} = R_Y(0) = \int_{-\infty}^{\infty} \int_{-\infty}^{\infty} h(\alpha)h(\beta)R_X(\alpha - \beta)\, d\alpha\, d\beta \quad (13.32)$$

Finally we may also wish to derive an expression for the mean of the output $Y(t)$, which can be obtained using the same methods:

$$m_Y = E\{Y(t)\} = E\left\{ \int_{-\infty}^{\infty} h(\alpha)X(t - \alpha)\, d\alpha \right\} = \int_{-\infty}^{\infty} h(\alpha)E\{X(t - \alpha)\}\, d\alpha$$

$$= m_X \int_{-\infty}^{\infty} h(\alpha)\, d\alpha \qquad\qquad (13.33)$$

The expressions provided in equations (13.31) and (13.32) cannot be simplified for the general case of an arbitrary random process $X(t)$. However, the calculation may be simplified if we assume that the random process has an autocorrelation function that is narrow relative to the impulse response function $h(\tau)$ of the system. In this case we can approximate such a narrow autocorrelation function by an impulse function, and we call this approximating process "white noise."

Gaussian Random Process

Since all distribution functions of a Gaussian random process are Gaussian and remain Gaussian after linear operations, if we pass a Gaussian random process through a linear system, then the output process will also be a Gaussian random process. Therefore once we obtain the mean and autocorrelation function of the output process, we know all its density functions, as they are completely determined by these functions. An important model of a Gaussian noise process is the white noise, which we shall define next.

White Noise

A special case of a noise random process is called white noise (we shall see why it is called that in the next chapter), and it is obtained as an approximation in the limit of a random process with very narrow autocorrelation function. In such a case, when we go to the limit as the width of the autocorrelation function approaches zero, we have to assume that the area under the autocorrelation function remains finite, so that the result is an impulse function. Consider for example the case of the random telegraph signal when the switching rate λ is very high but the amplitude of the signal is also high. The autocorrelation of the random telegraph signal has been derived in equation (12.47) to be given by

$$R_X(\tau) = a^2 \exp(-2\lambda|\tau|) \qquad\qquad (13.34)$$

We now let the rate λ tend to infinity while the square of amplitude tends also to infinity at the same rate as λ, so that the area remains finite; that is,

$$a^2 = A\lambda \tag{13.35}$$

This means that the autocorrelation of the process as λ tends to infinity becomes an impulse of magnitude A. In this case, while the magnitude of the autocorrelation at $\tau = 0$ (the average power of the process) is infinite, its integral will still be finite and equal to A. In the limit, we can express the autocorrelation function of the process as

$$R_X(\tau) = A\delta(\tau) \tag{13.36}$$

A detailed but brief introduction of the impulse function and its uses in linear systems is provided in Appendix D.

Another such example is the binary random signal whose autocorrelation function was given by equation (12.51). In this case its autocorrelation function becomes an impulse function if its width T tends to zero and it amplitude a tends to infinity as $a^2 = A/T$. You may wish to verify that the resulting function approaches an impulse function with magnitude A as T tends to zero.

We call such a process **white noise**. The reason for this name will be clarified in the next chapter. Additional examples of white noise processes will then be considered as well. What is important to note at this time is the value of the average power of the output when such a process is used as an input to a linear system with impulse response $h(\tau)$ as expressed by equation (13.32). In this case the average power of the output becomes

$$E\{[Y(t)]^2\} = R_Y(0) = \int_{-\infty}^{\infty} \int_{-\infty}^{\infty} h(\alpha)h(\beta)A\delta(\alpha - \beta)\, d\alpha\, d\beta$$

$$= \int_{-\infty}^{\infty} h(\alpha)h(\alpha)A\, d\alpha = A \int_{-\infty}^{\infty} [h(\alpha)]^2\, d\alpha \tag{13.37}$$

To arrive at the simplified expression of equation (13.37), we used the basic property of the impulse function:

$$\int_{-\infty}^{\infty} h(\alpha)\delta(\alpha - \beta)\, d\alpha = h(\beta)$$

More details are provided in Appendix D.

If we are dealing with white Gaussian noise as the input $X(t)$ to a linear system, then we can write the probability density function of the output $Y(t)$ in this case, since it will be Gaussian with mean m_Y and variance given by equation (13.37). In Section 14.7 we shall discuss an example of such a white Gaussian noise process.

13.4 APPLICATION TO ESTIMATION

We wish to estimate a constant m that is measured in additive noise $X(t)$, which is assumed to be a zero-mean process with autocorrelation function $R_X(\tau)$. We obtain the estimate of m by integrating the observations $Z(t)$ over an interval of time and dividing by its length:

$$Z(t) = m + X(t) \tag{13.38}$$

The estimate is defined as

$$\hat{m} = \frac{1}{2T} \int_{-T}^{T} Z(t)\, dt \tag{13.39}$$

We now find the MSE between m and its estimate:

$$\text{MSE} = E\{(\hat{m} - m)^2\} = E\left\{ \left[\frac{1}{2T} \int_{-T}^{T} Z(t)\, dt - m \right]^2 \right\}$$

$$= E\left\{ \left[\frac{1}{2T} \int_{-T}^{T} X(t)\, dt \right]^2 \right\} \tag{13.40}$$

We have the same expression we obtained before for $Y(t)$ with $h(t) = 0$ outside $|t| > T$ and equal to $(1/2T)$ for $|t| < T$. Hence we can use equation (13.32) to obtain the value of the MSE:

$$\text{MSE} = \frac{1}{4T^2} \int_{-T}^{T} \int_{-T}^{T} R_X(\alpha - \beta)\, d\alpha\, d\beta = \frac{1}{2T} \int_{-2T}^{2T} R_X(\tau)\left(1 - \frac{|\tau|}{2T}\right) d\tau \tag{13.41}$$

We skipped several steps in the simplification of the result in equation (13.41), and the complete derivation is shown in Appendix E. Note that the result of equation (13.41) is true for a general autocorrelation function.

We now consider the special case for which the autocorrelation function of $X(t)$ is very narrow but has a very large value at zero (as we have done previously when discussing white noise). Consider, for example, a random binary signal with a small pulsewidth B, while its area is finite and is equal to A, as in equation (12.51) with B replacing T and $a^2 = A/B$:

$$R_X(\tau) = \frac{A}{B}\left(1 - \frac{|\tau|}{B}\right),\ \text{for } |\tau| < B, \text{ and is zero elsewhere} \tag{13.42}$$

Note that in this special case we can evaluate the integral in equation (13.41) explicitly as a function of A, B, and T. The resulting expression is quite complicated. However, for B very small, we may approximate $R_X(\tau)$ by an impulse function $A\delta(\tau)$, since $X(t)$ then becomes a white noise process. As B tends to zero, the expression for the MSE becomes in this case.

$$\text{MSE} = \frac{A}{2T} \tag{13.43}$$

It is left as an exercise to verify that the exact expression obtained by using equation (13.41) and (13.42) reduces to equation (13.43) when B tends to zero.

We see that even though the variance of the "noise" $X(t)$ is large (it is equal to A/B with B very small), the MSE tends to zero as T tends to infinity. The reason for this result is that the noise exhibits very small correlation from one instant to the next, which, when integrated, results in reduced variance. This is the same type of behavior exhibited when finding sample averages of independent or uncorrelated samples.

The preceding is just a simple example to illustrate the way we use the properties of the noise and the signal to recover useful data from noisy measurements by using linear operations on the observations. The example also illustrates how the result becomes simplified when we assume that the noise is white.

Example 13.2

Consider the linear system with impulse response

$$h(t) = \exp(-\lambda t), \text{ for } t > 0 \tag{13.44}$$

Let us suppose that the input to the system contains a useful signal $X(t)$, which may be a random process or a nonrandom signal. We also shall assume that the signal is corrupted by an additive noise signal, which we shall denote as $N(t)$. Our objective is to determine the signal-to-noise ratio (SNR) at the output of the system. The output of the system also contains a sum of two signals (since the system is linear), and we shall denote them by $X_0(t)$ and $N_0(t)$ to represent the output due to the signal and noise, respectively, as illustrated in Figure 13.3.

We shall consider two cases for the signal $X(t)$, but we shall assume that the noise $N(t)$ is white with parameter A, as in equation (13.36).

Case a: Let $X(t)$ be the sinusoidal signal defined in equation (12.39) with constant nonrandom amplitude a and random phase that is uniformly distributed, as in equation (12.42):

$$X(t) = a \cos(\omega_0 t + \Theta) \tag{13.45}$$

In this case we can find that the output signal $X_0(t)$ is also sinusoidal with the same frequency but with different amplitude and phase. However, since we wish to find only the average signal power at the output, all we need to do is to use the equation (13.32) with

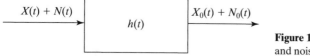

Figure 13.3   A linear system with signal and noise input

the appropriate autocorrelation of $X(t)$ and the system response $h(t)$. The autocorrelation of the signal $X(t)$ is given by equation (12.46):

$$R_X(\tau) = 0.5a^2 \cos(\omega_0\tau)$$

If we substitute the expression for $h(t)$ and the autocorrelation into equation (13.32), the result can be shown to yield

$$E\{[X_0(t)]^2\} = \int_0^\infty \int_0^\infty \exp(-\lambda\alpha)\exp(-\lambda\beta)0.5a^2\cos[\omega_0(\alpha - \beta)]\, d\alpha\, d\beta$$

$$= \frac{0.5a^2}{(\omega_0^2 + \lambda^2)} \tag{13.46}$$

Now we can find the average output noise power using the same equation, but with the autocorrelation given by equation (13.36). Since $N(t)$ is a white noise process, we can use the result given by equation (13.37):

$$E\{[N_0(t)]^2\} = \int_0^\infty \int_0^\infty \exp(-\lambda\alpha)\exp(-\lambda\beta)A\delta(\alpha - \beta)\, d\alpha\, d\beta$$

$$= A\int_0^\infty [\exp(-\lambda\alpha)]^2\, d\alpha = A/(2\lambda) \tag{13.47}$$

The output SNR can be evaluated by taking the ratio of the two average powers to yield

$$\text{SNR} = \frac{0.5a^2}{(\omega_0^2 + \lambda^2)}/[A/(2\lambda)] = \frac{a^2\lambda}{A(\omega_0^2 + \lambda^2)} \tag{13.48}$$

We can now try to optimize the system response by selecting the value of λ that maximizes the SNR. By taking the derivative with respect to λ and setting it equal to zero, we find that the optimal value of λ is:

$$\lambda_{\text{optimal}} = \omega_0 \tag{13.49}$$

The resulting maximum SNR is then given by

$$\text{SNR}_{\text{max}} = \frac{a^2}{A2\omega_0} \tag{13.50}$$

Case b: In this case we assume that the signal $X(t)$ is just a deterministic signal, given as a square pulse of amplitude a and width T as shown in Figure 13.4:

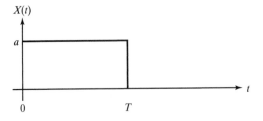

Figure 13.4   The input signal for Example 13.2

The output signal, which in this case is not random, will be given by the expression

$$X_0(t) = \begin{cases} (a/\lambda)[1 - \exp(-\lambda t)], & \text{for } 0 < t < T \\ (a/\lambda)[1 - \exp(-\lambda T)] \exp[-\lambda(t - T)], & \text{for } T < t \end{cases} \quad (13.51)$$

Equation (13.51) was obtained by using the convolution integral with $X(t)$ as the input and $h(t)$ as the impulse response. The noise power remains as in Case a, and is given by equation (13.47). The output signal amplitude is the largest at the time instant $t = T$, so we shall use that value to determine the signal power:

$$\text{Signal Power} = [X_0(T)]^2 = \{(a/\lambda)[1 - \exp(-\lambda T)]\}^2 \quad (13.52)$$

Therefore, for this case the SNR becomes

$$\text{SNR} = \{(a/\lambda)[1 - \exp(-\lambda T)]\}^2/[A/(2\lambda)] = \frac{2a^2[1 - \exp(-\lambda T)]^2}{A\lambda} \quad (13.53)$$

We see that as λ tends either to zero or to infinity the SNR tends to zero. Hence, there should be a value of the parameter λ that maximizes the SNR. We can obtain that value by taking the derivative and equating it to zero to obtain an equation to be solved for λ (the algebraic details have been skipped):

$$2(\lambda T) \exp(-\lambda T) - [1 - \exp(-\lambda T)] = 0 \quad (13.55)$$

The solution for the optimal value of λ can be obtained only numerically and is shown to be

$$\lambda_{\text{optimal}} = 1.26/T \quad (13.56)$$

In this case the resulting maximum value of the SNR becomes

$$\text{SNR}_{\text{max}} = 0.8145(a^2T/A) \quad (13.57)$$

The example illustrates the use of linear systems and other linear operation as a means of extracting useful information from noisy communication channels. A more systematic approach to such problems uses frequency domain methods that are considered in the next chapter.

Example 13.3

Consider the case of a linear system, having the impulse response shown in Figure 13.5 with white noise input $X(t)$ whose autocorrelation function is given by equation (13.36).

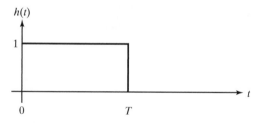

Figure 13.5 Impulse response for Example 13.3

With $u(t)$ used to denote the unit step function, the impulse response has the expression

$$h(t) = u(t) - u(t - T) \tag{13.58}$$

If we wish to find the autocorrelation of the output, $Y(t)$, we have to use equation (13.31) and utilize the property of the impulse function to obtain

$$\begin{aligned}
R_Y(\tau) &= \int_{-\infty}^{\infty} \int_{-\infty}^{\infty} h(\alpha)h(\beta)R_X(\tau + \alpha - \beta)\, d\alpha\, d\beta \\
&= \int_{-\infty}^{\infty} \int_{-\infty}^{\infty} h(\alpha)h(\beta)\delta(\tau + \alpha - \beta)\, d\alpha\, d\beta \\
&= \int_{-\infty}^{\infty} h(\alpha)h(\tau + \alpha)\, d\alpha \tag{13.59}
\end{aligned}$$

If we now use the expression for $h(t)$ in equation (13.59) and consider various ranges of the variable τ, we obtain the following result for the output autocorrelation function:

$$\begin{aligned}
R_Y(\tau) &= \int_{\tau}^{T} 1 \times 1\, d\alpha = (T - \tau), \qquad \text{for } 0 < \tau < T \\
R_Y(\tau) &= 0, \qquad \text{for } T < \tau
\end{aligned}$$

Since the autocorrelation function is symmetric (an even function), we find that we can express the autocorrelation function as

$$R_Y(\tau) = (T - |\tau|), \qquad \text{for } 0 < |\tau| < T \text{ and is zero elsewhere.} \tag{13.60}$$

What is interesting is that we obtained the same autocorrelation function as the one we obtained for the random binary signal. It should be clear from this example that the autocorrelation alone does not uniquely describe a random signal.

Example 13.4

We consider another example of the same white noise as in Example 13.3 through a linear system with impulse response $h(t)$ as follows:

$$h(t) = \exp(-\lambda t), \qquad \text{for } 0 < t, \text{ and is zero for } t < 0. \tag{13.61}$$

We again use equation (13.59) to find the expression for the output autocorrelation function for positive values of τ:

$$R_Y(\tau) = \int_{-\infty}^{\infty} h(\alpha)h(\tau + \alpha)\, d\alpha = \int_{0}^{\infty} \exp(-\lambda\alpha) \exp[-\lambda(\tau + \alpha)]\, d\alpha$$

$$= \frac{1}{2\lambda} \exp(-\lambda\tau), \text{ for } \tau > 0$$

Since the autocorrelation function is even, we can write the final expression for all values of τ as follows:

$$R_Y(\tau) = \frac{1}{2\lambda}\exp(-\lambda|\tau|) \tag{13.62}$$

We again see that the autocorrelation we obtained is the same as the one obtained for the random telegraph signal, except with different parameters.

13.5 SUMMARY

Mean and variance for linear discrete-time processing:

$$Y = b + \sum_{i=0}^{N} a_i X(kT - iT)$$

$$m_Y = b + m_X \sum_{i=0}^{N} a_i$$

$$\sigma_Y^2 = \sum_{j=0}^{N}\sum_{i=0}^{N} a_j a_i C_X(jT - iT)$$

Mean and autocorrelation function for continuous-time processing:

$$Y(t) = \int_{-\infty}^{\infty} h(\alpha)X(t - \alpha)\, d\alpha$$

$$m_Y = E\{Y(t)\} = m_X \int_{-\infty}^{\infty} h(\alpha)\, d\alpha$$

$$R_{XY}(\tau) = E\{X(t)Y(t + \tau)\} = \int_{-\infty}^{\infty} h(\alpha)R_X(\tau - \alpha)\, d\alpha$$

$$R_Y(\tau) = \int_{-\infty}^{\infty}\int_{-\infty}^{\infty} h(\alpha)h(\beta)R_X(\tau + \alpha - \beta)\, d\alpha\, d\beta$$

13.6 PROBLEMS

MATLAB Problems:

1. Generate 500 sample functions of the random telegraph signal as in Problem 2 of Chapter 12, but use only times between 0 and 4 (instead of 12). Sample the process using a sampling period of $T = 0.05$, and extrapolate the value in the midpoint of the sampling period (pick an arbitrary period). Compare the extrapolated value with the true value of the process and find the sample variance of the error (averaging over the 500 samples of the process).

2. Repeat Problem 1 to predict the value of the process at times $0.01, 0.02, 0.03, 0.04$, and 0.05, using one past sample value. Find the sample variances of the prediction errors.

3. Repeat Problem 1 for the sinusoidal signal of Problem 12.3 but with a frequency of 1 Hz, using the same sampling instants as in Problem 1.

4. Repeat Problem 2 for the sinusoidal signal you used in Problem 3.

Regular Problems:

5. Solve the extrapolation problem of a sampled random telegraph signal using two future samples and two past samples. Show that the result depends only on the immediate neighboring samples.

6. Solve the prediction problem of a sampled random telegraph signal, using two past samples. Show that the result depends only on the immediate past sample.

7. A sinusoidal random signal as given in equation (12.39) with $A = a$ and the phase uniformly distributed in $(0, 2\pi)$ is processed by a continuous-time linear system with impulse response $h(t) = u(t) - u(t - T)$, where $u(t)$ is a unit step function. Find the cross-correlation between the signal and the system output. Find the autocorrelation of the output as well as the average output power.

8. A random signal $X(t)$ with autocorrelation $R_X(\tau) = 4\exp(-0.5|\tau|)$ is processed by a continuous-time linear system with impulse response $h(t) = \exp(-t)u(t)$ (where $u(t)$ is the unit step function). Find the cross-correlation between the input and the output. Find the autocorrelation of the output and the average output power.

9. Solve the prediction problem for the random binary signal whose period is $T = 3$. Assume that we use five past samples $(k, k - 1, k - 2, k - 3,$ and $k - 4)$ and the sampling period is 0.5. We wish to predict the value of the process at $k + 0.5\alpha$, where $0 < \alpha < 1$.

   a. Write the equation for the prediction MSE as a function of the coefficients.
   b. Find the five coefficients that minimize the MSE and compute the resulting MSE.
   c. Plot the prediction MSE as a function of the prediction interval α. It is important to note that the prediction error is zero when $\alpha = 0$, and it becomes larger as α increases.
   d. For two values of the prediction interval $\alpha = 0.5$ and $\alpha = 1.0$, simulate the process and its prediction by using MATLAB and 500 samples of the process. Compare the results with the computed ones.

10. A discrete-time random process X_k is defined by the following recursive relationship:

$$X_{k+1} = \alpha X_k + W_k, \qquad \text{for } k = 0, 1, 2, \ldots$$

The $\{W_k\}$ are independent random variables with mean zero and variance σ^2. The initial value X_0 is assumed to be a random variable with zero mean and variance 1, and is assumed to be independent of the W_k. The parameter $\alpha < 1$.

   a. Find a recursive relationship for the correlation between the signal X_{k+1} and W_k.
   b. Find a recursive relationship for the correlation between X_{k+1} and X_k.
   c. Use the relationships you derived to find an expression for the correlation function of the process X_k in the steady state (as k becomes large).
   d. Use the result of part (c) to obtain an expression for the average power of the process $E\{[X_k]^2\}$ in the steady state.

11. A random telegraph signal $X(t)$ with unknown nonzero mean m_X and switching rate λ, is sampled every T seconds. These samples are used to compute an estimate of the unknown mean m_X. The estimate is obtained using the following expression:

$$\hat{m}_X = \frac{1}{n} \sum_{k=1}^{n} X(kT)$$

Find an expression for the MSE between the true mean and its estimate. Compute the result for $n = 100$, $n = 1000$ and for the following values of $\lambda T = 0.5$; 1; and 2. What can you conclude from these results?

12. Consider a discrete-time random process X_k with a known autocorrelation function. A new process Y_k is defined as follows:

$$Y_k = X_k - X_{k-1}$$

Find the autocorrelation function of the process Y_k. Compute for the case when X_k is obtained by sampling the random telegraph signal given Problem 11.

14

Power Spectrum

14.1 SPECTRUM OF DETERMINISTIC SIGNALS

When dealing with deterministic signals, we know that we have two alternative descriptions of their properties, either in the time domain, which provides information on the shape of the waveform representing the signal, or in the frequency domain, which provides information on the frequency content of the signals. Given a time function $g(t)$, we define its Fourier transform by the following expression:

$$G(\omega) = \int_{-\infty}^{\infty} g(t)e^{-j\omega t}\, dt \qquad (14.1)$$

The limits of the integral are taken over all values of t for which the function $g(t)$ is not zero. If the signal exists over all time, then an infinite interval is used, while if the signal is causal (i.e., it is zero for $t < 0$), then the lower limit starts at $t = 0$. The transform $G(\omega)$ is in general complex for real values of the radian frequency ω. As such, it has real and imaginary parts representing magnitude and phase, respectively.

$$G(\omega) = |G(\omega)|\, \exp[j\angle G(\omega)] \qquad (14.2)$$

The magnitude spectrum $|G(\omega)|$ represents the strength of the signal at various frequencies and is even as a function of the frequency ω if we assume that the signal $g(t)$ is real. The signal itself can be recovered from its transform by using the inverse Fourier transform:

$$g(t) = \frac{1}{2\pi} \int_{-\infty}^{\infty} G(\omega)e^{j\omega t}\, d\omega \tag{14.3}$$

The usefulness of the frequency domain representation is that linear systems may also be represented by their frequency response rather than their impulse response. Given a system with impulse response $h(t)$, we define its frequency response as

$$H(\omega) = \int_{-\infty}^{\infty} h(t)e^{-j\omega t}\, dt \tag{14.4}$$

The frequency response can also be described in terms of its magnitude response and phase response. If we now apply a deterministic signal $g_i(t)$ to a linear system with impulse response $h(t)$, then the output signal $g_o(t)$ is given by the convolution integral shown in equation (13.28), where the input and output were denoted by $X(t)$ and $Y(t)$, respectively:

$$g_o(t) = \int_{-\infty}^{\infty} g_i(t - \tau)h(\tau)\, d\tau = \int_{-\infty}^{\infty} g_i(\tau)h(t - \tau)\, d\tau \tag{14.5}$$

What is more useful is the way the input and output are related in the frequency domain, which is the product of the frequency response and the input transform:

$$G_o(\omega) = H(\omega)G_i(\omega) \tag{14.6}$$

The relation between the magnitude spectra of the input and the output is of particular interest, as it may suppress or amplify certain frequencies that the input signal contains:

$$|G_o(\omega)| = |H(\omega)||G_i(\omega)| \tag{14.7}$$

We usually call the square of the magnitude spectrum $|G(\omega)|^2$ the energy spectrum of the signal $g(t)$ if the signal is assumed to have finite energy. If we wish to find the signal energy at the output as related to the signal energy of the input, we find the following useful relationship:

$$E_o = \int_{-\infty}^{\infty} |g_o(t)|^2\, dt = \frac{1}{2\pi} \int_{-\infty}^{\infty} |G_o(\omega)|^2\, d\omega$$

$$= \frac{1}{2\pi} \int_{-\infty}^{\infty} |G_i(\omega)|^2 |H(\omega)|^2\, d\omega \tag{14.8}$$

Equation (14.8) relating the energy of a signal in the time domain and frequency domain, is commonly referred to as Parseval's Theorem. We see that the output energy depends only on the input energy spectrum and on the magnitude response of the linear system. This means that by amplifying or attenuating certain frequencies, we can affect what parts of the input signal are propagated to the output.

A note about our use of the term "energy" of the signal is in order. In general, we may consider two types of signals. Signals for which the integral E_0 is finite are called energy signals. On the other hand, signals for which the integral E_0 is infinite but the average of the integral over time is finite are called power signals. Periodic signals are typical power signals. In the preceding discussion we have dealt with energy signals.

The question is whether we can characterize random signals in terms of their frequency content. Then, if such characterization is possible, does the use of the frequency response of a linear system have the same effect as in the deterministic case? Our objective in this chapter is to allow us to define frequency content of random signals and how these concepts can be used for the processing of random signals, with particular application to the filtering of useful signals from noise.

14.2 POWER SPECTRUM OF RANDOM SIGNALS

Since random signals do not behave in any predictable fashion, as do deterministic signals, nor are they represented by a single time function, it is unlikely that we can define the spectrum of random signals by taking their Fourier transforms. However, we did note that the autocorrelation of random signals describes in some way whether the signal changes rapidly or slowly. (See for example the random telegraph signal for different values of the switching rate.) Also, unlike deterministic signals with Fourier transforms, which usually are finite energy signals, stationary random signals have finite power rather than finite energy; hence we have to deal with the power carried by the signal rather than the energy we considered in the deterministic case. We shall start by first defining the power spectrum and then see why it makes sense.

> **Definition:** Given a wide-sense stationary random signal $X(t)$ with autocorrelation function $R_X(\tau)$, we define the **power spectrum** $S_X(\omega)$ of the random signal as the Fourier transform of the autocorrelation function:
>
> $$S_X(\omega) = \int_{-\infty}^{\infty} R_X(\tau)e^{-j\omega\tau}\, d\tau \qquad (14.9)$$

It should be noted that we are defining the power spectrum in terms of the autocorrelation function of the random signal. One rationale for this approach may be based on the fact that if we have a deterministic power signal, we can define its time-autocorrelation function by taking time averages as defined in equation (12.56). The power spectrum in such a case is indeed the Fourier transform of the time-autocorrelation function. It therefore makes sense to define the power spectrum of random signals in the same manner, provided we assume ergodic properties that allow the derivation of the autocorrelation function by using the time-autocorrelation function.

Since the autocorrelation function can be obtained from its transform by the inverse Fourier transform, we have the following relationship:

$$R_X(\tau) = \frac{1}{2\pi} \int_{-\infty}^{\infty} S_X(\omega) e^{j\omega\tau} \, d\omega \tag{14.10}$$

Before we consider examples, let us consider the properties of the power spectrum and why they are important and useful.

Properties of the Power Spectrum

We know that the autocorrelation function is even; therefore the power spectrum, which is its transform, must also be real and even as a function of the frequency.

Property 1: The power spectrum is real and even:

$$S_X(-\omega) = S_X(\omega) \tag{14.11}$$

$$[S_X(\omega)]^* = S_X(\omega) \tag{14.12}$$

We use $S^*(\omega)$ to denote complex conjugate value of $S(\omega)$. In order to prove these two properties, we use the definition (14.9) and the fact that the autocorrelation is an even function:

$$S_X(\omega) = \int_{-\infty}^{\infty} R_X(\tau) e^{-j\omega\tau} \, d\tau = \int_{-\infty}^{\infty} R_X(\tau) \{\cos(\omega\tau) + j \sin(\omega\tau)\} \, d\tau$$

$$= \int_{-\infty}^{\infty} R_X(\tau) \cos(\omega\tau) \, d\tau + 0 = 2 \int_{0}^{\infty} R_X(\tau) \cos(\omega\tau) \, d\tau \tag{14.13}$$

In the preceding derivation we used the fact that the second integral involving the sine function is zero as the function is odd, and the first integral can be performed over only the positive values of τ, since the function is even. Thus equation (14.13) proves that the power spectrum is even and real.

Property 2: The power spectrum is nonnegative:

$$S_X(\omega) \geq 0 \tag{14.14}$$

The proof of this will be deferred until later, after we discuss how linear systems affect the power spectrum.

Property 3: The average power of the random signal is equal to the integral of the power spectrum—that is, the area under the power spectrum curve:

$$E\{[X(t)]^2\} = R_X(0) = \frac{1}{2\pi} \int_{-\infty}^{\infty} S_X(\omega) \, d\omega = \frac{1}{\pi} \int_{0}^{\infty} S_X(\omega) \, d\omega \tag{14.15}$$

The proof follows from the inverse transform shown in equation (14.10) and the fact that the average power in equation (14.15) is simply $R_X(0)$.

Property 4: If the random signal has nonzero mean m_X, then the power spectrum contains an impulse at zero frequency of magnitude $2\pi[m_X]^2$.

The proof follows from the fact that the autocorrelation in such a case is equal to the autocovariance function $C_X(\tau) + [m_X]^2$. Now when we take the Fourier transform of a constant $[m_X]^2$, we obtain

$$\int_{-\infty}^{\infty} m_X^2 e^{-j\omega\tau}\, d\tau = 2\pi[m_X]^2\delta(\omega) \tag{14.16}$$

It is easier to verify this relation if we take the inverse transform of the right-hand side. By virtue of the delta-function property, we then obtain the expected result. More details on the impulse function are provided in Appendix D.

Property 5: The Fourier transform of the autocovariance function of the random process is itself also a power spectrum, and usually does not contain an impulse component at zero frequency.

This property follows from the fact that if we subtract the mean from a random process with nonzero mean, we obtain a new process with zero mean whose autocorrelation function is equal to the autocovariance function of the original process. We can summarize this property as follows: Let $X(t)$ be a random process with mean m_X and autocovariance function $C_X(\tau)$, and let $Y(t)$ be defined by

$$Y(t) = X(t) - m_X \tag{14.17}$$

Then the autocorrelation of $Y(t)$ is given by

$$R_Y(\tau) = E\{Y(t)Y(t+\tau)\} = E\{[X(t) - m_X][X(t+\tau) - m_X]\} = C_X(\tau) \tag{14.18}$$

Hence, the power spectrum of $Y(t)$ is given by

$$S_Y(\omega) = \int_{-\infty}^{\infty} R_Y(\tau)e^{-j\omega\tau}\, d\tau = \int_{-\infty}^{\infty} C_X(\tau)e^{-j\omega\tau}\, d\tau \tag{14.19}$$

The preceding then implies that the Fourier transform of the autocovariance function is indeed a power spectrum. Furthermore, we find that the power spectrum of $X(t)$ is expressed as

$$\begin{aligned}
S_X\omega) &= \int_{-\infty}^{\infty} R_X(\tau)e^{-j\omega\tau}\, d\tau = \int_{-\infty}^{\infty} \{C_X(\tau) + m_X^2\}e^{-j\omega\tau}\, d\tau \\
&= \int_{-\infty}^{\infty} C_X(\tau)e^{-j\omega\tau}\, d\tau + 2\pi m_X^2\delta(\omega) \\
&= S_Y(\omega) + 2\pi m_X^2\delta(\omega) \tag{14.20}
\end{aligned}$$

In the next section we derive the power spectrum of the various key examples of random signals that we encountered in Chapter 12.

14.3 EXAMPLES OF POWER SPECTRUM

14.3.1 Random Sinusoidal Signal

Consider the sinusoidal signal defined in equation (12.39), where the phase is assumed to be uniformly distributed in the interval $[0, 2\pi]$:

$$X(t) = A \cos(\omega_0 t + \Theta) \tag{14.21}$$

For simplicity we assume that the amplitude A has mean zero and variance σ^2. We derived the autocorrelation function in equation (12.45), and it is expressed as

$$R_X(\tau) = 0.5\sigma^2 \cos(\omega_0 \tau) = R_X(0) \cos(\omega_0 \tau) \tag{14.22}$$

The power spectrum of this signal then becomes

$$S_X\omega) = \int_{-\infty}^{\infty} R_X(0) \cos(\omega_0 \tau) e^{-j\omega\tau}\, d\tau = R_X(0)\pi\{\delta(\omega - \omega_0) + \delta(\omega + \omega_0)\} \tag{14.23}$$

Since this signal contains only one frequency, ω_0, its power spectrum, as expected, is just two impulses, one at ω_0 and one at $-\omega_0$. Since the negative frequency appears due only to the even property of the power spectrum, it is clear that all power is concentrated at the frequency of the sinusoidal signal. While this is a very simple example, it does illustrate that the power spectrum indeed represents the way the power in the random signal is distributed among the various frequencies. We shall see later that if we also use linear systems in order to amplify or attenuate certain frequencies, the results mirror what we expect to parallel the deterministic case.

14.3.2 Random Telegraph Signal

This signal was considered in Section 12.4.4(c). The autocorrelation function of the random telegraph signal was derived in equation (12.47) and is given by

$$R_X(\tau) = R_X(0) \exp(-2\lambda|\tau|) \tag{14.24}$$

Recall that the parameter λ reflects the rate at which the signal switches between $+a$ and $-a$. Hence, we expect the frequency content to be dependent on the switching rate λ so that, as λ becomes larger, the signal will contain power at higher frequencies. The power spectrum may be derived directly to yield

$$S_X(\omega) = \int_{-\infty}^{\infty} R_X(0) e^{-2\lambda|\tau|} e^{-j\omega\tau}\, d\tau$$

$$= R_X(0)\left\{ \int_{-\infty}^{0} e^{2\lambda\tau} e^{-j\omega\tau}\, d\tau + \int_{0}^{\infty} e^{-2\lambda\tau} e^{-j\omega\tau}\, d\tau \right\}$$

$$= R_X(0)\left\{ \frac{1}{2\lambda - j\omega} + \frac{1}{2\lambda + j\omega} \right\} = \frac{4\lambda R_X(0)}{\omega^2 + (2\lambda)^2} \tag{14.25}$$

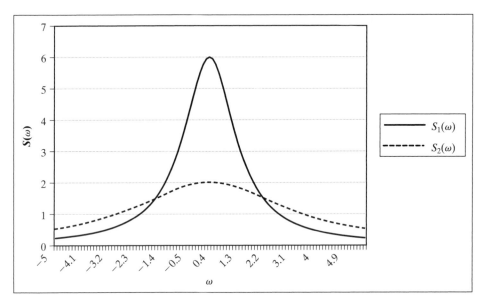

Figure 14.1   Power spectrum for the random telegraph signal for $\lambda_1 = 0.5$ and $\lambda_2 = 1.5$ with $R_X(0) = 3$

The power spectrum is shown in Figure 14.1 for two values of the switching rate, λ. It is clear that for larger values of λ the power spectrum is still large for higher values of frequencies. For smaller values of the switching rate the power is concentrated at lower frequencies.

We see that the spectrum looks like a low-pass type of signal that starts at zero frequency and decays as the frequency increases. If we define the bandwidth (positive frequency only) of the signal as the frequency for which the power spectrum is half its value at the origin (zero frequency), we see that for the case of $\lambda_1 = 0.5$ the bandwidth is 1 radian/sec ($1/(2\pi)$ Hz), while for $\lambda_2 = 1.5$ the bandwidth is 3 radian/sec ($3/(2\pi)$ Hz), which confirms our understanding that as the switching rate increases, the bandwidth of the signal spectrum increases. The bandwidth just defined is also called the 3dB bandwidth of the signal.

14.3.3 Modulated Signal

To push the concept of the meaning of the frequency content of random signals further, let us consider a sinusoidal signal modulated by another random signal, which contains low frequencies. Suppose $X(t)$ is a signal with autocorrelation function given in equation (14.24) and power spectrum given by equation (14.25). Let us define a new random process $Y(t)$ as follows:

$$Y(t) = X(t)\cos(\omega_0 t + \Theta) \tag{14.26}$$

We assume that the phase angle in equation (14.26) is a random variable uniformly distributed in the interval $[0, 2\pi]$ and is independent of $X(t)$. We find the autocorrelation function of $Y(t)$ using the usual approach by taking the expectations:

$$
\begin{aligned}
R_Y(\tau) &= E\{Y(t)Y(t + \tau)\} \\
&= E\{X(t)\cos(\omega_0 t + \Theta)X(t + \tau)\cos[\omega_0(t + \tau) + \Theta]\} \\
&= E\{X(t)X(t + \tau)\}E\{0.5\cos(\omega_0\tau) + 0.5\cos[\omega_0(2t + \tau) + 2\Theta]\} \\
&= 0.5R_X(\tau)\cos(\omega_0\tau) = 0.5R_X(0)\exp(-2\lambda|\tau|)\cos(\omega_0\tau) \qquad (14.27)
\end{aligned}
$$

The autocorrelation function is shown for $\lambda = 0.5$ and $\omega_0 = 20$ in Figure 14.2.
 To see the resulting power spectrum we use its definition to obtain

$$
S_Y(\omega) = \int_{-\infty}^{\infty} 0.5R_X(\tau)\cos(\omega_0\tau)e^{-j\omega\tau}\, d\tau
$$

$$
\begin{aligned}
&= 0.25\int_{-\infty}^{\infty} R_X(\tau)[e^{j\omega_0\tau} + e^{-j\omega_0\tau}]e^{-j\omega\tau}\, d\tau \\
&= 0.25\{S_X(\omega - \omega_0) + S_X(\omega + \omega_0)\} \qquad (14.28)
\end{aligned}
$$

We see that the resulting power spectrum is shifted to the modulating frequency ω_0 and its negative value. The power spectrum for the values shown in Figure 14.2 is shown in Figure 14.3.
 The figure is shown in two parts, one for positive frequencies and one for negative frequencies. If the value of ω_0 were smaller, we could fit it in the same figure. It should be noted that the negative frequency plot provides no additional information since the power spectrum is even.

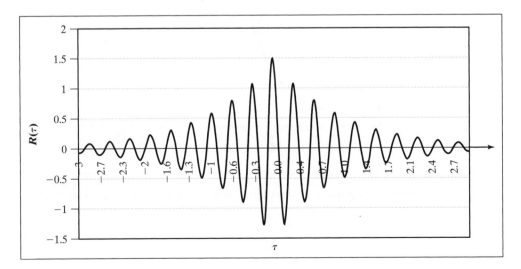

Figure 14.2   Autocorrelation function of the modulated signal $Y(t)$, for $\lambda = 0.5$ and $\omega_0 = 20$

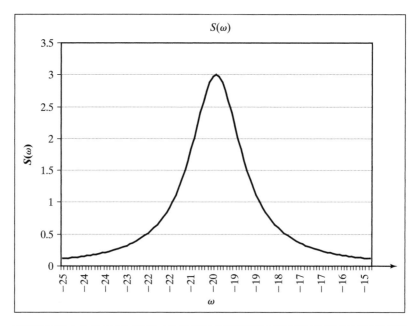

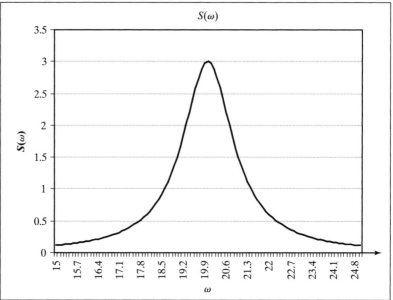

Figure 14.3   The power spectrum of $Y(t)$ for negative frequencies (top figure) and positive frequencies (bottom figure)

14.3.4 Random Binary Signal

This random signal was considered in Section 12.4.4(d). It represented the transmission of random square pulses, which are either positive or negative, every T seconds. The autocorrelation function was given in equation (12.51) and is expressed as

$$R_X(\tau) = a^2\left\{1 - \frac{|\tau|}{T}\right\}, \qquad \text{for } |\tau| < T \qquad (14.29)$$

The power spectrum is again obtained directly by using the definition, except that we may have to use the Fourier transform or integral tables to arrive at the final answer:

$$
\begin{aligned}
S_X(\omega) &= \int_{-T}^{T} a^2\left[1 - \frac{|\tau|}{T}\right]e^{-j\omega\tau}\,d\tau \\
&= a^2\left\{\int_{-T}^{0}\left[1 + \frac{\tau}{T}\right]e^{-j\omega\tau}\,d\tau + \int_{0}^{T}\left[1 - \frac{\tau}{T}\right]e^{-j\omega\tau}\,d\tau\right\} \\
&= a^2 T\left(\frac{\sin\left(\frac{\omega T}{2}\right)}{\left(\frac{\omega T}{2}\right)}\right)^2 = a^2 T\left[\operatorname{sinc}\left(\frac{\omega T}{2}\right)\right]^2 \qquad (14.30)
\end{aligned}
$$

At zero frequency the value of the power spectrum is just equal to $a^2 T$, while the first time it reaches zero is at the frequency $(2\pi/T)$ radian/sec, which is equal to $1/T$ Hz. We can conclude from this observation that the bandwidth of the signal is approximately $1/T$ Hz, which agrees with the fact that as we make the period of the square pulses smaller, the signal will be changing faster, thus requiring or occupying larger bandwidth. The power spectrum for $a = 3$ and $T = 2$ is shown in Figure 14.4. We see that the value at zero frequency is indeed $a^2 T = 18$, and it becomes zero at π radian/sec. If we approximate the area under the spectrum by an area of a triangle with base 2π and height 18, then after dividing the area by 2π, we obtain the value of the autocorrelation at the origin (the average power of the signal), which is equal to $a^2 = 9$ as expected.

14.3.5 White Noise

In Section 13.3 we discussed the random process that we called **"white noise."** In that section we considered random signals whose autocorrelation function was very narrow but whose value at the origin was quite high. In the limit the autocorrelation function of these signals was represented by the impulse function as in equation (13.36) and we defined that as the autocorrelation of white noise. While such a model of a random signal is only an idealization, as it has infinite average power, it was useful when we considered integrating such a signal with a very narrow autocorrelation function in order to estimate an unknown mean or signal amplitude. Here, we shall study the spectrum of this type of random signal. We can see that in the limit both the random binary signal and the random telegraph signal can

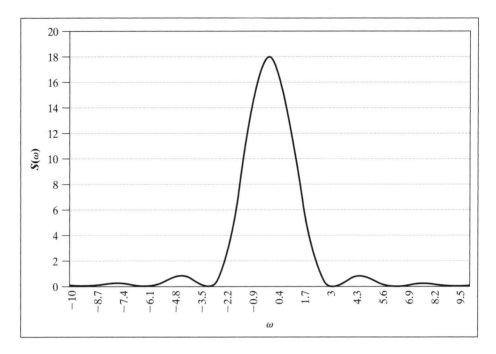

Figure 14.4   Power spectrum of the random binary signal

approach the white noise model as they switch faster between symbols or levels, respectively. In other words, as the autocorrelation functions of these processes become narrower, they approach a white noise model as we observed in Chapter 13.

Consider the random binary signal first, when the period T becomes smaller, while the amplitude increases as the inverse of the square root of T, $a = C/\sqrt{T}$. In this case the autocorrelation in equation (14.29) becomes

$$R_X(\tau) = \frac{C}{T}\left\{1 - \frac{|\tau|}{T}\right\}, \qquad \text{for } |\tau| < \text{T} \qquad (14.31)$$

The area under the autocorrelation is fixed at C, so that as T becomes smaller, then the autocorrelation tends to the impulse function, $C\delta(\tau)$. The power spectrum in this case becomes

$$S_X(\omega) = C\left(\frac{\sin\left(\frac{\omega T}{2}\right)}{\left(\frac{\omega T}{2}\right)}\right)^2 \longrightarrow C \text{ as } T \longrightarrow 0 \qquad (14.32)$$

It is important to note that in the expression for the power spectrum, as T becomes smaller the frequency at which the power spectrum reaches zero becomes higher.

In the limit the power spectrum becomes just a flat spectrum whose value is equal to C. The fact that the power spectrum is flat for all frequencies gives rise to the "white noise" name used for such models, since it contains all frequencies with equal amount.

Let us consider the autocorrelation of the random telegraph signal as the switching rate becomes large. In this case, while the rate λ approaches infinity, we also have to increase the amplitude as the square root of λ, which means that we increase $R_X(0)$ linearly with increasing λ. The autocorrelation function thus becomes

$$R_X(\tau) = C\lambda \exp(-2\lambda|\tau|) \tag{14.33}$$

Again, the autocorrelation function will have an area equal to C as λ increases, so that it tends to an impulse function when λ approaches infinity. The resulting power spectrum in equation (14.25) then becomes

$$S_X(\omega) = \frac{4C\lambda^2}{\omega^2 + (2\lambda)^2} = \frac{C}{1 + \left(\dfrac{\omega}{2\lambda}\right)^2} \longrightarrow C \text{ as } \lambda \longrightarrow \infty \tag{14.34}$$

We see that the power spectrum is again flat for all frequencies, and thus deserves the white noise designation.

To obtain the same results, we could obtain the power spectrum of the white noise model given by equation (13.36) directly via the definition of the power spectrum and the property of the impulse function.

An important note about white noise is that theoretically it is assumed to have infinite average power. Obviously, there is no real signal with infinite power. As we shall see later, we usually process signals using linear systems, and such systems pass only certain frequencies; hence, as far as the output of linear systems with white noise input is concerned, the model works very well, since while we assume that the power spectrum is flat for all frequencies, in practice the power spectrum decays eventually, but that decay may occur at frequencies that are higher than the frequency response region of the linear system we are using.

Now that we have seen how the behavior of the autocorrelation function is reflected in the power spectrum of the random signal, we are ready to look at how the results translate when processing random signals with linear systems. However, as we have seen in the time domain, we first need to define the cross-power spectrum in order to be able to consider the input–output properties of the signals involved.

14.4 CROSS-POWER SPECTRUM

Suppose we have two random signals $X(t)$ and $Y(t)$ that we are adding together. We defined the cross-correlation function in equation (12.58) of Section 12.5 as follows:

$$R_{XY}(\tau) = E\{X(t)Y(t + \tau)\} \tag{14.35}$$

If we now add these two signals we find that the autocorrelation function of their sum $Z(t)$ is given by

$$R_Z(\tau) = R_X(\tau) + R_Y(\tau) + R_{XY}(\tau) + R_{YX}(\tau) \tag{14.36}$$

If we now wish to find the power spectrum of $Z(t)$, we find that we need to define something new as the Fourier transform of the last two terms in equation (14.36). We call the resulting quantity the **cross-power spectrum** of $X(t)$ and $Y(t)$.

> **Definition:** Given two jointly wide-sense stationary random processes with known autocorrelation and cross-correlation functions, we define the **cross-power spectrum** $S_{XY}(\omega)$ of $X(t)$ and $Y(t)$ as the Fourier transform of the cross-correlation function:

$$S_{XY}(\omega) = \int_{-\infty}^{\infty} R_{XY}(\tau)e^{-j\omega\tau}\, d\tau \tag{14.37}$$

As we saw earlier, we have two such functions but they are related as follows:

$$R_{YX}(\tau) = R_{XY}(-\tau) \tag{14.38}$$

The preceding relation implies that the two cross-power spectra are related as follows:

$$S_{YX}(\omega) = S_{XY}(-\omega) = [S_{XY}(\omega)]^* \tag{14.39}$$

Example 14.1

Let $X(t)$ be a wide-sense stationary random process with twice differentiable autocorrelation function $R_X(\tau)$, and we define $Y(t)$ as its derivative. We wish to find the cross-power spectrum of $X(t)$ and $Y(t)$ and the power spectrum of $Y(t)$.

In Section 12.5 we obtained the cross-correlation function of $X(t)$ and its derivative in equation (12.65). We repeat the equation here:

$$R_{XY}(\tau) = \frac{d}{d\tau}R_X(\tau) \tag{14.40}$$

We now use the basic property of the Fourier transform of the derivative to find the cross-power spectrum of $X(t)$ and $Y(t)$. We get

$$S_{XY}(\omega) = j\omega S_X(\omega) \tag{14.41}$$

Obviously, the other cross-power spectrum follows from equation (14.39) and is

$$S_{YX}(\omega) = -j\omega S_X(\omega) \tag{14.42}$$

Finally, in order to obtain the expression for the power spectrum of $Y(t)$, we use equation (12.67), which related the autocorrelation of $Y(t)$ to that of $X(t)$:

$$R_Y(\tau) = -\frac{d^2}{d\tau^2} R_X(\tau) \tag{14.43}$$

The power spectrum of $Y(t)$ may again be derived using the derivative property of the Fourier transform to yield

$$S_Y(\omega) = -(j\omega)^2 S_X(\omega) = \omega^2 S_X(\omega) \tag{14.44}$$

We see from equation (14.44) that the power spectrum is still real, even, and nonnegative as expected, while from equation (14.41) we observe that the cross-power spectrum does not have any such special properties.

Example 14.2

As a special case of the power spectrum of a signal and its derivative, let us consider $X(t)$ with power spectrum

$$S_X(\omega) = \frac{36}{(4 + \omega^2)(1 + \omega^2)} \tag{14.45}$$

The autocorrelation function of $X(t)$ may be obtained from Fourier transform tables:

$$R_X(\tau) = 3\{2 \exp(-|\tau|) - \exp(-2|\tau|)\} \tag{14.46}$$

We can verify that the average power of $X(t)$, which is equal to $R(0) = 3$, is also equal to the area under the power spectrum. Now if we consider the derivative $Y(t)$, then its cross-power spectrum with $X(t)$ is equal to

$$S_{XY}(\omega) = j\omega S_X(\omega) = \frac{36j\omega}{(4 + \omega^2)(1 + \omega^2)} \tag{14.47}$$

We can now verify that the inverse transform of the cross-power spectrum is indeed equal to the cross-correlation function as obtained by the derivative of the autocorrelation function:

$$R_{XY}(\tau) = \begin{cases} 6\{\exp(\tau) - \exp(2\tau)\}, & \text{for } \tau < 0 \\ -6\{\exp(-\tau) - \exp(-2\tau)\}, & \text{for } \tau > 0 \end{cases} \tag{14.48}$$

In this case we find that the cross-correlation function is an odd function, as is also seen from the fact that its Fourier transform is purely imaginary and odd. It should be noted that even though equation (14.48) has two different expressions for positive and negative values of τ, the function is continuous and differentiable at the origin $\tau = 0$. That is a critical observation, since otherwise the derivative $Y(t)$ would not have existed.

The power spectrum of the derivative $Y(t)$ is expressed from equation (14.44) as

$$S_Y(\omega) = \frac{36\omega^2}{(4 + \omega^2)(1 + \omega^2)} \tag{14.49}$$

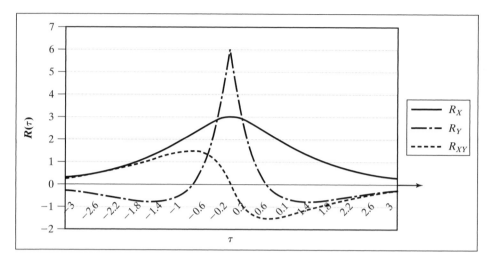

Figure 14.5a Autocorrelation and cross-correlation of a signal and its derivative

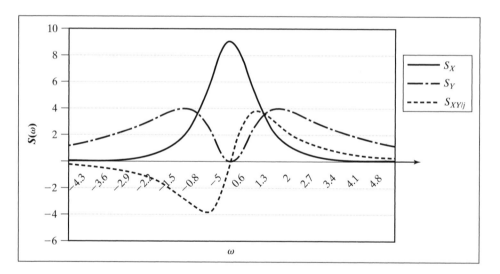

Figure 14.5b Power spectrum and cross-power spectrum of a signal and its derivative

The autocorrelation function of the derivative $Y(t)$ can again be obtained directly from the inverse transform of equation (14.49) or by taking the second derivative of the autocorrelation of $X(t)$ as in equation (14.43). The answer can be confirmed to be the same, whichever approach we use:

$$R_Y(\tau) = 6\{2 \exp(-2|\tau|) - \exp(-|\tau|)\} \tag{14.50}$$

The average power of $Y(t)$ is therefore equal to $R_Y(0) = 6$ and is also equal to the area under the power spectrum.

The power spectrum of $X(t)$ and $Y(t)$ and their autocorrelation and cross-correlation functions are shown in Figure 14.5. We see from the power spectrum that the derivative tends to have more power at higher frequencies than the original signal has and has no power component at zero frequency. This agrees with our intuition that when we differentiate a signal we have more high-frequency components.

14.5 RANDOM SIGNALS IN LINEAR SYSTEMS

In Section 13.3 we considered time-domain approaches to the analysis of random signals when processed by linear systems. Here we extend the result to the use of power spectrum and frequency-domain methods. We found that we can derive the cross-correlation of the output and the input, and also the output autocorrelation function. In this section we find the results for the power spectrum. Suppose $X(t)$ is a wide-sense stationary process and is used as the input to a linear system with impulse response $h(t)$, and we denote the output as $Y(t)$. The input–output relation was given by the convolution of equation (13.28). We found the cross-correlation function of $X(t)$ and $Y(t)$ by equation (13.29), and the output autocorrelation was given by equation (13.30) or equation (13.31). We now turn to the cross-power spectrum of $X(t)$ and $Y(t)$, and here we use the property that a convolution in the time domain yields a product in the frequency domain. In this case we find that

$$S_{XY}(\omega) = H(\omega)S_X(\omega) \tag{14.51}$$

Similarly, since the cross-power spectrum satisfies equation (14.39), we also find that

$$S_{YX}(\omega) = H^*(\omega)S_X(\omega) = H(-\omega)S_X(\omega) \tag{14.52}$$

Finally we use equation (13.29) to obtain the power spectrum of the output:

$$S_Y(\omega) = H(\omega)S_{YX}(\omega) = H(\omega)H^*(\omega)S_X(\omega) = |H(\omega)|^2S_X(\omega) \tag{14.53}$$

The result expressed in equation (14.53) is very important, as it shows how a linear system affects the different frequency components of the signal power even if the signal is a random signal. The result also allows us to prove the property (Property 2) that the power spectrum cannot be negative. Before we do so, however, let us find the average power of the output signal, for which we use equation (14.15):

$$E\{[Y(t)]^2\} = \frac{1}{2\pi} \int_{-\infty}^{\infty} S_Y(\omega)\,d\omega = \frac{1}{2\pi} \int_{-\infty}^{\infty} |H(\omega)|^2 S_X(\omega)\,d\omega \tag{14.54}$$

Now we are ready to prove Property 2. In this case we pass the signal $X(t)$ through a linear system whose frequency response is nonzero only for a very narrow frequency range of width Δ at any frequency ω_0, and its magnitude is 1 in that narrow range, as shown in Figure 14.6. Then the average power of the output is given by the following expression, for a small enough value of the width Δ:

$$E\{[Y(t)]^2\} \cong \frac{2}{2\pi} S_X(\omega_0)\Delta \tag{14.55}$$

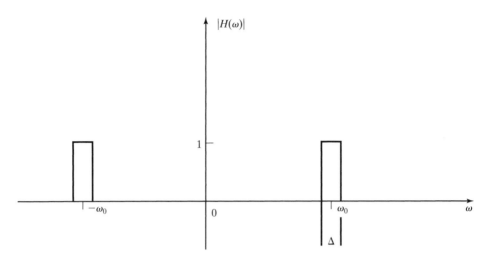

Figure 14.6 A narrow-band system

Since the average power shown in equation (14.55) must be nonnegative, the value of $S_X(\omega_0)$ must be nonnegative for any frequency ω_0, which is what we wished to show. We can also determine the power spectrum of the derivative of a random process by using the fact that the frequency response of a differentiator is just $H(\omega) = j\omega$. It is left as an exercise to show the results of Example 14.2.

   We can now use the results derived so far to analyze linear systems with random inputs. In particular, if we are interested in recovering useful information about a desired signal that is corrupted by noise, we may try to find the best linear system that reduces the error between the desired signal and the signal we obtain by filtering the noisy observation signal. In other situations, we may wish to decide if a known signal is present in noisy observations (which may contain the signal plus noise or noise alone). In such a case we also try to filter the signal out of the noisy observations, but we are interested only in obtaining the largest signal-to-noise ratio at the time instants when we make the decision. We shall discuss the two cases in the following section, after we consider two examples.

Example 14.3

   A sinusoidal signal is observed in additive white noise. The observed signal is passed through a linear filter in order to improve the signal-to-noise ratio. The example is illustrated as in Figure 14.7. In this case we are given that the desired signal is a sine wave:

$$s(t) = A\cos(\omega_0 t + \Theta) \tag{14.56}$$

The observed signal is $Y(t)$, which is just the sum of $s(t)$ and the noise $N(t)$. We assume that the noise is white with power spectrum N_0. The output is composed of two components: the signal component $s_0(t)$ and a noise component $N_1(t)$, as shown in the figure.

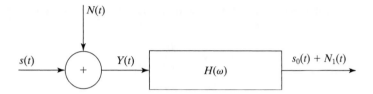

Figure 14.7   Sinusoidal signal in additive white noise

We wish to find the signal-to-noise ratio at the output if we know the frequency response of the linear system. The selection of the frequency response of the filter is a very important problem, and some approaches in the general case will be discussed later in this chapter. For this example we shall consider a simple low-pass filter having the frequency response

$$H(\omega) = \frac{a}{a + j\omega} \qquad (14.57)$$

We know that the signal component at the output is also sinusoidal with amplitude and phase given by the frequency response of the system. Since the phase does not affect the signal power, we shall not bother to derive the output phase, so that we have

$$s_0(t) = A|H(\omega_0)| \cos(\omega_0 t + \Theta_0) \qquad (14.58)$$

Hence the output signal power is obtained as the output magnitude squared and divided by 2:

$$\text{Signal Power} = 0.5 A^2 |H(\omega_0)|^2 \qquad (14.59)$$

The noise power is really the average noise power and is obtained from equation (14.54), where the input is $N(t)$ and the input power spectrum is just N_0. In this case we have

$$E\{[N_1(t)]^2\} = \frac{1}{2\pi} \int_{-\infty}^{\infty} |H(\omega)|^2 S_N(\omega)\, d\omega = \frac{1}{2\pi} \int_{-\infty}^{\infty} |H(\omega)|^2 N_0\, d\omega \qquad (14.60)$$

The signal-to-noise ratio, which we denote by SNR, is obtained as the ratio of the two quantities derived in equations (14.59) and (14.60):

$$\text{SNR} = \frac{0.5 A^2 |H(\omega_0)|^2}{\dfrac{N_0}{2\pi} \displaystyle\int_{-\infty}^{\infty} |H(\omega)|^2\, d\omega} \qquad (14.61)$$

For the special case of the system described in equation (14.57), the expressions for the signal and noise powers become

$$\text{Signal power} = \frac{0.5A^2a^2}{a^2 + \omega_0^2} \tag{14.62}$$

$$E\{[N_1(t)]^2\} = \frac{N_0}{2\pi} \int_{-\infty}^{\infty} \frac{a^2}{a^2 + \omega^2} d\omega = 0.5aN_0 \tag{14.63}$$

The signal-to-noise ratio in equation (14.61) becomes

$$\text{SNR} = \frac{0.5a^2A^2}{(a^2 + \omega_0^2)0.5aN_0} = \frac{aA^2}{(a^2 + \omega_0^2)N_0} \tag{14.64}$$

We see here that the SNR is zero when $a = 0$, and is also zero when the value of a approaches infinity. This means that there is a value of the parameter a for which the SNR is the largest, and this value may be obtained by taking the derivative and equating it to zero:

$$\frac{d(\text{SNR})}{da} = 0 = \frac{A^2}{N_0} \frac{(a^2 + \omega_0^2) - 2aa}{(a^2 + \omega_0^2)^2} = \frac{A^2}{N_0} \frac{(\omega_0^2 - a^2)}{(a^2 + \omega_0^2)^2} \tag{14.65}$$

We see that the optimal solution is $a = \omega_0$, which yields the largest SNR at

$$(\text{SNR})_{\max} = \frac{A^2}{2\omega_0N_0} \tag{14.66}$$

The preceding example may appear rather simple, but it is a reasonable model of the case in which we wish to tune in to a sinusoidal carrier with some information contained in a modulated signal it carries. The time-domain version of this example was considered in Example 13.1(a).

Example 14.4

In this example we have a desired signal $X(t)$ that is a random process with power spectrum $S_X(\omega)$. Suppose for simplicity that the power spectrum is low pass and is given by the expression

$$S_X(\omega) = \frac{2aP}{a^2 + \omega^2} \tag{14.67}$$

It is left as an exercise to show that the average power of $X(t)$ is equal to P. The signal is observed in additive white noise $N(t)$ with power spectrum N_0, as in Example 14.3. We assume that the signal and noise are uncorrelated. In this case the objective is to obtain as close a reproduction of $X(t)$ as possible at the output of the linear system shown in Figure 14.8. In the figure we define the two components of the output as $X_1(t)$ due to the signal and $N_1(t)$ due to the noise.

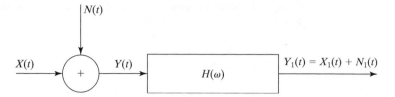

Figure 14.8   A random signal in additive white noise

Since we wish the output to be as close a reproduction of the desired signal as possible, this means that we wish the error between the output $Y_1(t)$ and the signal $X(t)$ be as small as possible. Since all the signals are random processes, the error is also a random process and our purpose is then to minimize the mean-squared value of the error (MSE)—that is, to minimize the average power of the error signal, which we shall denote by $Z(t)$:

$$Z(t) = Y_1(t) - X(t) = [X_1(t) - X(t)] + N_1(t) \qquad (14.68)$$

The MSE is then defined as

$$\begin{aligned} \text{MSE} &= E\{[Z(t)]^2\} = E\{[X_1(t) - X(t) + N_1(t)]^2\} \\ &= E\{[X_1(t) - X(t)]^2\} + E\{[N_1(t)]^2\} \end{aligned} \qquad (14.69)$$

We used the fact that the signal and noise are uncorrelated so as to ignore the cross term involving the product of the signal-dependent component, and the noise-dependent component of the error. All we have to do now is evaluate the two averages in equation (14.69) using equation (14.54). The term in equation (14.69) due to the noise is evaluated as in equation (14.60) in Example 14.3. The term due to the signal may be viewed as the result of passing the signal through a linear system with frequency response as shown in Figure 14.9:
Hence the average power of this term may be obtained also from equation (14.54) with the system response replaced by $[H(\omega) - 1]$ to yield the final expression for the MSE:

$$\text{MSE} = \frac{1}{2\pi} \int_{-\infty}^{\infty} |H(\omega) - 1|^2 S_X(\omega)\, d\omega + \frac{1}{2\pi} \int_{-\infty}^{\infty} |H(\omega)|^2 N_0\, d\omega \qquad (14.70)$$

In equation (14.70) we can identify the two terms as the error due to the signal distortion by the linear filter and the error due to the remaining noise at the output of the filter. We

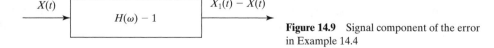

Figure 14.9   Signal component of the error in Example 14.4

see from that equation that if we select a system that passes nothing, the error due to noise is zero but the error due to the signal distortion is the largest. On the other hand, if we select a system that passes everything, then the distortion error is zero, while the error due to the output noise is the largest (and is even infinite). For our example, let us select an ideal low-pass filter with cutoff frequency ω_0 for the system

$$H(\omega) = 1, \qquad \text{for } |\omega| < \omega_0, \text{ and is zero elsewhere.}$$

For this case the MSE shown in equation (14.70) for the special case of $S_X(\omega)$ given in equation (14.67) reduces to

$$\text{MSE} = \frac{2}{2\pi} \int_{\omega_0}^{\infty} \frac{2aP}{a^2 + \omega^2} d\omega + \frac{2}{2\pi} \int_0^{\omega_0} N_0 \, d\omega = P\left\{1 - \frac{2}{\pi}\arctan\left(\frac{\omega_0}{a}\right)\right\} + \frac{N_0\omega_0}{\pi}$$

$$(14.71)$$

If we wish to find the cut-off frequency that minimizes the MSE, we obtain

$$\frac{d(\text{MSE})}{d\omega_0} = 0 = -\frac{2P}{\pi a(1 + \omega_0^2/a^2)} + \frac{N_0}{\pi} = \frac{N_0}{\pi}\left\{1 - \frac{\text{SNR}}{1 + \omega_0^2/a^2}\right\} \qquad (14.72)$$

Here we defined the SNR as $(2P/aN_0)$ since it represents a ratio of powers and hence is a nondimensional constant. The solution of equation (14.72) for the cut-off frequency that minimizes the MSE becomes

$$\omega_0 = a\sqrt{\text{SNR} - 1}, \text{ when SNR} > 1 \text{ and is zero when SNR} < 1.$$

It is clear that when the SNR is too low, we simply select a zero cut-off frequency and we do not pass the signal or the noise to the output. This is not the best system one can pick and was selected just to simplify the example. To see the behavior of this example as a function of the SNR, we show the relative value of the MSE (i.e., the ratio of the MSE to P) as a function of the SNR when we use the cut-off frequency derived in the example. The resulting MSE in equation (14.71) is then expressed as follows:

$$\text{MSE/P} = 1 - \frac{2}{\pi}\arctan\left(\sqrt{\text{SNR} - 1}\right) + \frac{2\sqrt{\text{SNR} - 1}}{\pi\text{SNR}} \qquad (14.73)$$

We see again that if the SNR is 1, the relative MSE is the largest at 1, and as the SNR approaches infinity, the MSE approaches zero, as expected. The results are shown in Figure 14.10 as a function of the SNR for SNR > 1.

General MMSE Filtering

We can obtain a more general expression for the problem considered in Example 14.4 if we assume an arbitrary system response $H(\omega)$, where we assume that the power spectrum of the signal and noise are given by $S_X(\omega)$ and $S_N(\omega)$, respectively. We are still interested in obtaining the expression for the mean-squared error (MSE) as in the example. The expression is obtained as in equation (14.70), except that the

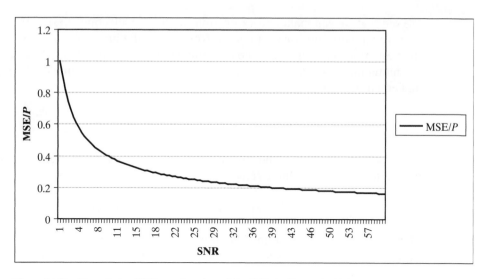

Figure 14.10   The relative MSE as a function of the SNR for Example 14.4

power spectrum of the noise is more general:

$$\text{MSE} = \frac{1}{2\pi} \int_{-\infty}^{\infty} |H(\omega) - 1|^2 S_X(\omega)\, d\omega + \frac{1}{2\pi} \int_{-\infty}^{\infty} |H(\omega)|^2 S_N(\omega)\, d\omega \quad (14.74)$$

Now we wish to find the $H(\omega)$ that minimizes the MSE. In general such a problem is difficult if we insist that the system response be causal (meaning that it operates only on past observation samples). For simplicity, we shall consider here the non-causal case, as it is simple to derive and it also provides a lower bound on the best MSE we can achieve. It should be noted that the integral in equation (14.74) contains only positive quantities. Hence, if we can make it as small as possible for every value of the frequency ω, the resulting MSE will be the smallest. Therefore, we shall find the frequency response $H(\omega)$ that minimizes the following expression for every frequency:

$$|H(\omega) - 1|^2 S_X(\omega) + |H(\omega)|^2 S_N(\omega) \quad (14.75)$$

For every frequency, we now write $H(\omega)$ as a sum of its real and imaginary parts, which we shall denote by $A(\omega)$ and $B(\omega)$:

$$H(\omega) = A(\omega) + jB(\omega) \quad (14.76)$$

The expression in equation (14.75) now becomes

$$[A(\omega) - 1]^2 S_X(\omega) + [A(\omega)]^2 S_N(\omega) + [B(\omega)]^2 [S_X(\omega) + S_X(\omega)] \quad (14.77)$$

We see that we can make the expression smaller by selecting $B(\omega) = 0$, as this will remove an entire positive expression from inside the integral. It is now left to find the best $A(\omega)$ that minimizes the remaining part of equation (14.77). We can obtain the minimum by differentiating with respect to A for every value of the frequency and equating to zero:

$$2[A(\omega) - 1]S_X(\omega) + 2[A(\omega)]S_N(\omega) = 0 \qquad (14.78)$$

We now solve for $A(\omega)$ and use the fact that B is identically zero to obtain the expression for optimal filter $H(\omega)$:

$$H_0(\omega) = S_X(\omega)/[S_X(\omega) + S_N(\omega)] \qquad (14.79)$$

This is what is called the optimal Wiener noncausal filter for recovering a signal from noisy observations. After some arithmetic operations, the resulting MSE becomes

$$\text{MSE} = \frac{1}{2\pi} \int_{-\infty}^{\infty} \frac{S_X(\omega)S_N(\omega)}{S_X(\omega) + S_N(\omega)} d\omega \qquad (14.80)$$

It is left as an exercise to check that with this optimal filter we can do much better than the ideal low-pass filter in Example 14.4.

14.6 MATCHED FILTER AND APPLICATION TO HYPOTHESIS TESTING

In this section we shall consider the problem of finding the optimal linear filter for maximizing an output signal-to-noise ratio. In this case we assume that our signal $s(t)$ is known, is nonzero in the interval $[0, T]$, and is corrupted by additive white Gaussian noise with power spectrum N_0. We now process the signal plus noise through a linear system with impulse response $h(\tau)$ and frequency response $H(\omega)$. The system is as shown in Figure 14.8, where $X(t) = s(t)$ is a known signal. We wish to maximize the SNR at the output at time $t = T$. In this case the signal at the output at $t = T$ is obtained by using the frequency response of the system and the Fourier transform of $s(t)$, which we shall denote by $S(\omega)$. The signal output, which we shall denote by $s_1(t)$ at time $t = T$ is given by

$$s_1(T) = \frac{1}{2\pi} \int_{-\infty}^{\infty} S_1(\omega)e^{j\omega T} d\omega = \frac{1}{2\pi} \int_{-\infty}^{\infty} S(\omega)H(\omega)e^{j\omega T} d\omega \qquad (14.81)$$

The noise power at the output is given by equation (14.6):

$$E\{[N_1(T)]^2\} = \frac{1}{2\pi} \int_{-\infty}^{\infty} |H(\omega)|^2 N_0 \, d\omega \qquad (14.82)$$

The output SNR is given by the ratio of the output signal squared to the average noise power:

$$\text{SNR} = \left| \frac{1}{2\pi} \int_{-\infty}^{\infty} S(\omega)H(\omega)e^{j\omega T}\, d\omega \right|^2 \Big/ \left\{ \frac{1}{2\pi} \int_{-\infty}^{\infty} |H(\omega)|^2 N_0 \, d\omega \right\} \qquad (14.83)$$

We now use the Schwartz inequality (see Appendix C) for the numerator of equation (14.83), with $F(\omega) = H(\omega)$ and $G(\omega) = S(\omega)e^{j\omega T}$, to yield

$$\left| \frac{1}{2\pi} \int_{-\infty}^{\infty} S(\omega)H(\omega)e^{j\omega T}\, d\omega \right|^2 \leq \left\{ \frac{1}{2\pi} \int_{-\infty}^{\infty} |H(\omega)|^2\, d\omega \right\} \left\{ \frac{1}{2\pi} \int_{-\infty}^{\infty} |S(\omega)e^{j\omega T}|^2\, d\omega \right\}$$

$$= \left\{ \frac{1}{2\pi} \int_{-\infty}^{\infty} |H(\omega)|^2\, d\omega \right\} \left\{ \frac{1}{2\pi} \int_{-\infty}^{\infty} |S(\omega)|^2\, d\omega \right\} \qquad (14.84)$$

If we use equation (14.84), together with equation (14.83), we obtain

$$\text{SNR} \leq \left\{ \frac{1}{2\pi N_o} \int_{-\infty}^{\infty} |S(\omega)|^2\, d\omega \right\}$$

$$= \frac{1}{N_0} \int_{o}^{T} [s(t)]^2\, dt = \frac{P_0}{N_0} \qquad (14.85)$$

Here we used Parseval's Theorem to represent the integral of the signal squared in the numerator of equation (14.85). The resulting integral is simply the signal energy, which we denoted by P_0. Note that this expression provides an upper bound on the largest SNR that we can achieve. The maximum is achieved by the rules of the Schwartz inequality as shown in Appendix C, namely when $F = KG^*$, which in this case means that the SNR achieves its maximum when

$$H(\omega) = KG^*(\omega) = K[S(\omega)e^{j\omega T}]^* = KS^*(\omega)e^{-j\omega T} \qquad (14.86)$$

If we take the inverse transform of equation (14.86), we obtain

$$h(t) = Ks(T - t) \qquad (14.87)$$

This is the optimal filter that yields the largest output SNR. It is called the **matched filter** since it is a shifted mirror image of the input signal $s(t)$ as shown in Figure 14.11

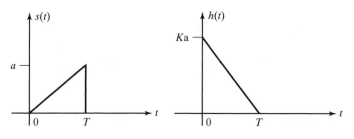

Figure 14.11   An illustration of the matched filter

for an input signal shaped like a triangle. The gain K that multiplies $s(t)$ in equation (14.87) is not important, as it amplifies the signal and noise by the same amount.

We now consider applications to signal detection (or as we called it in Chapter 10, hypothesis testing).

Example 14.5

We observe a random signal $X(t)$ in the interval $0 < t < T$. Under the hypothesis H_0 the signal contains a random noise signal $N(t)$. (We shall assume that it is white and Gaussian with power spectrum N_0.) Under the hypothesis H_1 the observed signal contains a known signal $s(t)$ in addition to the white noise $N(t)$. For simplicity, let us assume that $s(t)$ is just a constant signal of magnitude $A > 0$ over the observation interval.

$$\text{If } H_0 \text{ is true, } X(t) = N(t), \qquad\qquad 0 < t < T$$
$$\text{If } H_1 \text{ is true, } X(t) = N(t) + s(t) = N(t) + A, \qquad 0 < t < T$$

A simple solution is to filter the observation using a linear filter and make a decision based on the output value at $t = T$. Suppose we make our decision by comparing the output at time T with a threshold η and deciding in favor of H_1 if the output is larger than the threshold and in favor of H_0 if the output is smaller than the threshold. For the decision to be meaningful, we would like the signal component at $t = T$ to be large compared with the noise. We observed earlier in this section that at time $t = T$ we obtain the largest signal-to-noise ratio if we use the matched filter, which in this case is just a constant in the interval $0 < t < T$. The resulting detector may be implemented as shown in Figure 14.12.

Now we shall evaluate the two error probabilities for this case. Since the impulse response is just a constant (which we shall denote by K) over the interval $[0, T]$, if H_0 is true, the output $Y_0(T)$ is just the noise term:

$$Y_0(T) = \int_0^T KN(t)\, dt \tag{14.88}$$

It is therefore a Gaussian random variable with mean zero and variance

$$\sigma^2 = E\{[Y_0(T)]^2 | H_0\} = E\left\{ \int_0^T \int_0^T KN(\tau) KN(t)\, d\tau\, dt \right\}$$

$$= \int_0^T \int_0^T K^2 N_0 \delta(\tau - t)\, d\tau\, dt = K^2 N_0 T \tag{14.89}$$

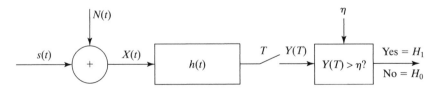

Figure 14.12   Block diagram of the detection problem of Example 14.5

Here we used the fact that the autocorrelation of the noise process is an impulse function with parameter N_0. A probability of false alarm (or type I error) is therefore equal to the probability that a Gaussian random variable with mean zero and variance σ^2 exceeds the threshold η, as described in Section 10.3:

$$\alpha = P\{Y_0(T) > \eta | H_0\} = \int_\eta^\infty \frac{\exp\{-y^2/(2\sigma^2)\}}{\sqrt{2\pi}\sigma} dy = 1 - \Phi(\eta/\sigma) \qquad (14.90)$$

Now if the hypothesis H_1 is true, then the output $Y_1(T)$ would contain two terms. The first is identical to $Y_0(T)$ and represents the noise term, and the second term is the signal component, which is a constant quantity that may be considered as the mean of $Y_1(T)$, given by

$$m_1 = E\{Y_1(T) | H_1\} = \int_0^T Ks(t)\, dt = \int_0^T KA\, dt = KAT \qquad (14.91)$$

The variance of $Y_1(T)$ is the same variance as $Y_0(T)$ and is therefore equal to σ^2. The power of the test (i.e., the probability of correctly deciding that H_1 is true) is therefore given by

$$1 - \beta = P\{Y_1(T) > \eta | H_1\} = \int_\eta^\infty \frac{\exp\{-(y - KAT)^2/(2\sigma^2)\}}{\sqrt{2\pi}\sigma} dy$$

$$= 1 - \Phi[(\eta - KAT)/\sigma] \qquad (14.92)$$

We again see that if we fix the acceptable value of α, we can determine the threshold by

$$\eta = \sigma\Phi^{-1}(1 - \alpha) = K\sqrt{N_0 T}\,\Phi^{-1}(1 - \alpha) \qquad (14.93)$$

We see that the threshold does not depend on the value of the amplitude A. On the other hand, we can check to verify that β does indeed depend on the value of A, so that stronger signals will have a higher probability of being correctly detected.

Example 14.6

We shall now consider more systematically the problem discussed in Example 14.5. In this case we assume that during the interval $[0, T]$ we observe either a signal of known shape but unknown amplitude, or noise only, without any signal present. This reflects a typical radar problem in which a return from a target is either present in what the receiver observes (if a target is present) or the receiver observes noise only when the target is not present.

In this case we can describe the received signal $X(t)$ by the following equation:

$$X(t) = As(t) + N(t), \quad 0 < t < T \qquad (14.94)$$

We assume that $N(t)$ is white Gaussian noise with power spectrum N_0 and $s(t)$ is a known signal that is nonzero only in the interval $[0, T]$. The amplitude A determines one of the following two hypotheses:

If H_0 is true, $A = 0$

If H_1 is true, $A > 0$

It should be noted that in such a formulation the value of A (if a target is present) represents the distance of the target or its size. Hence, while we can fix the false alarm rate α, since it involves the noise only, the probability of a miss and the power of the test will depend on the value of A if it is nonzero. The system we use for estimating A or for deciding which hypothesis is present is the same one shown in Figure 14.12.

Again the impulse response $h(\tau)$ that maximizes the signal-to-noise ratio for $Y(T)$ is the matched filter to $s(t)$. We can normalize the response so that we select the gain K to obtain as the output $Y(T)$ an estimate of the value of A:

$$h(t) = Ks(T - t) = (1/P_0)s(T - t), \quad 0 < t < T \tag{14.95}$$

Here we defined P_0 as the signal energy (when $A = 1$):

$$P_0 = \int_0^T [s(t)]^2 \, dt \tag{14.96}$$

In this case we can verify that the value of $Y(T)$ when the hypothesis H_1 is true, is indeed an estimate of the signal amplitude A:

$$Y(T) = \int_0^T As(t)h(T - t) \, dt + \int_0^T N(t)h(T - t) \, dt$$
$$= \frac{1}{P_0} \int_0^T As(t)s(t) \, dt + \frac{1}{P_0} \int_0^T N(t)s(t) \, dt = A + \frac{1}{P_0} \int_0^T N(t)s(t) \, dt \tag{14.97}$$

We can observe therefore that the mean of $Y(T)$ when the hypothesis H_1 is true is indeed equal to A, and it is zero when the hypothesis H_0 is true. The variance of $Y(T)$ is the same under both hypothesis and is obtained directly as

$$\text{Var}\{Y(T)\} = E\left\{\left[\frac{1}{P_0} \int_0^T N(t)s(t) \, dt\right]^2\right\}$$
$$= \frac{1}{P_0^2} \int_0^T \int_0^T E\{N(\tau)s(\tau)N(t)s(t)\} \, dt \, d\tau$$
$$= \frac{1}{P_0^2} \int_0^T \int_0^T N_0\delta(t - \tau)s(\tau)s(t) \, dt \, d\tau = N_0/P_0 = 1/\rho \tag{14.98}$$

Here we are denoting by ρ the signal-to-noise ratio at $Y(T)$ when $A = 1$. The decision to accept the hypothesis H_1 is made if $Y(T)$ is larger than the threshold η, and the value of the threshold is determined by the desired false alarm rate α. In this case, if the hypothesis H_0 is true, the false alarm rate is obtained from the Gaussian density with mean zero and variance $1/\rho$:

$$\alpha = P\{Y(T) > \eta | H_0\} = 1 - \Phi(\eta\sqrt{\rho}) \tag{14.99}$$

If we fix the false alarm rate, we obtain a threshold of

$$\eta = Z_\alpha/\sqrt{\rho} = \Phi^{-1}(1 - \alpha)/\sqrt{\rho} \tag{14.100}$$

We now consider the probability of a Type II error (a miss) when the signal present has amplitude A. In this case $Y(T)$ has mean A and variance $1/\rho$, and a miss occurs when its values does not exceed the threshold

$$\beta = P\{Y(T) < \eta | H_1\} = \Phi[(\eta - A)\sqrt{\rho}] \tag{14.101}$$

It should be noted that if we pick the threshold to be $A/2$, then both types of error probabilities become the same. If we substitute the value of the threshold from equation (14.93) into the equation (14.101) for β, we obtain the relationship between α and β in terms of the power of the test:

$$1 - \beta = 1 - \Phi[-A\sqrt{\rho} + \Phi^{-1}(1 - \alpha)] = 1 - \Phi[-d + \Phi^{-1}(1 - \alpha)] \tag{14.102}$$

Here we defined $d^2 = A^2\rho$ as the signal-to-noise ratio at $Y(T)$ for an arbitrary value of A. We see therefore that the expression for β is identical to the equation for the power of the test given in equation (10.29). It is then easy to see that the decision will have smaller error probabilities as d becomes larger (i.e., when the SNR becomes larger).

14.7 NOISE IN ELECTRICAL CIRCUITS

The current in electrical conductors is carried by free electrons, whose motion is not regimented. They are in constant motion due to the fact that the temperature is not absolute zero. Therefore, even without any voltage applied to the terminal of a resistor, there will be a voltage at the terminal of the resistor due the motion of the free electrons. This voltage is called thermal noise and is modeled as a random process $V(t)$. Suppose we have a resistor with resistance R. Then such a resistor may be modeled as a noise-free resistance R with a voltage source $V(t)$ connected in series to represent the thermal noise. This model is shown in Figure 14.13.

The derivation of the properties of the thermal noise process is beyond the scope of this textbook, so only the results will be provided here. Since the noise voltage results from the motion of a large number of electrons, where each induces a voltage across the terminal of the resistor, it would seem reasonable to assume that the resulting random process will be Gaussian. It can also be shown that the process has zero mean and is stationary, so we can describe it in terms of its power spectrum. The power spectrum of the noise voltage $V(t)$ will be almost white, in the sense that it stays flat for a wide range of frequencies from zero to the GHz range. Therefore, for the purpose of analyzing circuits whose bandwidth is smaller than such frequencies, we can model the random process $V(t)$ as white noise with power spectrum $S_V(\omega)$ given by the following expression:

$$S_V(\omega) = 2kTR \tag{14.103}$$

Here R is the resistance involved in ohms, T is the temperature of the resistor in degrees Kelvin, and k is the Boltzmann constant, which is equal to

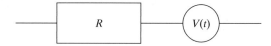

Figure 14.13 Representation of a resistance R with its thermal noise voltage

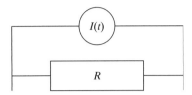

Figure 14.14   Representation of a resistance R with its thermal noise current

$k = 1.37 \times 10^{-23}$ Joules-degrees. The dimensions of the power spectrum are (for obvious reasons) in volts squared/Hz. This thermal noise process can therefore be modeled as a white Gaussian noise process. We next discuss how it behaves when it is involved in a circuit with other elements and other input signals.

Every circuit can have two representations—either as a voltage source in series or as a current source in parallel, with the resistance or impedance. If we use the current source model for the thermal noise shown in Figure 14.13, we obtain the model shown in Figure 14.14.

The relation between the current $I(t)$ and the voltage $V(t)$ is obtained from circuit theory as

$$I(t) = V(t)/R \qquad (14.104)$$

This relation implies that the power spectrum of $I(t)$ will also be approximately white; its value is

$$S_I(\omega) = S_V(\omega)/R^2 = 2kT/R \qquad (14.105)$$

In a circuit with more than one resistor, we can assume that each source is generated independently of the others, so that the noise sources of the various resistors are independent. There is a relationship that will not be derived here that provides the power spectrum of the equivalent voltage noise source in any passive circuit as having a power spectrum equal to $2kT$ times the real part of the impedance of the circuit. As an example of how the noise model discussed here is used, we shall consider a simple RC circuit.

Example 14.7

Consider a circuit involving just two elements R and C and an external signal source $X(t)$, as shown in Figure 14.15. For purposes of the contribution of the thermal noise, we have to add a voltage $V(t)$ to represent the noise; thus we obtain a model of a signal plus additive noise in the low-pass RC circuit shown.

The frequency response $H(\omega)$ of this circuit from the input $X(t)$ (which is in series with the noise source) to the output $Y(t)$ is given by

$$H(\omega) = 1/[1 + j\omega RC] \qquad (14.106)$$

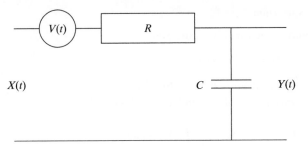

Figure 14.15   RC Circuit with input $X(t)$, output $Y(t)$, and noise $V(t)$

The output $Y(t)$ will be a sum of two components: $Y_0(t)$, representing the output due to the signal and $Y_n(t)$, representing the output due to the noise. The output power spectrum due to the signal input $X(t)$ is given by the usual expression:

$$S_0(\omega) = S_X(\omega)|H(\omega)|^2 = S_X(\omega)/[1 + (\omega RC)^2] \qquad (14.107)$$

The power spectrum of the output due to the noise is obtained similarly by

$$S_n(\omega) = S_V(\omega)|H(\omega)|^2 = 2kTR/[1 + (\omega RC)^2] \qquad (14.108)$$

We note here that even though the noise model is assumed to be white, the average power of the noise at the output is finite and is obtained by taking the integral under the power spectrum at the output:

$$E\{[Y_n(t)]^2\} = \frac{1}{2\pi} \int_{-\infty}^{\infty} 2kTR/[1 + (\omega RC)^2]\, d\omega = kT/C \qquad (14.109)$$

It is left as an exercise to show that the autocorrelation of the output noise has the same shape as that of the random telegraph signal. Also, if we know the power spectrum of the signal $X(t)$, we can find the average power of its output and compute the signal-to-noise ratio. Again, this will also be left as an exercise.

There are other noise models in electrical devices and solid-state gates, as well as other active circuits. The models in such cases may depend on using the Poisson arrival to model the current carried by minority carriers. This subject is beyond the scope of this textbook, and will not be addressed here.

14.8 SUMMARY

Power spectrum of random signals:

$$S_X(\omega) = \int_{-\infty}^{\infty} R_X(\tau)e^{-j\omega\tau}\, d\tau$$

$$R_X(\tau) = \frac{1}{2\pi} \int_{-\infty}^{\infty} S_X(\omega)e^{j\omega\tau}\, d\omega$$

Properties of the power spectrum:

Property 1: The power spectrum is real and even:

$$S_X(-\omega) = S_X(\omega) \quad \text{and} \quad [S_X(\omega)]^* = S_X(\omega)$$

Property 2: The power spectrum is nonnegative: $S_X(\omega) \geq 0$

Property 3: The average power of the random signal is equal to

$$E\{[X(t)]^2\} = \frac{1}{2\pi} \int_{-\infty}^{\infty} S_X(\omega)\, d\omega = \frac{1}{\pi} \int_0^{\infty} S_X(\omega)\, d\omega$$

Property 4: If $m_X \neq 0$, then $S_X(\omega)$ contains a component of $2\pi[m_X]^2\delta(\omega)$.

Cross-power spectrum:

$$S_{XY}(\omega) = \int_{-\infty}^{\infty} R_{XY}(\tau)e^{-j\omega\tau}\, d\tau$$

$$S_{YX}(\omega) = S_{XY}(-\omega) = [S_{XY}(\omega)]^*$$

Sum of random signals:

If $Z(t) = X(t) + Y(t)$, then

$$S_Z(\omega) = S_X(\omega) + S_Y(\omega) + S_{YX}(\omega) + S_{XY}(\omega) = S_X(\omega) + S_Y(\omega) + 2\text{Re}[S_{YX}(\omega)]$$

Linear systems with random inputs:

$X(t)$ and $Y(t)$ are the input and output of a linear system with frequency response $H(\omega)$:

$$S_{XY}(\omega) = S_X(\omega)H(\omega)$$
$$S_Y(\omega) = |H(\omega)|^2 S_X(\omega)$$

Thermal noise in a resistance R:

Power spectrum of a voltage source in series $= 2kTR$

Power spectrum of a current source in parallel $= 2kT/R$

14.9 PROBLEMS

1. Let a signal $X(t)$ and additive noise $N(t)$ pass as input through a low-pass filter with frequency response $H(\omega)$. The power spectra of the signal and noise are

$$S_X(\omega) = 2aP/(\omega^2 + a^2) \text{ and } S_N(\omega) = N_0$$

The system response is given by

$$H(\omega) = A/(j\omega + b)$$

Find the signal and noise power at the output of the system. Then obtain the values of A and b that maximize the signal-to-noise ratio at the output.

2. In Problem 1 we wish to minimize the mean-squared-error (MSE) as defined by equation (14.70). Evaluate the MSE and find the values of A and b that minimize the resulting MSE.

3. A white noise process $N(t)$ with power spectrum N_0 is used as input to the following linear system:

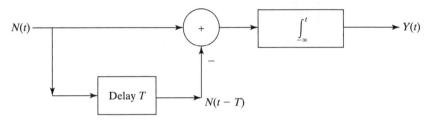

Find the power spectrum and autocorrelation function of the output $Y(t)$.

4. Compare the power spectrum obtained in Problem 3 with that of the binary random signal.

5. Repeat Problem 2 for $H(\omega) = A/(\omega^2 + b^2)$. Which system yields the lower MSE after selection of the optimal A and b?

6. Repeat Problem 1 for the following case:

Let $X(t) = a[u(t) - u(t - T)]$ be a deterministic signal, while $N(t)$ remains as defined in the problem. The signal-to-noise ratio at the output is defined as the ratio of the signal output at time $t = T$ squared and the average power of the noise at the output.

7. Consider Example 14.7 and assume that $C = 10 \, \mu F$ and $R = 1k$ ohm and that $T = 300$ (approximately room temperature). Let the signal $X(t)$ have a power spectrum given by

$$S_X(\omega) = A/[100 + \omega^2]$$

Find the signal-to-noise ratio at the output, where the noise is the thermal noise in the resistor R.

8. In the RLC circuits that follow, assume that the only voltage source is due to the thermal noise in the resistor R. For each circuit, find the current $I(t)$ through the resistor and derive its power spectrum. Since the power dissipated in the circuit is equal to Power $= [I(t)]^2 R$, find the average power dissipated in the circuit due to the thermal noise.

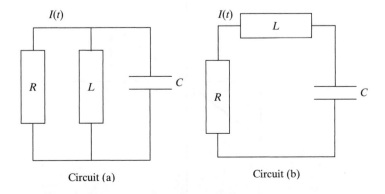

Circuit (a)   Circuit (b)

9. In order to find out how much noise power can be transferred from a circuit that is used to drive a load with impedance Z, consider the following two circuits:

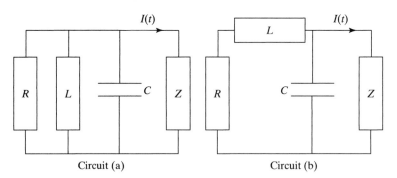

Circuit (a)   Circuit (b)

For each case, find the impedance Z that maximizes the power transfer from the thermal noise voltage to the load. For the load that satisfies the maximum power transfer, find the average power dissipated in the load. It should be noted that if we define $I(t)$ as the current through the load $Z(\omega)$, then the power spectrum of the power dissipated in the impedance is given by $S_1(\omega)\mathrm{Re}[Z(\omega)]$; hence the average power is just the integral over all frequencies.

10. Find the power spectrum of the process $Y(t)$ as defined by Problem 5 in Chapter 12.

11. Find the power spectrum, and cross-power spectrum of the processes $U(t)$ and $V(t)$ defined in Problem 7 in Chapter 12. Assume that the Fourier transforms of the functions $\alpha(\tau)$ and $\beta(\tau)$ are as shown in the following figures:

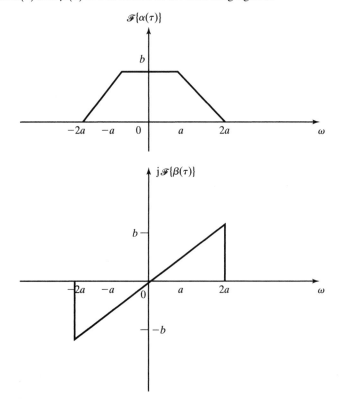

12. Consider the processes defined in Problem 11. We define a new process $Z(t)$ as follows:

$$Z(t) = U(t) \cos(\omega_0 t) - V(t) \sin(\omega_0 t)$$

Then we define a process $W(t)$ that we obtain from $Z(t)$ by passing $Z(t)$ through an ideal low-pass filter that passes all frequencies in the range $-2a < \omega < 2a$. Find the power spectrum of the output signal $W(t)$.

13. A binary channel uses square pulses of duration T and a positive amplitude A to send a "1" and square pulses of duration T and amplitude $-A$ to send a "0." The signal is corrupted by additive white Gaussian noise $N(t)$ with power spectrum N_0. The decision is made by passing the signal plus noise through a filter with impulse response $h(\tau) = \exp(-b\tau)u(\tau)$ and making a decision by comparing the value of the output at time T with a threshold. First find the value of b that maximizes the SNR at time T. Assume that H_0 applies to sending a "0".

    a. Find the threshold if we require a false alarm rate of α.
    b. Find the probability of a Type II error.
    c. Determine the threshold if we wish the two error rates to be the same for a given value of A.

14. Repeat Problem 13, assuming that we use the matched filter instead of the low-pass filter given in Problem 13. How much improvement do you obtain by using the matched filter?

Appendix

A. THE GAUSSIAN DISTRIBUTION AND CHARACTERISTIC FUNCTION

We show here that the integral of the unit Gaussian density function is indeed unity and then derive its characteristic function.

Consider the unit Gaussian density function and let us derive its integral, which we shall denote by C:

$$C = \int_{-\infty}^{\infty} \frac{1}{\sqrt{2\pi}} \exp\{-u^2/2\} \, du \qquad (A.1)$$

We first consider the squared value of the integral C:

$$C^2 = \left[\frac{1}{2\pi} \int_{-\infty}^{\infty} \exp\{-u^2/2\} \, du \right]^2$$

$$= \frac{1}{2\pi} \left[\int_{-\infty}^{\infty} \exp\{-u^2/2\} \, du \right] \left[\int_{-\infty}^{\infty} \exp\{-v^2/2\} \, dv \right] \qquad (A.2)$$

We wrote the square as the product of two integrals and we used different variables for the dummy integration variables in each integral. We can now combine both without causing any problem of confusing the variables of the different integrals:

$$C^2 = \frac{1}{2\pi} \int_{-\infty}^{\infty} \int_{-\infty}^{\infty} \exp\left\{ -\frac{u^2 + v^2}{2} \right\} \, du \, dv = \frac{1}{2\pi} \int_{0}^{\infty} \int_{0}^{2\pi} \exp\left\{ -\frac{r^2}{2} \right\} r \, d\varphi \, dr \qquad (A.3)$$

We arrived at the rightmost expression in equation (A.3) by changing the variables of integration from Cartesian coordinates, u and v, to polar coordinates, r and φ, with

$$u = r\cos(\varphi), \, v = r\sin(\varphi), \, du \, dv = r \, d\varphi \, dr \qquad (A.4)$$

We now perform the integration with respect to φ and change variables again with respect to r as follows:

$$w = r^2/2, \quad dw = r \, dr \qquad (A.5)$$

The result becomes

$$C^2 = \frac{1}{2\pi} \int_0^\infty \int_0^{2\pi} \exp\left\{-\frac{r^2}{2}\right\} r \, d\varphi \, dr = \int_0^\infty \exp\{-r^2/2\} r \, dr$$

$$= \int_0^\infty \exp\{-w\} \, dw = 1 \qquad (A.6)$$

The result proves that the area under the unit Gaussian density is indeed unity, since $C^2 = 1$ implies that $C = 1$.

We now derive the characteristic function of the unit Gaussian density function. In this case the integral is given by

$$\Phi_X(v) = \int_{-\infty}^\infty \exp\{jv\} \frac{\exp\{-u^2/2\}}{\sqrt{2\pi}} du = \int_{-\infty}^\infty \frac{\exp\{-[u^2 - 2jv]/2\}}{\sqrt{2\pi}} du \quad (A.7)$$

If we now add and subtract the term $-v^2 = (jv)^2$ inside the square bracket of the exponential function, we see that we shall obtain the following expression:

$$\Phi_X(v) = \int_{-\infty}^\infty \frac{\exp\{-[u^2 - 2jv + (jv)^2 - (jv)^2]/2\}}{\sqrt{2\pi}} du$$

$$= \int_{-\infty}^\infty \frac{\exp\{-[(u - jv)^2 - (jv)^2]/2\}}{\sqrt{2\pi}} du$$

$$= \exp(-v^2/2) \int_{-\infty}^\infty \frac{\exp\{-[(u - jv)^2/2\}}{\sqrt{2\pi}} du$$

$$= \exp(-v^2/2) \qquad (A.8)$$

The last equality is obtained from the fact that we recognize that the last integral is just the area under the Gaussian density, which is equal to unity.

B. FOURIER TRANSFORMS

Given a signal with finite energy $f(t)$, we define its Fourier transform $F(\omega)$ by

$$F(\omega) = \mathcal{F}\{f(t)\} = \int_{-\infty}^\infty f(t) e^{-j\omega t} \, dt \qquad (B.1)$$

The inverse Fourier transform provides us the function $f(t)$ from its transform:

$$f(t) = \mathcal{F}^{-1}\{F(\omega)\} = \frac{1}{2\pi} \int_{-\infty}^\infty F(\omega) e^{j\omega t} \, d\omega \qquad (B.2)$$

Properties:

$$F(\omega) = A(\omega) + jB(\omega) = |F(\omega)| \exp\{j\varphi(\omega)\} \qquad \text{(B.3)}$$

Here $|F(\omega)|$ is called the magnitude spectrum of $f(t)$ and $\varphi(\omega)$ is called the phase spectrum of $f(t)$. Some key properties of the Fourier transform are as follows:

$$|F(-\omega)| = |F(\omega)| \text{ and } \varphi(-\omega) = -\varphi(\omega) \qquad \text{(B.4)}$$

$$\mathcal{F}\{af(t) + bg(t)\} = a\mathcal{F}\{f(t)\} + b\mathcal{F}\{g(t)\} \qquad \text{(B.5)}$$

$$F\{f(at)\} = \frac{1}{|a|} F(\omega/a) \qquad \text{(B.6)}$$

In particular if $a = -1$, we obtain the time reversal property:

$$\mathcal{F}\{f(-t)\} = F(-\omega) = F^*(\omega) \qquad \text{(B.7)}$$

This property is important since, if we have a causal function (i.e., it is zero for negative time), its time reversal provides us with a time function that is zero for positive times. Their Fourier transforms are the complex conjugate of each other. As an example, consider the following two functions:

$$f(t) = \exp(-at)u(t)$$
$$f(-t) = \exp(at)u(-t) \qquad \text{(B.8)}$$

Here, we denote by $u(t)$ the unit step function. The first function is a decaying exponential starting at $t = 0$, and the other is its mirror image on the negative time axis. The Fourier transforms for the two cases are given by

$$\mathcal{F}\{f(t)\} = \frac{1}{a + j\omega}$$

$$\mathcal{F}\{f(-t)\} = \frac{1}{a - j\omega} \qquad \text{(B.9)}$$

What this means in general is that when we do time reversal, we obtain a signal with the same amplitude spectrum but different phase spectrum. The phase spectra are the negative of each other.

A key property of the Fourier transform is in passing signals through a linear system with impulse response $h(t)$. We call the Fourier transform of $h(t)$ the frequency response $H(\omega)$ of the system. If we denote the output by $g(t)$, then we know from linear systems theory that it is given as a convolution of $f(t)$ and $h(t)$:

$$g(t) = \int_{-\infty}^{\infty} f(\alpha)h(t - \alpha)\, d\alpha = \int_{-\infty}^{\infty} f(t - \alpha)h(\alpha)\, d\alpha \qquad \text{(B.10)}$$

The Fourier transform of $g(t)$ is given by

$$G(\omega) = \int_{-\infty}^{\infty} g(t)e^{-j\omega t}\, dt = \int_{-\infty}^{\infty} \int_{-\infty}^{\infty} f(t-\tau)h(\tau)e^{-j\omega t}\, d\tau\, dt$$

$$= \int_{-\infty}^{\infty} \int_{-\infty}^{\infty} f(t-\tau)h(\tau)e^{-j\omega(t-\tau)}\, dt\, e^{-j\omega\tau}\, d\tau = F(\omega)H(\omega) \qquad \text{(B.11)}$$

An important property of the Fourier transform is Parseval's Theorem. We first derive a more generic version:

$$\frac{1}{2\pi} \int_{-\infty}^{\infty} F(\omega)G^*(\omega)\, d\omega = \int_{-\infty}^{\infty} f(t)g(t)\, dt \qquad \text{(B.12)}$$

The proof is obtained by replacing the conjugate of $G(\omega)$ with its definition as a transform of $g(t)$ and changing the order of the integration:

$$\frac{1}{2\pi} \int_{-\infty}^{\infty} F(\omega)G^*(\omega)\, d\omega = \frac{1}{2\pi} \int_{-\infty}^{\infty} F(\omega) \int_{-\infty}^{\infty} g(t)e^{j\omega t}\, dt\, d\omega = \int_{-\infty}^{\infty} f(t)g(t)\, dt$$
$$\text{(B.13)}$$

Parseval's Theorem refers to the case for which $g(t) = f(t)$, so we obtain the result that the signal energy is equal to the integral of the square of the magnitude spectrum:

$$\int_{-\infty}^{\infty} |f(t)|^2\, dt = \frac{1}{2\pi} \int_{-\infty}^{\infty} F(\omega)F^*(\omega)\, d\omega = \frac{1}{2\pi} \int_{-\infty}^{\infty} |F(\omega)|^2\, d\omega \quad \text{(B.14)}$$

The expression in equation (B.12) may also be written as

$$\frac{1}{2\pi} \int_{-\infty}^{\infty} F(\omega)G(\omega)\, d\omega = \int_{-\infty}^{\infty} f(t)g(-t)\, dt = \int_{-\infty}^{\infty} f(-t)g(t)\, dt \quad \text{(B.15)}$$

Note also that since the right-hand side of these equations is real, the integral in the frequency domain is also real.

C. SCHWARTZ'S INEQUALITY

This inequality is important in the derivation of the matched filter in Section 14.6.

It is stated as follows: Let $f(t)$ and $g(t)$ be any real functions with finite energy, and let their Fourier transforms be given by $F(\omega)$ and $G(\omega)$, respectively. Then the inequality states that the following bound is always satisfied:

$$\left| \int_{-\infty}^{\infty} F(\omega)G(\omega)\, d\omega \right|^2 \leq \left\{ \int_{-\infty}^{\infty} |F(\omega)|^2\, d\omega \right\}\left\{ \int_{-\infty}^{\infty} |G(\omega)|^2\, d\omega \right\} \quad \text{(C.1)}$$

These expressions are equal if and only if

$$F(\omega) = kG^*(\omega) \qquad \text{(C.2)}$$

In order to prove the inequality, we shall denote the energy of the signals F and G by α^2 and β^2, respectively:

$$\alpha^2 = \int_{-\infty}^{\infty} |F(\omega)|^2 \, d\omega \text{ and } \beta^2 = \int_{-\infty}^{\infty} |G(\omega)|^2 \, d\omega \qquad \text{(C.3)}$$

Let us now consider the following integral, which must be nonnegative, since it involves the integral of an absolute value:

$$C = \int_{-\infty}^{\infty} |[F(\omega)/\alpha] \pm [G^*(\omega)/\beta]|^2 \, d\omega \geq 0 \qquad \text{(C.4)}$$

We now write the absolute value inside the integral as multiplying the expression inside the absolute value by its complex conjugate:

$$C = \int_{-\infty}^{\infty} \{[F(\omega)/\alpha] \pm [G^*(\omega)/\beta]\}\{[F^*(\omega)/\alpha] \pm [G(\omega)/\beta]\} \, d\omega \geq 0 \qquad \text{(C.5)}$$

Now we multiply the expressions and note that the portion of the integral involving the product of F and G are real, as shown in equation (B.15):

$$C = \left[\int_{-\infty}^{\infty} |F(\omega)|^2 \, d\omega \right]/\alpha^2 + \left[\int_{-\infty}^{\infty} |G(\omega)|^2 \, d\omega \right]/\beta^2$$

$$\pm \left[\int_{-\infty}^{\infty} F^*(\omega)G^*(\omega) \, d\omega \right]/\alpha\beta$$

$$\pm \left[\int_{-\infty}^{\infty} F(\omega)G(\omega) \, d\omega \right]/\alpha\beta \geq 0 \qquad \text{(C.6)}$$

We now use the fact that the last two terms are identical and real, as in equation (B.15), while the first two terms are equal to unity. (This follows from the definition of the energy in equation (C.3). We obtain

$$C = 2 \pm 2 \left[\int_{-\infty}^{\infty} F(\omega)G(\omega) \, d\omega \right]/\alpha\beta \geq 0 \qquad \text{(C.7)}$$

We now use the expression resulting from each of the $\pm$ signs to yield two inequalities:

$$1 \geq \left[\int_{-\infty}^{\infty} F(\omega)G(\omega) \, d\omega \right]/\alpha\beta \geq -1 \qquad \text{(C.8)}$$

The result implies that $\left| \int_{-\infty}^{\infty} F(\omega)G(\omega)\,d\omega \right| \leq \alpha\beta$, which, after squaring both sides, yields the inequality (C.1) we started to prove. Note that if we set $F = kG^*$, then the two sides are equal and the bound is achieved.

D. THE IMPULSE FUNCTION

The impulse function (also called the **delta** function) is useful in many applications in electrical engineering. It is an approximation of real pulses, but the impulse function itself is not a practically realizable function or signal.

The definition of the impulse function is based on its relation to other functions. We write the impulse function as $\delta(t)$, and it is defined by its satisfaction of the following property for any function $f(t)$ that is continuous at $t = 0$:

$$\int_{-\infty}^{\infty} f(t)\delta(t)\,dt = f(0) \tag{D.1}$$

We usually draw the delta function as a bold arrow occurring at $t = 0$ and with unity magnitude, as shown in Figure D.1.

If we shift the function and multiply by a constant, we obtain an impulse function of magnitude α occurring at time $t = \beta$ (also shown in the figure):

$$\alpha\delta(t - \beta) \tag{D.2}$$

Properties of the impulse function:

$$f(t)\delta(t - \beta) = f(\beta)\delta(t - \beta) \tag{D.3}$$

$$f(t)\delta(t/\beta) = \beta f(0)\delta(t) \tag{D.4}$$

$$\int_{-\infty}^{t} \delta(\tau)\,d\tau = u(t), \text{ where } u(t) \text{ is the unit step function} \tag{D.5}$$

$$\mathcal{F}\{\delta(t)\} = 1 \tag{D.6}$$

$$\mathcal{F}(1) = 2\pi\delta(\omega) \tag{D.7}$$

Many functions tend in the limit to an impulse function, and here are a few examples. The first is just a square pulse of width a and magnitude $1/a$, so that its area is 1:

$$f(t) = 1/a, \text{ for } 0 < t < a, \text{ and } f(t) \text{ is zero elsewhere.} \tag{D.8}$$

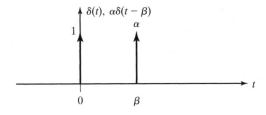

Figure D.1 Pictorial representation of the impulse function

It tends to a delta function as the width a tends to zero.

$$f(t) = \alpha \exp(-\alpha t), \text{ for } 0 < t \text{ and is zero for } t < 0. \tag{D.9}$$

This is an exponential function whose area is unity and time constant is $1/\alpha$. It tends to a delta function as α tends to infinity (time constant tends to zero):

$$f(t) = (1/T)(1 - |t|/T), \text{ for } 0 < t < |T|, \text{ and is zero elsewhere.} \tag{D.10}$$

This is a triangular pulse with width T and unity area. It tends to a delta function as the width T tends to zero:

$$f(t) = \sin(\alpha t)/(\pi t) \tag{D.11}$$

This function has magnitude α/π at $t = 0$ and its first zeros occur at $t = \pm\pi/\alpha$. It also tends to a delta function as α tends to infinity (the width of the first lobe $2\pi/\alpha$ tends to zero).

Finally, consider the Gaussian probability density function with mean zero and standard deviation σ:

$$f(t) = \frac{1}{\sqrt{2\pi}\sigma} \exp\left[-\frac{t^2}{2\sigma^2}\right] \tag{D.12}$$

This function has unity area regardless of the value of σ, and it tends to an impulse function as σ tends to zero.

E. DERIVATION OF EQUATION (13.41)

We are interested in obtaining an expression for the variance of the time-average of a random process $X(t)$ whose mean is zero, which was shown to be given by equation (13.41). Let the random variable Y be defined as

$$Y = \frac{1}{2T} \int_{-T}^{T} X(t)\, dt \tag{E.1}$$

We are interested in finding the mean-squared value of Y:

$$E\{Y^2\} = E\left\{\left[\frac{1}{2T} \int_{-T}^{T} X(t)\, dt\right]^2\right\} = \frac{1}{4T^2} \int_{-T}^{T} \int_{-T}^{T} E\{X(\alpha)X(\beta)\}\, d\alpha\, d\beta$$

$$= \frac{1}{4T^2} \int_{-T}^{T} \int_{-T}^{T} R_X(\alpha - \beta)\, d\alpha\, d\beta \tag{E.2}$$

If we change the integration variables by using $\tau = \alpha - \beta$ and β, we obtain the following expression, since the limits will be obtained from its definition by replacing α with its limits of $-T$ and $+T$:

$$E\{Y^2\} = \frac{1}{4T^2} \int_{-T}^{T} \int_{-T-\beta}^{T-\beta} R_X(\tau)\, d\tau\, d\beta \tag{E.3}$$

The region of integration is shown in Figure E.1.

We now change the order of integration by integrating over the β variable first. We see that we need to divide the region in two, since the limits for β are different when τ is positive than when it is negative. In the figure we also show via dashed lines how the limits of the integration over the β variable are obtained in the two regions. In this case we obtain the following expressions, where we also take the liberty of moving $R_X(\tau)$ into the last integral since it does not depend on β:

$$
\begin{aligned}
E\{Y^2\} &= \frac{1}{4T^2}\left\{ \int_{-2T}^{0} R_X(\tau) \int_{-T-\tau}^{T} d\beta\, d\tau + \int_{0}^{2T} R_X(\tau) \int_{-T}^{T-\tau} d\beta\, d\tau \right\} \\
&= \frac{1}{4T^2}\left\{ \int_{-2T}^{0} R_X(\tau)[T - (-T - \tau)]\, d\tau \right. \\
&\qquad + \left. \int_{0}^{2T} R_X(\tau)[(T - \tau) - (-T)]\, d\tau \right\} \\
&= \frac{1}{2T}\left\{ \int_{-2T}^{0} R_X(\tau)[1 + \tau/2T]\, d\tau + \int_{0}^{2T} R_X(\tau)[1 - \tau/2T]\, d\tau \right\} \\
&= \frac{1}{2T} \int_{-T}^{T} R_X(\tau)\left(1 - \frac{|\tau|}{2T}\right) d\tau
\end{aligned} \tag{E.4}
$$

This is the result presented in equation (13.41).

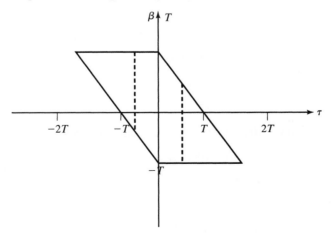

Figure E.1   Region of integration for equation (E.3)

Answers to Selected Problems

CHAPTER 2:

2-7. (c) $P(A) = 0.125$, $P(C \cup D) = 0.5$

2-8. (a) 0.95; (c) 0.1; (e) 0.1; (g) 0.15; (i) 0.05

2-10. $P\{F_2 \cap F_3\} = 0.02$; $P(F_1) = 0.01$

2-11. (a) $P(F) = 0.0521$; (b) $P(F) = 0.016065$

2-12. (a) $P(D) = 0.0035$; (b) $P(A_1|D) = 0.1429$

2-13. (a) 1.225×10^{-5}; (b) 2.05×10^{-5}

2-15. (a) 0.01; (b) 0.18; (c) 0.81

2-16. $P(\text{Failure}) = 0.087$

2-17. With parity: 0.01252; Without parity: 0.14924

2-18. (b) $P(F) = 0.160106$; (c) 0.165476

2-19. $P(F) = 0.125$

2-20. (c) $P\{\text{output is "0"}\} = 1/16$

2-22. $P\{\text{Fuse trips}\} = 0.0298$

2-23.   (a) 0.56; (b) 0.964; (c) 0.44; (d) 0.864

2-25.   Parallel: $P(\text{open}) = 0.1936$; Series: $P(\text{Open}) = 0.6864$

CHAPTER 3:

3-6.   System (a): $P(X = 0) = 0.0298$; $P(X = 4) = 0.0792$; $P(X = 6) = 0.1782$; $P(X = 10) = 0.7128$

3-6.   System (b): $P(X = 0) = 0.0028$; $P(X = 4) = 0.0072$; $P(X = 10) = 0.2772$; $P(X = 14) = 0.7128$

3-8. $P\{X = 18\} = 0.125$; $P\{X = 20\} = 0.25$; $P\{X = 22\} = 0.125$

3-9.   (a) and (d) Valid

3-10.   (b), (c), and (d) Valid

3-11. $P\{0 < X < 3\} = 0.3780$; $P\{X < 5\} = 0.8413$

3-12.   (a) 0.135335; (c) 0.1954; (e) 0.05 seconds

3-13.   (a) 0.07776; (c) 0.9533

3-14.   (a) 0.368; (c) 0.2386

3-15.   (a) 0.63212; (c) For System 6(a): 0.48737

3-16.   (a) 0.203; (c) Rating of 52.5 Amp

3-17.   (a) 0.0073; (c) 0.472

3-19.   (b) $P\{\text{False Alarm}\} = 0.0062$

CHAPTER 4:

4-6.   (a) 4; (b) 5

4-7.   (b) 0.12

4-8.   (b) $\sigma_Y^2 = 9.297$; (c) $P\{Y = 0\} = 0.495$; $P\{Y = 10\} = 0.023$

4-9.   (a) $f_Y(u) = \sqrt{\dfrac{2}{u}}e^{-2\sqrt{2u}}$, (b) 0.25

4-11. $E\{X\} = 6$; $\sigma_X = 4.9$

4-12. $E\{X\} = 20$; $\sigma_X = 8.9$

4-14.   (b) $P\{Y = 9\} = 0.0455$

4-15. (a) 1.259

4-16. (a) $E\{Y\} = 73T$; (b) $P\{Y = 0\} = 0.2$; $P\{Y = 512T\} = (0.8)^{10}$

4-17. (a) $f_Y(v) = 111/v^3$, for $3.178 < v < 3.514$; (b) $E\{Y\} = 3.334$ kHz

CHAPTER 5:

5-6. (a) $C = 0.25$; (b) $f_X(u) = [1 + 2u]/2, 0 < u < 1$;

     (e) $P\{0.25 < X < 0.5, 1 < Y < 1.5\} = 0.0625$

5-8. (a) $f_X(u) = \dfrac{2\sqrt{9 - u^2}}{9\pi}$, for $|u| \le 3$; (c) $f_{X|Y}(u|Y = v) = \dfrac{1}{2\sqrt{9 - v^2}}$, for

     $|u| \le \sqrt{9 - v^2}$

5-9. (b) $f_X(u) = 5 \exp(-5u)$; $f_Y(v) = 25v \exp(-5v)$; (c) 0.828; (d) 0.9084

5-10. (a) $P\{Y = 1\} = 0.0253$; (c) 0.3085

5-12. $C = 12$;   (a) $f_X(u) = 6\{\exp(-3u) - \exp(-6u)\}, 0 < u < \infty$ °;

     (c) $P\{X < 1, Y < 1\} = 0.8558$

5-14. (a) $f_X(u) = 0.01 \exp(-u/30) + 0.07 \exp(-u/10)$; (b) $P\{V|X=20\}=0.35147$;

     (c) $P\{D|X < 15\} = 0.82165$; (d) $P\{V|X > 25\} = 0.6941$

CHAPTER 6:

6-6. (b) 7/6; (c) 1/3; (d) 1.5; (e) $\rho = -0.0909$

6-7. (d) 1/3; (e) 0.297; (f) $\rho = -0.5$

6-9. $\rho = 0.8$; MSE $= 0.05$

6-10. (d) $\hat{X} = \dfrac{a^2}{(6 + a^2)} Y$; MSE $= (a^2/3)\dfrac{6}{(6 + a^2)}$

6-11. (b) $\lambda = \dfrac{n}{(t + 0.5)}$; (c) $E\{\Lambda|T = t\} = \dfrac{n + 1}{(t + 0.5)}$

6-13. (a) $E\{Z\} = 3338$ Hz

CHAPTER 7:

7-1. $f_Z(u) = \dfrac{\alpha + \beta}{\pi[u^2 + (\alpha + \beta)^2]}$

7-3. $f_Y(u) = (\lambda^2 u)\exp(-\lambda u), \quad 0 < u$

CHAPTER 8:

8-5. $E\{Z\} = 9; E\{W\} = -10; \mathrm{Cov}(Z, W) = 0$

8-6. (a) $E\{X\} = 0.625T$; (b) $E\{X\} = 0.375T$

8-7. (a) $E\{X\} = 0.8T$; (b) $E\{X\} = (1/3)T$

8-8. (a) $E\{X\} = (5/12)T$; (b) $E\{X\} = (7/12)T$

8-10. (a) $E\{X\} = [2n/(2n + 1)]T$;

8-11. (a) $f_R(w) = 0.0000625(330 - w)^2$; (b) 0.1406; (c) $\mathrm{Var}\{R\} = 100$

8-12. (b) $\mathrm{Var}\{Z\} = 1$

8-13. (a) $\rho_{UV} = -0.4472$;

8-14. (a) $\rho_{UV} = 0.3829$;

8-16. For $p = 0.5$: $E\{Y\} = 0$ and $\mathrm{Var}\{Y\} = \lambda t$

8-17. Approximate value of $P\{10 < X < 20\} = 0.932$; Exact value $= 0.901$

8-18. $P\{\text{A call is blocked}\} = 0.014$

8-19. (a) $E\{Y\} = 10.5$ minutes; (b) Variance $= 5.25$ minutes^2;
       (c) $P\{Y > 1.05T\} = 0.409$

CHAPTER 9:

9-4. (c) 0.962334; (d) $n = 577$

9-5. (a) p is in the range: $(0.00052, 0.00188)$ (b) $C = 0.228$; (c) $n = 1{,}080{,}000$

9-6. (b) 0.935 ± 0.16; (c) $n = 38$; (d) 68.3%

9-7. $r_{xy} = 0.0317$; $r_{xz} = 0.824$; residual variance 0.044

9-8. (a) λ is in the range $(0.0152, 0.0348)$; (b) 0.6827; (c) 3,842 hours

9-9.   (a) m = 0.784; (b) C = 0.789; (c) n = 24,586

9-10. (a) p will be in the range 0.2 ± 0.078; (b) C = 86.6%; (c) n = 385

CHAPTER 10:

10-1. (a) Accept H_1 if we count 49 or more drops; (b) β = 0.007; (c) n = 65

10-2. (a) x_c = 2.64; (b) β = 0.236; (c) n = 214

10-4. (a) x_c = 31.94; (b) β = 0.0014; (c) n = 54

CHAPTER 11:

11-3. (b) $E\{X\} = (2/3)T$

11-4. System (a): $R(t) = 1 - F_X(t) = 2e^{-2\lambda t} - e^{-3\lambda t}$; $E\{X\} = 2/(3\lambda)$

System (b): $R(t) = \exp(-\lambda t) + \exp(-2\lambda t) - \exp(-3\lambda t)$; $E\{X\} = 1.167/\lambda$

11-5. System (a): $R(t) = 2 \exp(-3t) - \exp(-5t)$; $E\{X\} = (7/15)$

System (b): $R(t) = \exp(-t) + \exp(-1.5t) - \exp(-2.5t)$; $E\{X\} = (19/15)$

11-6. System (a): $E\{X\} = 0.843$

11-7. $E\{T\} = 2.438$

CHAPTER 12:

12-4. $m_X(t) = 2u(t) - 3u(t - 2)$

12-5. $R_Y(\tau) = 2 \exp(-3|\tau|) \cos(\omega_0 \tau)$

12-6. $R_{ZW}(\tau) = 4 \exp(-2|\tau|) - 9 \exp(-|\tau|)$

12-7. $R_U(\tau) = R_V(\tau) = \alpha(\tau) \cos(\omega_0 \tau) + \beta(\tau) \sin(\omega_0 \tau)$;

$R_{UV}(\tau) = -\alpha(\tau) \sin(\omega_0 \tau) + \beta(\tau) \cos(\omega_0 \tau)$

12-8. $C_X(\tau) = p(1 - p)(a - b)^2 \left[1 - \dfrac{|\tau|}{T} \right]$, for $|\tau| < T$

12-9. $C_X(\tau) = 0.25(a - b)^2 \exp(-2\lambda|\tau|)$

12-10. $C_X(\tau) = 0.25(a - b)^2 \exp(-2\lambda p|\tau|)$

12-13. $E\{X(t)\} = 0$; $R_X(\tau) = a^2(1 - 2|\tau|)$, for $|\tau| < 1$, and is periodic with period 2.

CHAPTER 13:

13-7. $a_1 = 0, a_0 = \exp(-\alpha\lambda T)$

13-8. $R_Y(0) = 8/3$

13-9. (c) For $\alpha = 0.5$, MSE $= 0.15625$; For $\alpha = 1$, MSC $= 0.291667$

13-10. (b) $R_x(m) = \alpha^m R_X(0)$;

(d) $R_X(0) = \dfrac{\sigma^2}{1 - \alpha^2}$

13-11. For n $= 100$, λT $= 0.5$, MSE $= 0.021455$

13-12. $R_Y(0) = 2C_X(0)[1 - \exp(-2\lambda T)]$

CHAPTER 14:

14-3. $R_Y(\tau) = N_0 T(1 - |\tau|/T)$, for $|\tau| < T$

14-4. $R_Y(0) = N_0 T$

14-6. $(SNR)_{max} = 0.814(a^2 T)/N_0$, for b $= 1.2564/T$

14-7. SNR $= 1.193A \times 10^{14}$

14-8. Circuit (b)Power $= kTR/L$

14-9. $S_Y(\omega) = \dfrac{6}{9 + (\omega - \omega_0)^2} + \dfrac{6}{9 + (\omega + \omega_0)^2}$

14-12. $R_W(\tau) = \alpha(\tau)$

14-13. (c) $\alpha = \beta = \Phi\left(-\sqrt{\dfrac{0.814 A^2 T}{N_0}}\right)$

14-14. (c) $\alpha = \beta = \Phi\left(-\sqrt{\dfrac{A^2 T}{N_0}}\right)$

Index